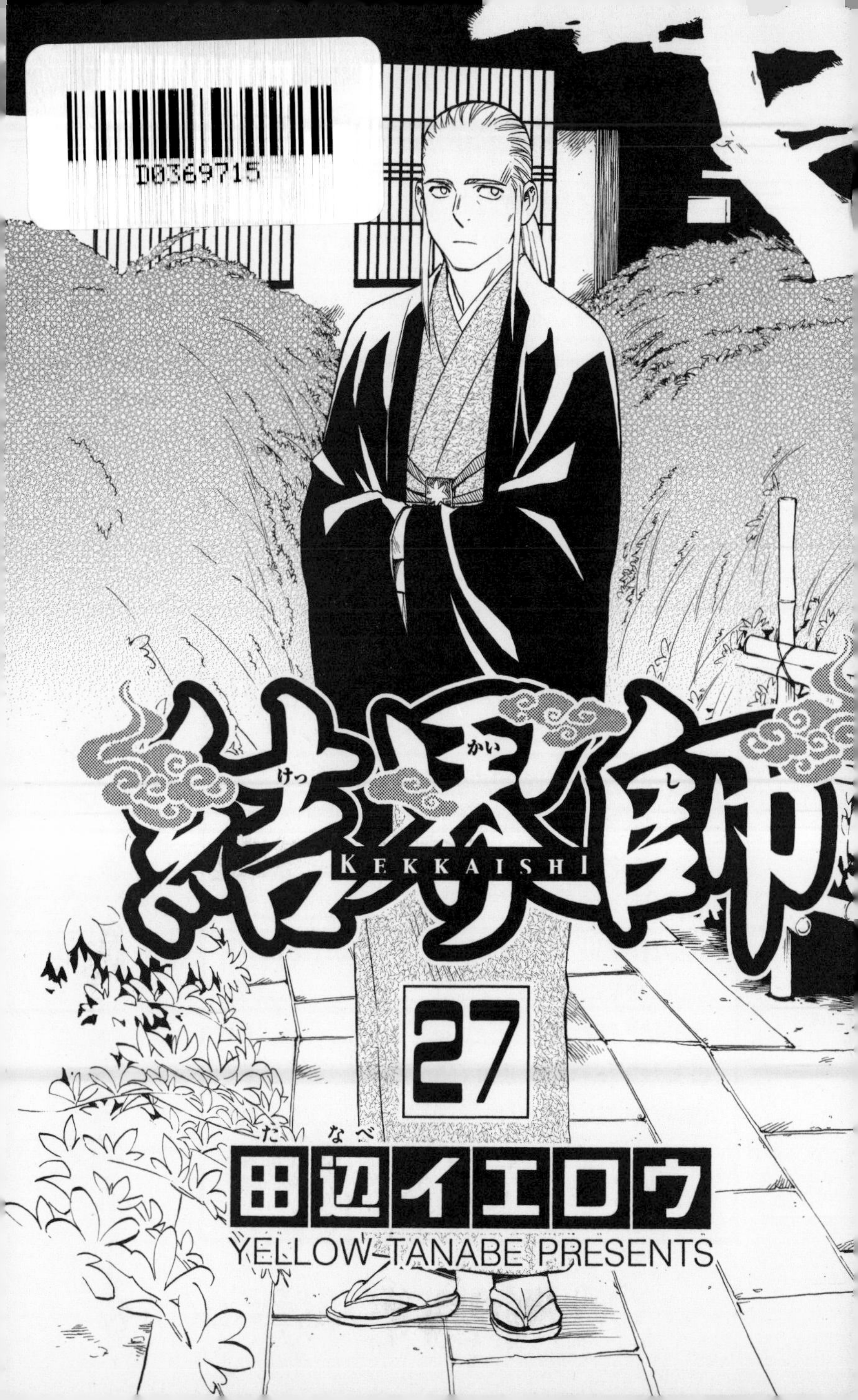

結界師
けっかいし
KEKKAISHI
27
田辺イエロウ
たなべ
YELLOW TANABE PRESENTS

THE STORY THUS FAR

Increasingly worried about the attacks on the Karasumori Site, Yoshimori struggles to grasp the essence of kekkai magic. After intensive training, he comes very close to mastering the critical technique of emptying his mind...

Meanwhile, the truth about the mystical site attacks begins to emerge. The supreme leader of the Shadow Organization, Nichinaga Omi, is the prime suspect. The case against Omi grows when it is revealed that he commissioned the assassinations of key members of the Council of Twelve.

Yoshimori's training is not yet complete when two witches descend upon the Karasumori Site and amaze Yoshimori and the others by levitating the *entire* school...

KEKKAISHI VOL. 27

TABLE OF CONTENTS

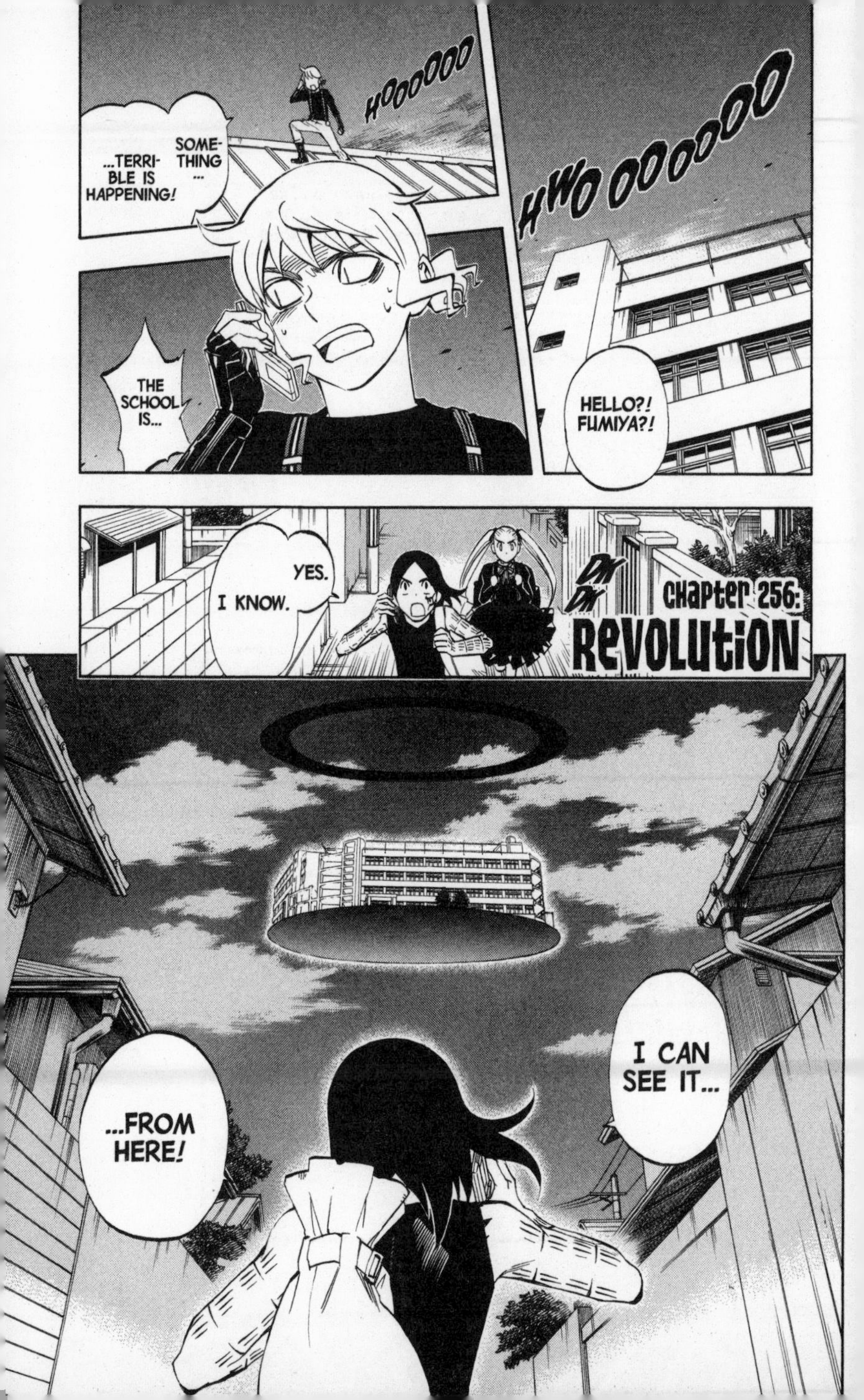
HWOOOOOOOOO
HELLO?! FUMIYA?!
HOOOOOO
SOME-THING... ...TERRI-BLE IS HAPPENING!
THE SCHOOL IS...
DK DK
Chapter 256: Revolution
YES. I KNOW.
I CAN SEE IT...
...FROM HERE!

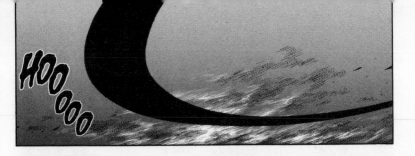

HOO OOO

CHAPTER 256: REVOLUTION

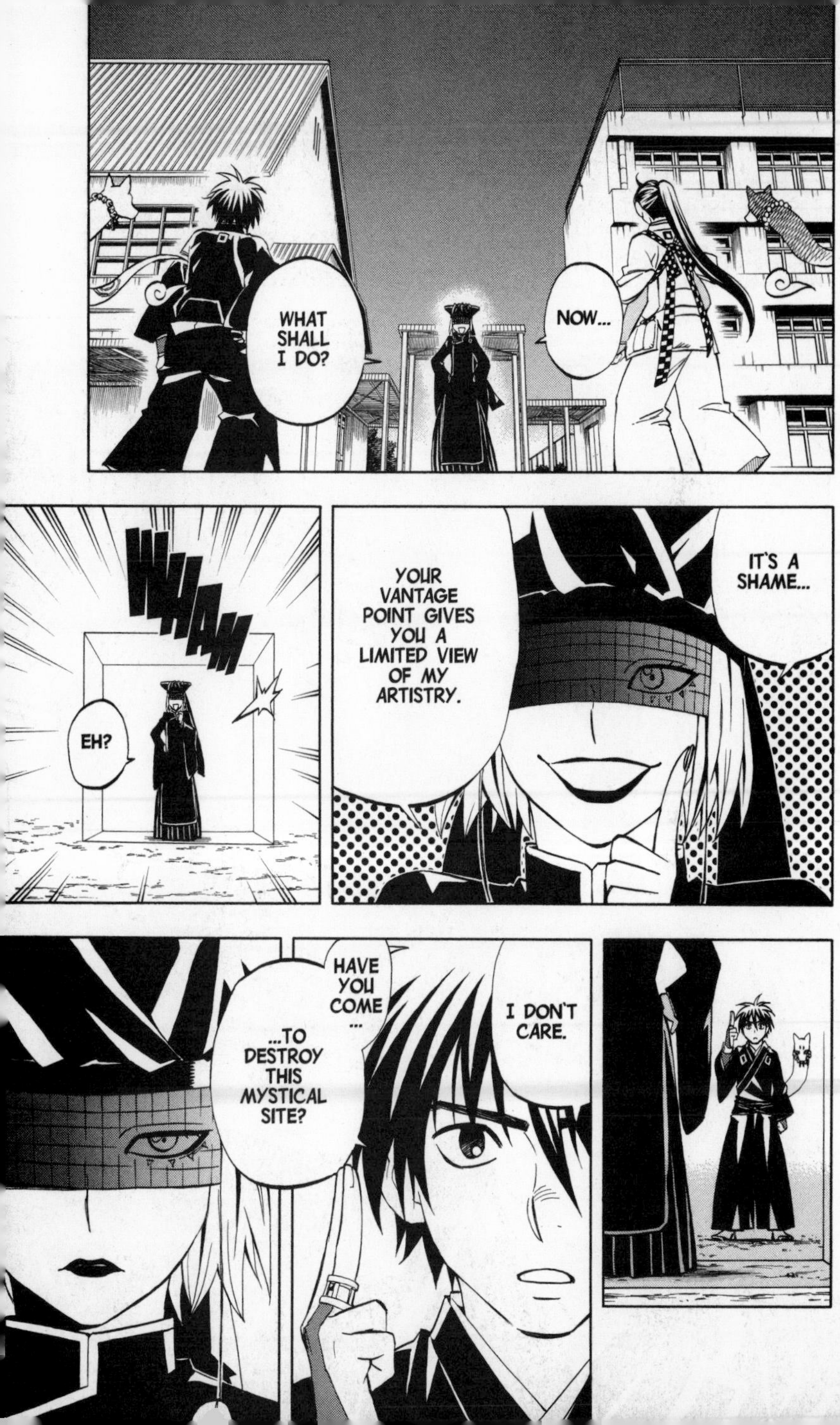
NOW...
WHAT SHALL I DO?
IT'S A SHAME...
YOUR VANTAGE POINT GIVES YOU A LIMITED VIEW OF MY ARTISTRY.
WHAM
EH?
I DON'T CARE.
HAVE YOU COME ...
...TO DESTROY THIS MYSTICAL SITE?

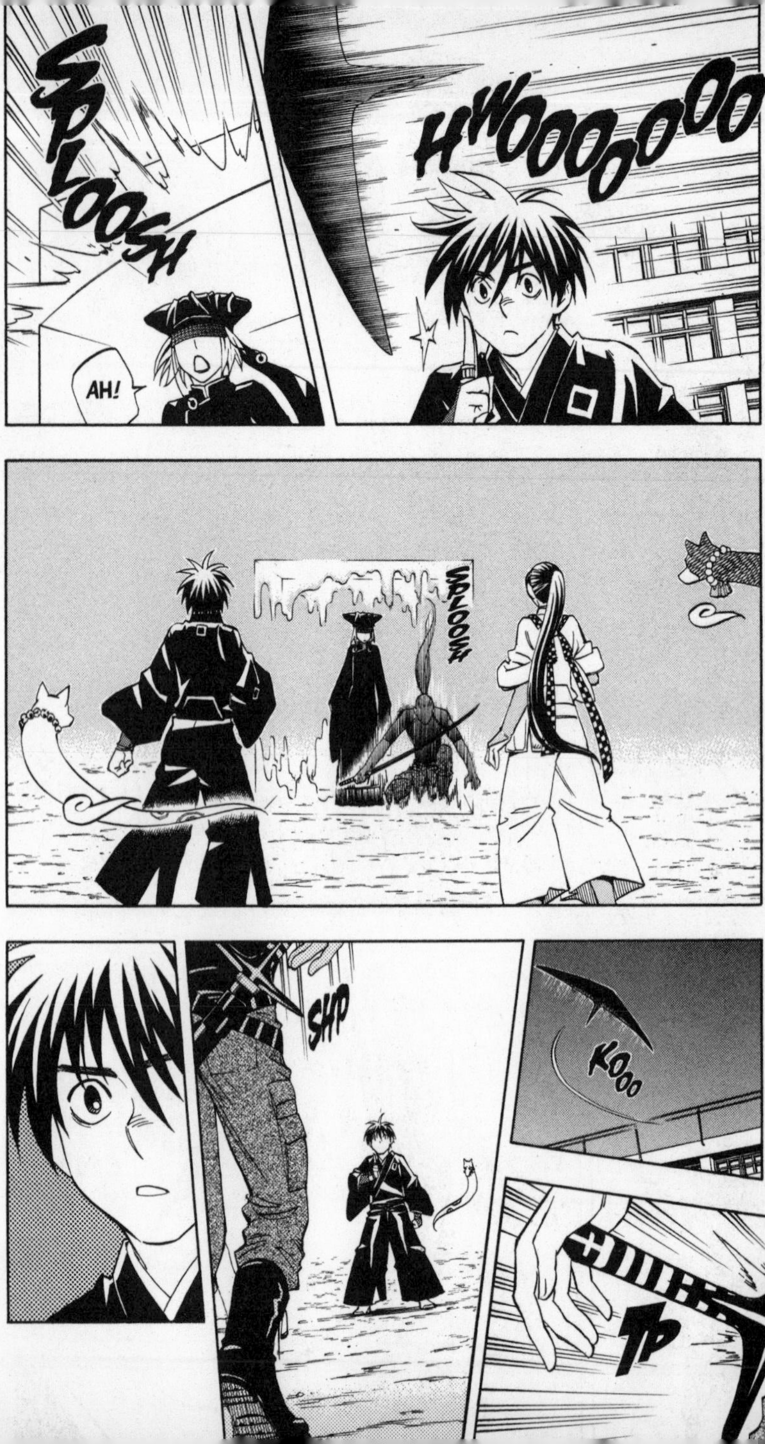
HWOOOOOOO
SPLOOSH
AH!
SPLOOSH
KOOO
TP
SHP

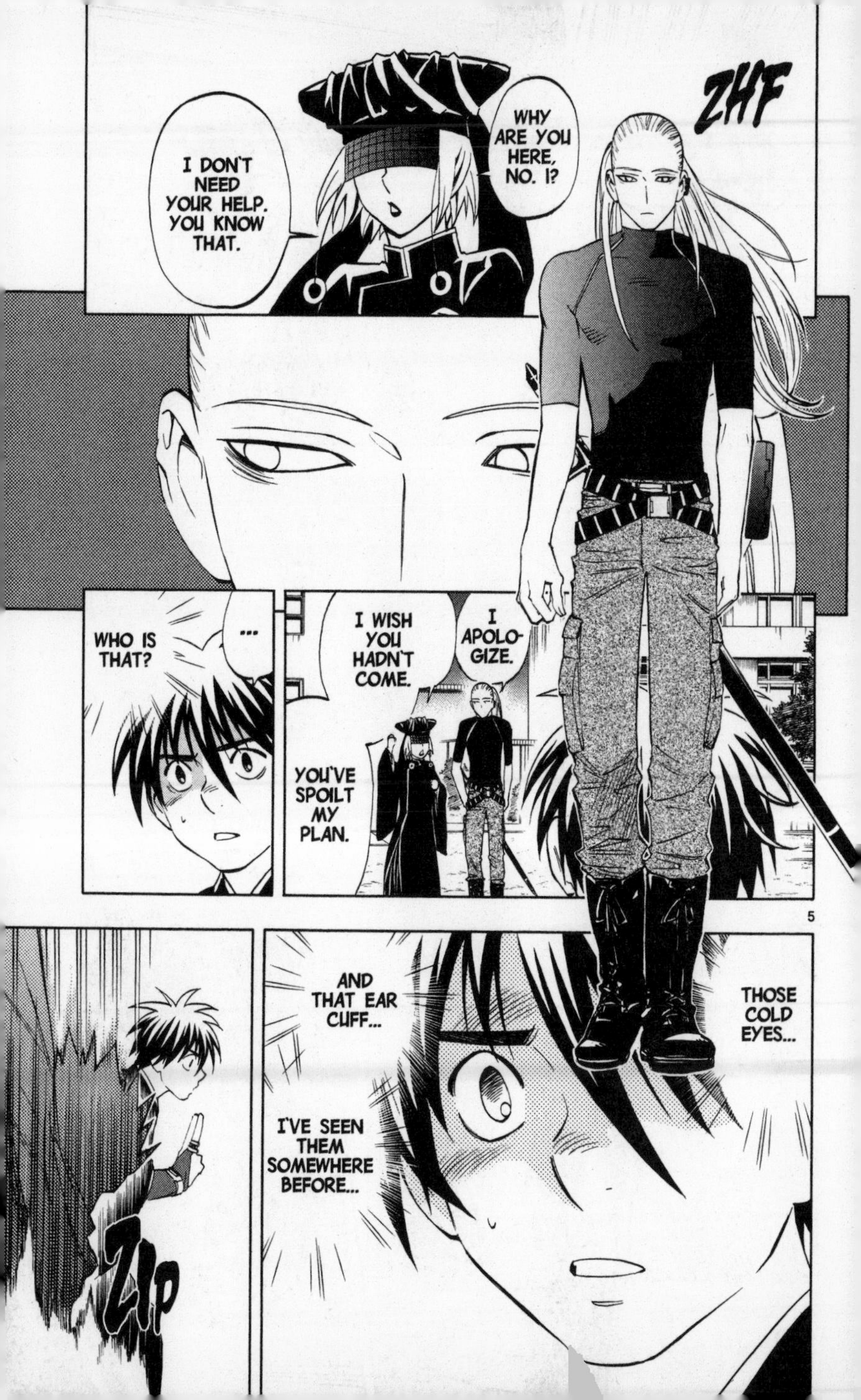
ZHF
WHY ARE YOU HERE, NO. 1?
I DON'T NEED YOUR HELP. YOU KNOW THAT.
I APOLOGIZE.
I WISH YOU HADN'T COME.
YOU'VE SPOILT MY PLAN.
...
WHO IS THAT?
THOSE COLD EYES...
AND THAT EAR CUFF...
I'VE SEEN THEM SOMEWHERE BEFORE...
ZIP

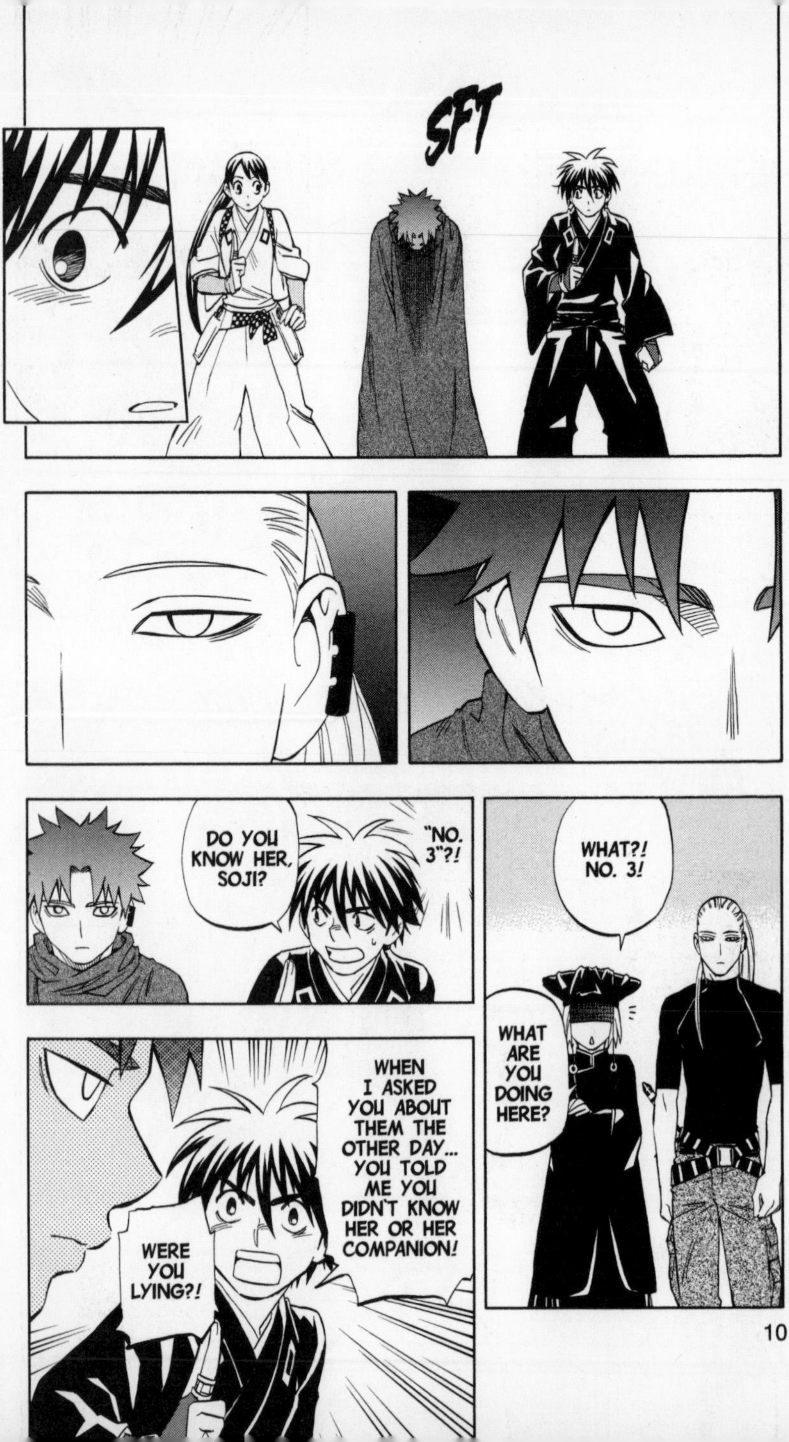
SFT
WHAT?! NO. 3!
WHAT ARE YOU DOING HERE?
"NO. 3"?!
DO YOU KNOW HER, SOJI?
WHEN I ASKED YOU ABOUT THEM THE OTHER DAY... YOU TOLD ME YOU DIDN'T KNOW HER OR HER COMPANION!
WERE YOU LYING?!

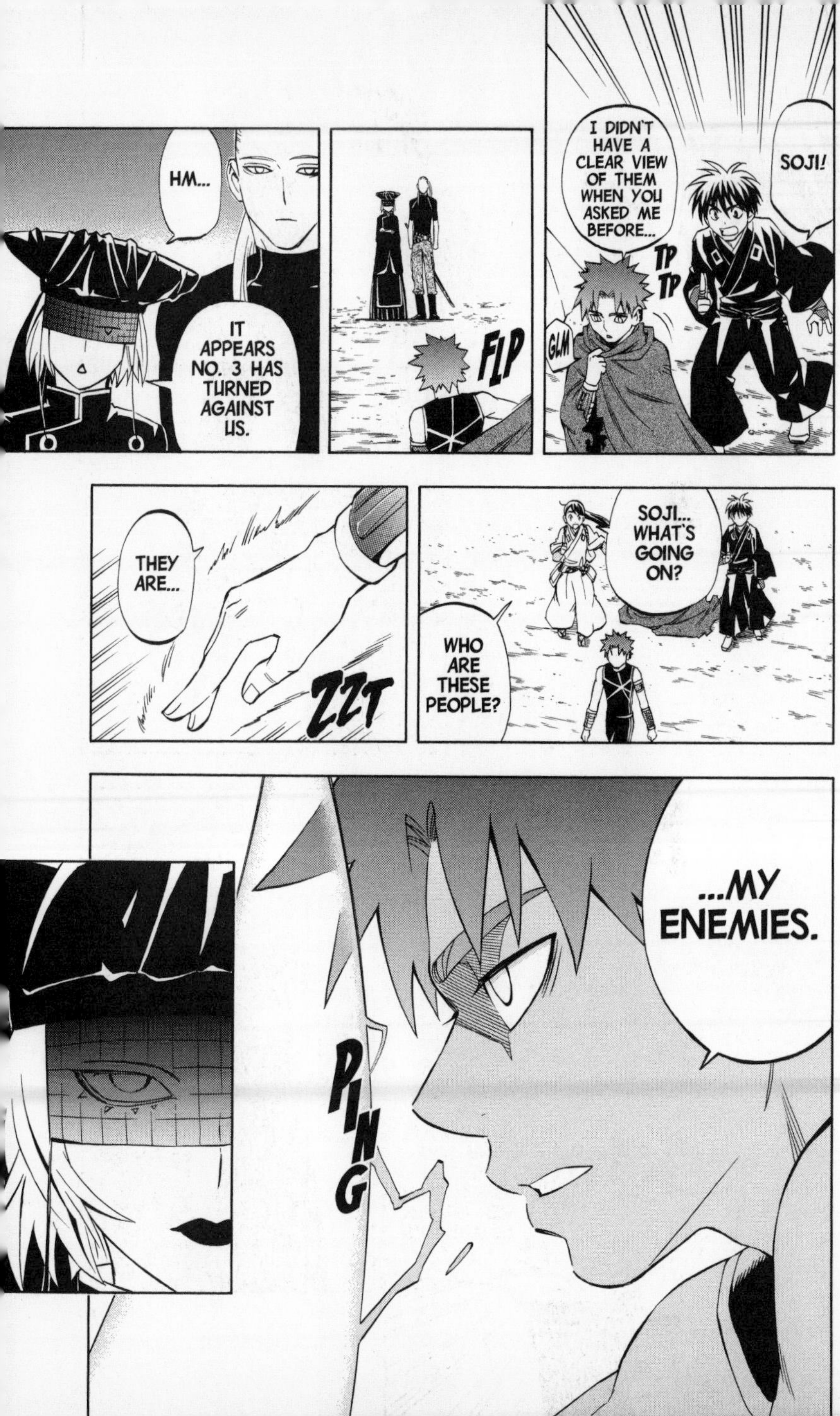
SOJI!
I DIDN'T HAVE A CLEAR VIEW OF THEM WHEN YOU ASKED ME BEFORE...
TP TP
GLM
FLP
HM...
IT APPEARS NO. 3 HAS TURNED AGAINST US.
SOJI... WHAT'S GOING ON?
WHO ARE THESE PEOPLE?
THEY ARE...
ZZT
...MY ENEMIES.
PING

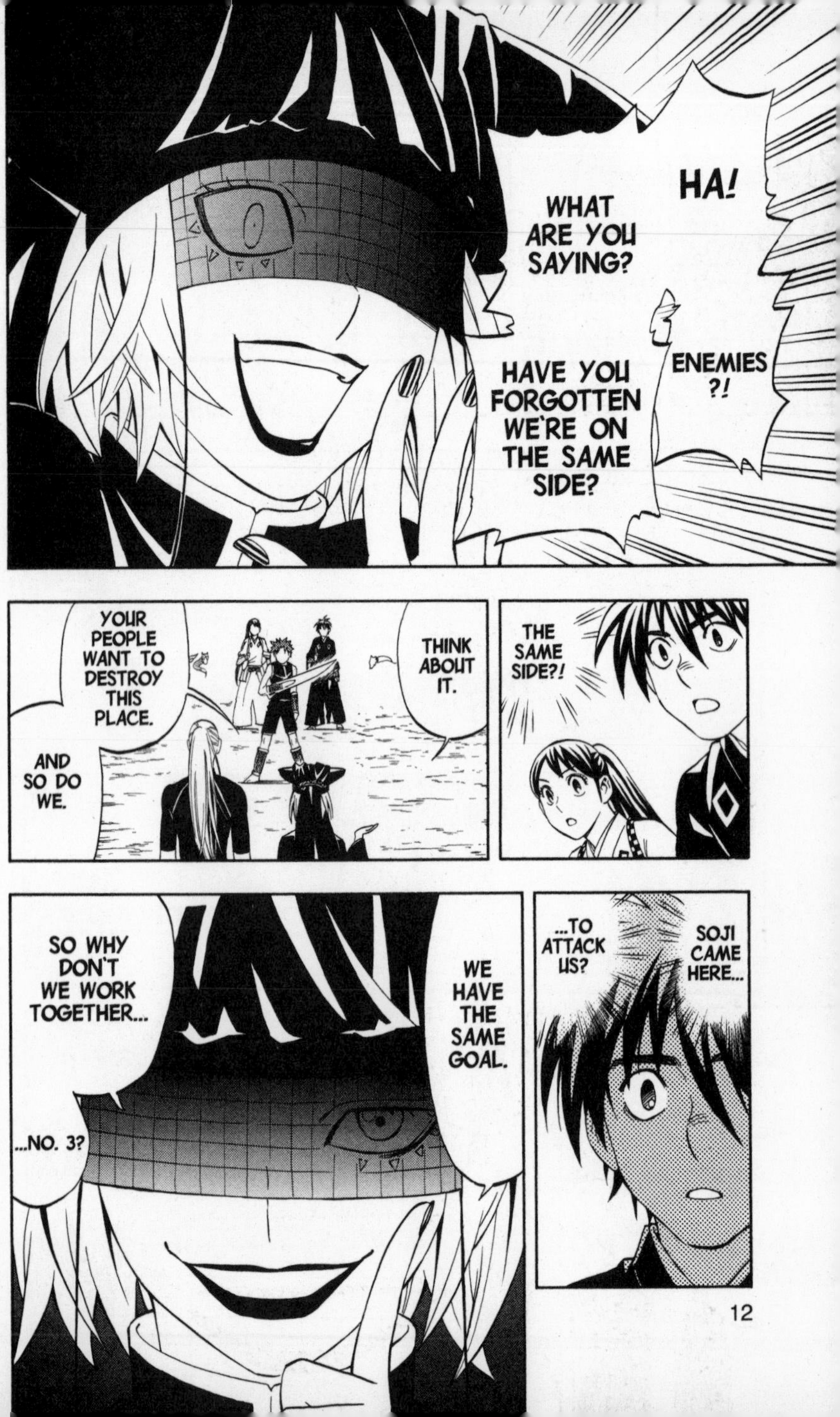
HA!
ENEMIES ?!
WHAT ARE YOU SAYING?
HAVE YOU FORGOTTEN WE'RE ON THE SAME SIDE?
THE SAME SIDE?!
THINK ABOUT IT.
YOUR PEOPLE WANT TO DESTROY THIS PLACE.
AND SO DO WE.
SOJI CAME HERE...
...TO ATTACK US?
WE HAVE THE SAME GOAL.
SO WHY DON'T WE WORK TOGETHER...
...NO. 3?

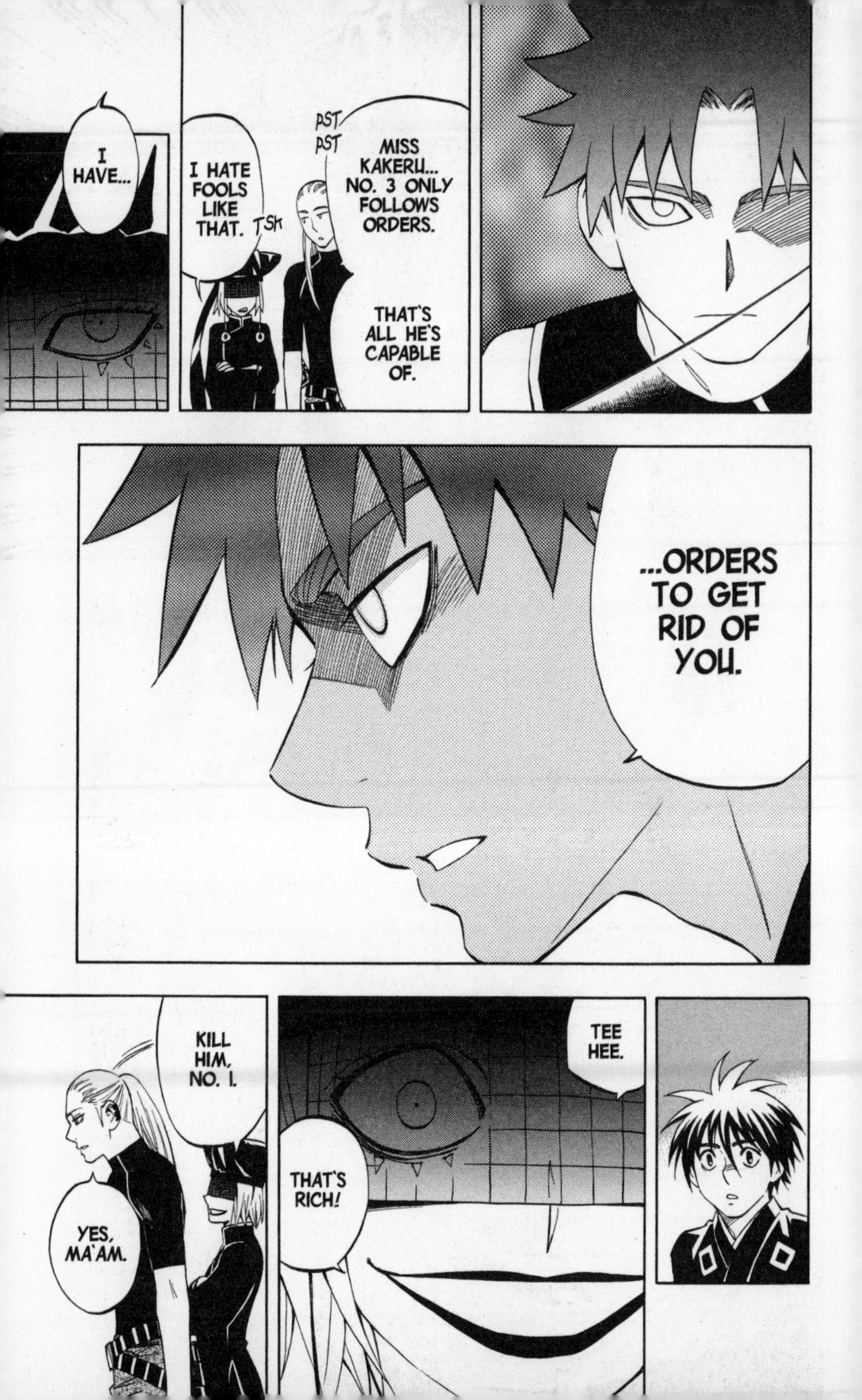
PST PST
MISS KAKERU... NO. 3 ONLY FOLLOWS ORDERS.
THAT'S ALL HE'S CAPABLE OF.
I HATE FOOLS LIKE THAT.
TSK
I HAVE...
...ORDERS TO GET RID OF YOU.
TEE HEE.
THAT'S RICH!
KILL HIM, NO. 1.
YES, MA'AM.

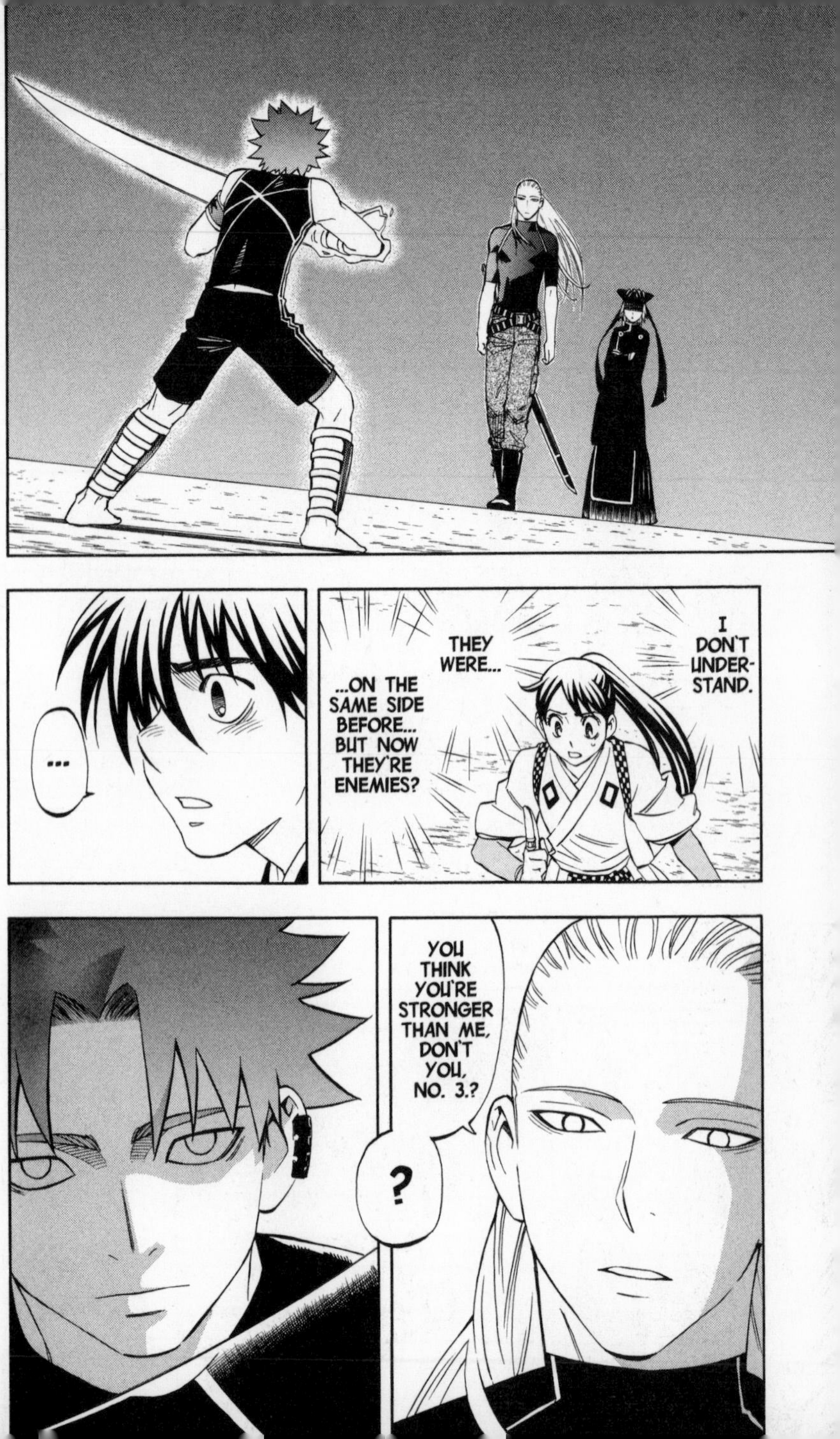
I DON'T UNDERSTAND.
THEY WERE...
...ON THE SAME SIDE BEFORE... BUT NOW THEY'RE ENEMIES?
...
YOU THINK YOU'RE STRONGER THAN ME, DON'T YOU, NO. 3.?
?

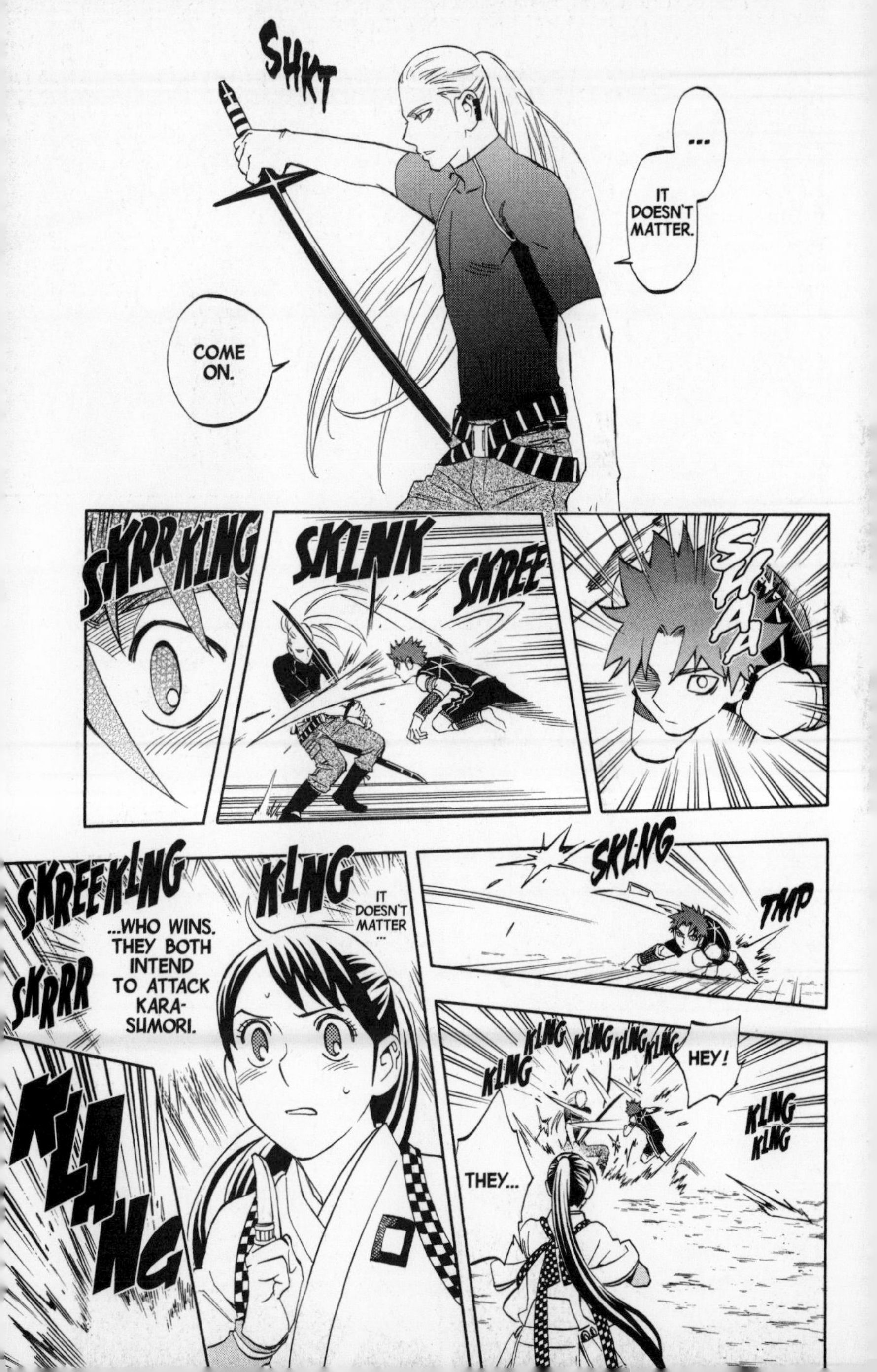
...
IT DOESN'T MATTER.
SHKT
COME ON.
SHAA
SKREE
SKLNK
SKRR KLNG
SKLNG
TMP
HEY!
KLNG KLNG
KLNG KLNG KLNG KLNG KLNG
THEY...
IT DOESN'T MATTER...
KLNG
SKREE KLNG
...WHO WINS. THEY BOTH INTEND TO ATTACK KARASUMORI.
SKRRR
KLANG

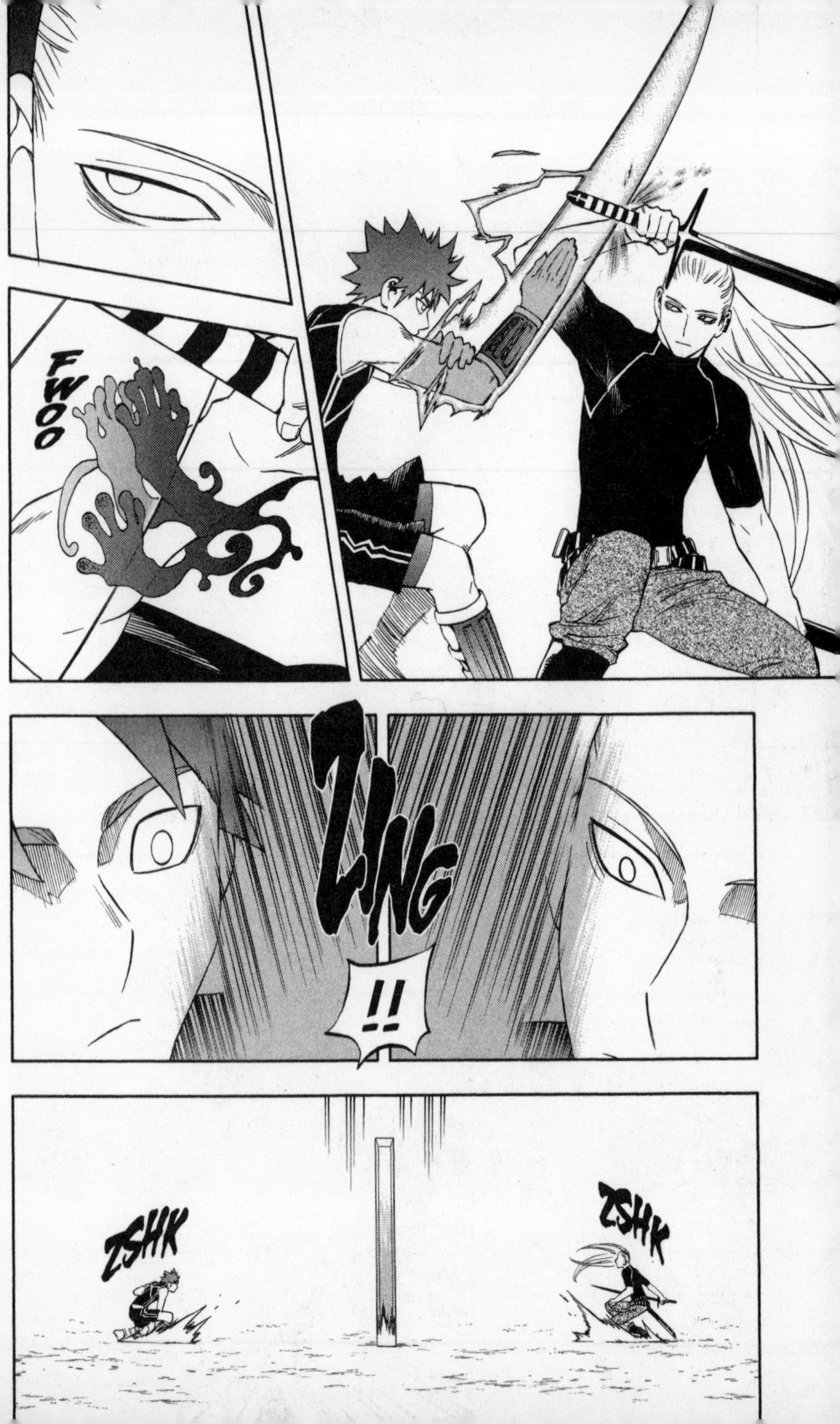
FWOO
ZING
!!
ZSHK
ZSHK

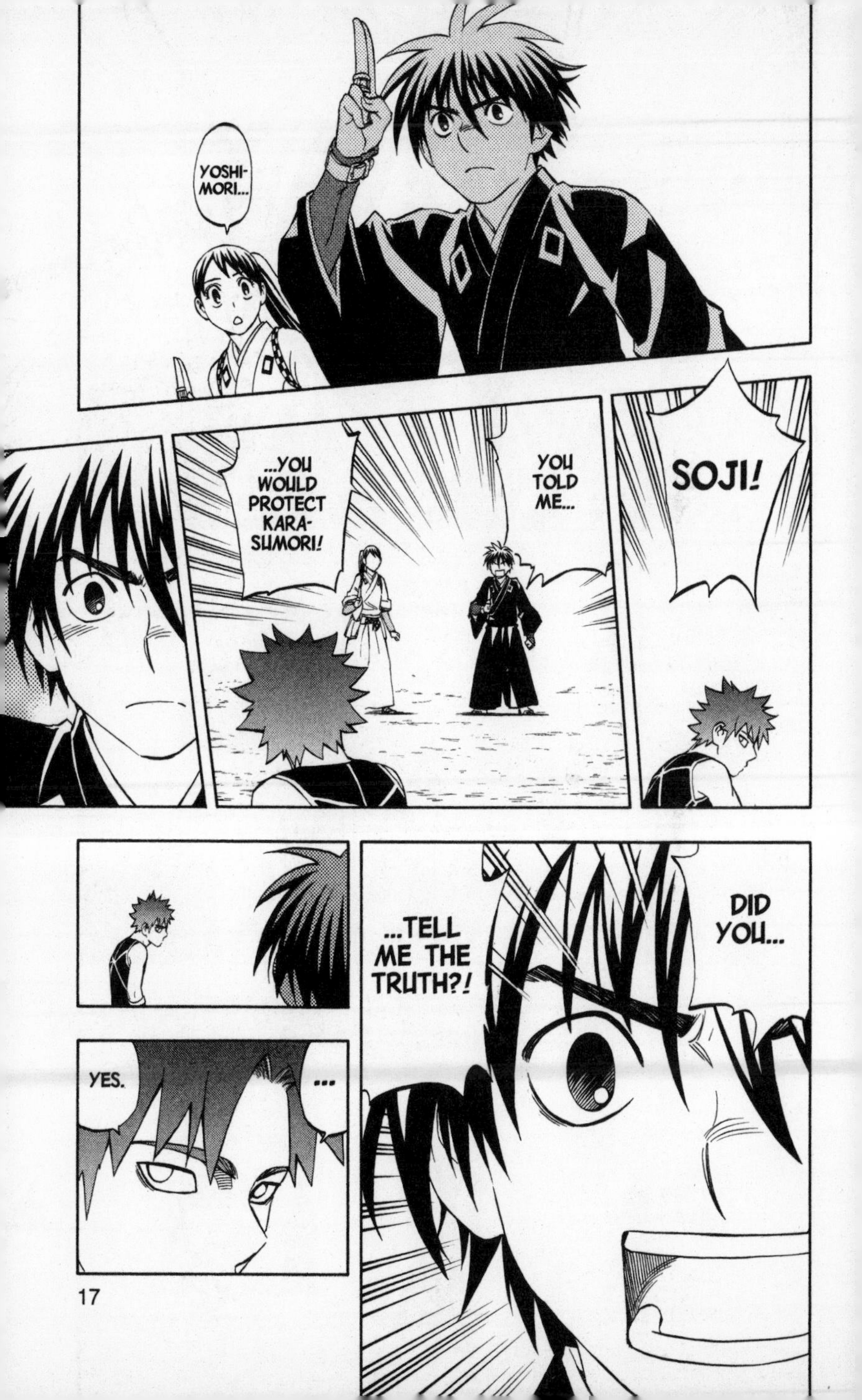
YOSHI-MORI...
SOJI!
YOU TOLD ME...
...YOU WOULD PROTECT KARA-SUMORI!
DID YOU...
...TELL ME THE TRUTH?!
...
YES.

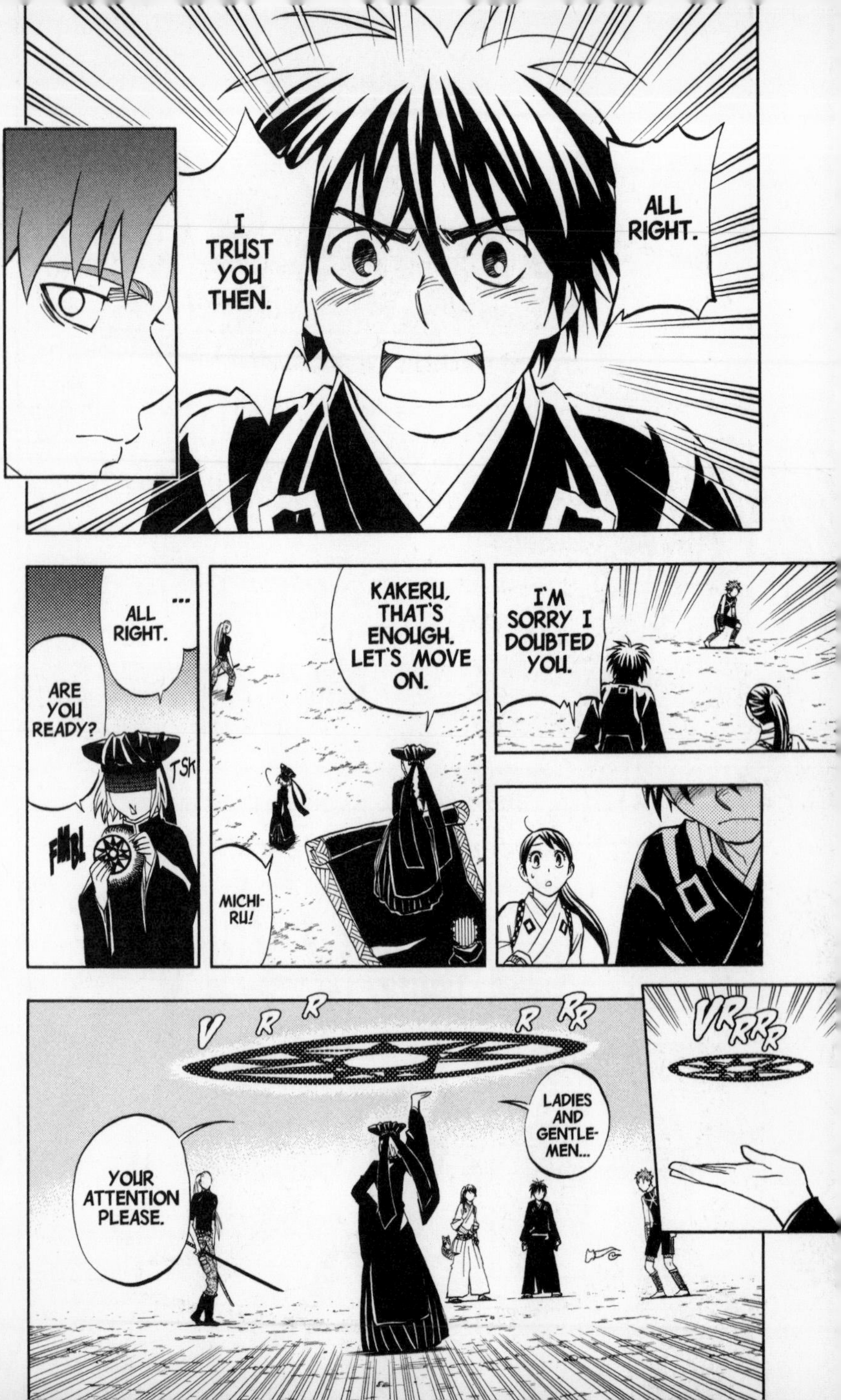
ALL RIGHT.
I TRUST YOU THEN.
I'M SORRY I DOUBTED YOU.
KAKERU, THAT'S ENOUGH. LET'S MOVE ON.
MICHI-RU!
... ALL RIGHT.
ARE YOU READY?
TSK
FMBL
VRRRR
VRRRRR
LADIES AND GENTLE-MEN...
YOUR ATTENTION PLEASE.

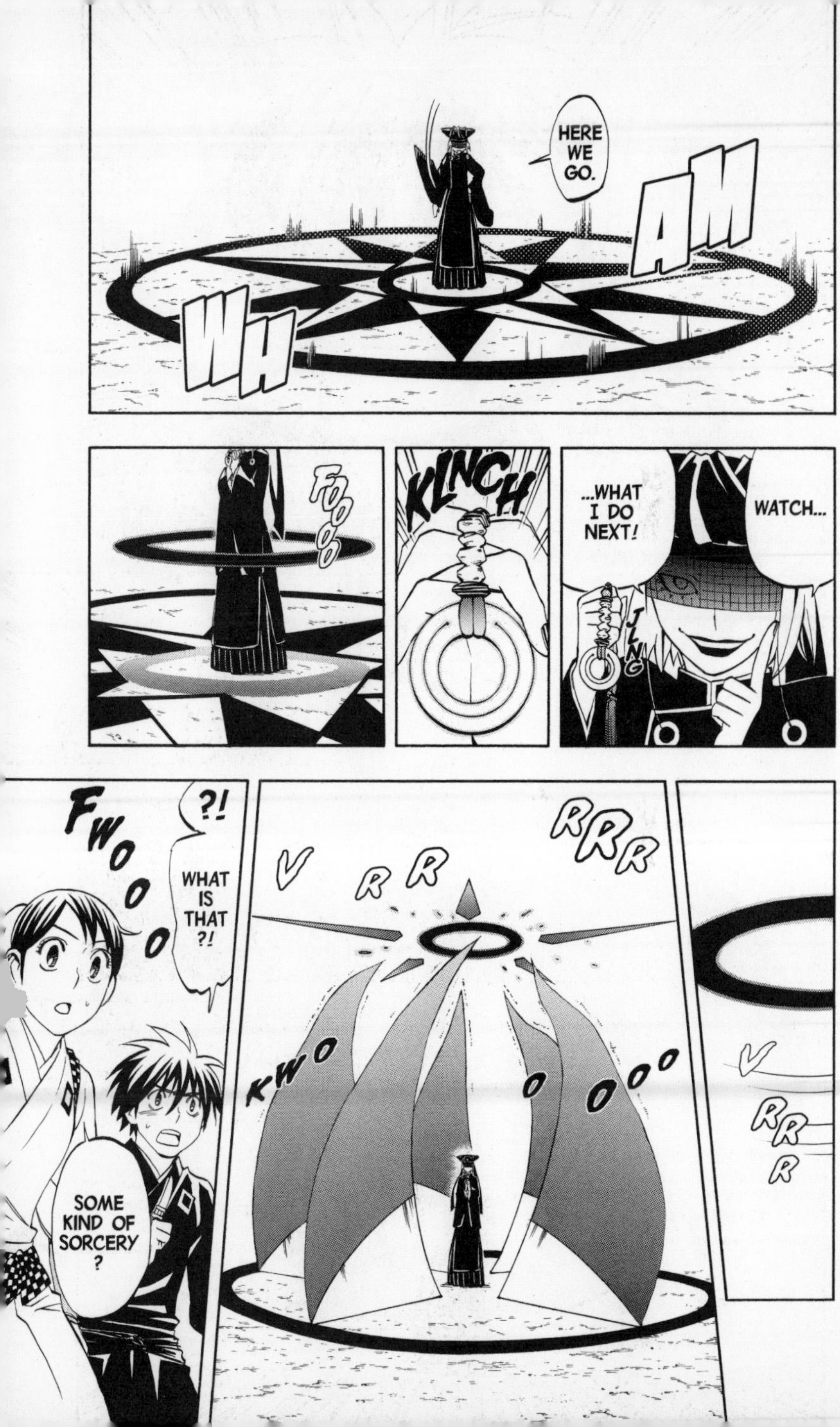
HERE WE GO.
WHAM
WATCH...
...WHAT I DO NEXT!
JING
KLINCH
FOOOOO
VRRR
RRRR
VRR
KWOOOOO
?!
WHAT IS THAT?!
FWOOOO
SOME KIND OF SORCERY?

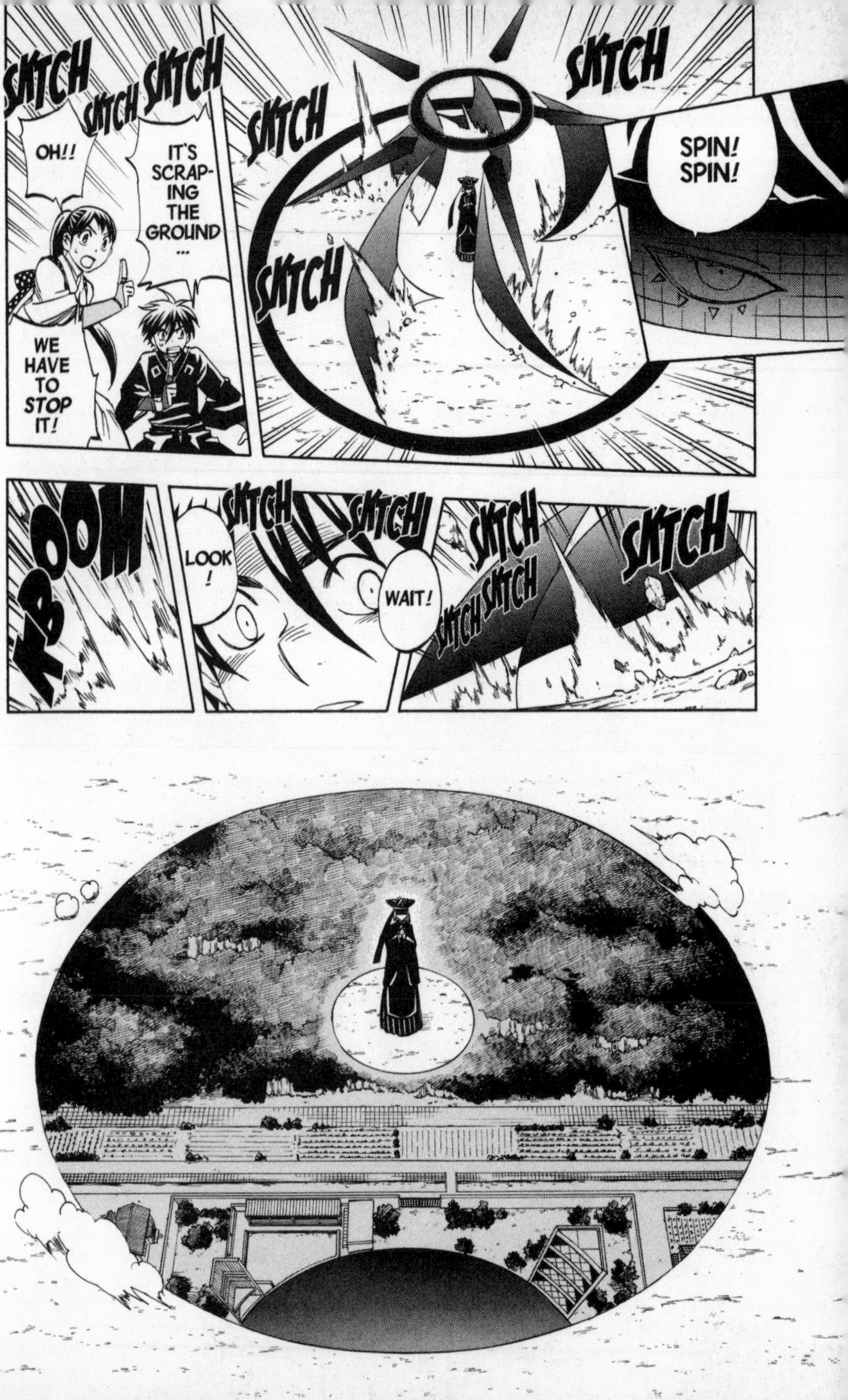
SKTCH
SPIN! SPIN!
SKTCH
SKTCH
SKTCH
SKTCH SKTCH
IT'S SCRAPING THE GROUND...
OH!!
WE HAVE TO STOP IT!
SKTCH
SKTCH
SKTCH SKTCH
SKTCH!
WAIT!
SKTCH
LOOK!
KBOOM

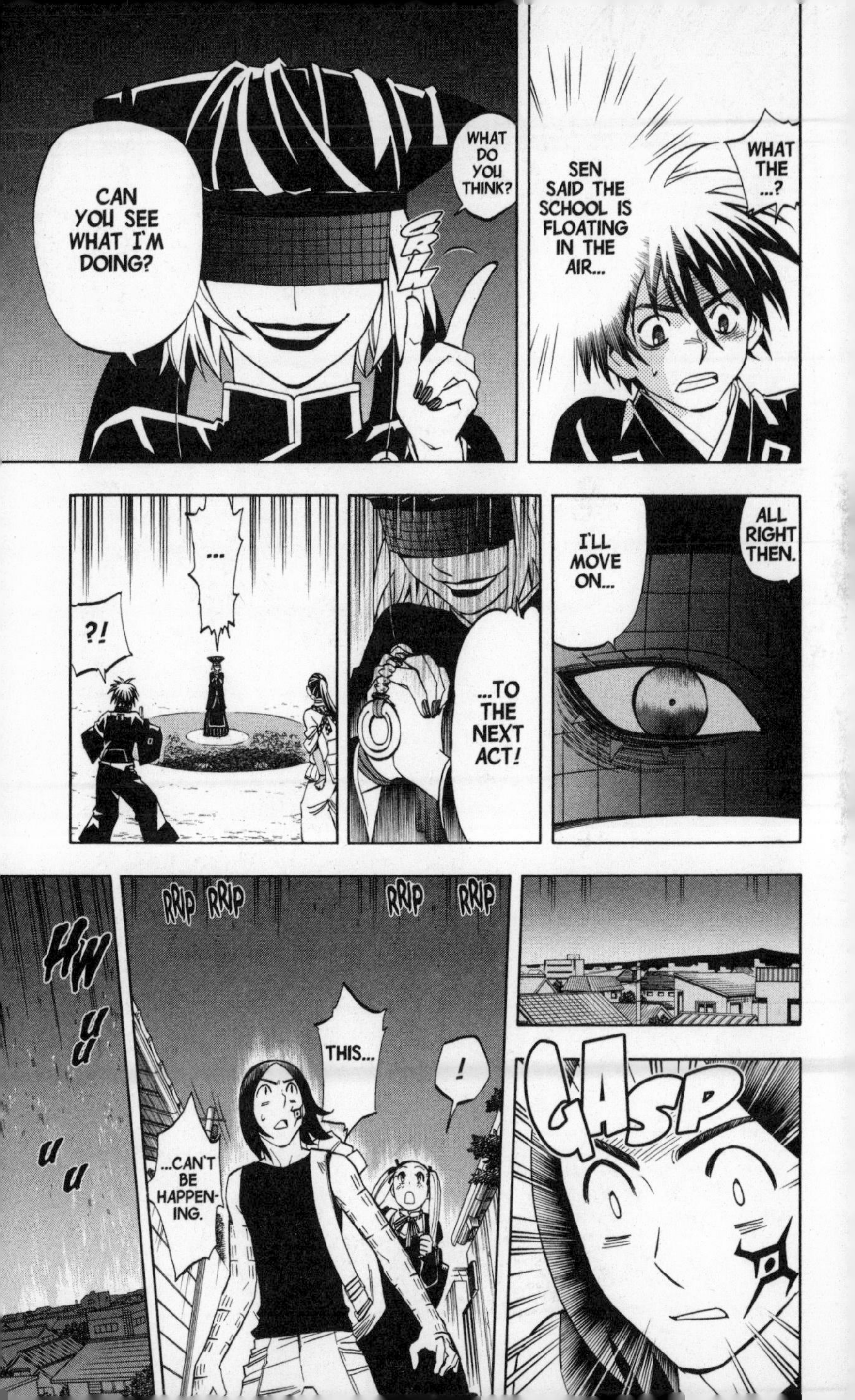
WHAT THE ...?
SEN SAID THE SCHOOL IS FLOATING IN THE AIR...
WHAT DO YOU THINK?
GRIN
CAN YOU SEE WHAT I'M DOING?
ALL RIGHT THEN.
I'LL MOVE ON...
...TO THE NEXT ACT!
...
?!
GASP
RRIP RRIP
RRIP RRIP
!
THIS...
...CAN'T BE HAPPEN-ING.
HWuuuu

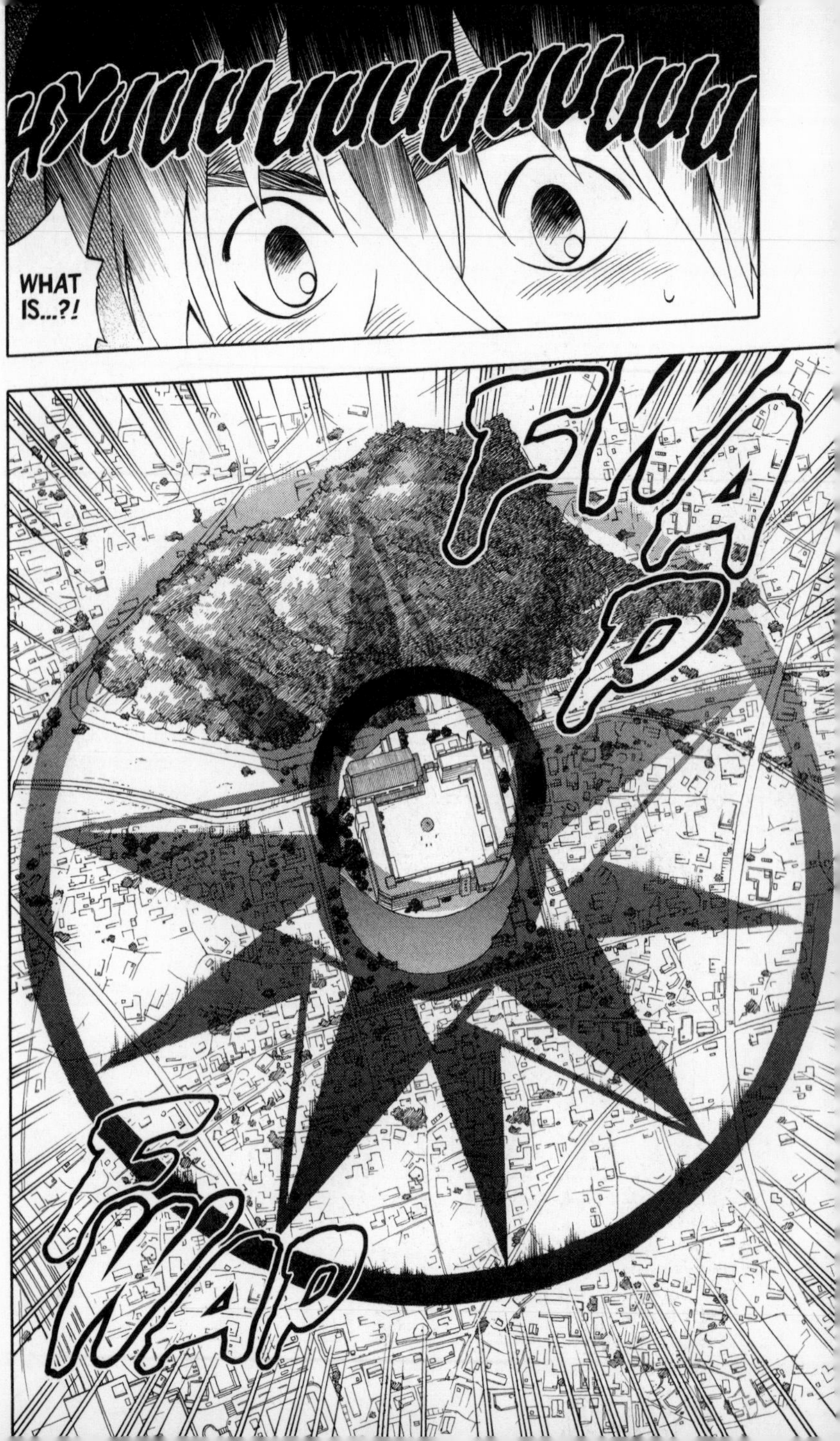
WHAT IS...?!
FWAP
FWAP

Chapter 257: Prodigy

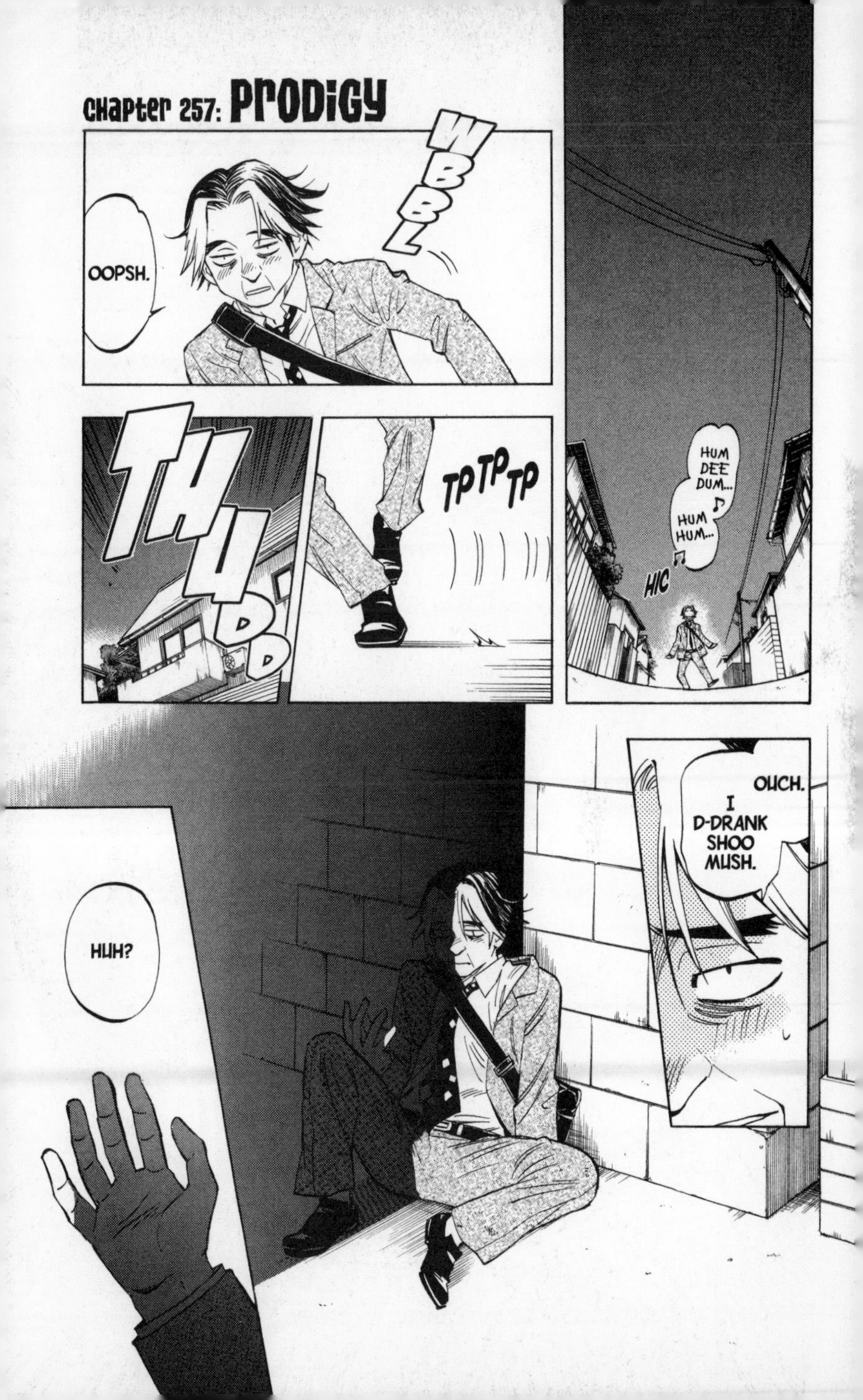
HUM DEE DUM... ♪
HUM HUM... ♪
HIC
WBBL
OOPSH.
TP TP TP
THUDD
OUCH.
I D-DRANK SHOO MUSH.
HUH?

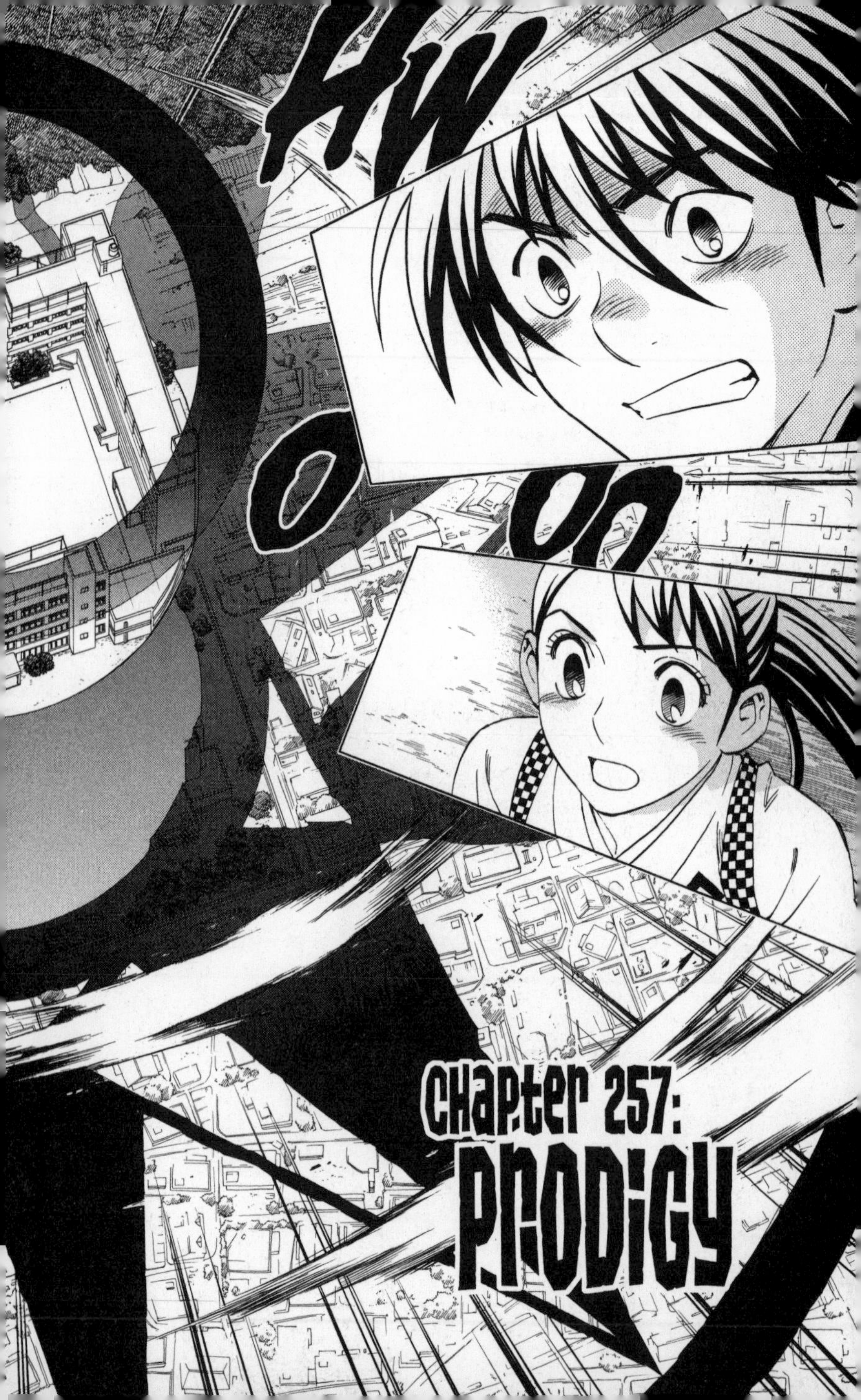
HWOON
CHAPTER 257:
PRODIGY

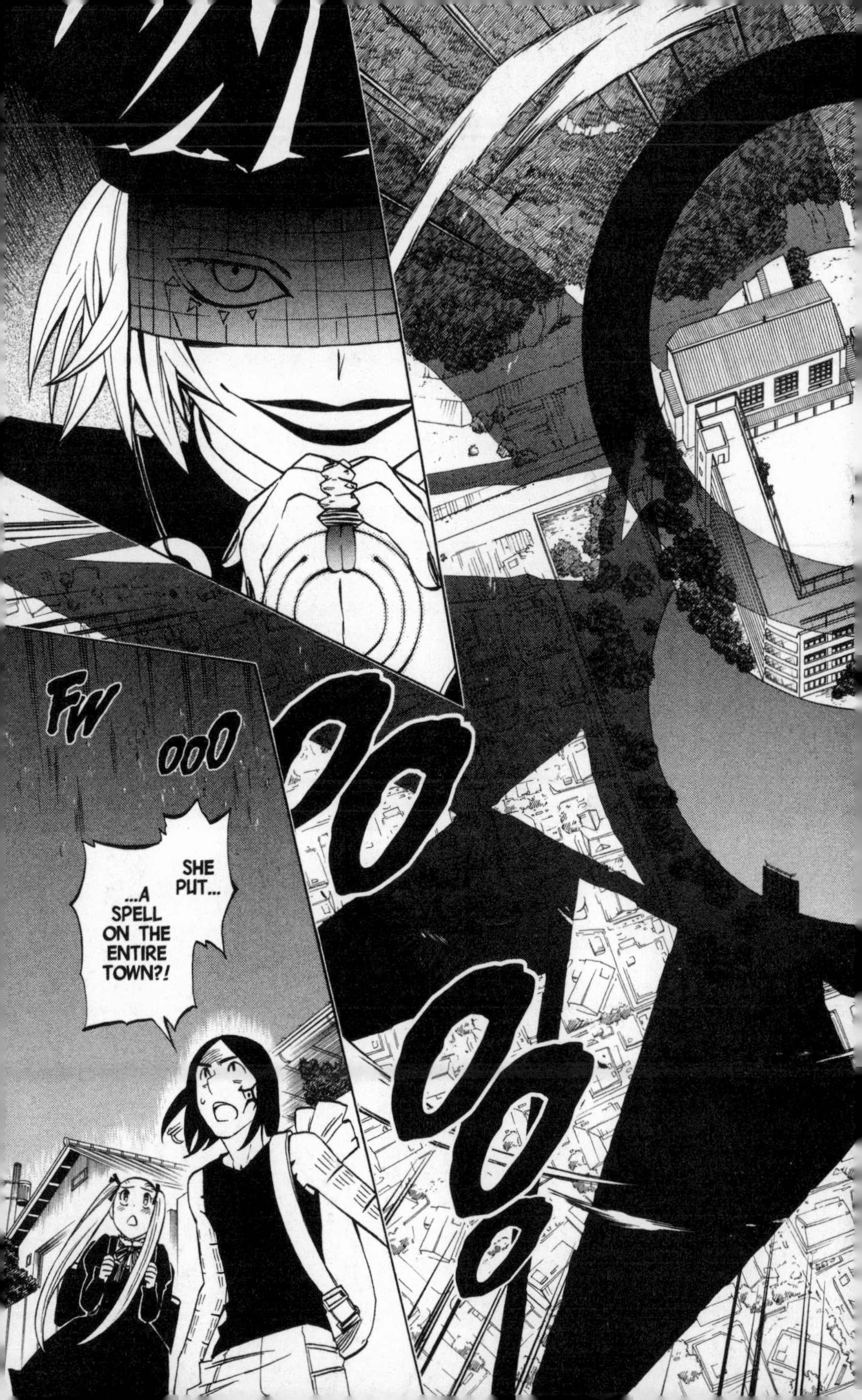
FWOOOOOOOOOOOOO
SHE PUT... ...A SPELL ON THE ENTIRE TOWN?!

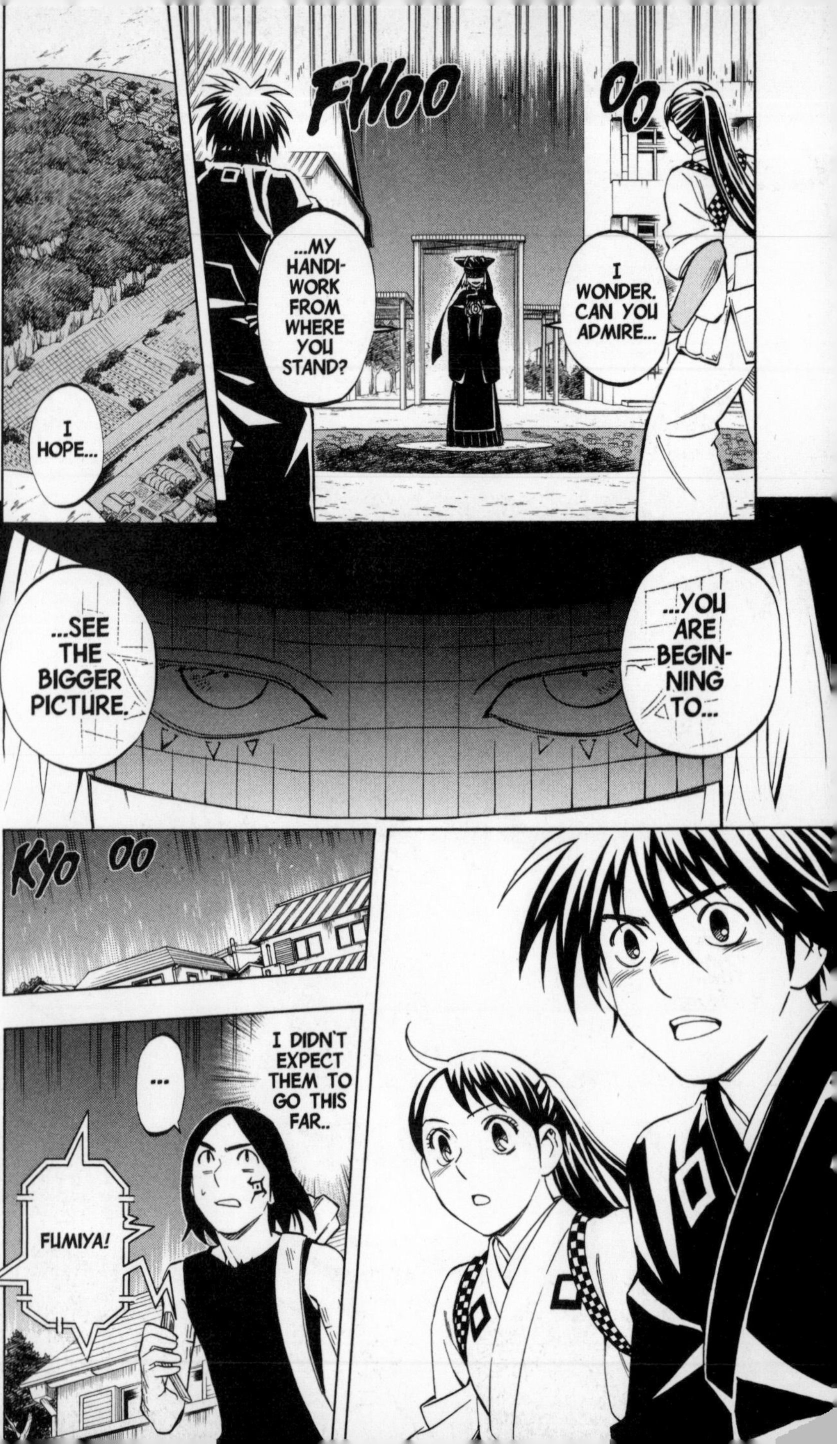
FWOOOO
I WONDER. CAN YOU ADMIRE...
...MY HANDIWORK FROM WHERE YOU STAND?
I HOPE...
...YOU ARE BEGINNING TO...
...SEE THE BIGGER PICTURE.
KYOOO
I DIDN'T EXPECT THEM TO GO THIS FAR..
...
FUMIYA!

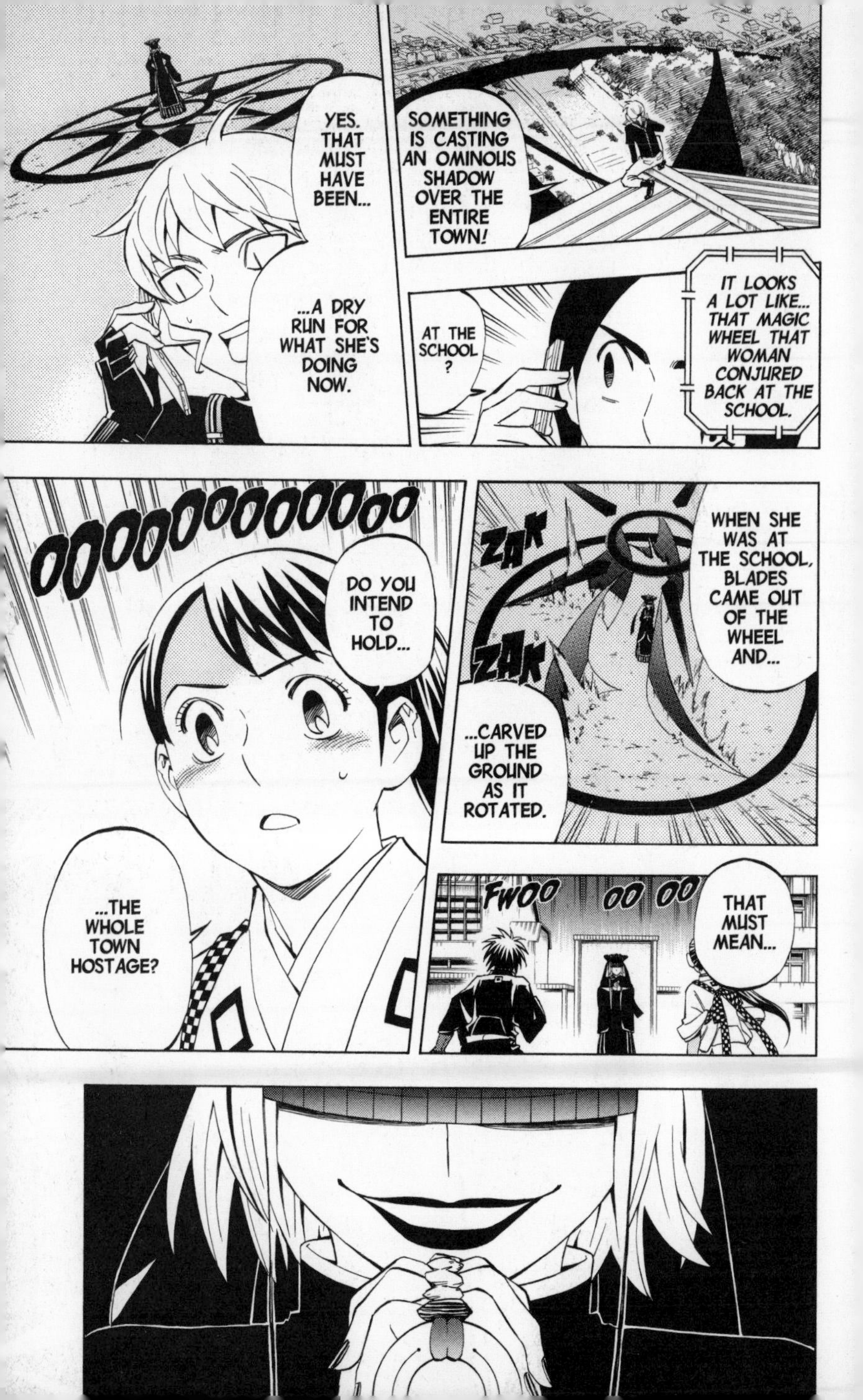
SOMETHING IS CASTING AN OMINOUS SHADOW OVER THE ENTIRE TOWN!
IT LOOKS A LOT LIKE... THAT MAGIC WHEEL THAT WOMAN CONJURED BACK AT THE SCHOOL.
AT THE SCHOOL?
YES. THAT MUST HAVE BEEN...
...A DRY RUN FOR WHAT SHE'S DOING NOW.
WHEN SHE WAS AT THE SCHOOL, BLADES CAME OUT OF THE WHEEL AND...
ZAK
ZAK
...CARVED UP THE GROUND AS IT ROTATED.
THAT MUST MEAN...
FWOO OO OO
OOOOOOOOOOOOOO
DO YOU INTEND TO HOLD...
...THE WHOLE TOWN HOSTAGE?

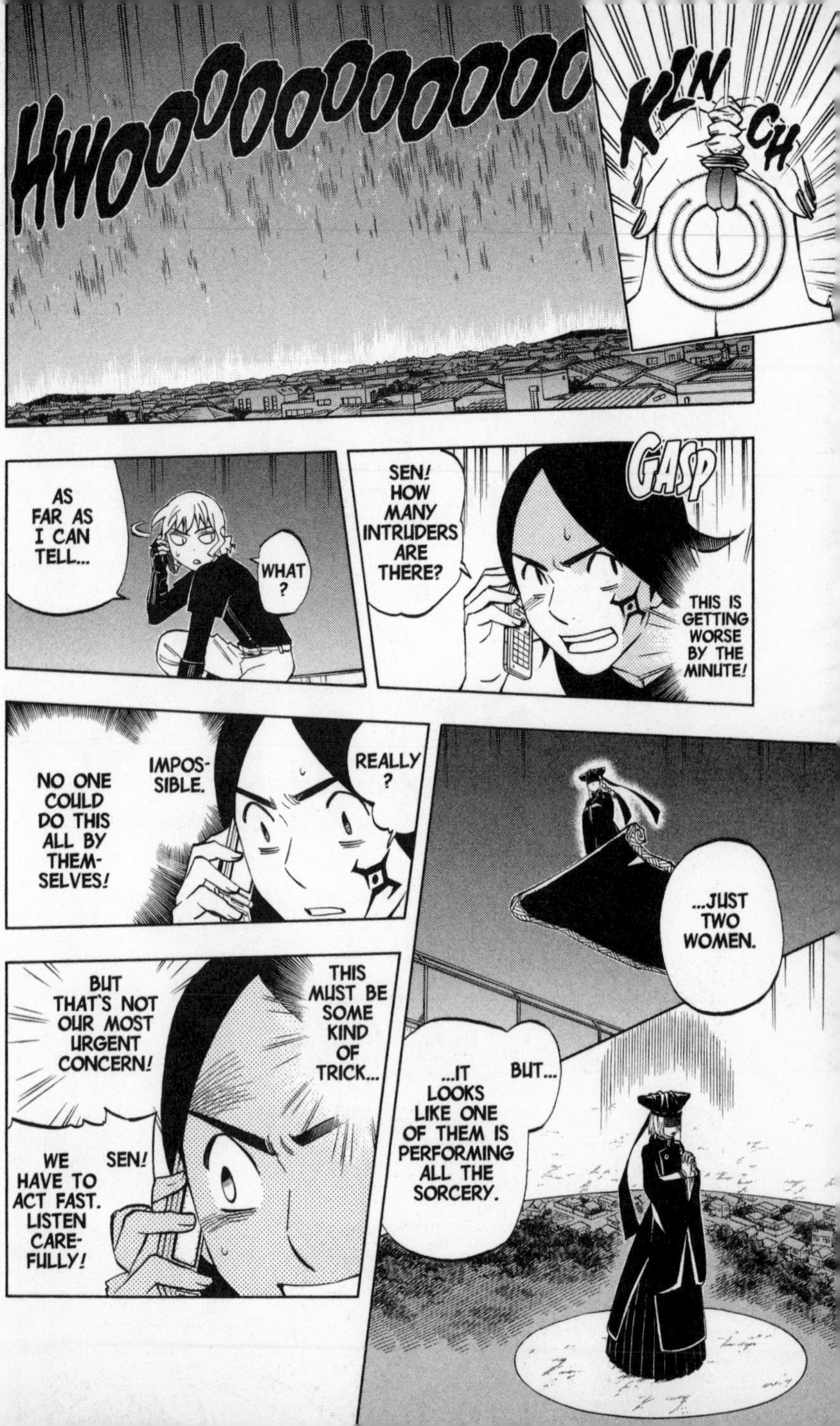
KLNCH
HWOOOOOOOOOOO
GASP
SEN! HOW MANY INTRUDERS ARE THERE?
THIS IS GETTING WORSE BY THE MINUTE!
WHAT?
AS FAR AS I CAN TELL...
...JUST TWO WOMEN.
BUT...
...IT LOOKS LIKE ONE OF THEM IS PERFORMING ALL THE SORCERY.
REALLY?
IMPOSSIBLE.
NO ONE COULD DO THIS ALL BY THEMSELVES!
THIS MUST BE SOME KIND OF TRICK...
BUT THAT'S NOT OUR MOST URGENT CONCERN!
SEN!
WE HAVE TO ACT FAST. LISTEN CAREFULLY!

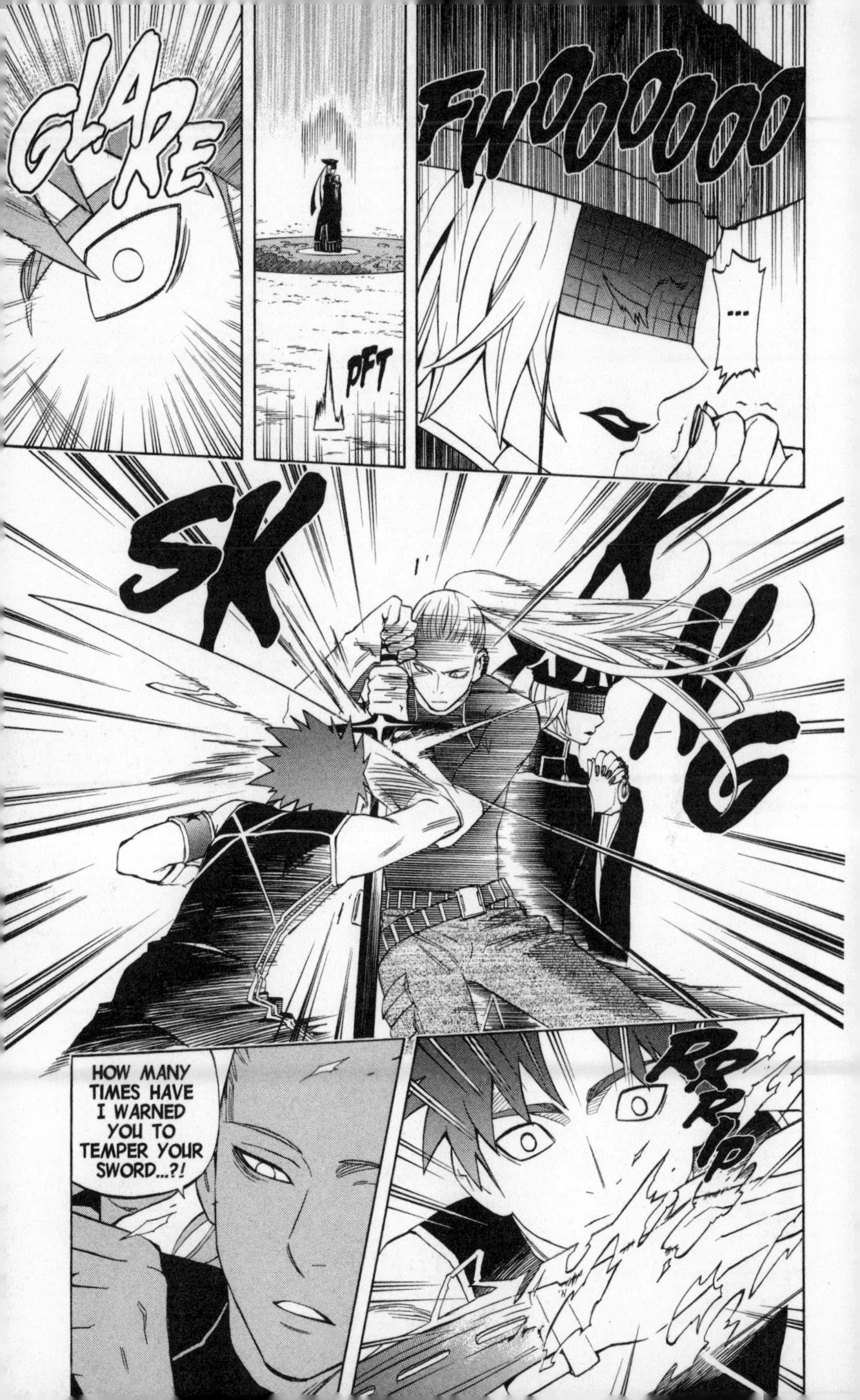
FWOOOOOO
...
PFT
GLARE
SKKNG
RRRIP
HOW MANY TIMES HAVE I WARNED YOU TO TEMPER YOUR SWORD...?!

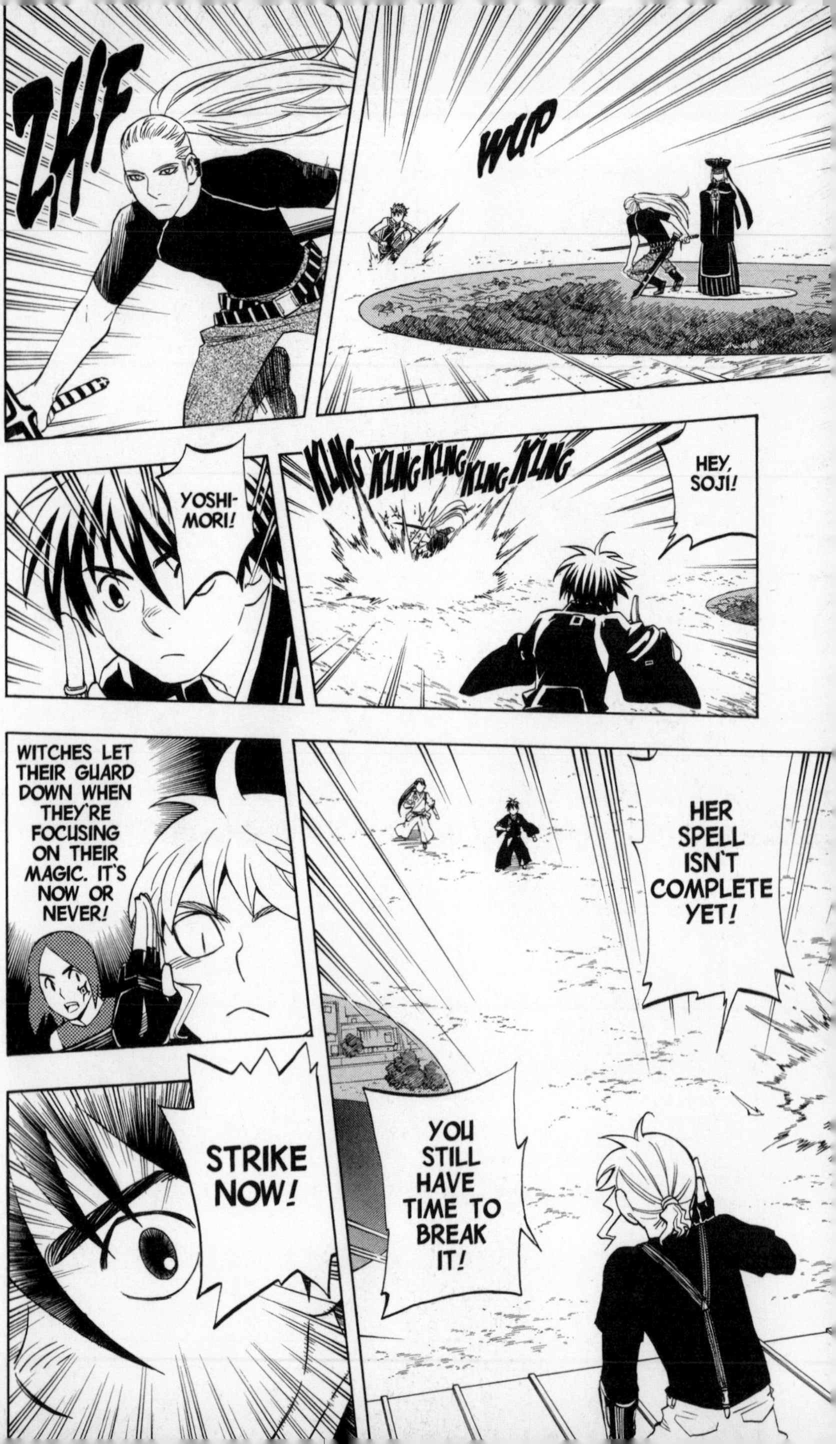
WUP
ZHF
HEY, SOJI!
KLING KLING KLING KLING KLING
YOSHI-MORI!
HER SPELL ISN'T COMPLETE YET!
YOU STILL HAVE TIME TO BREAK IT!
WITCHES LET THEIR GUARD DOWN WHEN THEY'RE FOCUSING ON THEIR MAGIC. IT'S NOW OR NEVER!
STRIKE NOW!

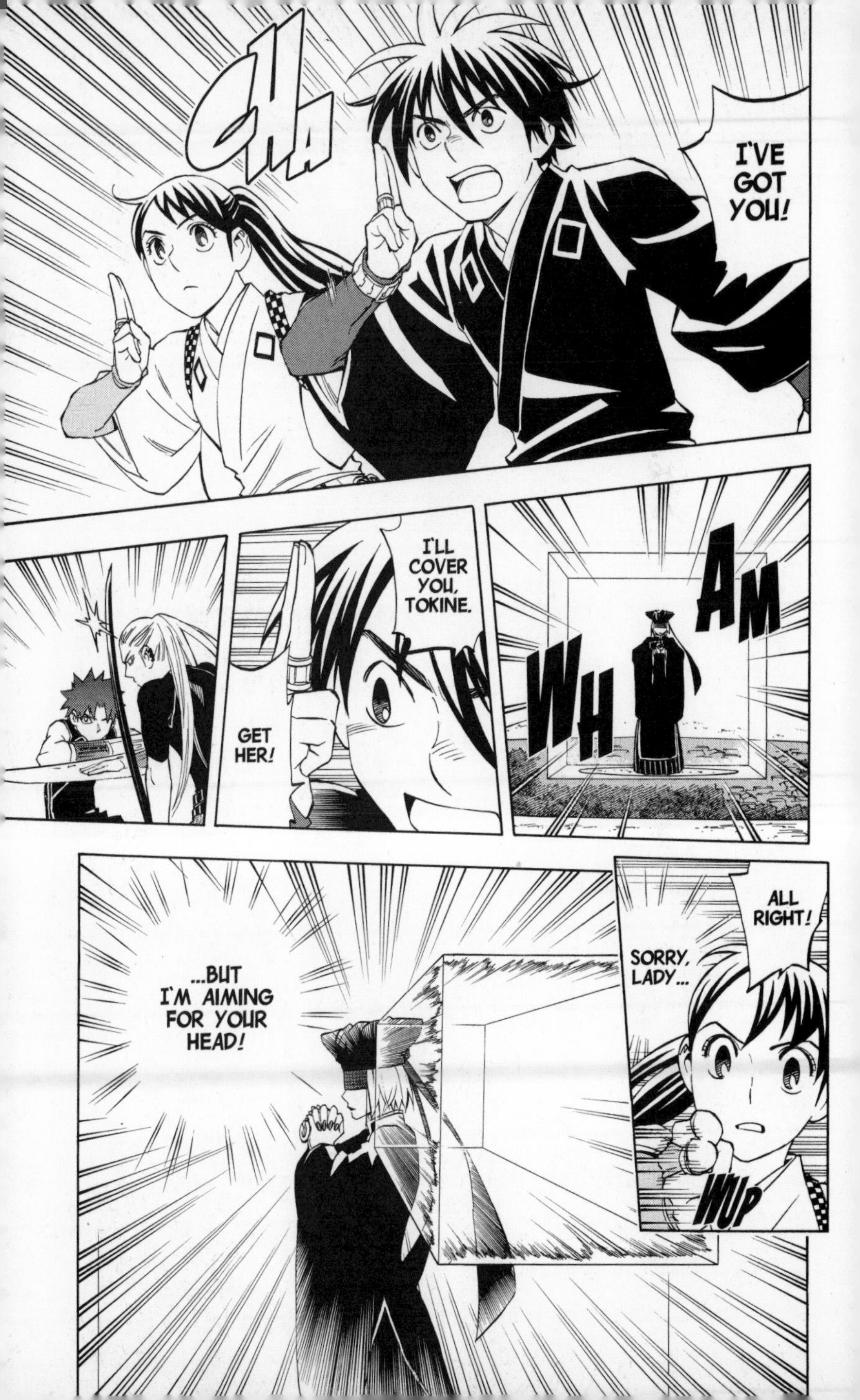
I'VE GOT YOU!
CHA
WHAM
I'LL COVER YOU, TOKINE.
GET HER!
ALL RIGHT!
SORRY, LADY...
WUP
...BUT I'M AIMING FOR YOUR HEAD!

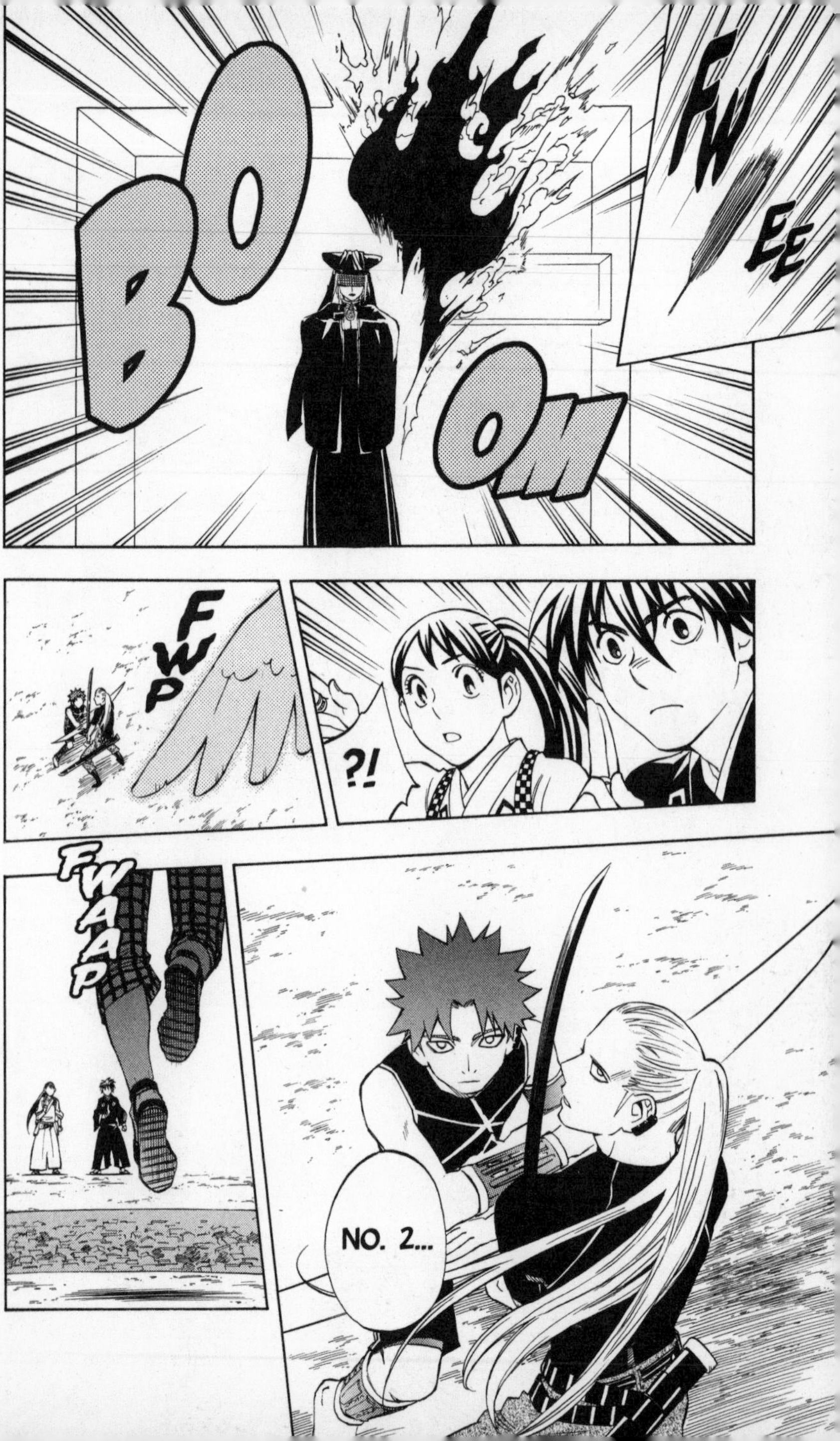
FWEE
BOOM
?!
FWP
NO. 2...
FWAAP

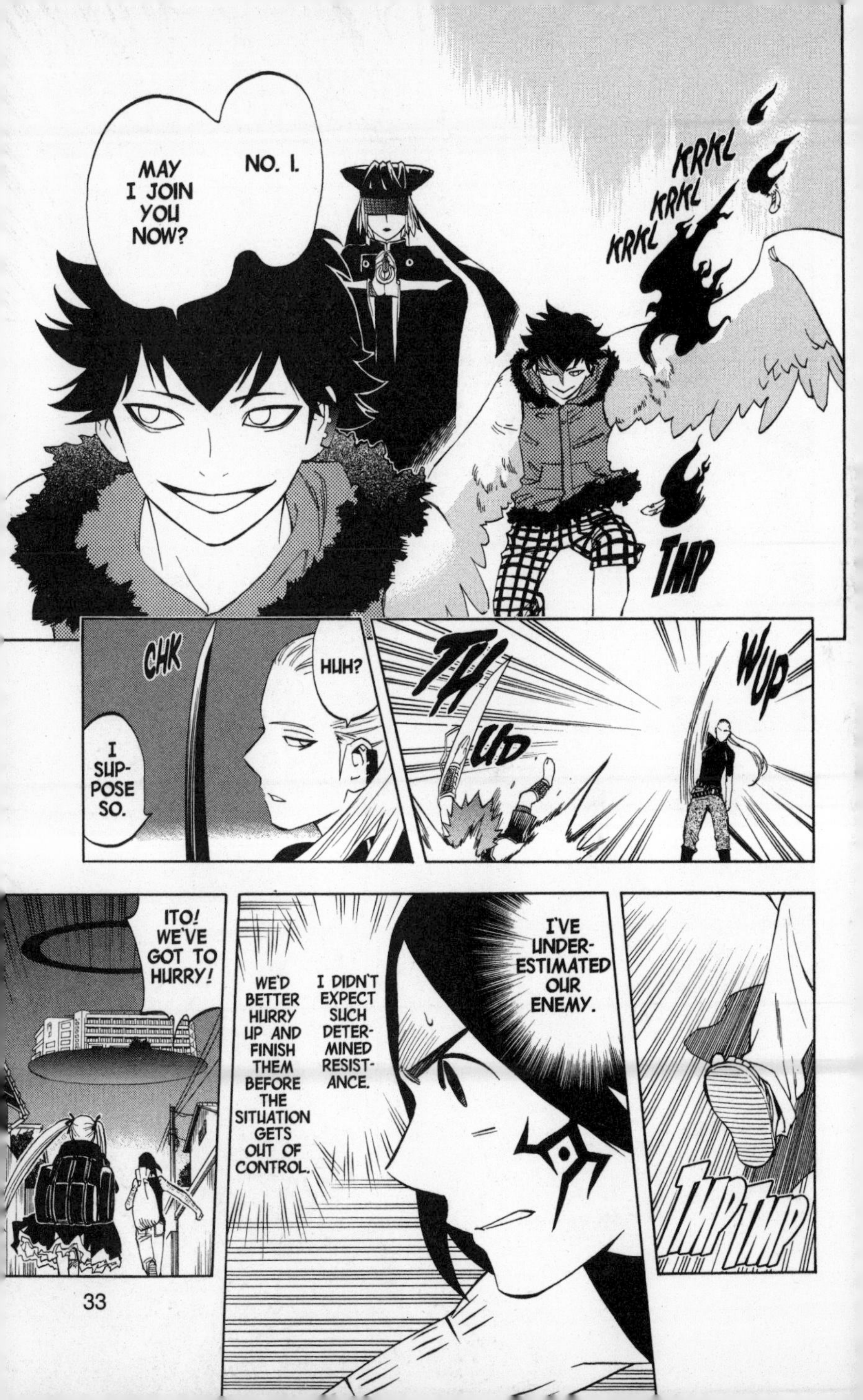
NO. I.
MAY I JOIN YOU NOW?
KRKL KRKL KRKL
TMP
WUP
THUD
HUH?
I SUPPOSE SO.
CHK
TMP TMP
I'VE UNDERESTIMATED OUR ENEMY.
I DIDN'T EXPECT SUCH DETERMINED RESISTANCE.
WE'D BETTER HURRY UP AND FINISH THEM BEFORE THE SITUATION GETS OUT OF CONTROL.
ITO! WE'VE GOT TO HURRY!

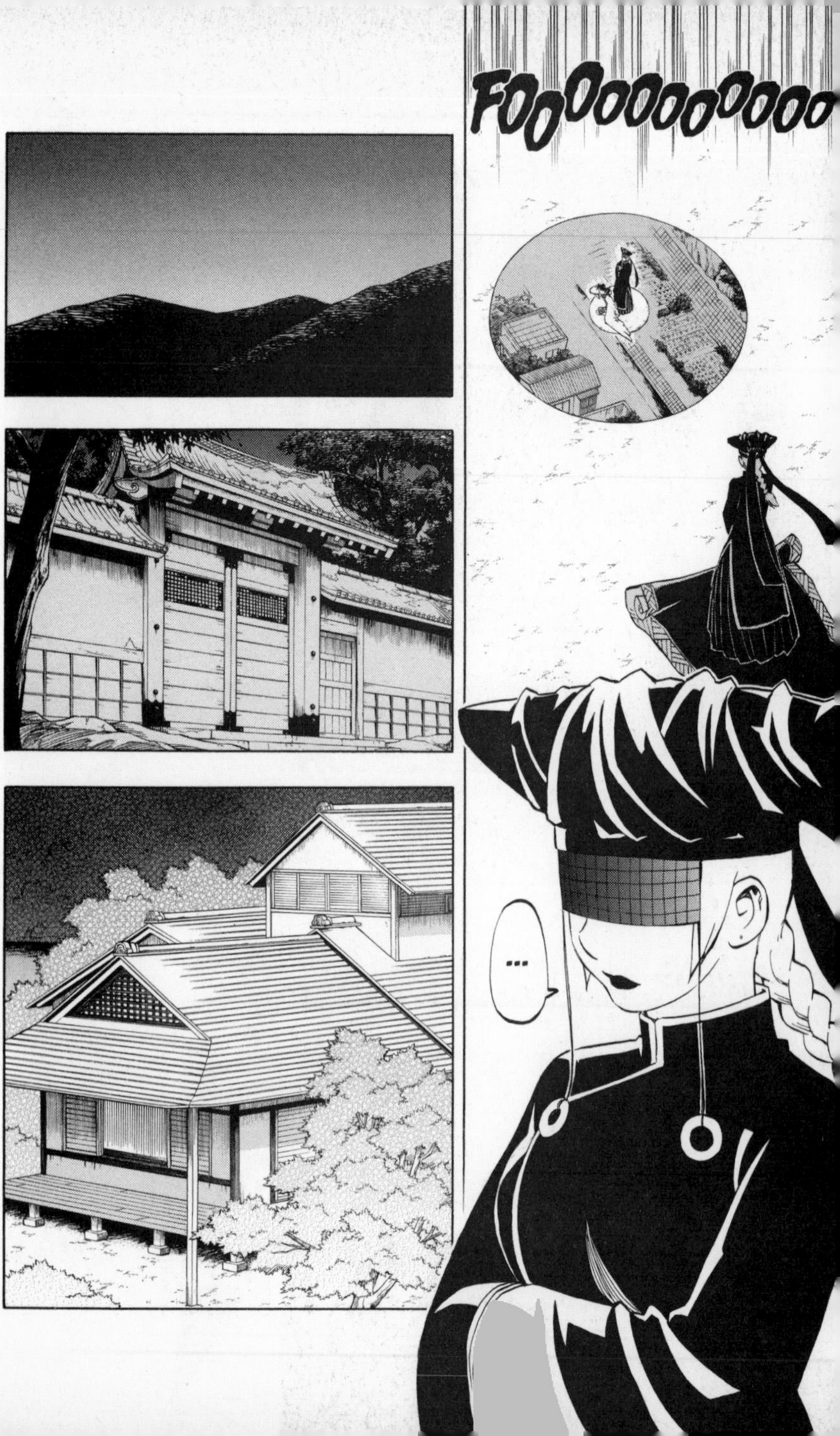
FOOOOOOOOOOO
...

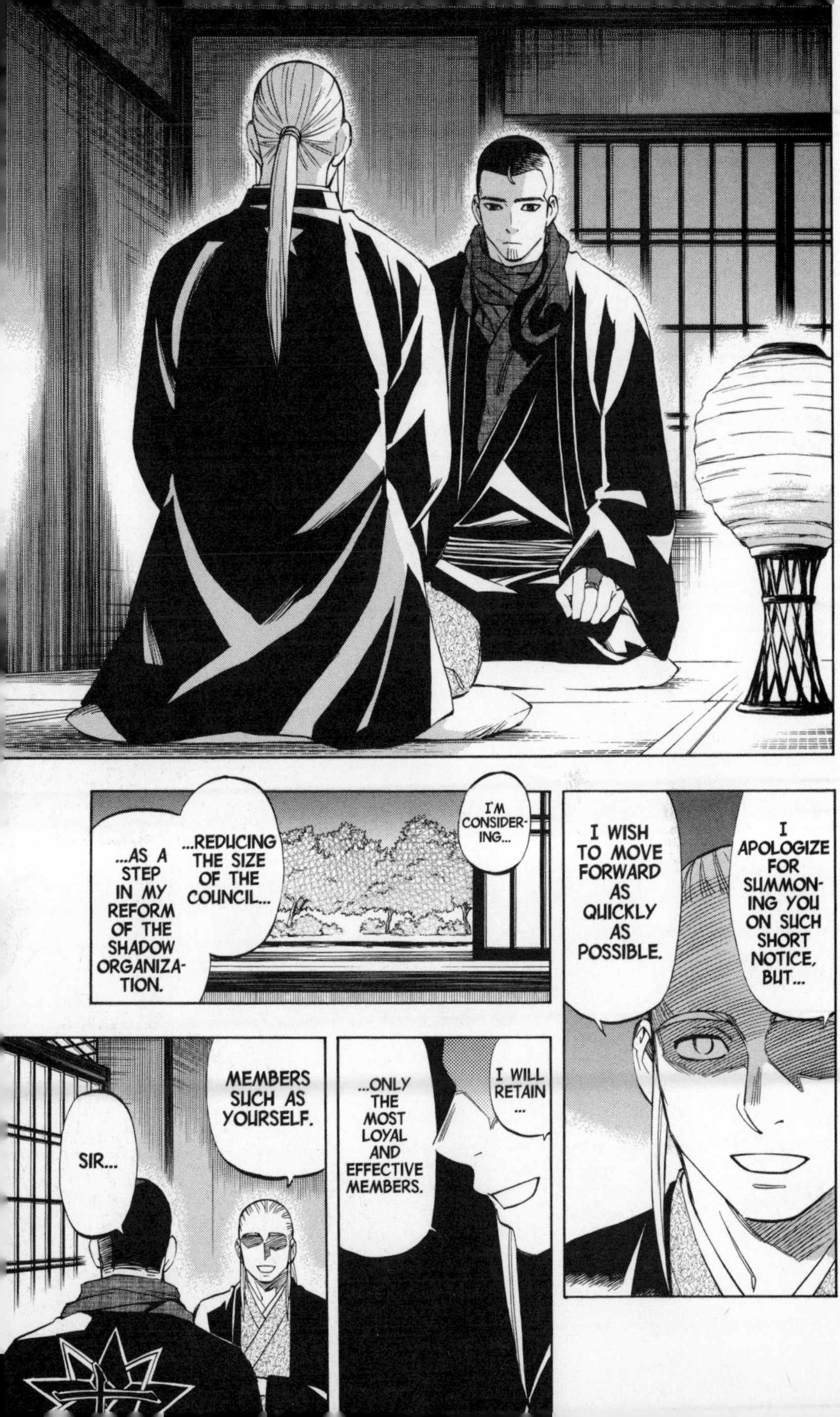
I APOLOGIZE FOR SUMMONING YOU ON SUCH SHORT NOTICE, BUT...
I WISH TO MOVE FORWARD AS QUICKLY AS POSSIBLE.
I'M CONSIDERING...
...REDUCING THE SIZE OF THE COUNCIL...
...AS A STEP IN MY REFORM OF THE SHADOW ORGANIZATION.
I WILL RETAIN...
...ONLY THE MOST LOYAL AND EFFECTIVE MEMBERS.
MEMBERS SUCH AS YOURSELF.
SIR...

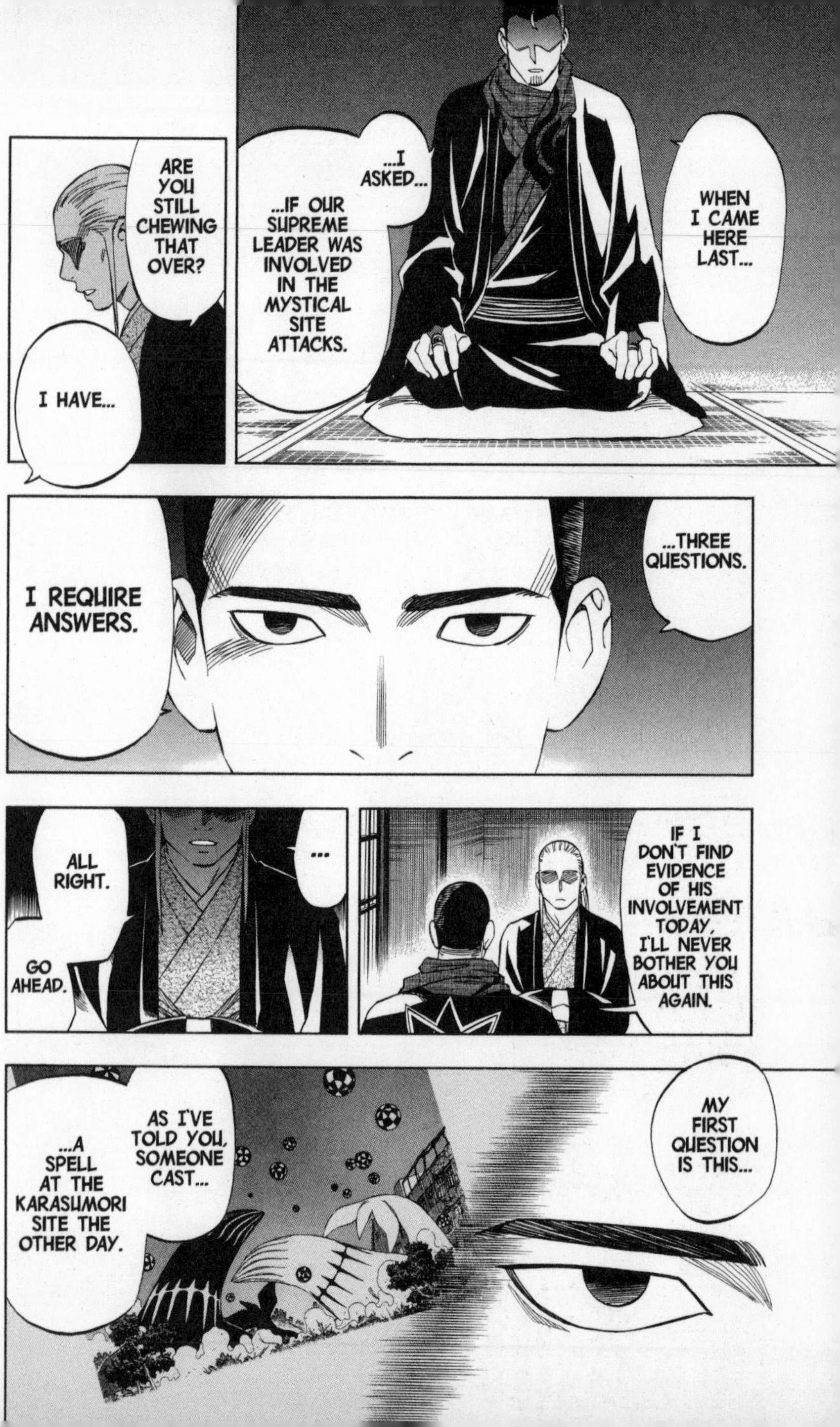
WHEN I CAME HERE LAST...
...I ASKED...
...IF OUR SUPREME LEADER WAS INVOLVED IN THE MYSTICAL SITE ATTACKS.
ARE YOU STILL CHEWING THAT OVER?
I HAVE...
...THREE QUESTIONS.
I REQUIRE ANSWERS.
IF I DON'T FIND EVIDENCE OF HIS INVOLVEMENT TODAY, I'LL NEVER BOTHER YOU ABOUT THIS AGAIN.
...
ALL RIGHT.
GO AHEAD.
MY FIRST QUESTION IS THIS...
AS I'VE TOLD YOU, SOMEONE CAST...
...A SPELL AT THE KARASUMORI SITE THE OTHER DAY.

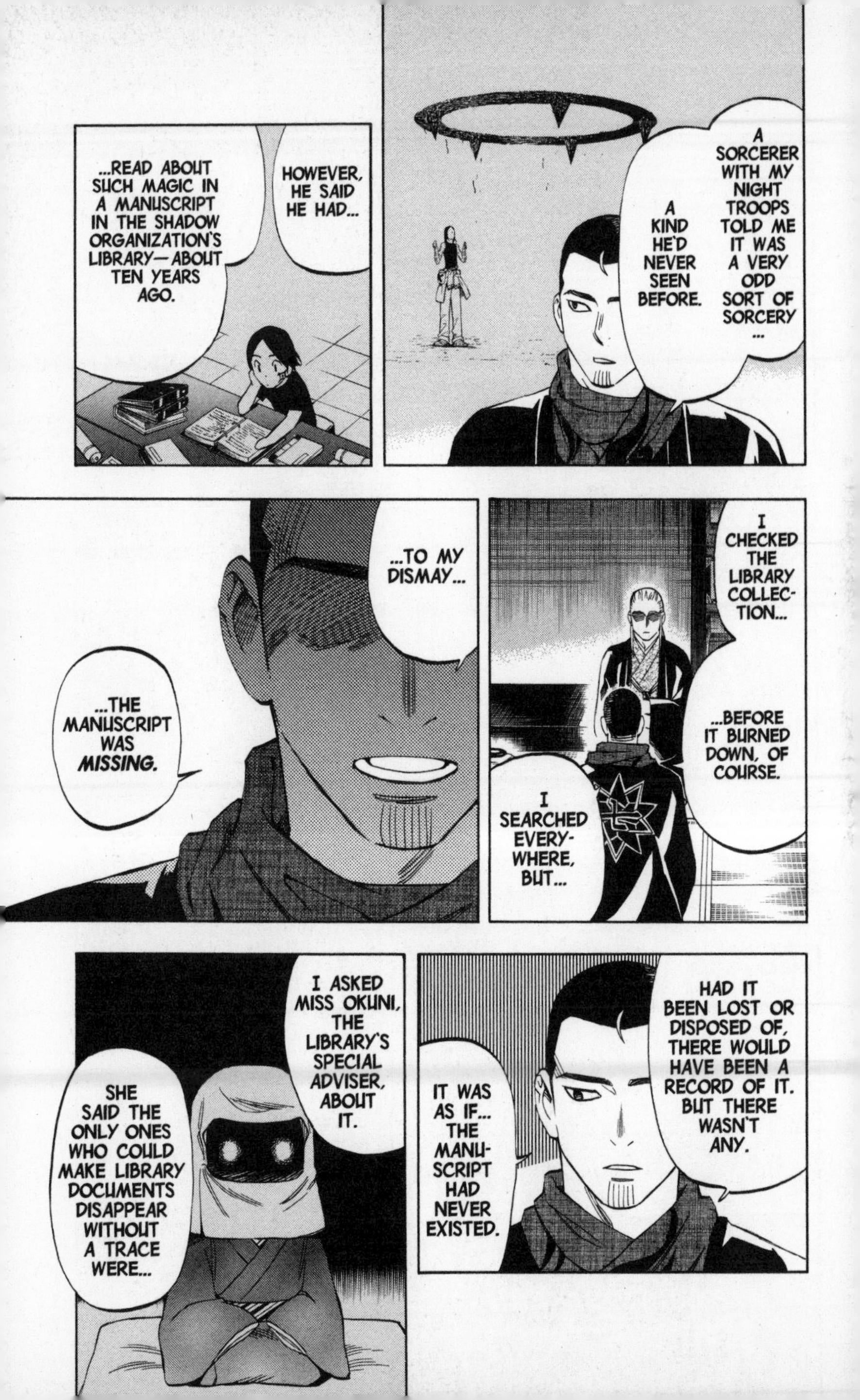
A SORCERER WITH MY NIGHT TROOPS TOLD ME IT WAS A VERY ODD SORT OF SORCERY...
A KIND HE'D NEVER SEEN BEFORE.
HOWEVER, HE SAID HE HAD...
...READ ABOUT SUCH MAGIC IN A MANUSCRIPT IN THE SHADOW ORGANIZATION'S LIBRARY—ABOUT TEN YEARS AGO.
I CHECKED THE LIBRARY COLLECTION...
...BEFORE IT BURNED DOWN, OF COURSE.
I SEARCHED EVERY-WHERE, BUT...
...TO MY DISMAY...
...THE MANUSCRIPT WAS *MISSING.*
HAD IT BEEN LOST OR DISPOSED OF, THERE WOULD HAVE BEEN A RECORD OF IT. BUT THERE WASN'T ANY.
IT WAS AS IF... THE MANU-SCRIPT HAD NEVER EXISTED.
I ASKED MISS OKUNI, THE LIBRARY'S SPECIAL ADVISER, ABOUT IT.
SHE SAID THE ONLY ONES WHO COULD MAKE LIBRARY DOCUMENTS DISAPPEAR WITHOUT A TRACE WERE...

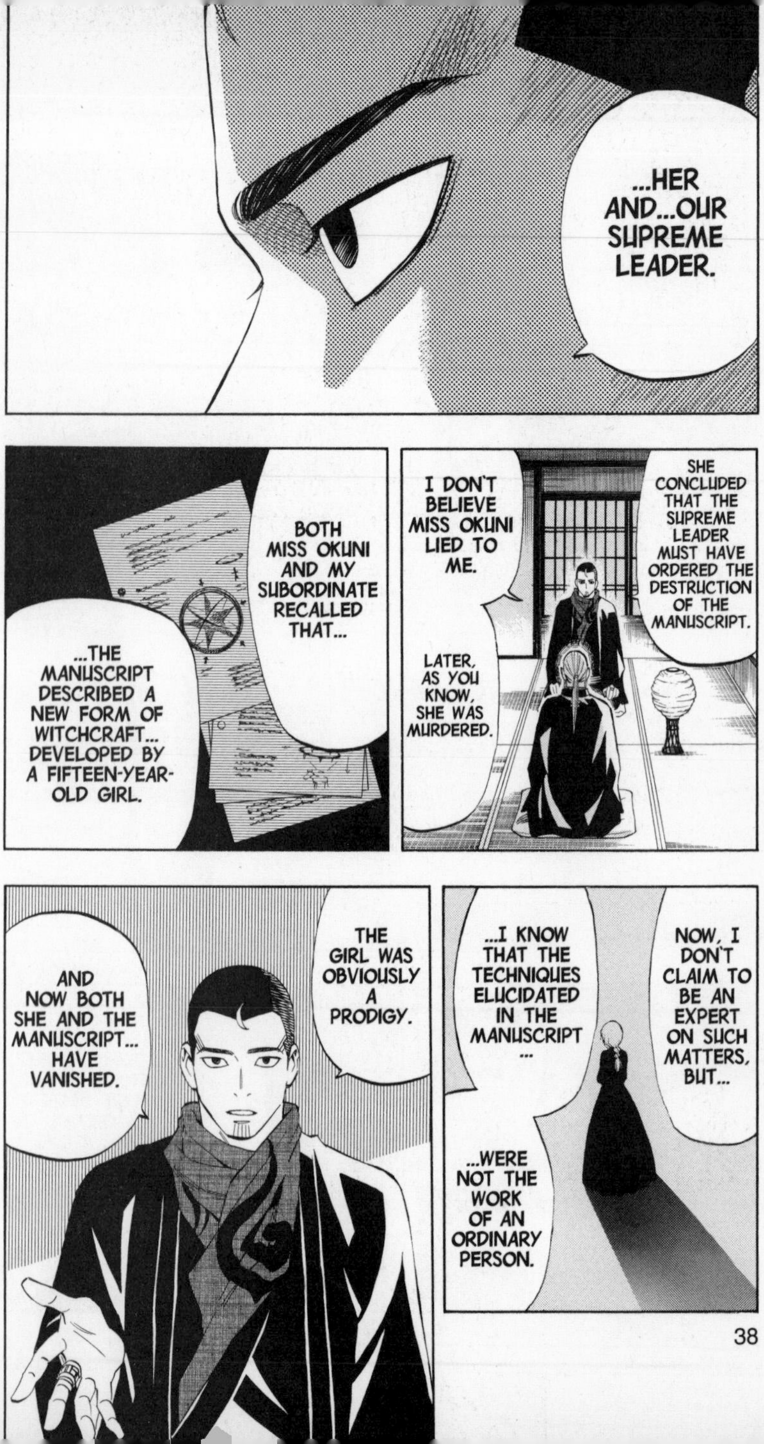
...HER AND...OUR SUPREME LEADER.
SHE CONCLUDED THAT THE SUPREME LEADER MUST HAVE ORDERED THE DESTRUCTION OF THE MANUSCRIPT.
I DON'T BELIEVE MISS OKUNI LIED TO ME.
LATER, AS YOU KNOW, SHE WAS MURDERED.
BOTH MISS OKUNI AND MY SUBORDINATE RECALLED THAT...
...THE MANUSCRIPT DESCRIBED A NEW FORM OF WITCHCRAFT... DEVELOPED BY A FIFTEEN-YEAR-OLD GIRL.
NOW, I DON'T CLAIM TO BE AN EXPERT ON SUCH MATTERS, BUT...
...I KNOW THAT THE TECHNIQUES ELUCIDATED IN THE MANUSCRIPT...
...WERE NOT THE WORK OF AN ORDINARY PERSON.
THE GIRL WAS OBVIOUSLY A PRODIGY.
AND NOW BOTH SHE AND THE MANUSCRIPT... HAVE VANISHED.

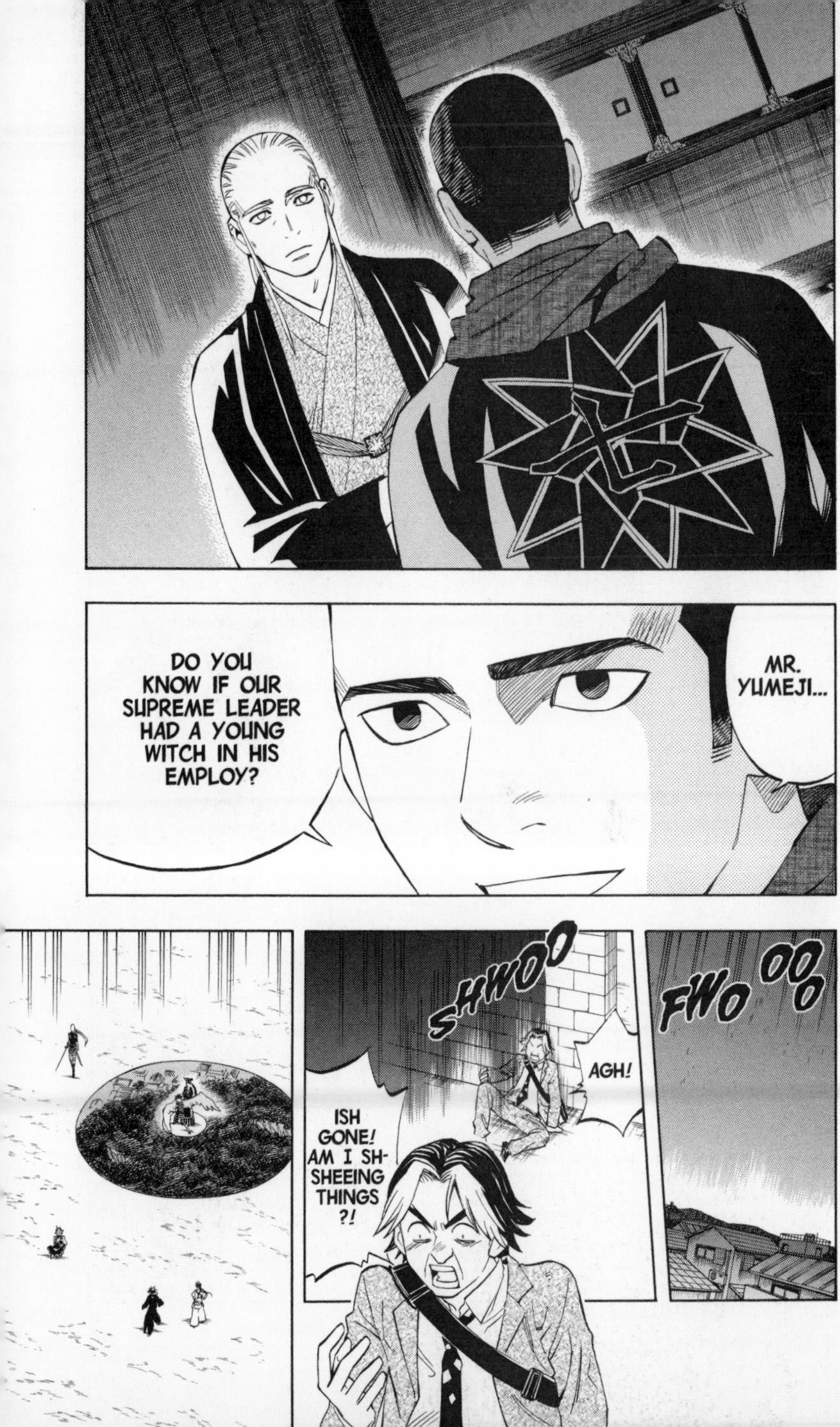
MR. YUMEJI...
DO YOU KNOW IF OUR SUPREME LEADER HAD A YOUNG WITCH IN HIS EMPLOY?
FWOOOO
SHWOO
AGH!
ISH GONE! AM I SH-SHEEING THINGS?!

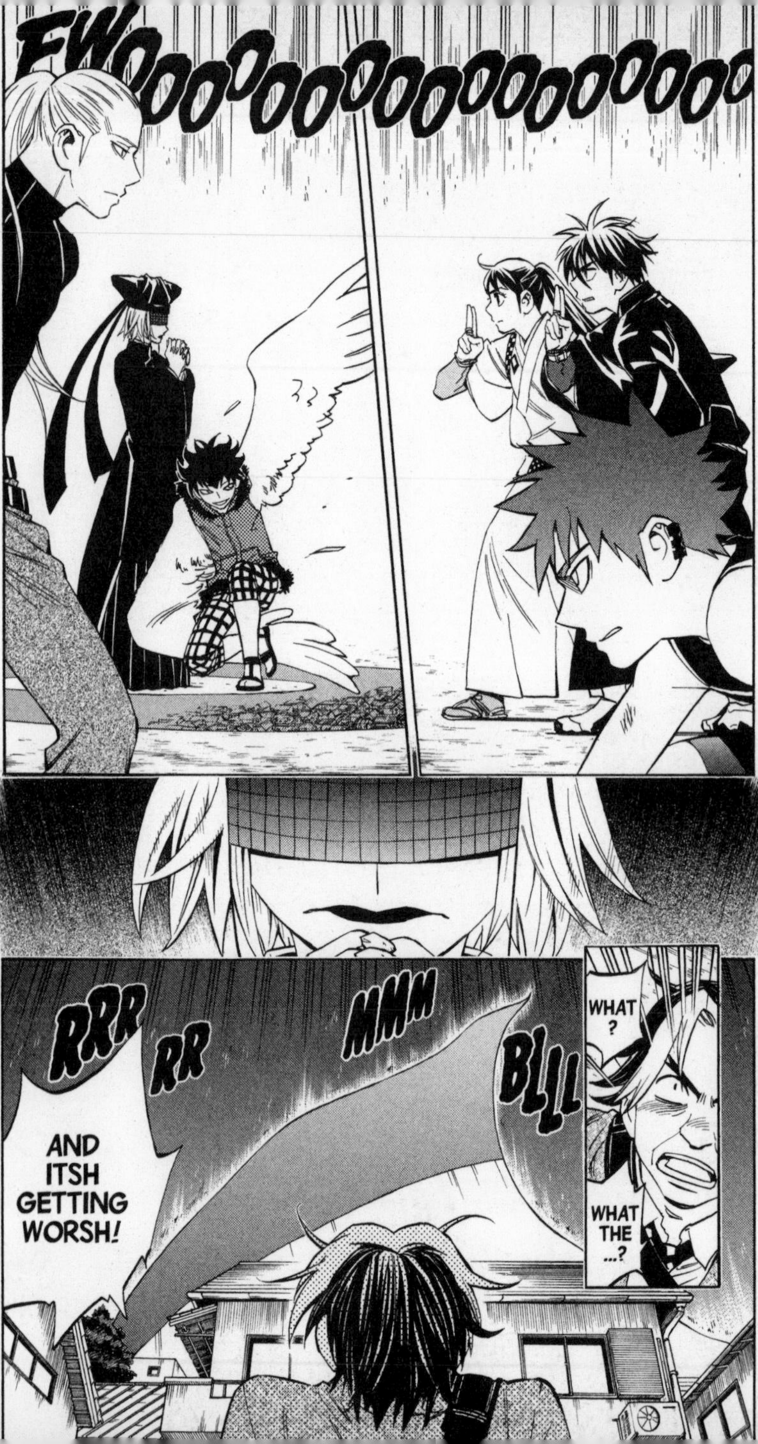
FWOOOOOOOOOOOOOOOOOO
WHAT?
WHAT THE ...?
RRR RR MMM BLLL
AND ITSH GETTING WORSH!

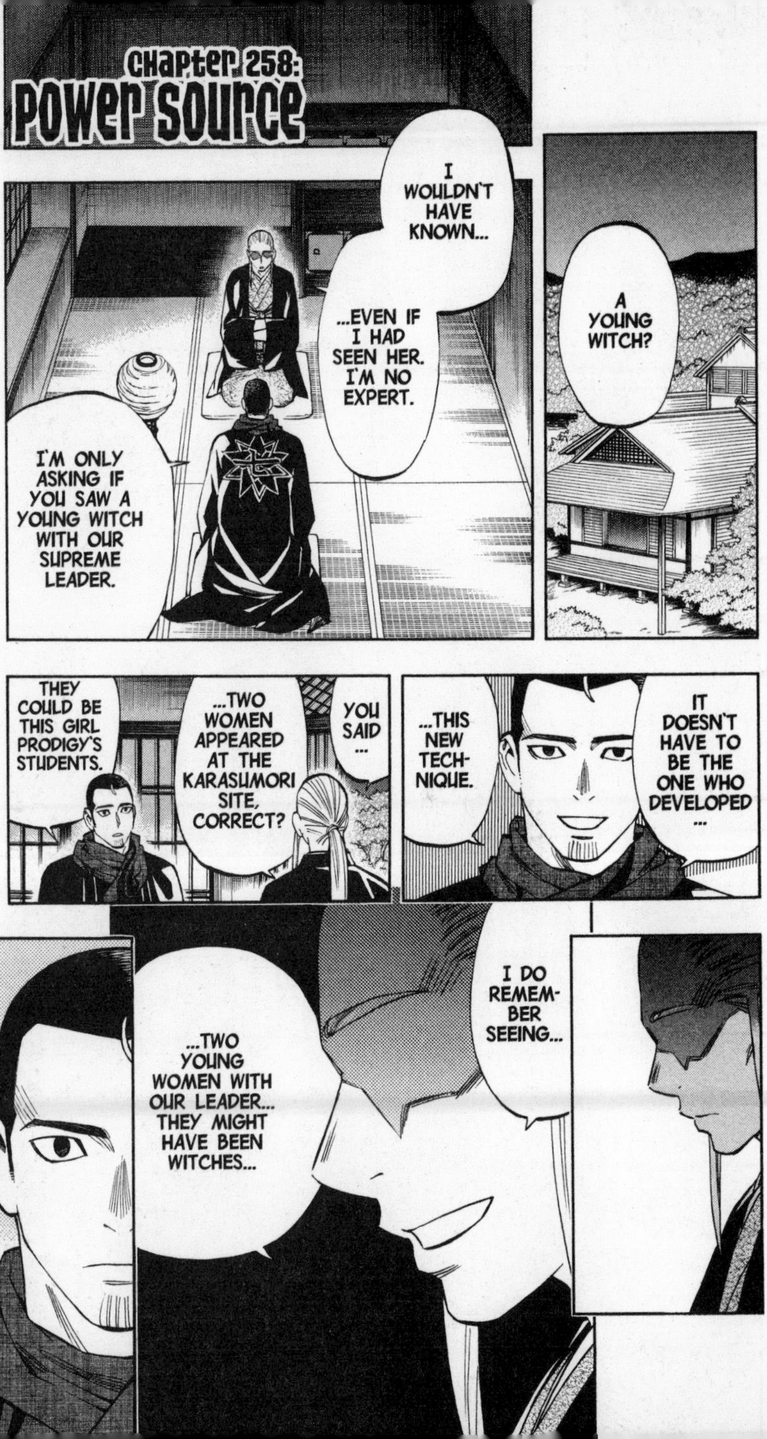
Chapter 258:
Power Source
A young witch?
I wouldn't have known...
...even if I had seen her. I'm no expert.
I'm only asking if you saw a young witch with our supreme leader.
It doesn't have to be the one who developed...
...this new technique.
You said...
...two women appeared at the Karasumori site, correct?
They could be this girl prodigy's students.
I do remember seeing...
...two young women with our leader... they might have been witches...

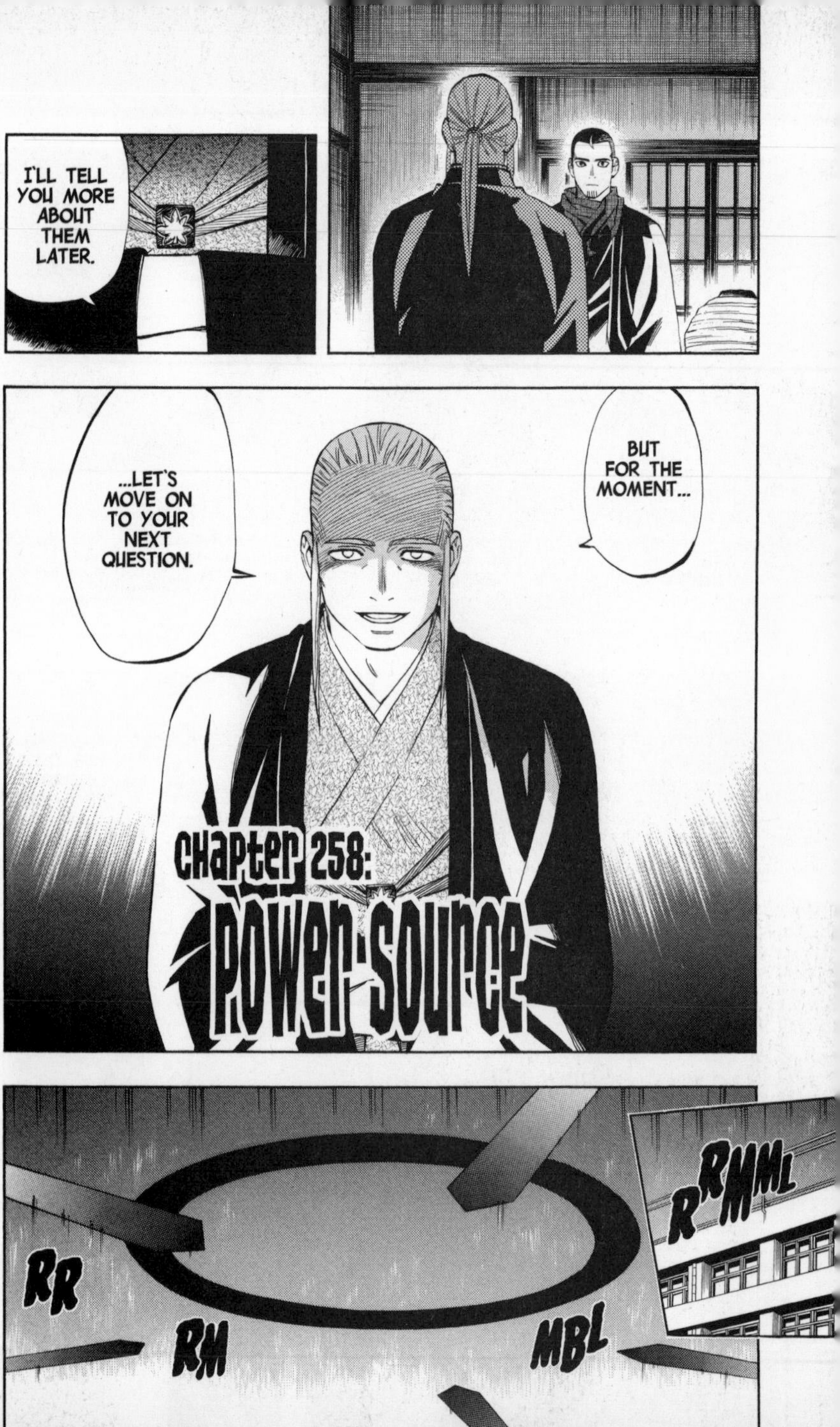
I'LL TELL YOU MORE ABOUT THEM LATER.
BUT FOR THE MOMENT...
...LET'S MOVE ON TO YOUR NEXT QUESTION.
Chapter 258: Power Source
RRMML
RR
RM
MBL

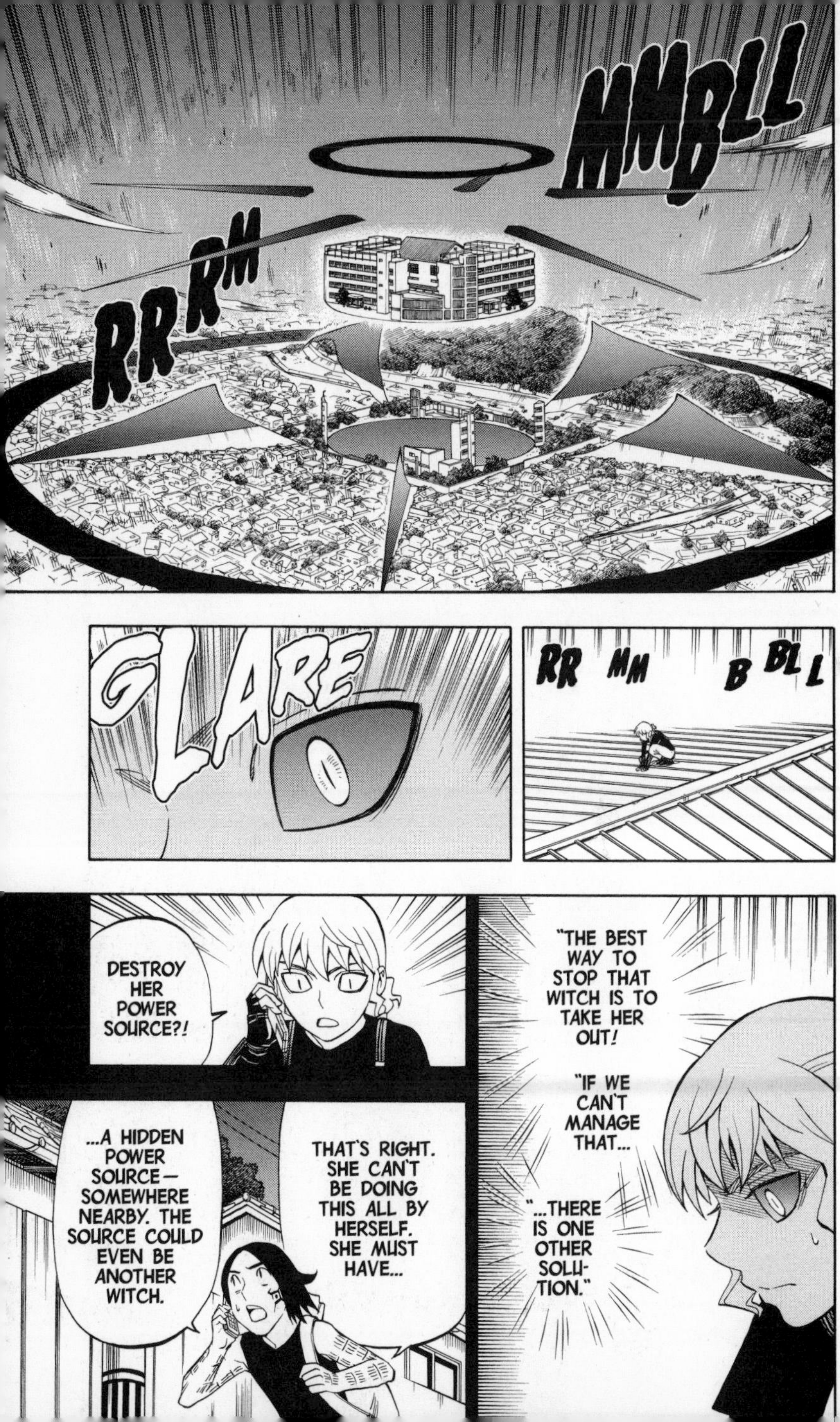
MMBLL
RRRM
RR MM B BL L
GLARE
"THE BEST WAY TO STOP THAT WITCH IS TO TAKE HER OUT!
"IF WE CAN'T MANAGE THAT...
"...THERE IS ONE OTHER SOLU-TION."
DESTROY HER POWER SOURCE?!
THAT'S RIGHT. SHE CAN'T BE DOING THIS ALL BY HERSELF. SHE MUST HAVE...
...A HIDDEN POWER SOURCE—SOMEWHERE NEARBY. THE SOURCE COULD EVEN BE ANOTHER WITCH.

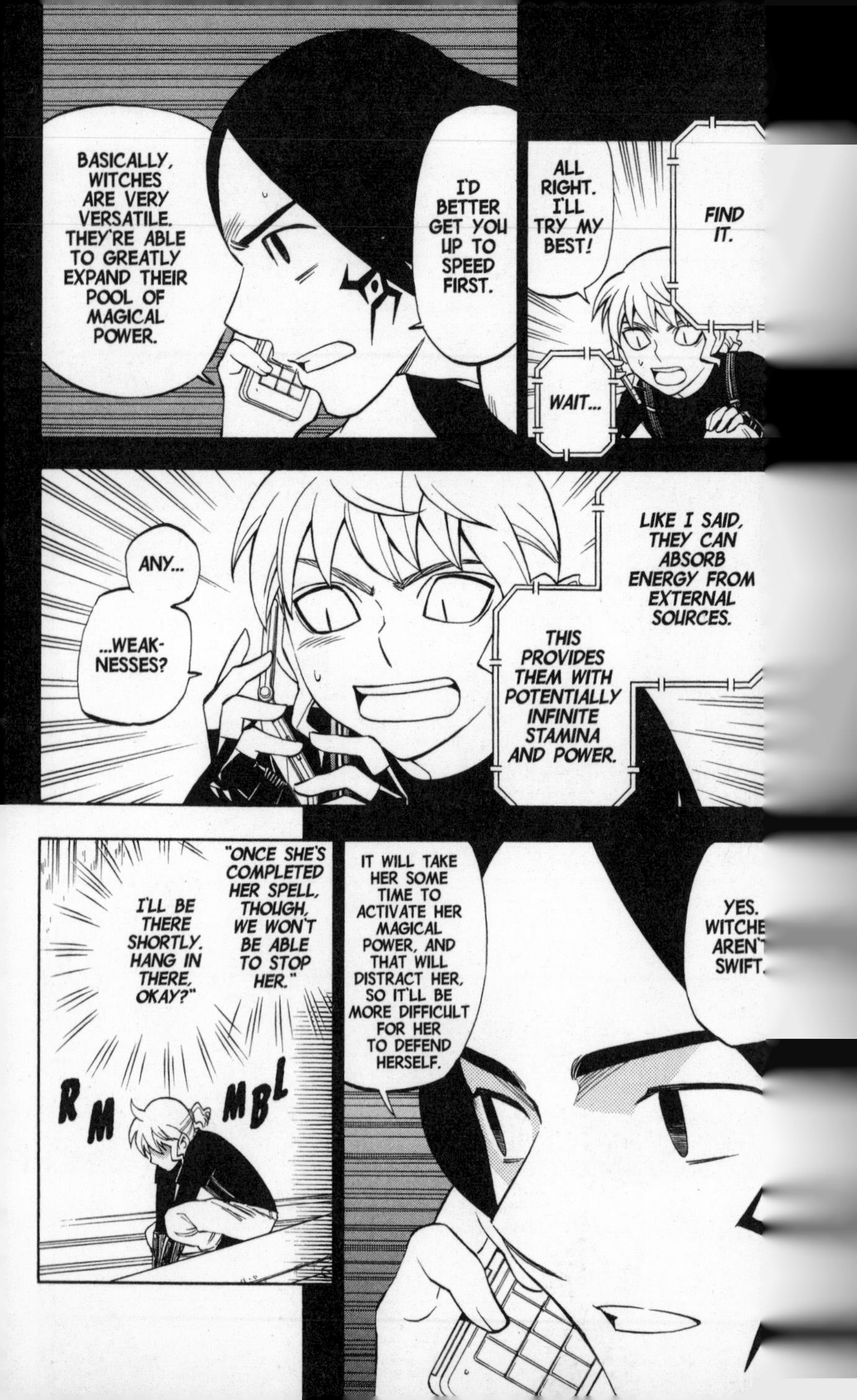
FIND IT.
ALL RIGHT. I'LL TRY MY BEST!
WAIT...
I'D BETTER GET YOU UP TO SPEED FIRST.
BASICALLY, WITCHES ARE VERY VERSATILE. THEY'RE ABLE TO GREATLY EXPAND THEIR POOL OF MAGICAL POWER.
LIKE I SAID, THEY CAN ABSORB ENERGY FROM EXTERNAL SOURCES.
THIS PROVIDES THEM WITH POTENTIALLY INFINITE STAMINA AND POWER.
ANY...
...WEAK-NESSES?
YES. WITCHE AREN'T SWIFT.
IT WILL TAKE HER SOME TIME TO ACTIVATE HER MAGICAL POWER, AND THAT WILL DISTRACT HER, SO IT'LL BE MORE DIFFICULT FOR HER TO DEFEND HERSELF.
"ONCE SHE'S COMPLETED HER SPELL, THOUGH, WE WON'T BE ABLE TO STOP HER."
I'LL BE THERE SHORTLY. HANG IN THERE, OKAY?"
RMMBL

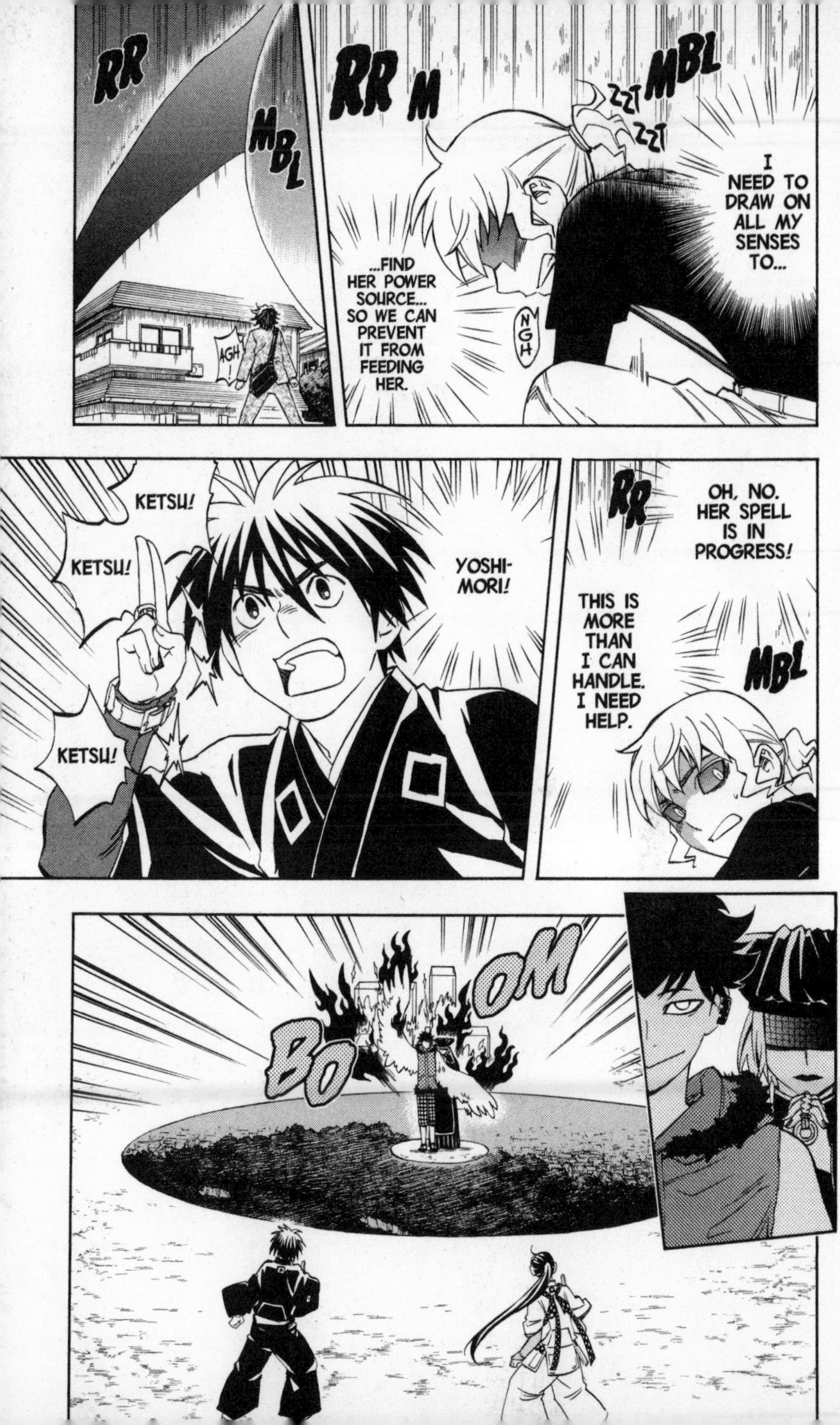
RR M
MBL
ZZZT
ZZZT
I NEED TO DRAW ON ALL MY SENSES TO...
NGH
...FIND HER POWER SOURCE... SO WE CAN PREVENT IT FROM FEEDING HER.
RR
MBL
AGH!
RR
OH, NO. HER SPELL IS IN PROGRESS!
THIS IS MORE THAN I CAN HANDLE. I NEED HELP.
MBL
YOSHI-MORI!
KETSU!
KETSU!
KETSU!
BOOM

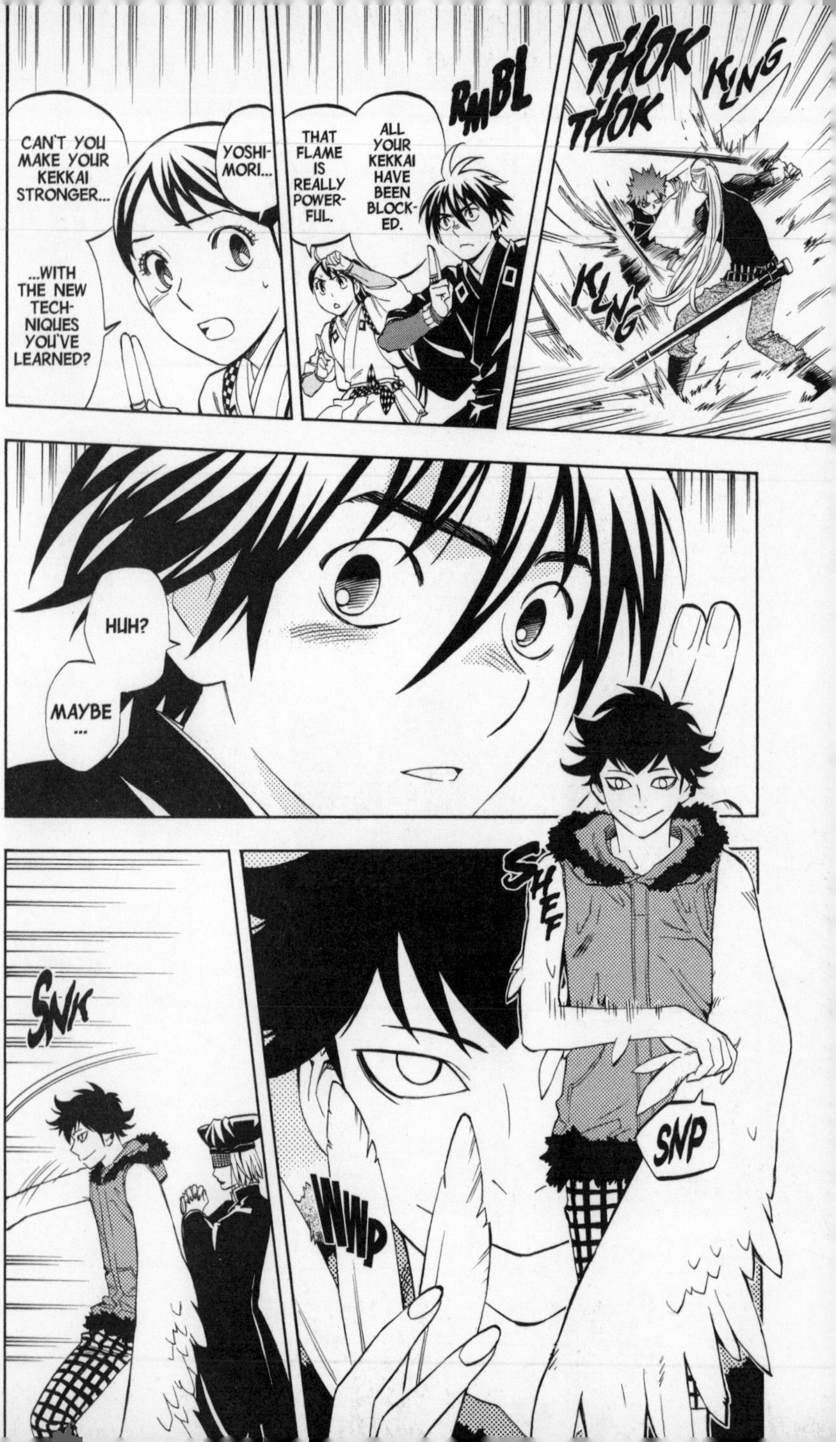
THOK THOK
KLING
KLING
RMBL
ALL YOUR KEKKAI HAVE BEEN BLOCKED.
THAT FLAME IS REALLY POWERFUL.
YOSHIMORI...
CAN'T YOU MAKE YOUR KEKKAI STRONGER...
...WITH THE NEW TECHNIQUES YOU'VE LEARNED?
HUH?
MAYBE...
SHEF
SNP
WWP
SNK

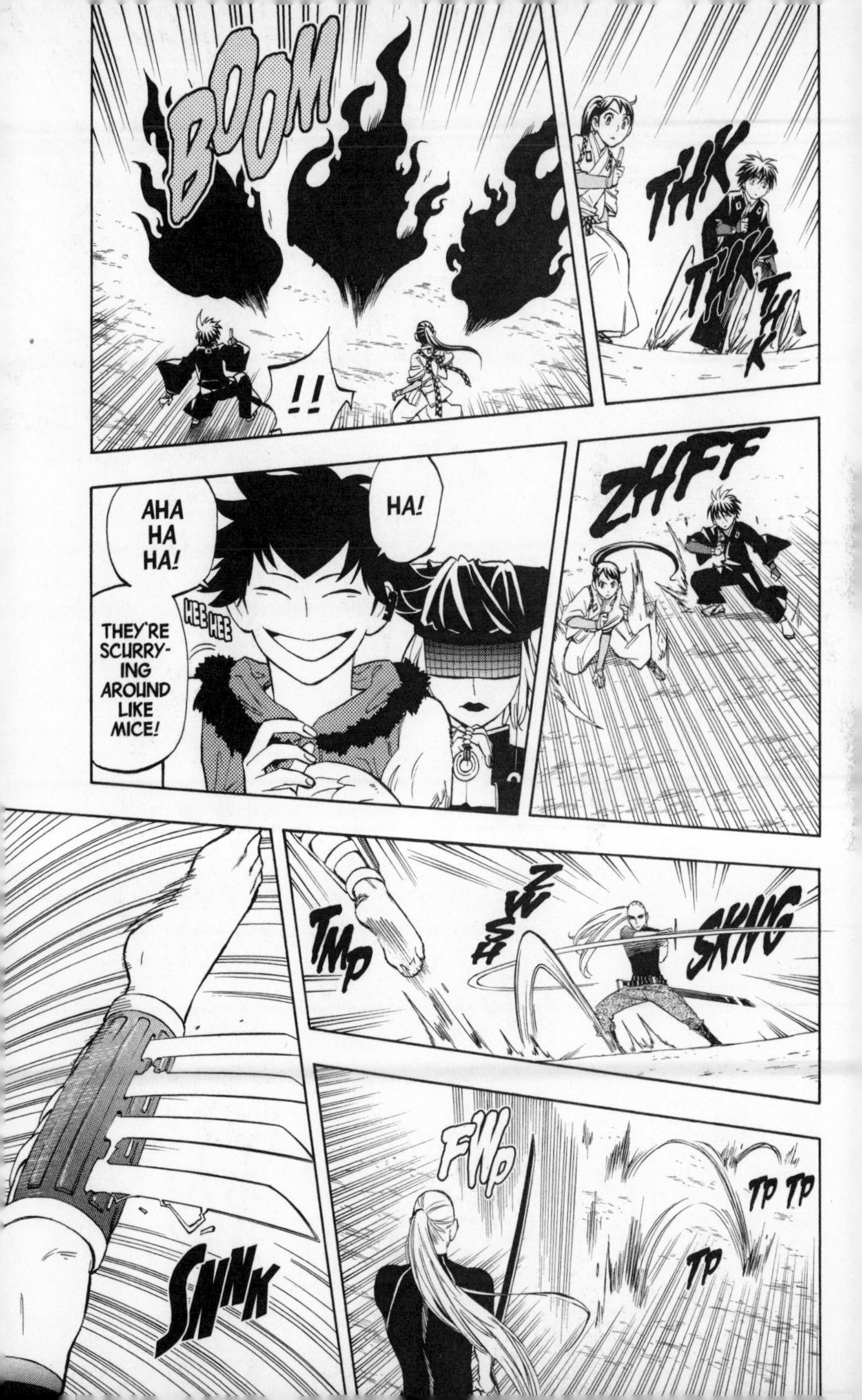
THK
THK
THK
BOOM
!!
ZHFF
HA!
AHA HA HA!
HEE HEE
THEY'RE SCURRYING AROUND LIKE MICE!
SKING
WSH
TMP
TP TP
TP
FWP
SNNK

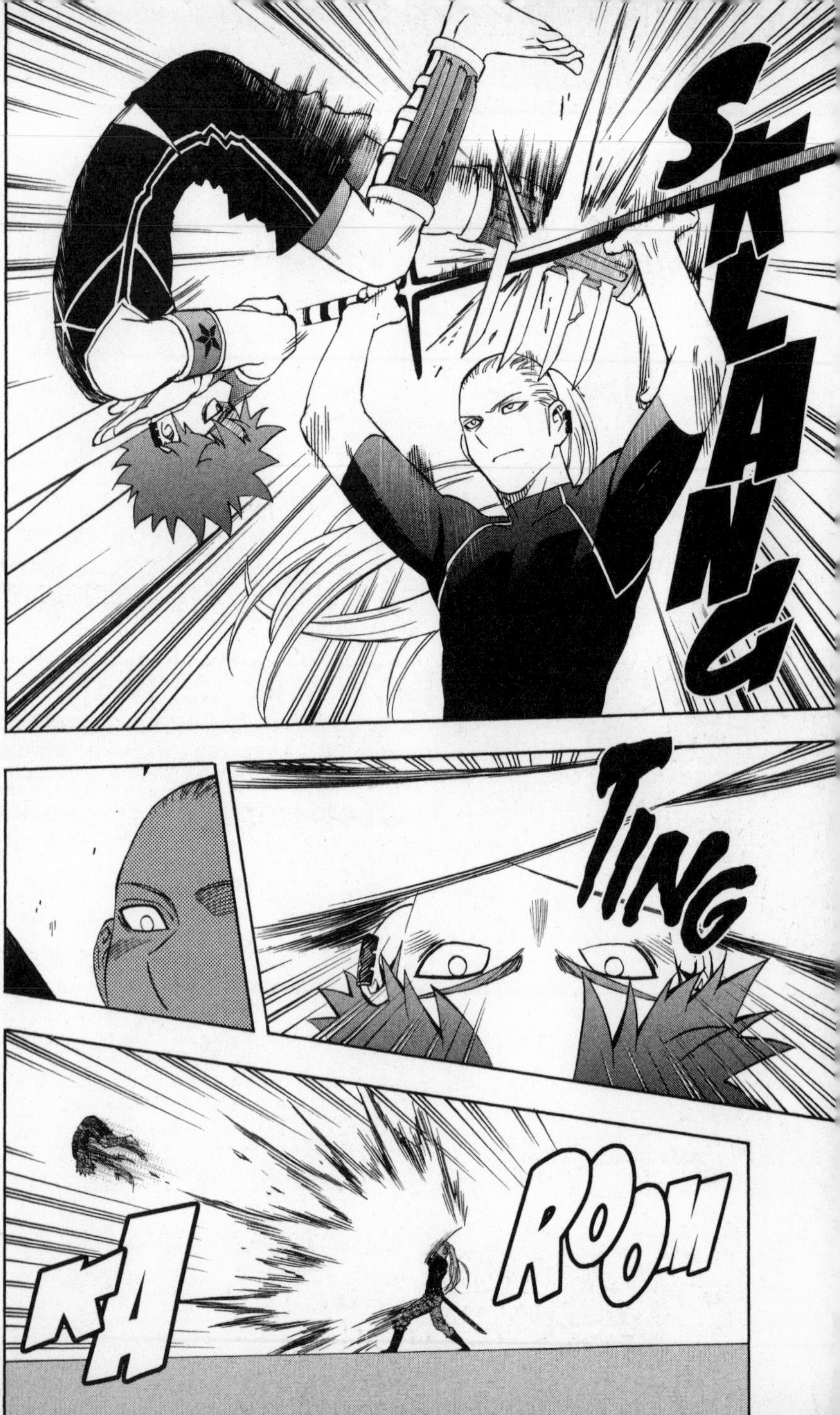
SKLANG
TING
KA
ROOM

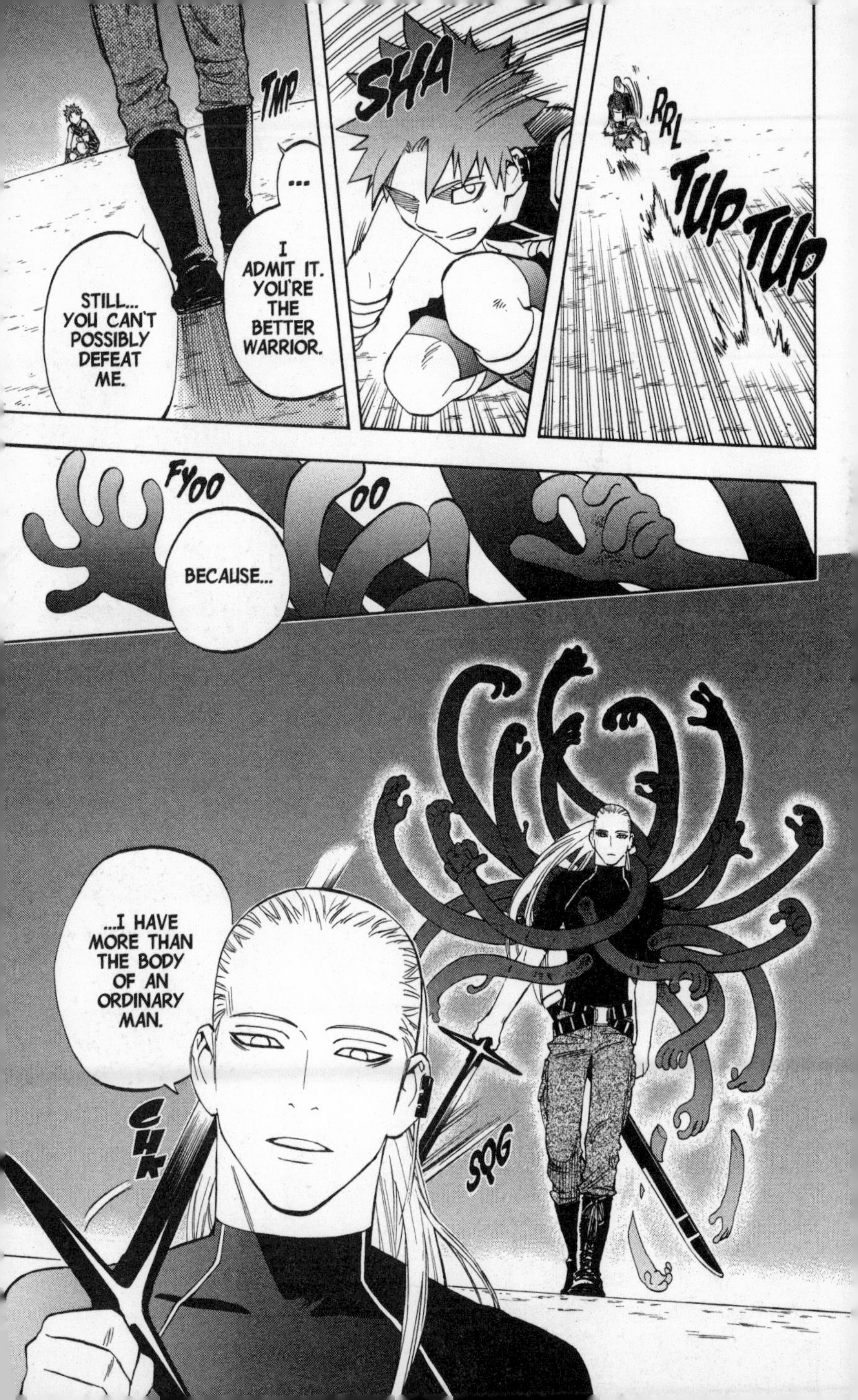
RRL
TUP TUP
SHA
TMP
...
I ADMIT IT. YOU'RE THE BETTER WARRIOR.
STILL... YOU CAN'T POSSIBLY DEFEAT ME.
OO
FYOO
BECAUSE...
...I HAVE MORE THAN THE BODY OF AN ORDINARY MAN.
SQG
CHK

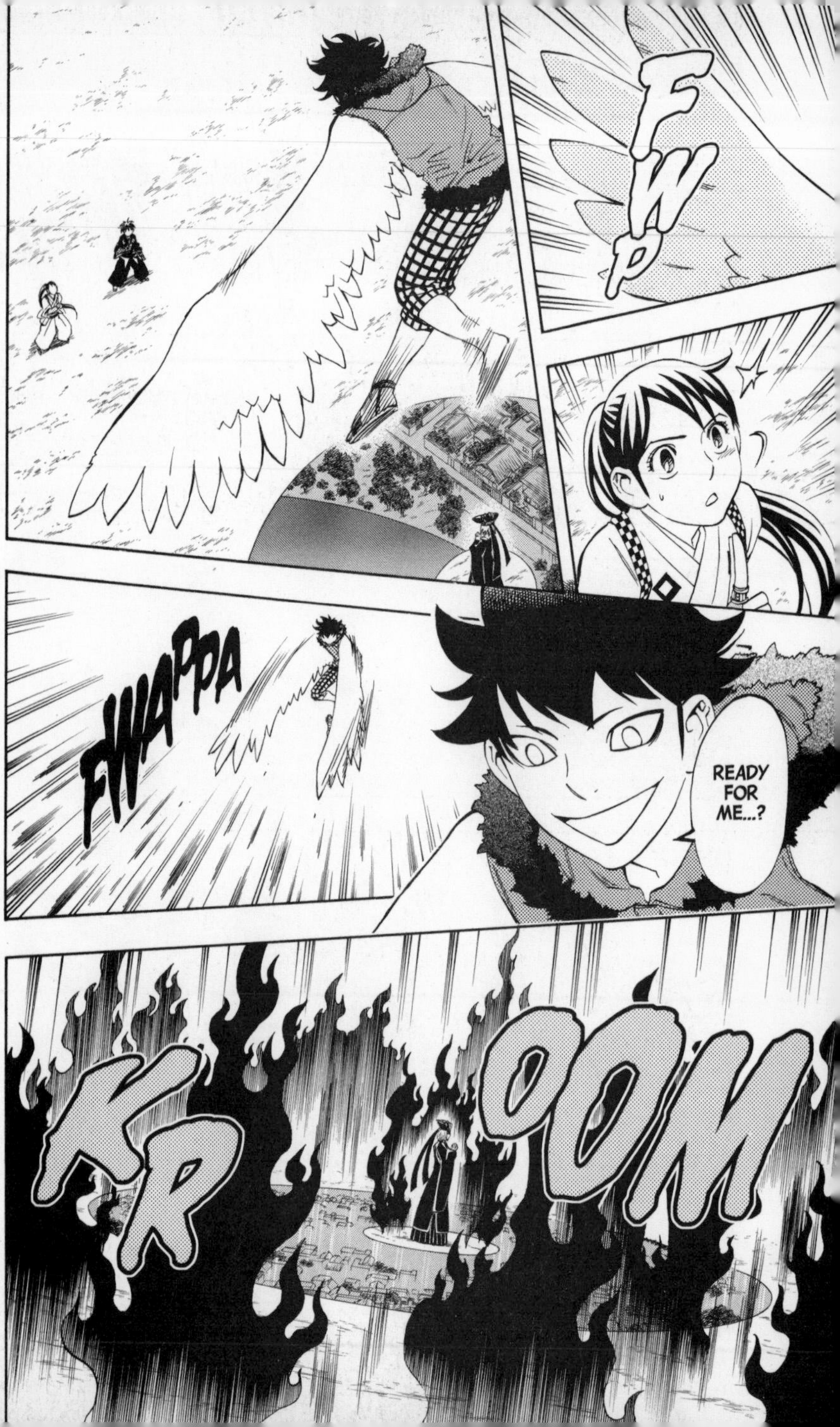
FWP
READY FOR ME...?
FWAPPA
KR
OOM

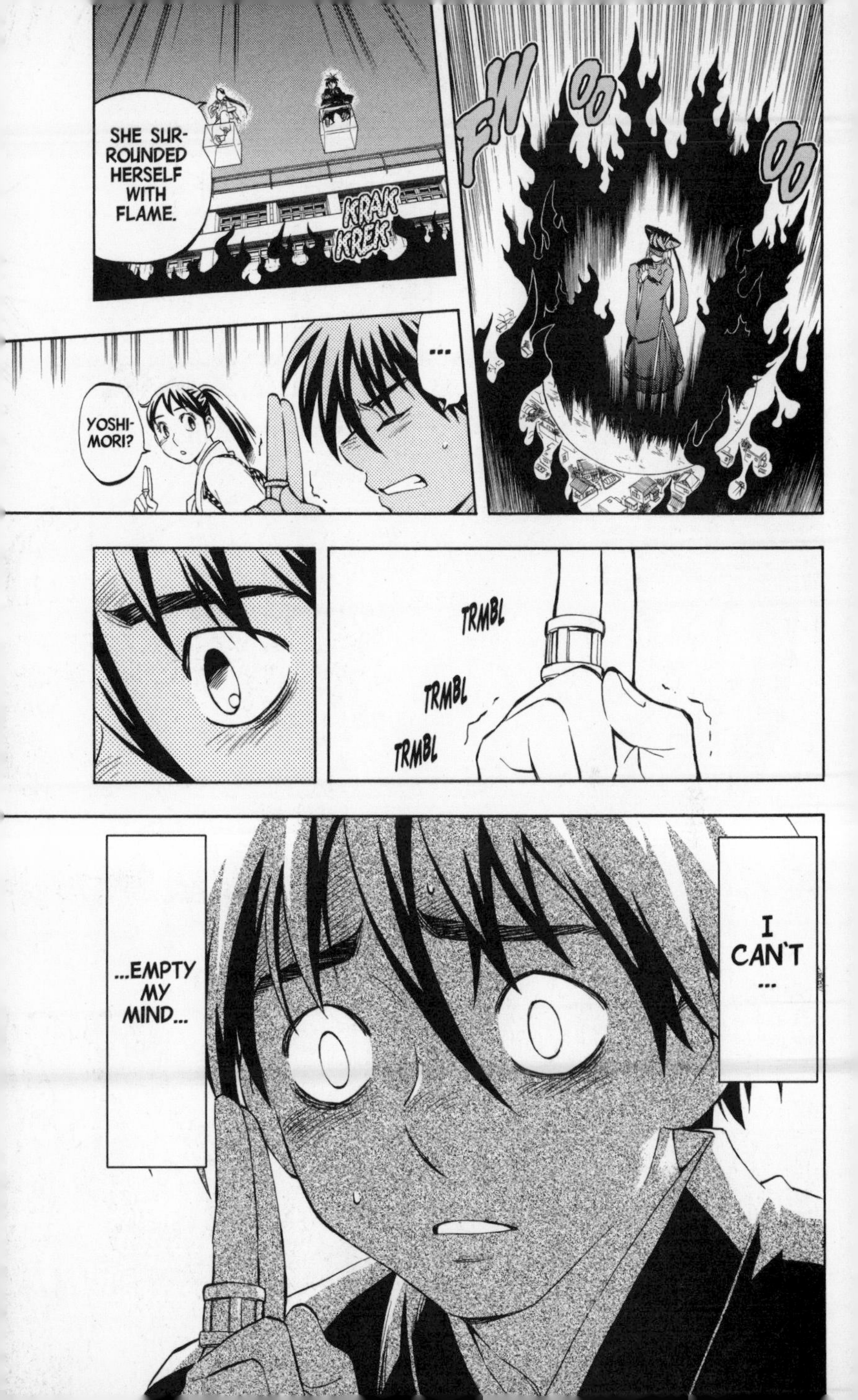
FWOOOO
SHE SURROUNDED HERSELF WITH FLAME.
KRAK KREK
...
YOSHIMORI?
TRMBL
TRMBL
TRMBL
I CAN'T ...
...EMPTY MY MIND...

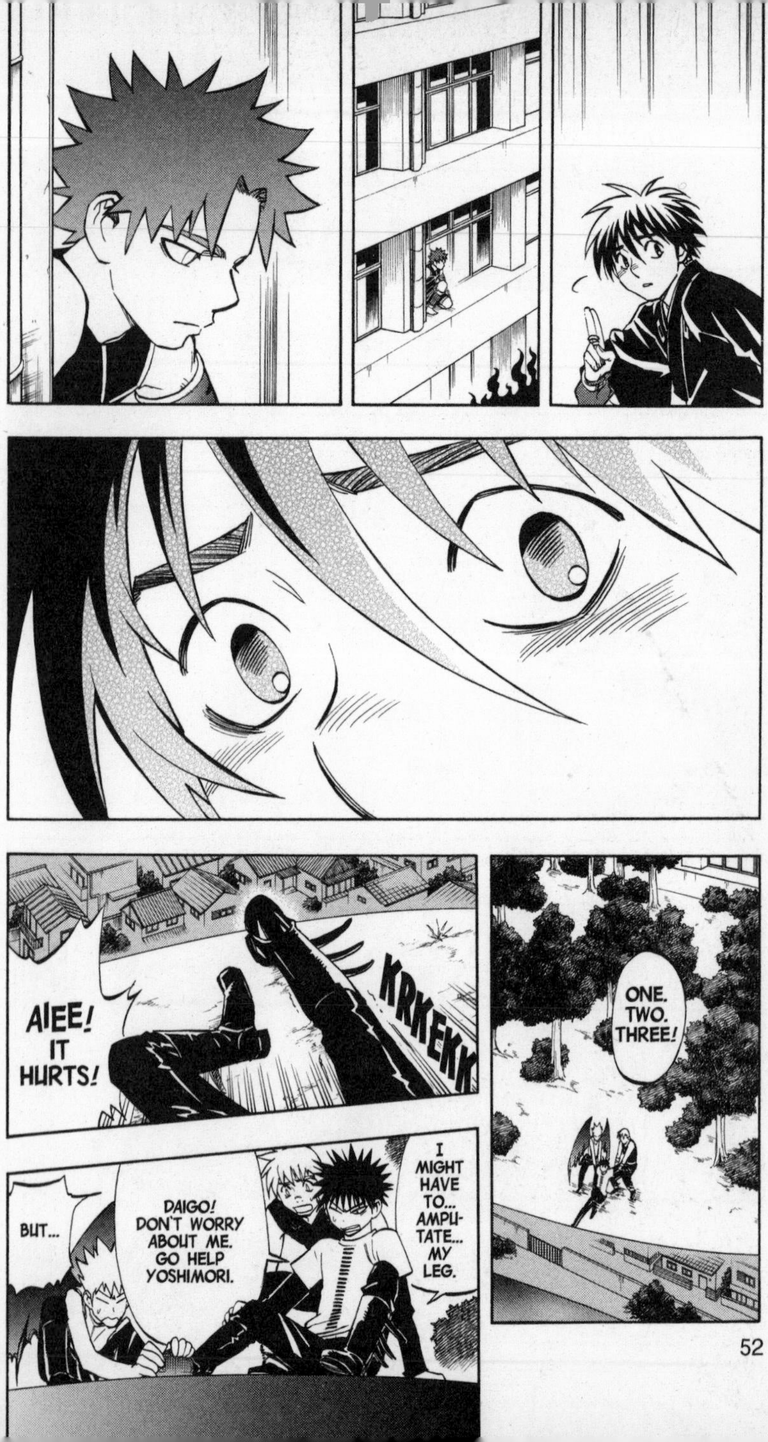
ONE. TWO. THREE!
KRKEKK
AIEE! IT HURTS!
I MIGHT HAVE TO... AMPUTATE... MY LEG.
DAIGO! DON'T WORRY ABOUT ME. GO HELP YOSHIMORI.
BUT...

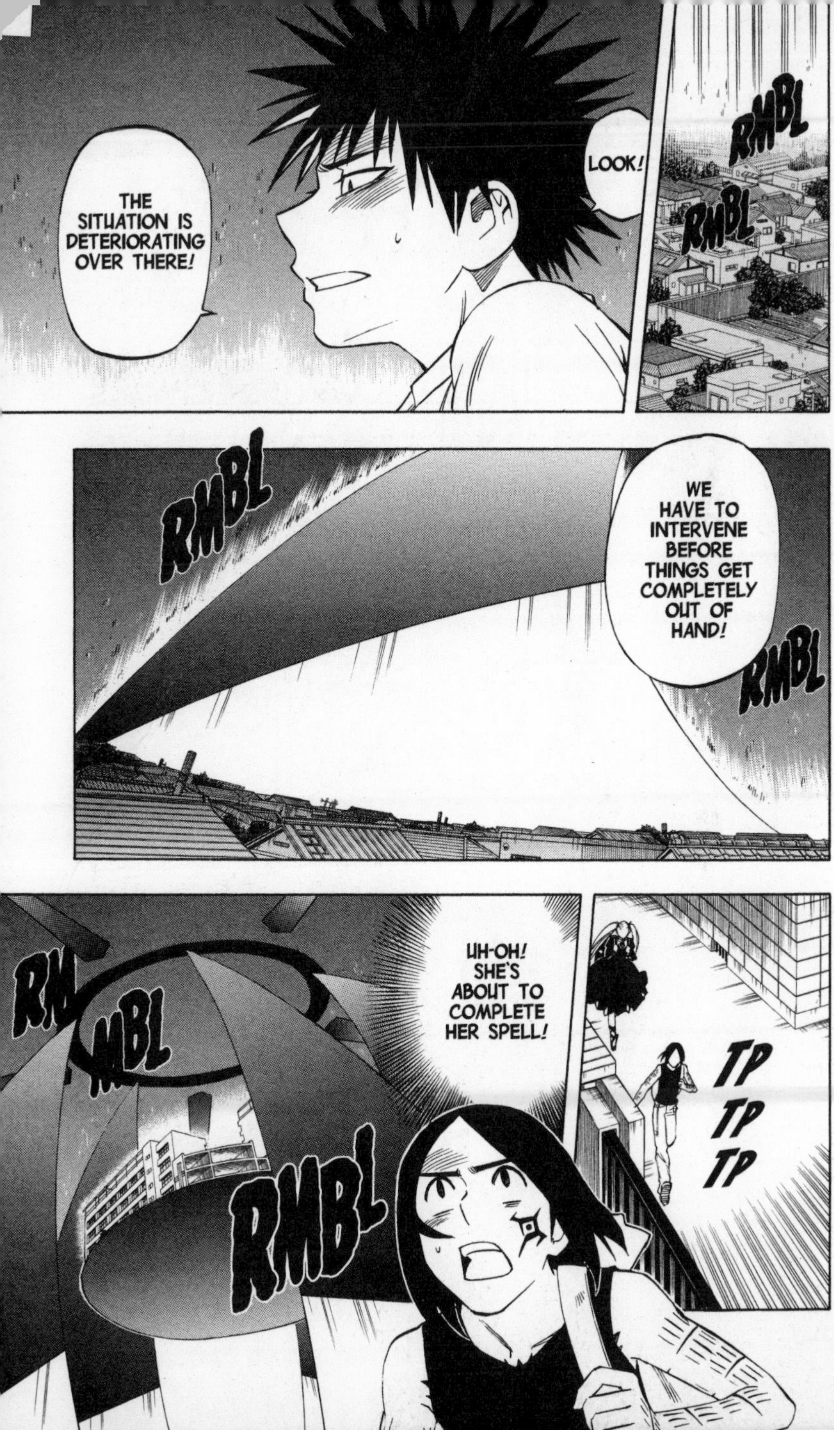
RMBL
RMBL
LOOK!
THE SITUATION IS DETERIORATING OVER THERE!
WE HAVE TO INTERVENE BEFORE THINGS GET COMPLETELY OUT OF HAND!
RMBL
RMBL
TP TP TP
UH-OH! SHE'S ABOUT TO COMPLETE HER SPELL!
RMBL
RMBL
RMBL

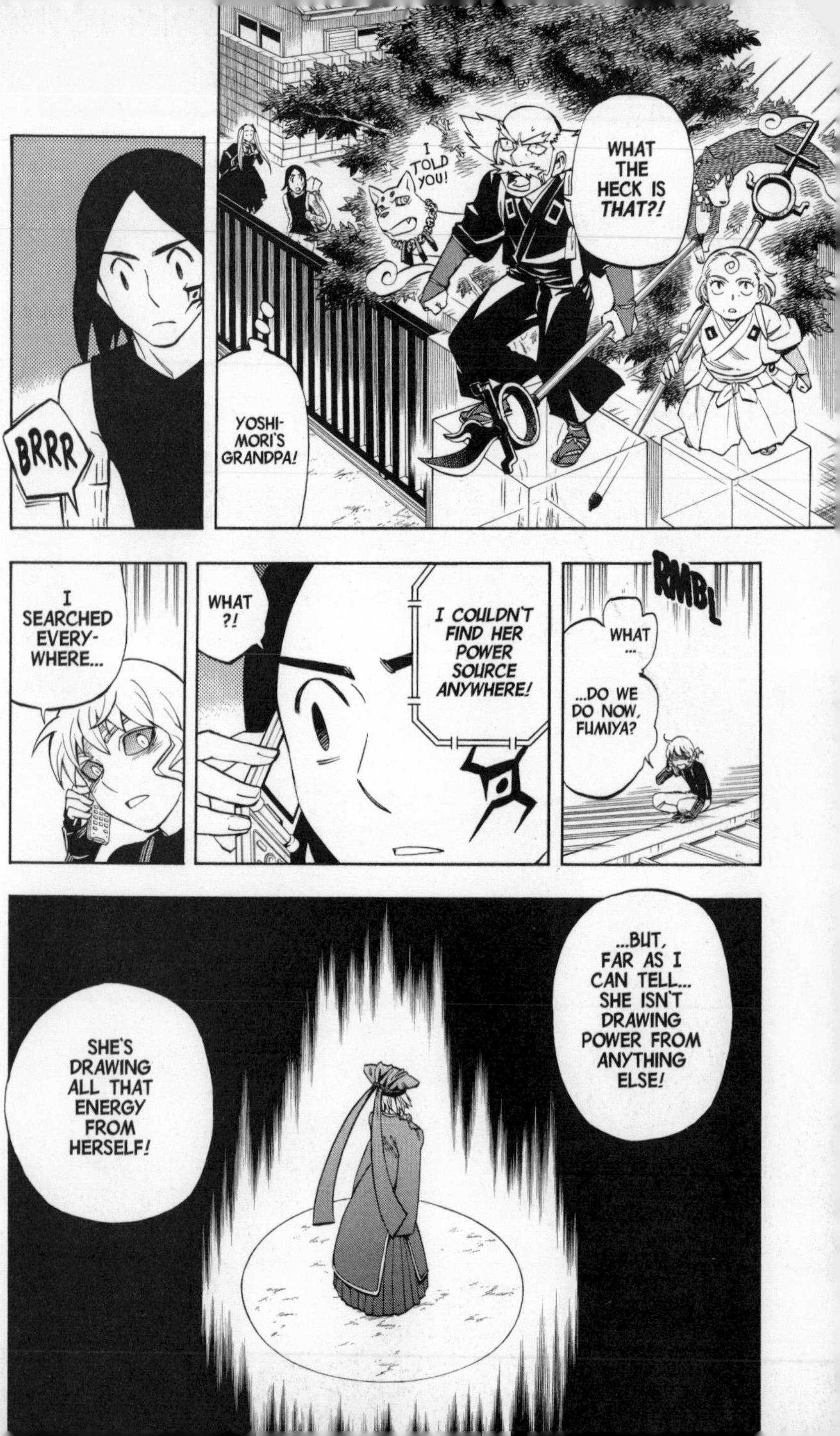
WHAT THE HECK IS THAT?!
I TOLD YOU!
YOSHIMORI'S GRANDPA!
BRRR
RMBL
WHAT...
...DO WE DO NOW, FUMIYA?
I COULDN'T FIND HER POWER SOURCE ANYWHERE!
WHAT?!
I SEARCHED EVERYWHERE...
...BUT, FAR AS I CAN TELL... SHE ISN'T DRAWING POWER FROM ANYTHING ELSE!
SHE'S DRAWING ALL THAT ENERGY FROM HERSELF!

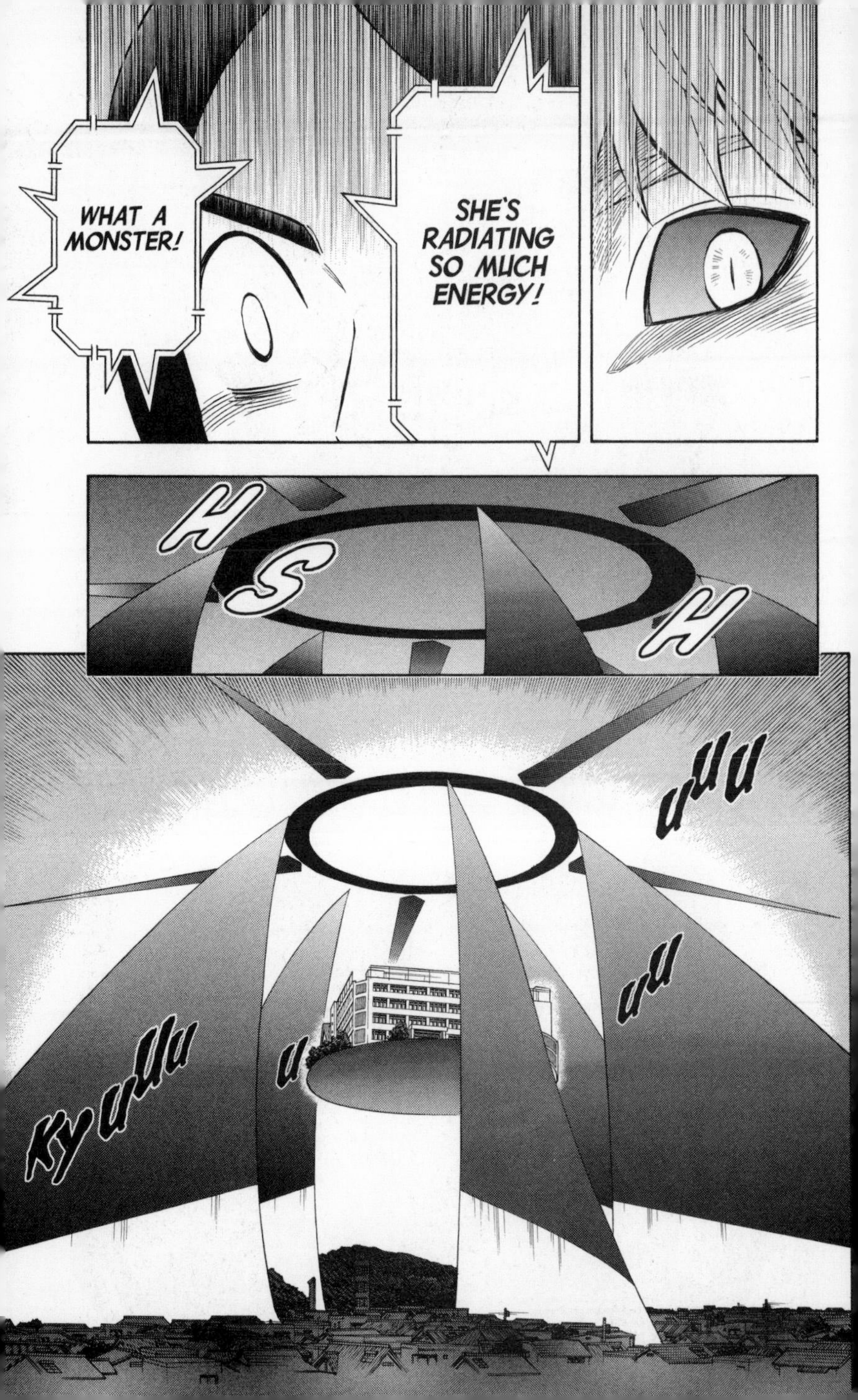
SHE'S RADIATING SO MUCH ENERGY!
WHAT A MONSTER!
HSH
Kyuuu
u
uu
uuu

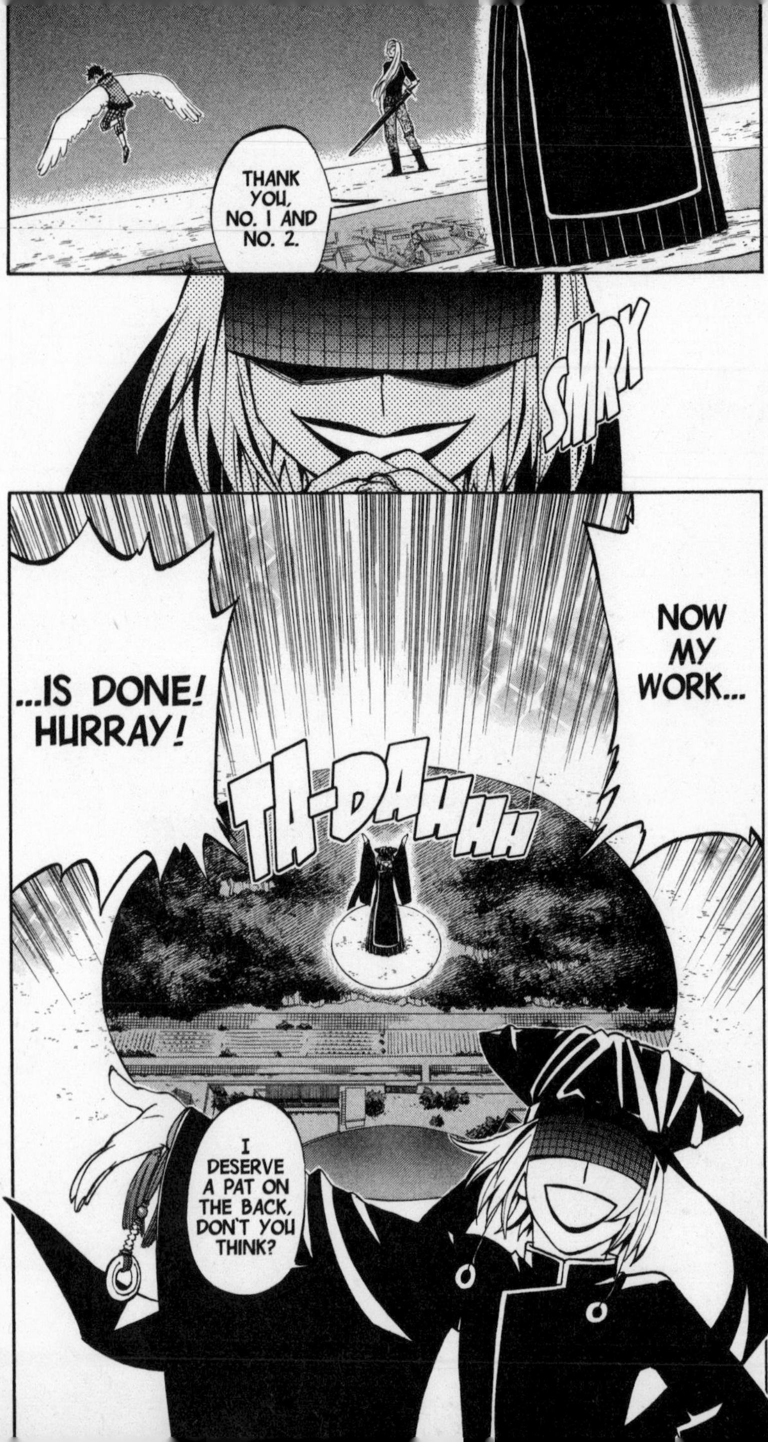
THANK YOU, NO. 1 AND NO. 2.
SMRK
NOW MY WORK...
...IS DONE! HURRAY!
TA-DAHHHH
I DESERVE A PAT ON THE BACK, DON'T YOU THINK?

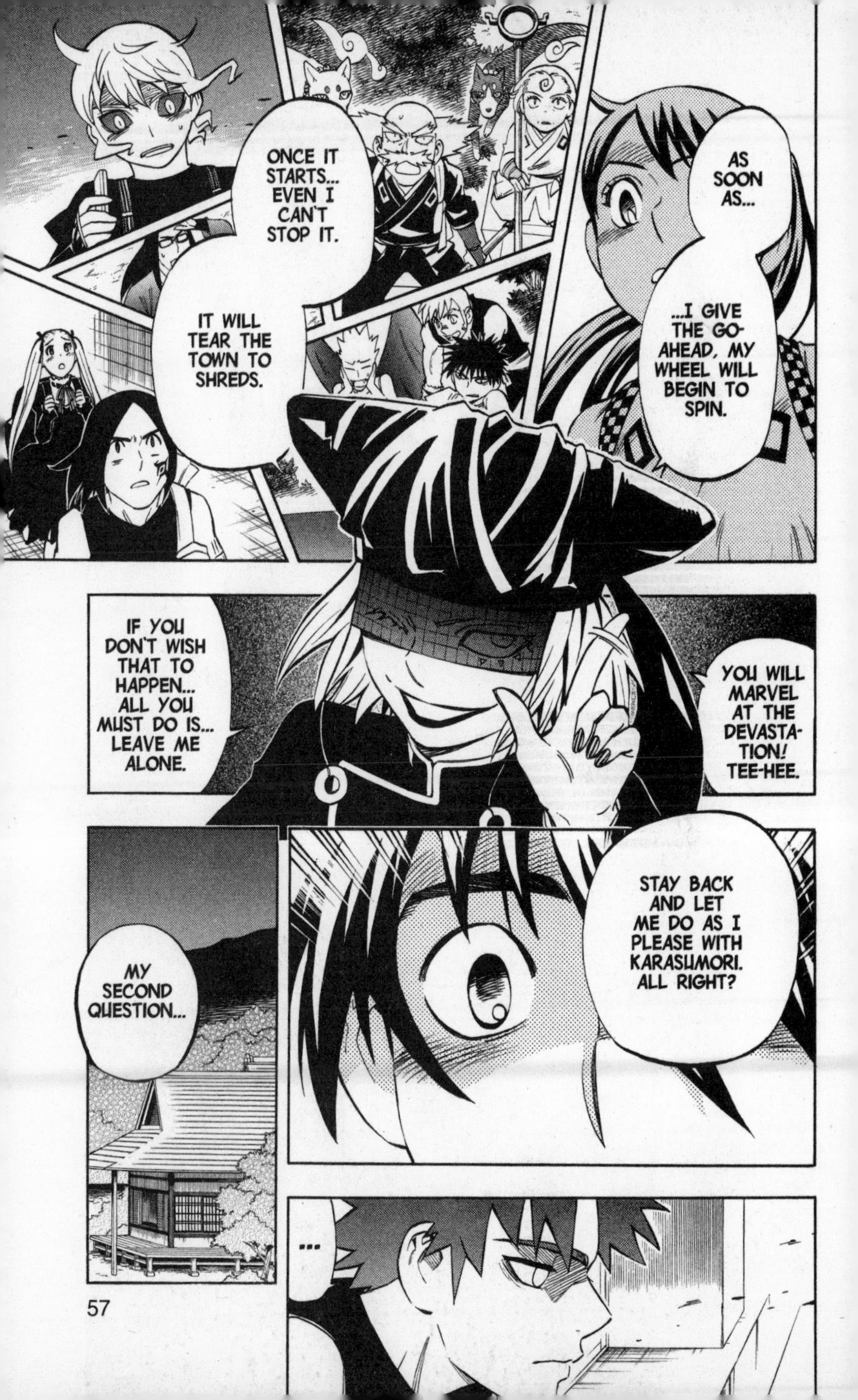
AS SOON AS...
...I GIVE THE GO-AHEAD, MY WHEEL WILL BEGIN TO SPIN.
ONCE IT STARTS... EVEN I CAN'T STOP IT.
IT WILL TEAR THE TOWN TO SHREDS.
YOU WILL MARVEL AT THE DEVASTATION! TEE-HEE.
IF YOU DON'T WISH THAT TO HAPPEN... ALL YOU MUST DO IS... LEAVE ME ALONE.
STAY BACK AND LET ME DO AS I PLEASE WITH KARASUMORI. ALL RIGHT?
MY SECOND QUESTION...
...

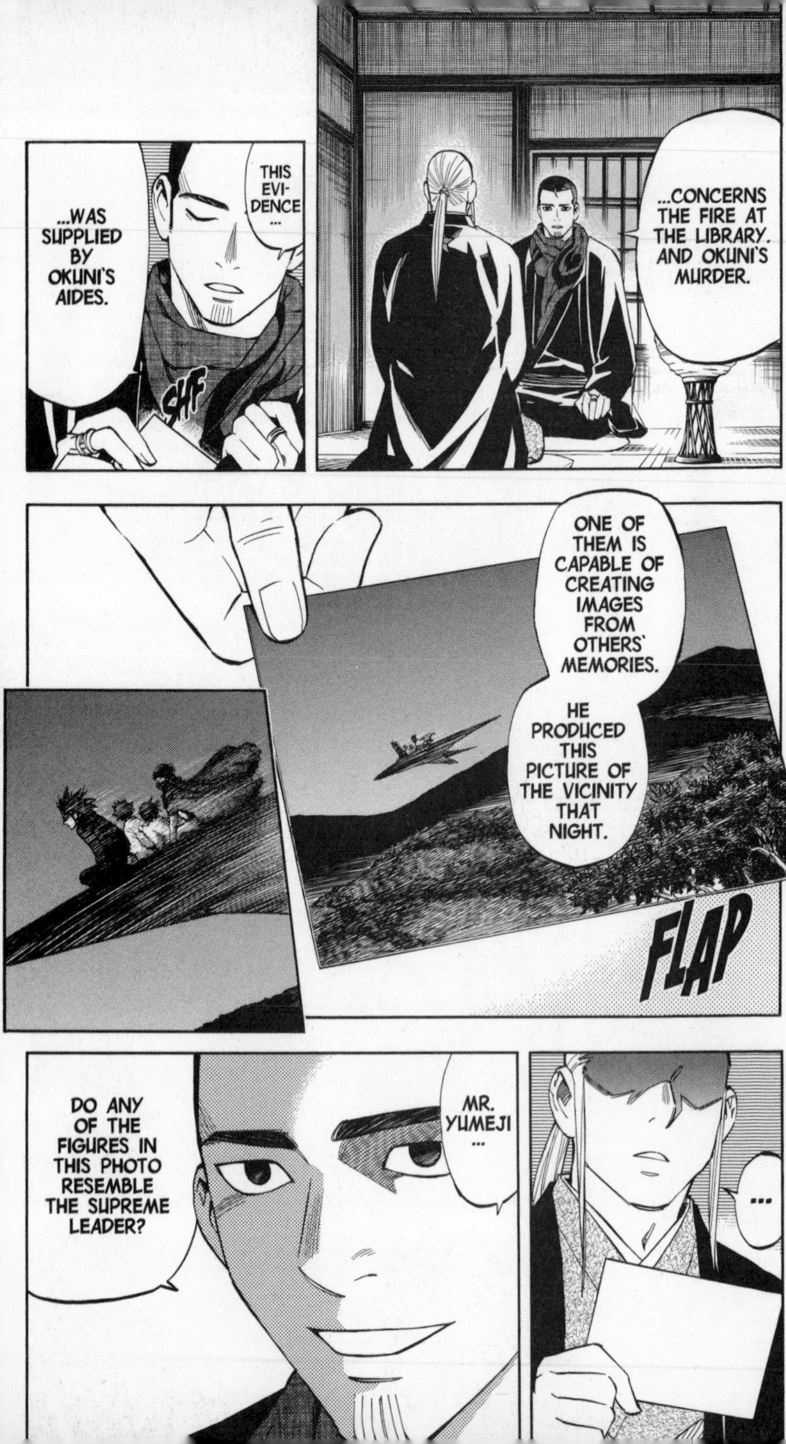
...CONCERNS THE FIRE AT THE LIBRARY. AND OKUNI'S MURDER.
THIS EVIDENCE...
...WAS SUPPLIED BY OKUNI'S AIDES.
SHF
ONE OF THEM IS CAPABLE OF CREATING IMAGES FROM OTHERS' MEMORIES.
HE PRODUCED THIS PICTURE OF THE VICINITY THAT NIGHT.
FLAP
...
MR. YUMEJI...
DO ANY OF THE FIGURES IN THIS PHOTO RESEMBLE THE SUPREME LEADER?

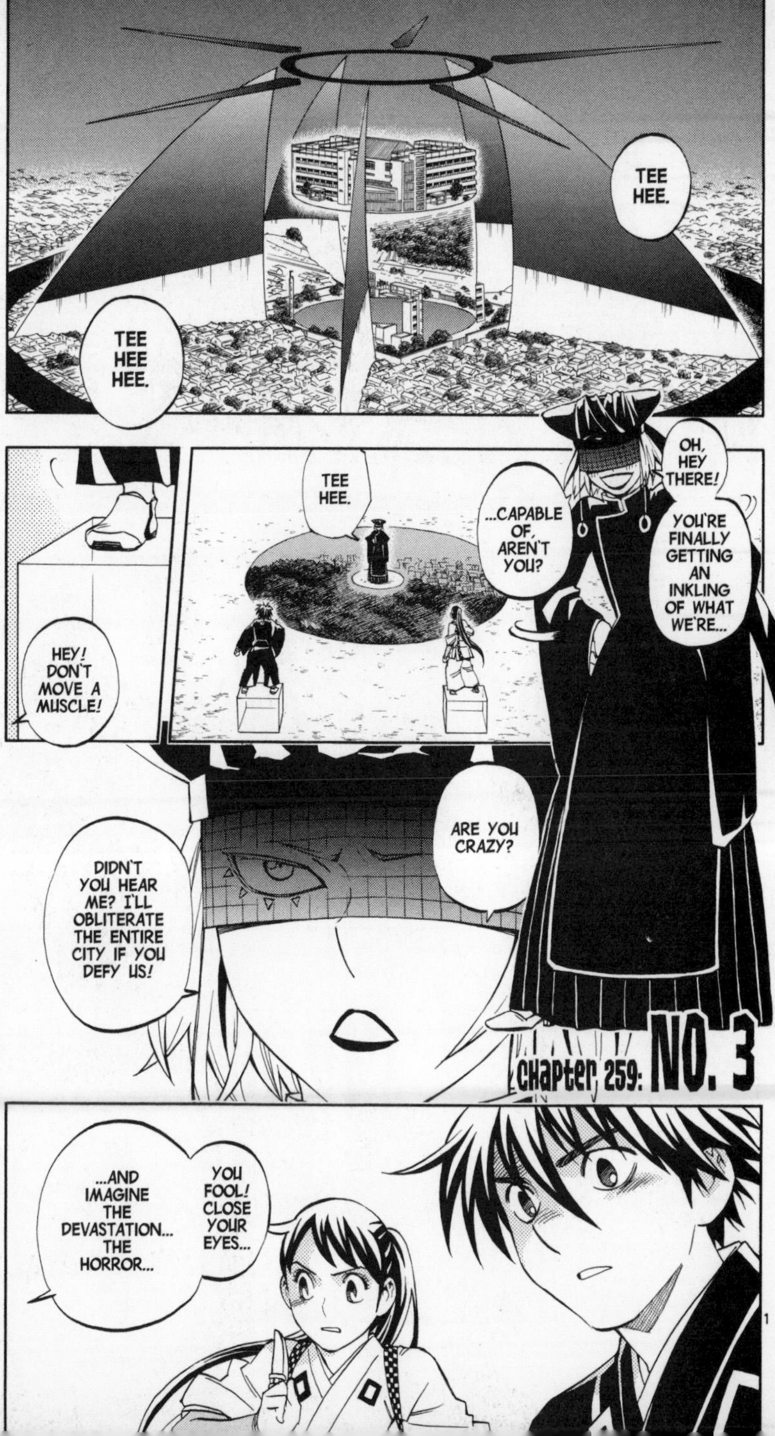
TEE HEE.
TEE HEE HEE.
OH, HEY THERE!
YOU'RE FINALLY GETTING AN INKLING OF WHAT WE'RE...
...CAPABLE OF, AREN'T YOU?
TEE HEE.
HEY! DON'T MOVE A MUSCLE!
ARE YOU CRAZY?
DIDN'T YOU HEAR ME? I'LL OBLITERATE THE ENTIRE CITY IF YOU DEFY US!
Chapter 259: NO. 3
YOU FOOL! CLOSE YOUR EYES...
...AND IMAGINE THE DEVASTATION... THE HORROR...

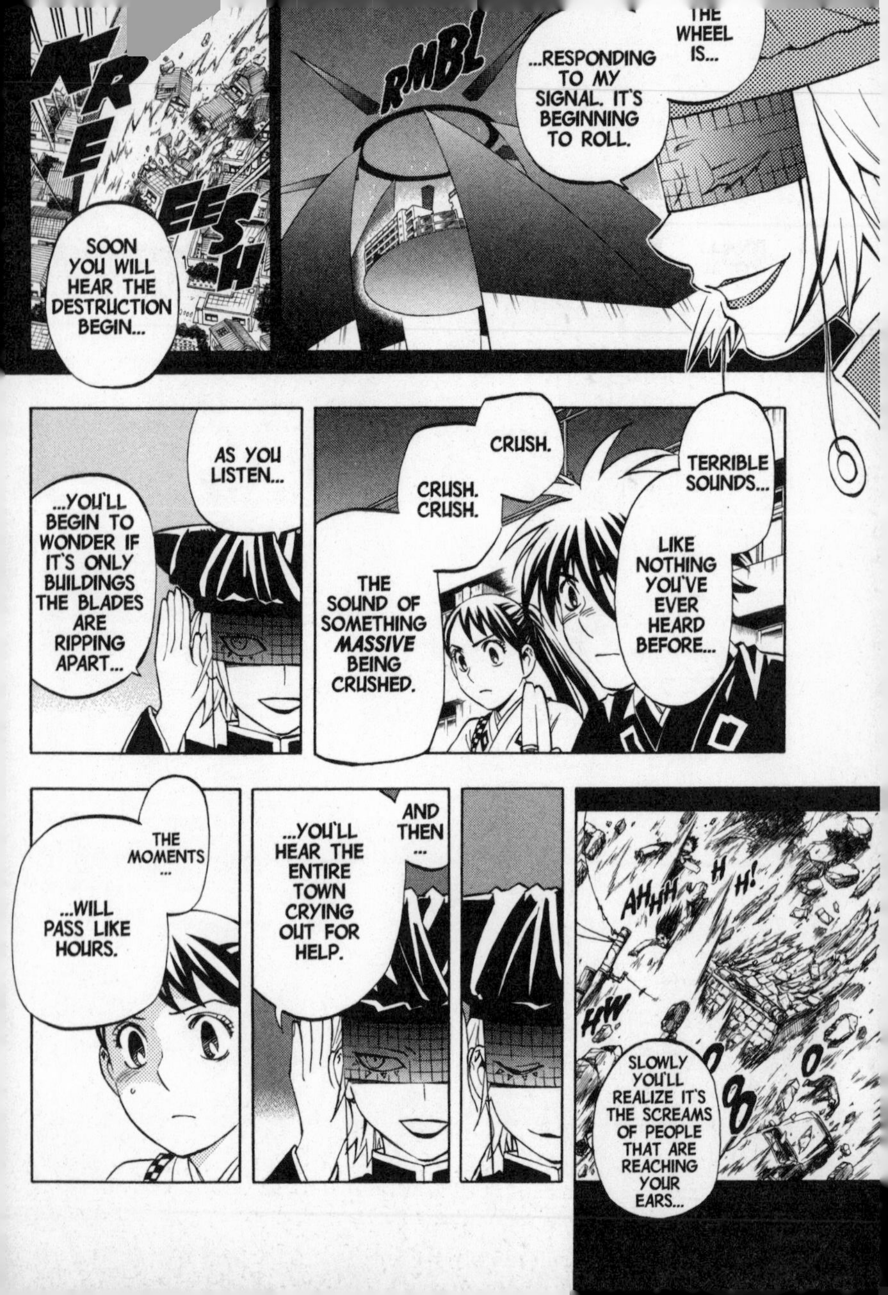
THE WHEEL IS...
...RESPONDING TO MY SIGNAL. IT'S BEGINNING TO ROLL.
RMBL
KREEESH
SOON YOU WILL HEAR THE DESTRUCTION BEGIN...
TERRIBLE SOUNDS...
LIKE NOTHING YOU'VE EVER HEARD BEFORE...
CRUSH.
CRUSH. CRUSH.
THE SOUND OF SOMETHING *MASSIVE* BEING CRUSHED.
AS YOU LISTEN...
...YOU'LL BEGIN TO WONDER IF IT'S ONLY BUILDINGS THE BLADES ARE RIPPING APART...
AHHHH H H!
HW
SLOWLY YOU'LL REALIZE IT'S THE SCREAMS OF PEOPLE THAT ARE REACHING YOUR EARS...
AND THEN...
...YOU'LL HEAR THE ENTIRE TOWN CRYING OUT FOR HELP.
THE MOMENTS...
...WILL PASS LIKE HOURS.

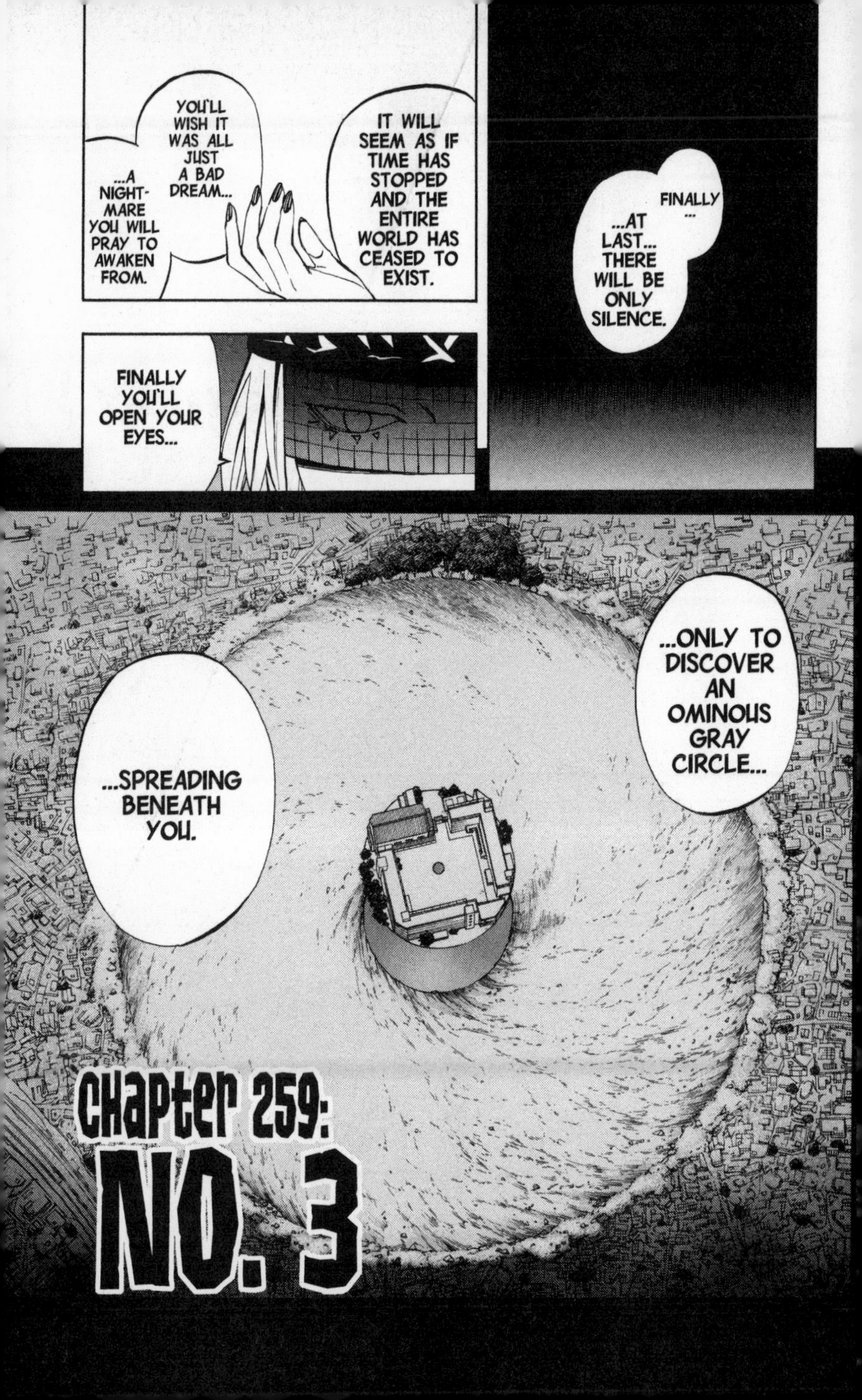
FINALLY...
...AT LAST... THERE WILL BE ONLY SILENCE.
IT WILL SEEM AS IF TIME HAS STOPPED AND THE ENTIRE WORLD HAS CEASED TO EXIST.
YOU'LL WISH IT WAS ALL JUST A BAD DREAM...
...A NIGHT-MARE YOU WILL PRAY TO AWAKEN FROM.
FINALLY YOU'LL OPEN YOUR EYES...
...ONLY TO DISCOVER AN OMINOUS GRAY CIRCLE...
...SPREADING BENEATH YOU.

Chapter 259: NO. 3

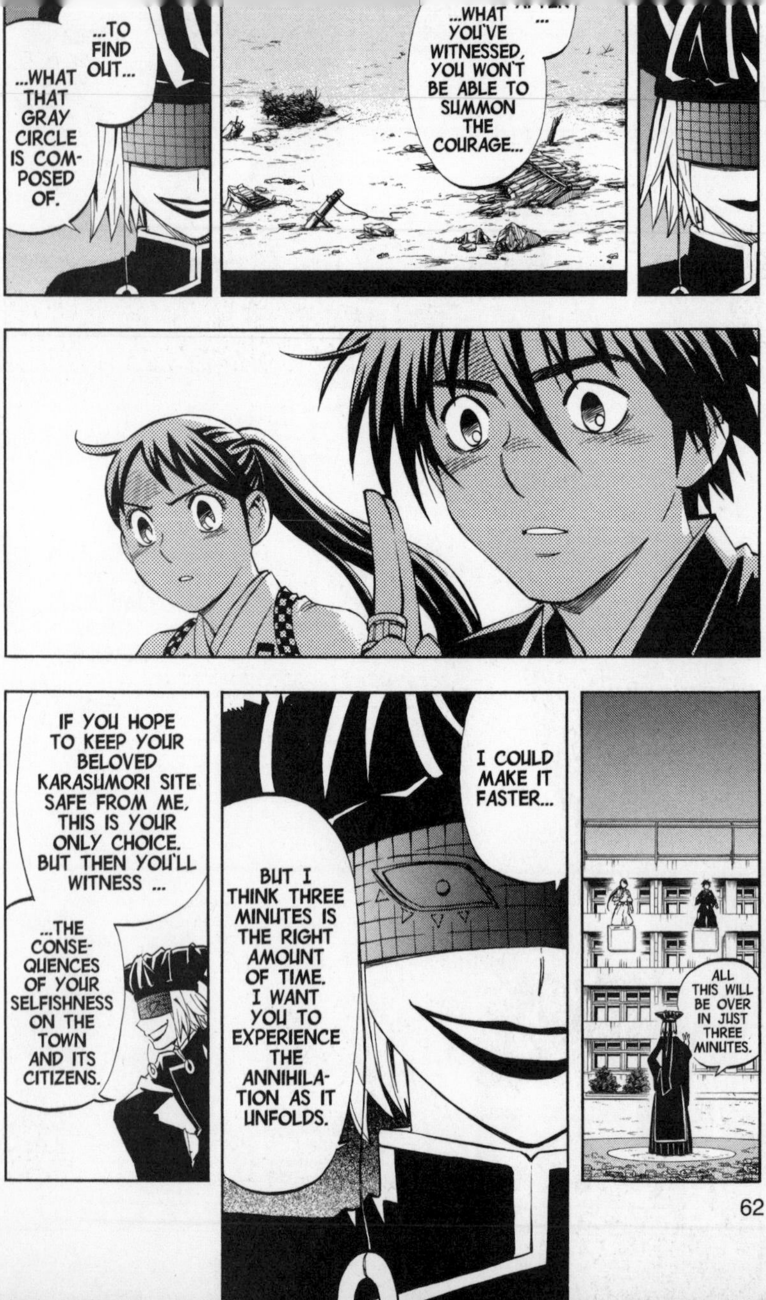

...WHAT YOU'VE WITNESSED, YOU WON'T BE ABLE TO SUMMON THE COURAGE...
...TO FIND OUT...
...WHAT THAT GRAY CIRCLE IS COMPOSED OF.
ALL THIS WILL BE OVER IN JUST THREE MINUTES.
I COULD MAKE IT FASTER...
BUT I THINK THREE MINUTES IS THE RIGHT AMOUNT OF TIME. I WANT YOU TO EXPERIENCE THE ANNIHILATION AS IT UNFOLDS.
IF YOU HOPE TO KEEP YOUR BELOVED KARASUMORI SITE SAFE FROM ME, THIS IS YOUR ONLY CHOICE. BUT THEN YOU'LL WITNESS ...
...THE CONSEQUENCES OF YOUR SELFISHNESS ON THE TOWN AND ITS CITIZENS.

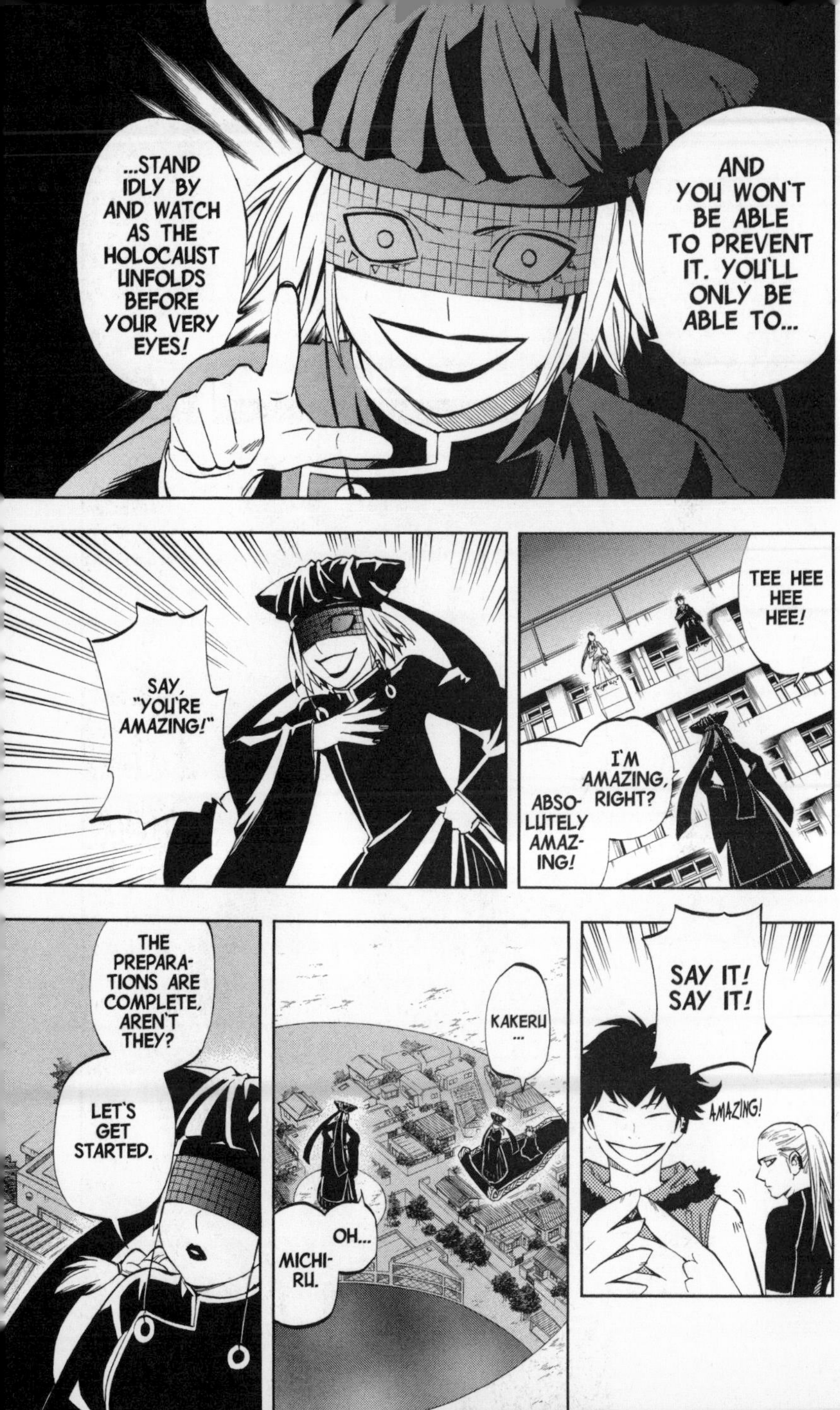
AND YOU WON'T BE ABLE TO PREVENT IT. YOU'LL ONLY BE ABLE TO...
...STAND IDLY BY AND WATCH AS THE HOLOCAUST UNFOLDS BEFORE YOUR VERY EYES!
TEE HEE HEE HEE!
I'M AMAZING, RIGHT?
ABSO-LUTELY AMAZ-ING!
SAY, "YOU'RE AMAZING!"
SAY IT! SAY IT!
AMAZING!
KAKERU...
OH... MICHI-RU.
THE PREPARA-TIONS ARE COMPLETE, AREN'T THEY?
LET'S GET STARTED.

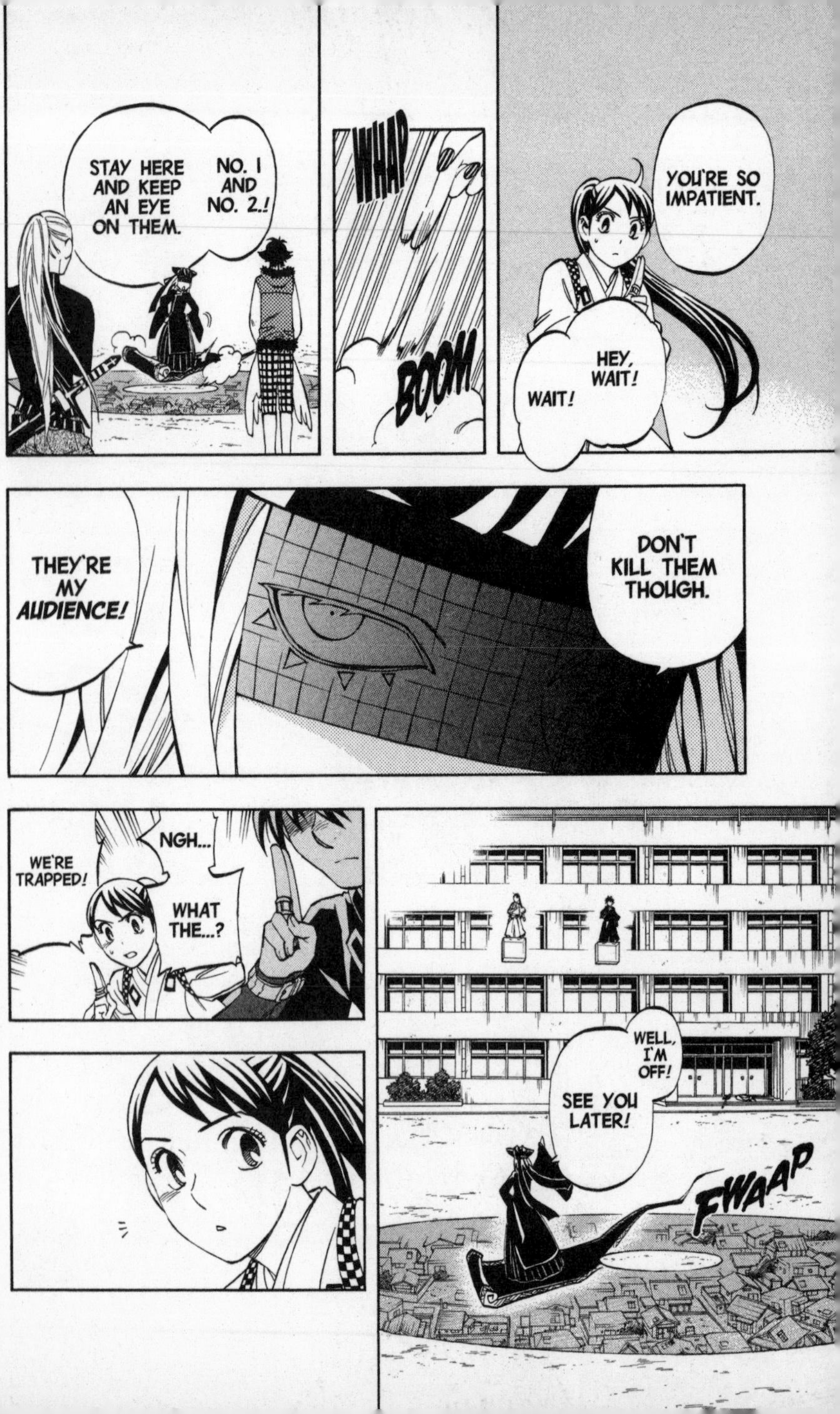
YOU'RE SO IMPATIENT.
HEY, WAIT!
WAIT!
WHAP
BOOM
NO. 1 AND NO. 2.!
STAY HERE AND KEEP AN EYE ON THEM.
DON'T KILL THEM THOUGH.
THEY'RE MY AUDIENCE!
WELL, I'M OFF!
SEE YOU LATER!
FWAAP
NGH...
WE'RE TRAPPED!
WHAT THE...?

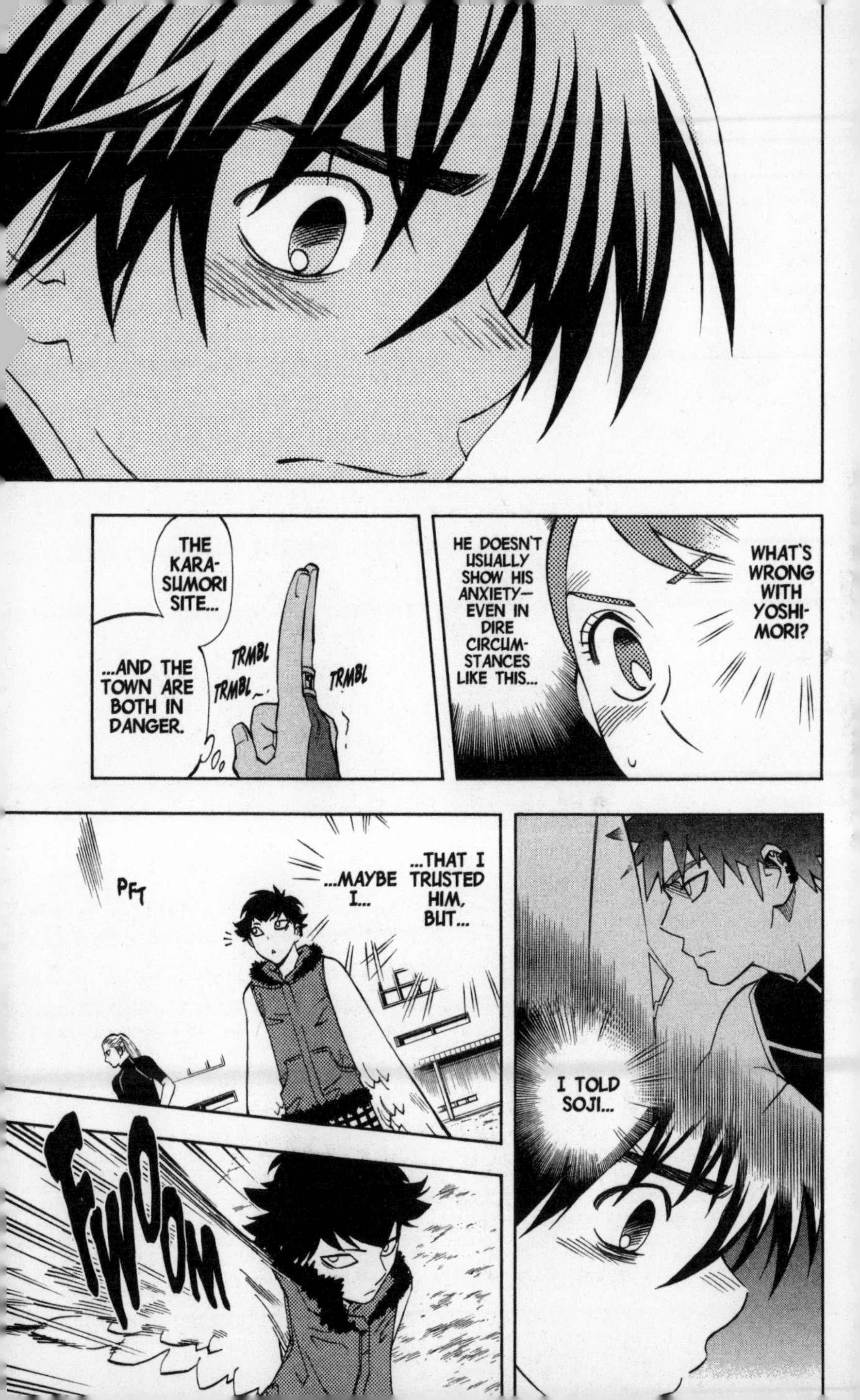
WHAT'S WRONG WITH YOSHIMORI?
HE DOESN'T USUALLY SHOW HIS ANXIETY— EVEN IN DIRE CIRCUMSTANCES LIKE THIS...
THE KARASUMORI SITE...
TRMBL
TRMBL
TRMBL
...AND THE TOWN ARE BOTH IN DANGER.
I TOLD SOJI...
...THAT I TRUSTED HIM, BUT...
...MAYBE I...
PFT
FWOOM

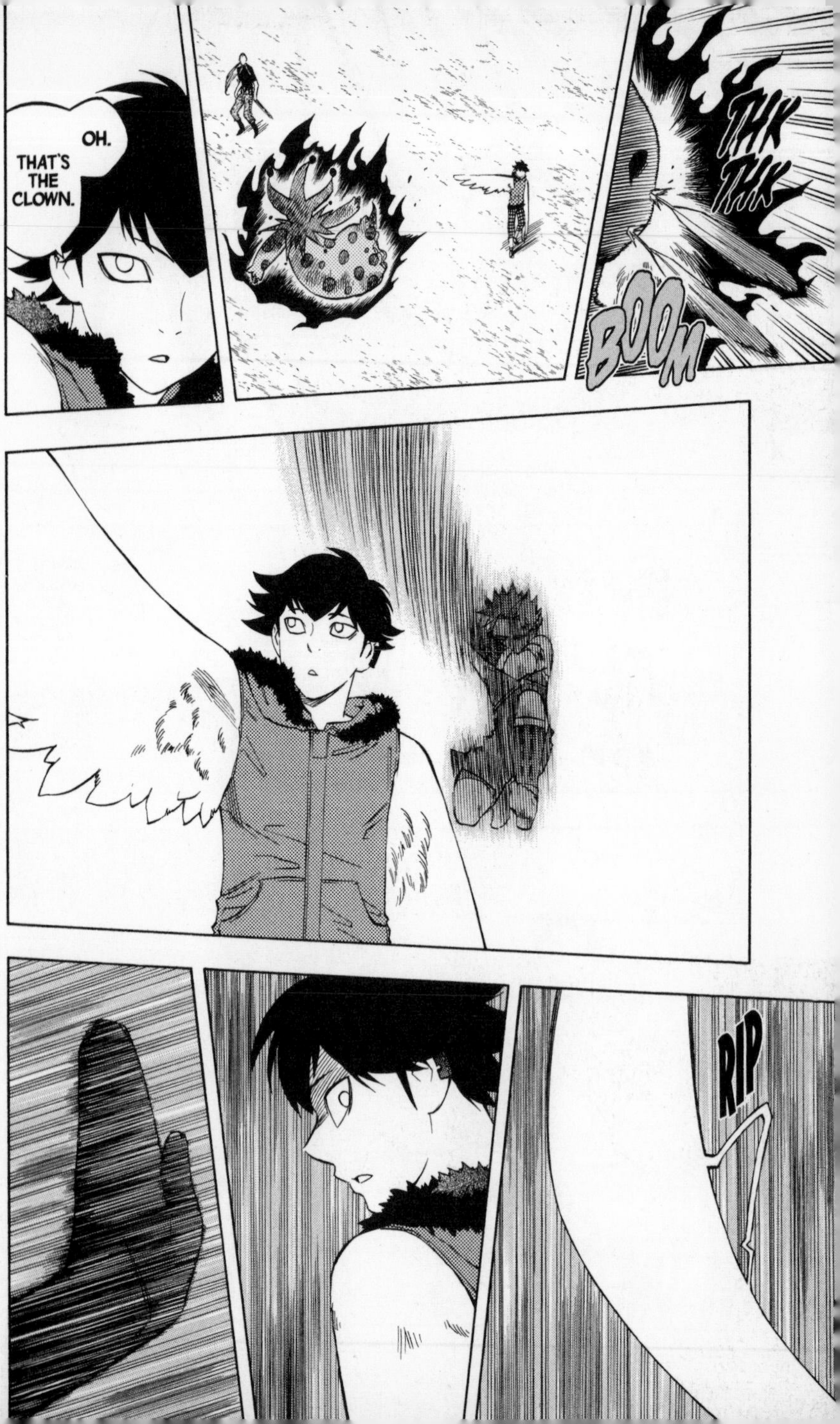
THK THK
BOOM
OH. THAT'S THE CLOWN.
RIP

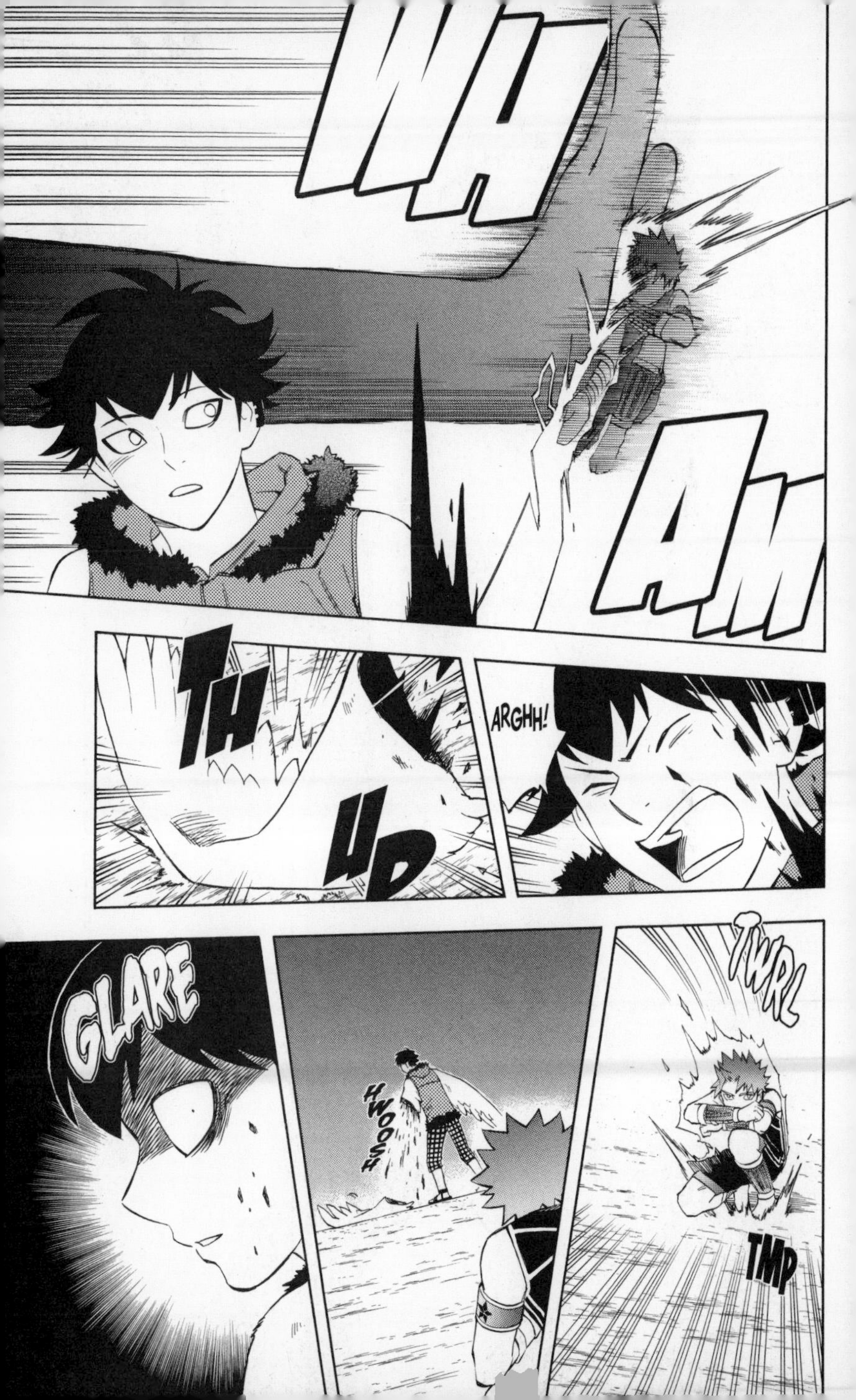
WHAM
THUD
ARGHH!
TWRL
TMP
HWOOSH
GLARE

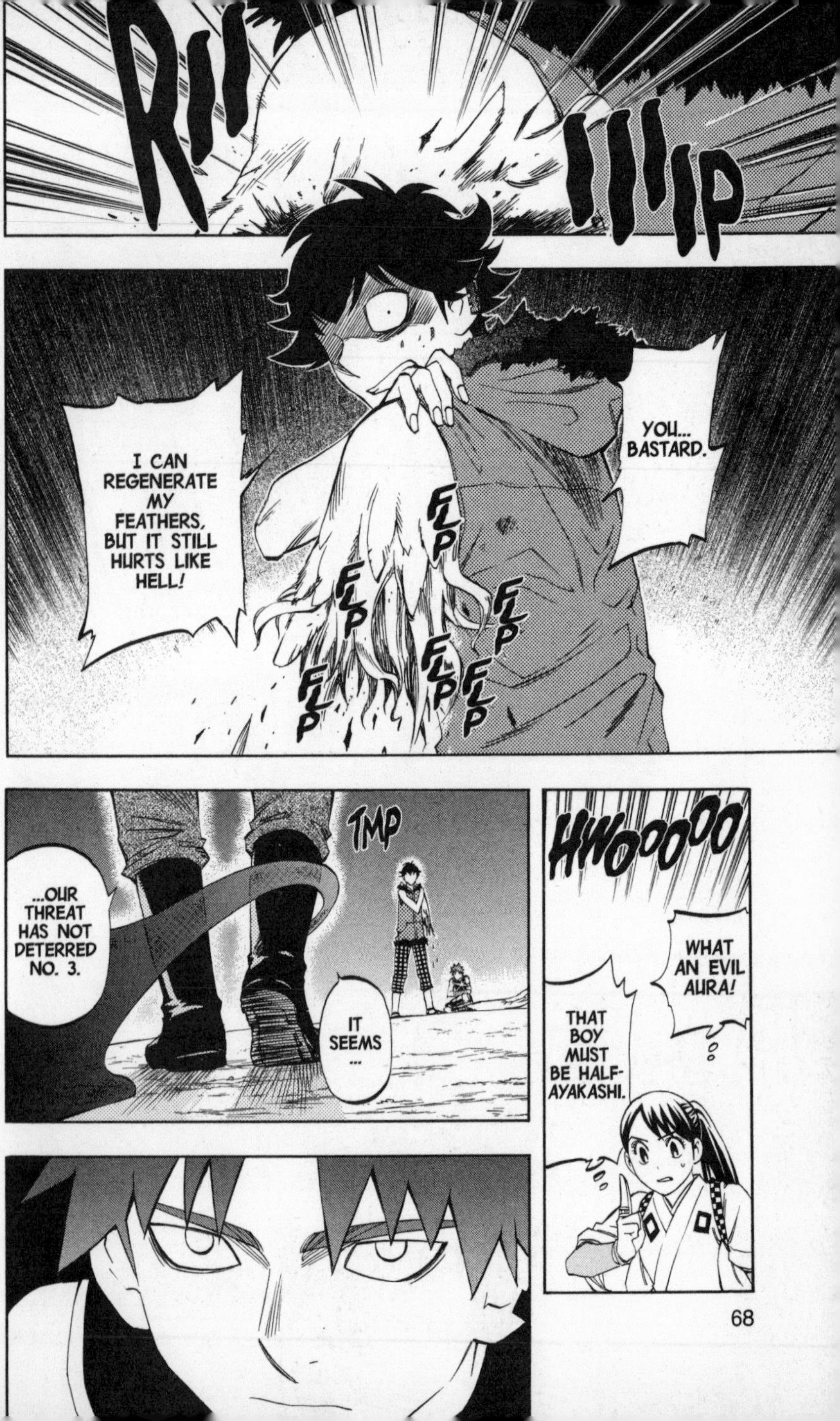
RIIIIIP
YOU... BASTARD.
I CAN REGENERATE MY FEATHERS, BUT IT STILL HURTS LIKE HELL!
FLP FLP FLP FLP FLP FLP
HWOOOOO
WHAT AN EVIL AURA!
THAT BOY MUST BE HALF-AYAKASHI.
TMP
IT SEEMS...
...OUR THREAT HAS NOT DETERRED NO. 3.

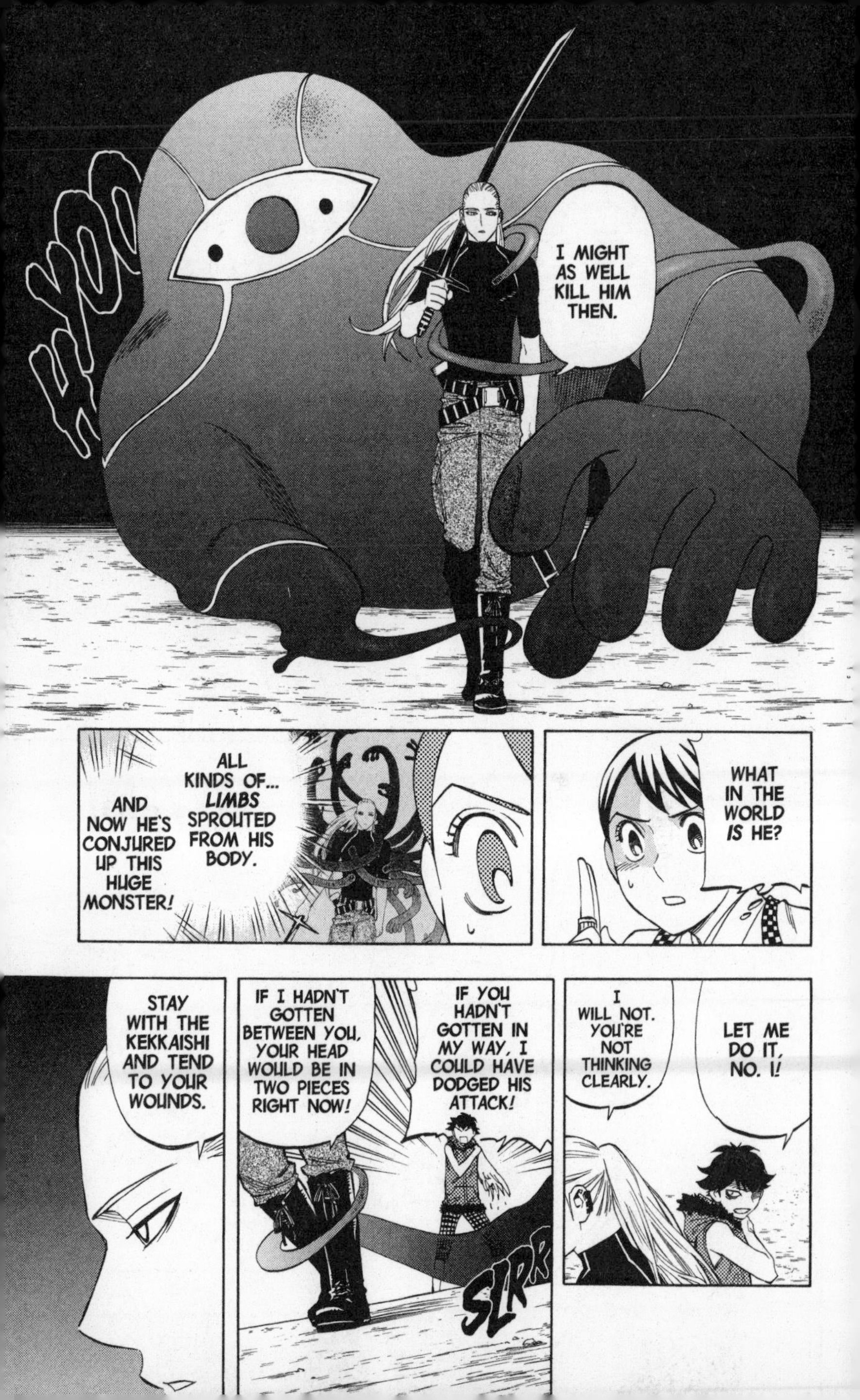
KYOO
I MIGHT AS WELL KILL HIM THEN.
WHAT IN THE WORLD IS HE?
ALL KINDS OF... LIMBS SPROUTED FROM HIS BODY.
AND NOW HE'S CONJURED UP THIS HUGE MONSTER!
LET ME DO IT, NO. I!
I WILL NOT. YOU'RE NOT THINKING CLEARLY.
IF YOU HADN'T GOTTEN IN MY WAY, I COULD HAVE DODGED HIS ATTACK!
IF I HADN'T GOTTEN BETWEEN YOU, YOUR HEAD WOULD BE IN TWO PIECES RIGHT NOW!
SLRR
STAY WITH THE KEKKAISHI AND TEND TO YOUR WOUNDS.

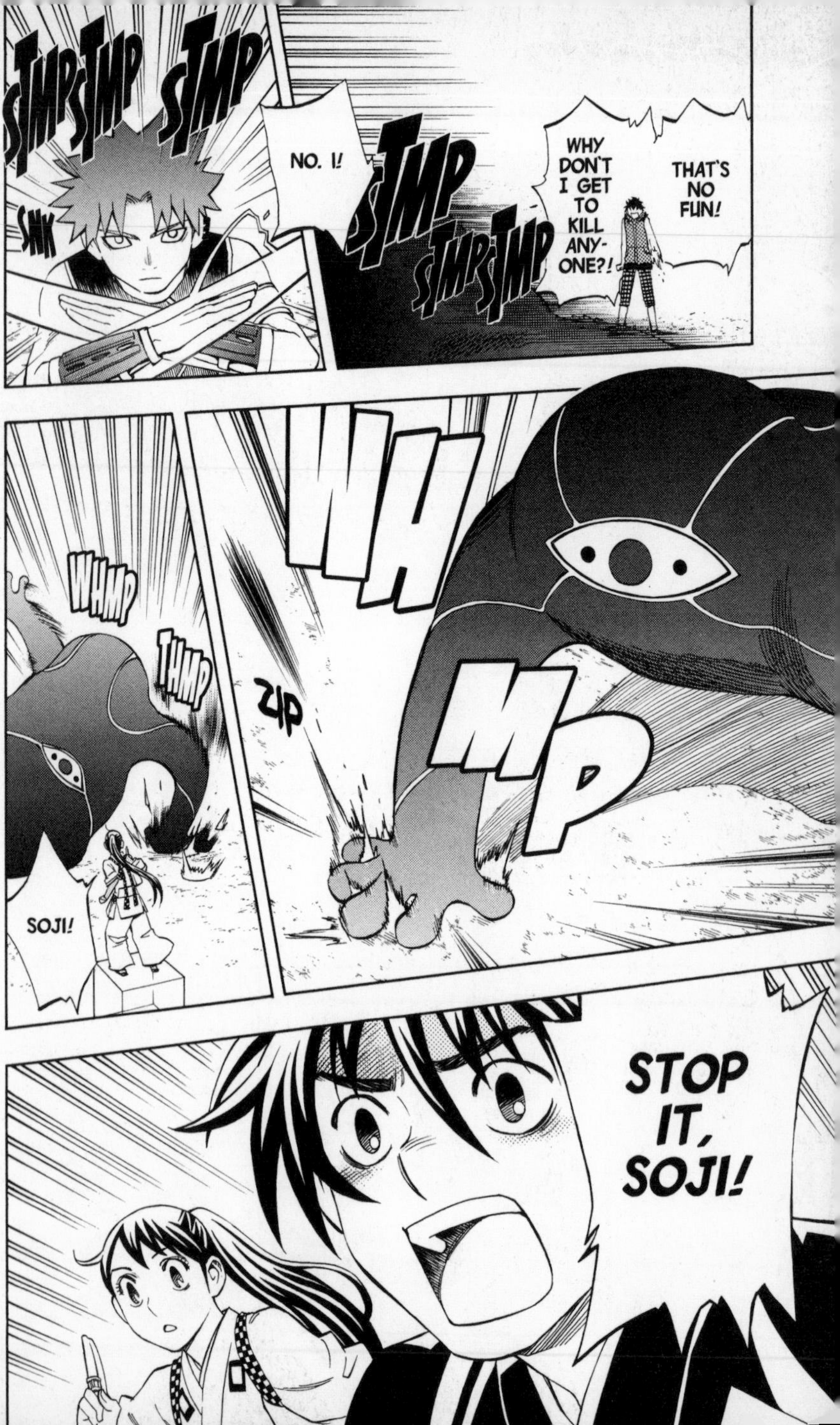
WHY DON'T I GET TO KILL ANY-ONE?!
THAT'S NO FUN!
STMP STMPSTMP
STMPSTMP STMP
NO. I!
SNK
WHMP
ZIP
WHMP
THMP
SOJI!
STOP IT, SOJI!

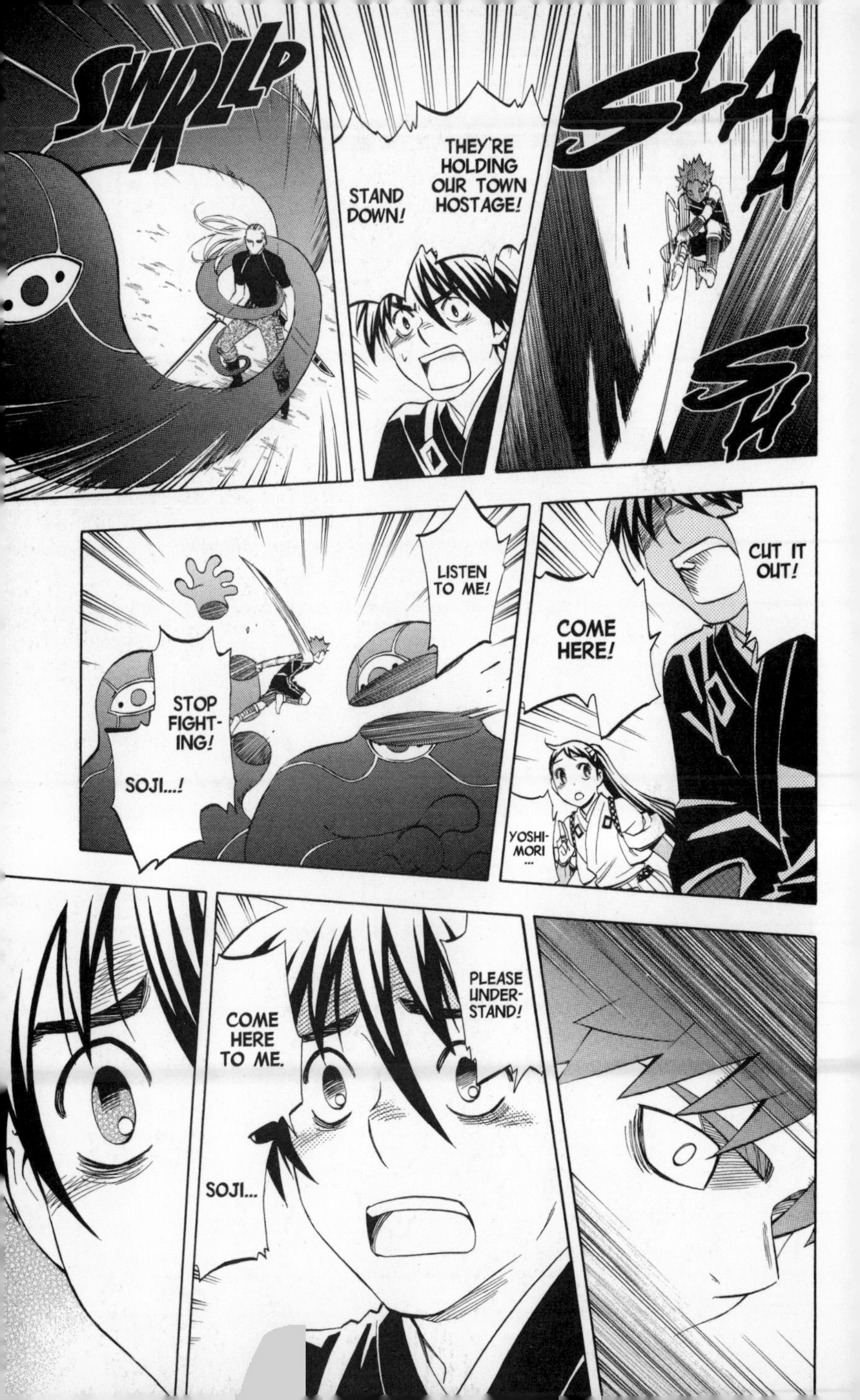
SLAASH
THEY'RE HOLDING OUR TOWN HOSTAGE!
STAND DOWN!
SWHLLP
CUT IT OUT!
COME HERE!
YOSHIMORI...
LISTEN TO ME!
STOP FIGHTING!
SOJI...!
PLEASE UNDERSTAND!
COME HERE TO ME.
SOJI...

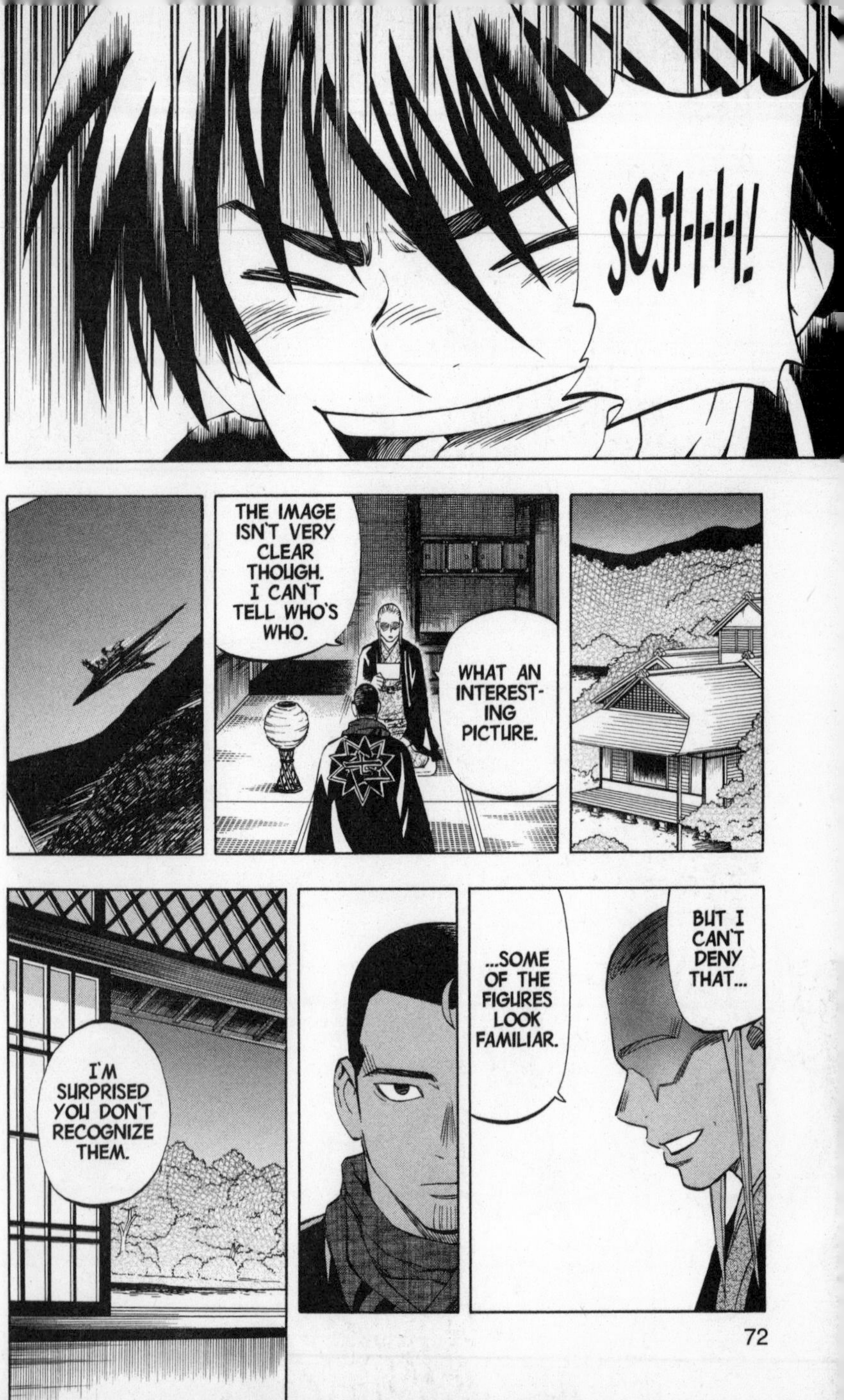
SOJI-I-I-I!
WHAT AN INTEREST-ING PICTURE.
THE IMAGE ISN'T VERY CLEAR THOUGH. I CAN'T TELL WHO'S WHO.
BUT I CAN'T DENY THAT...
...SOME OF THE FIGURES LOOK FAMILIAR.
I'M SURPRISED YOU DON'T RECOGNIZE THEM.

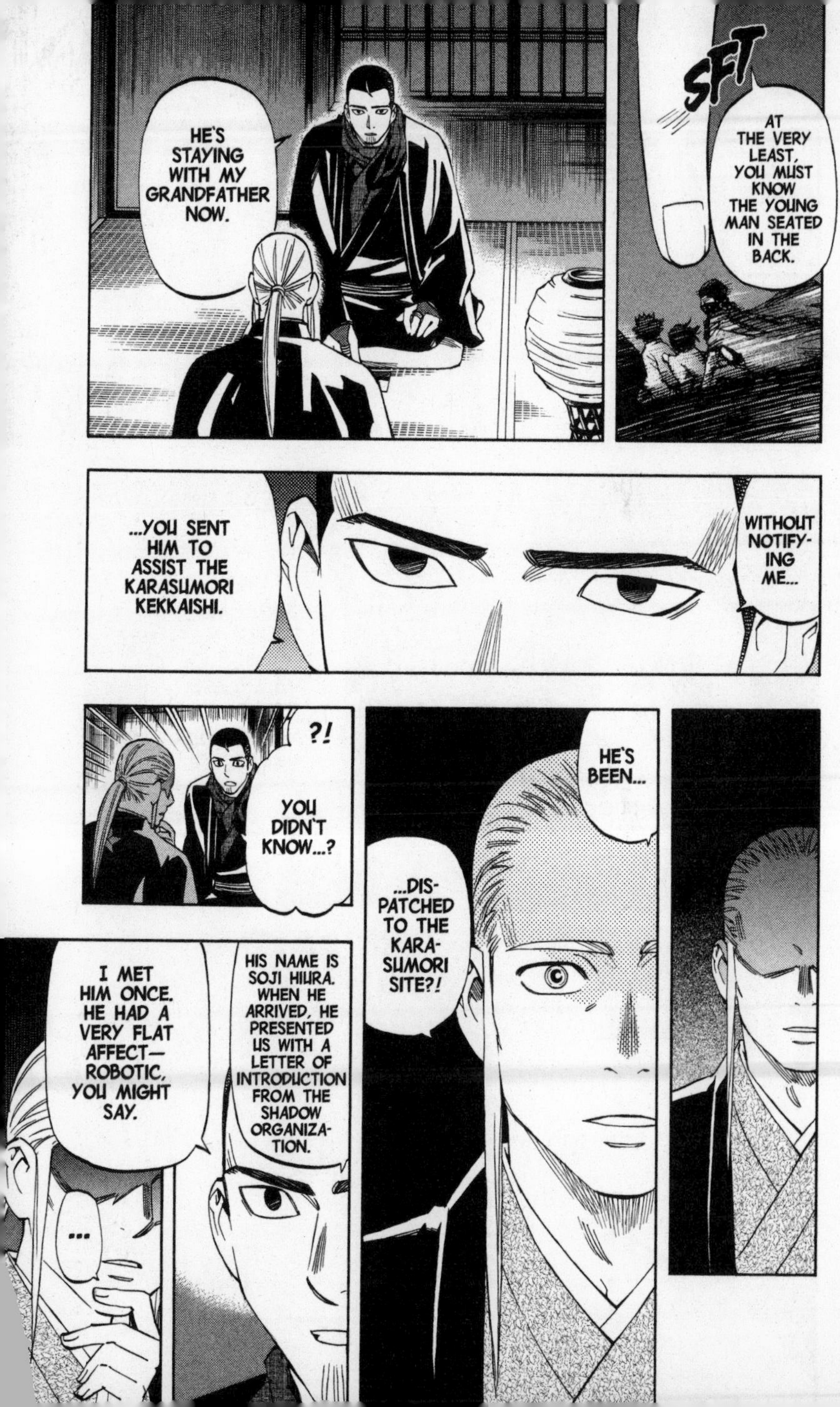

SFT
AT THE VERY LEAST, YOU MUST KNOW THE YOUNG MAN SEATED IN THE BACK.
HE'S STAYING WITH MY GRANDFATHER NOW.
WITHOUT NOTIFYING ME...
...YOU SENT HIM TO ASSIST THE KARASUMORI KEKKAISHI.
HE'S BEEN...
...DISPATCHED TO THE KARASUMORI SITE?!
?!
YOU DIDN'T KNOW...?
HIS NAME IS SOJI HIURA. WHEN HE ARRIVED, HE PRESENTED US WITH A LETTER OF INTRODUCTION FROM THE SHADOW ORGANIZATION.
I MET HIM ONCE. HE HAD A VERY FLAT AFFECT—ROBOTIC, YOU MIGHT SAY.
...

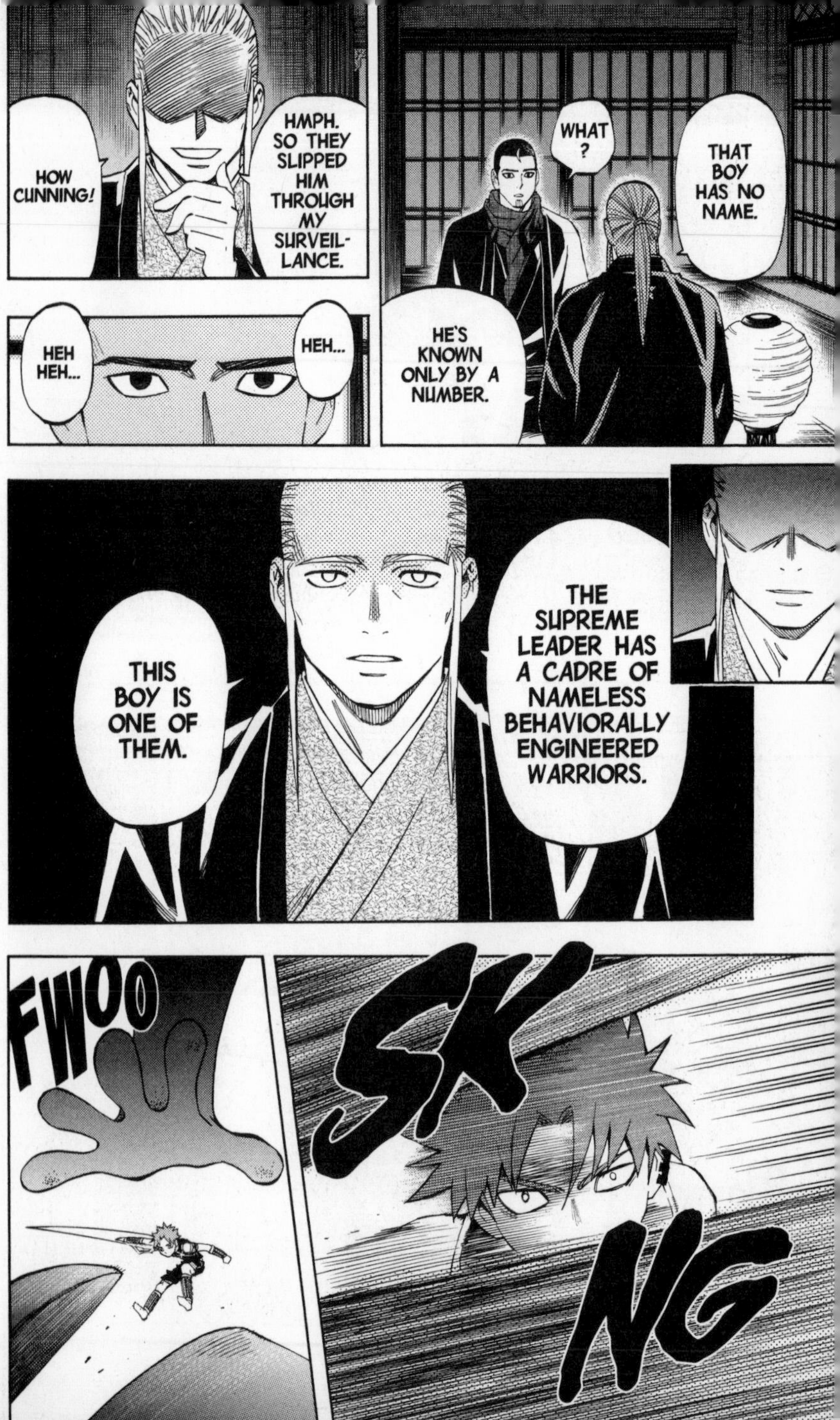
THAT BOY HAS NO NAME.
WHAT?
HE'S KNOWN ONLY BY A NUMBER.
HMPH. SO THEY SLIPPED HIM THROUGH MY SURVEIL-LANCE.
HOW CUNNING!
HEH...
HEH HEH...
THE SUPREME LEADER HAS A CADRE OF NAMELESS BEHAVIORALLY ENGINEERED WARRIORS.
THIS BOY IS ONE OF THEM.
SKING
FWOO

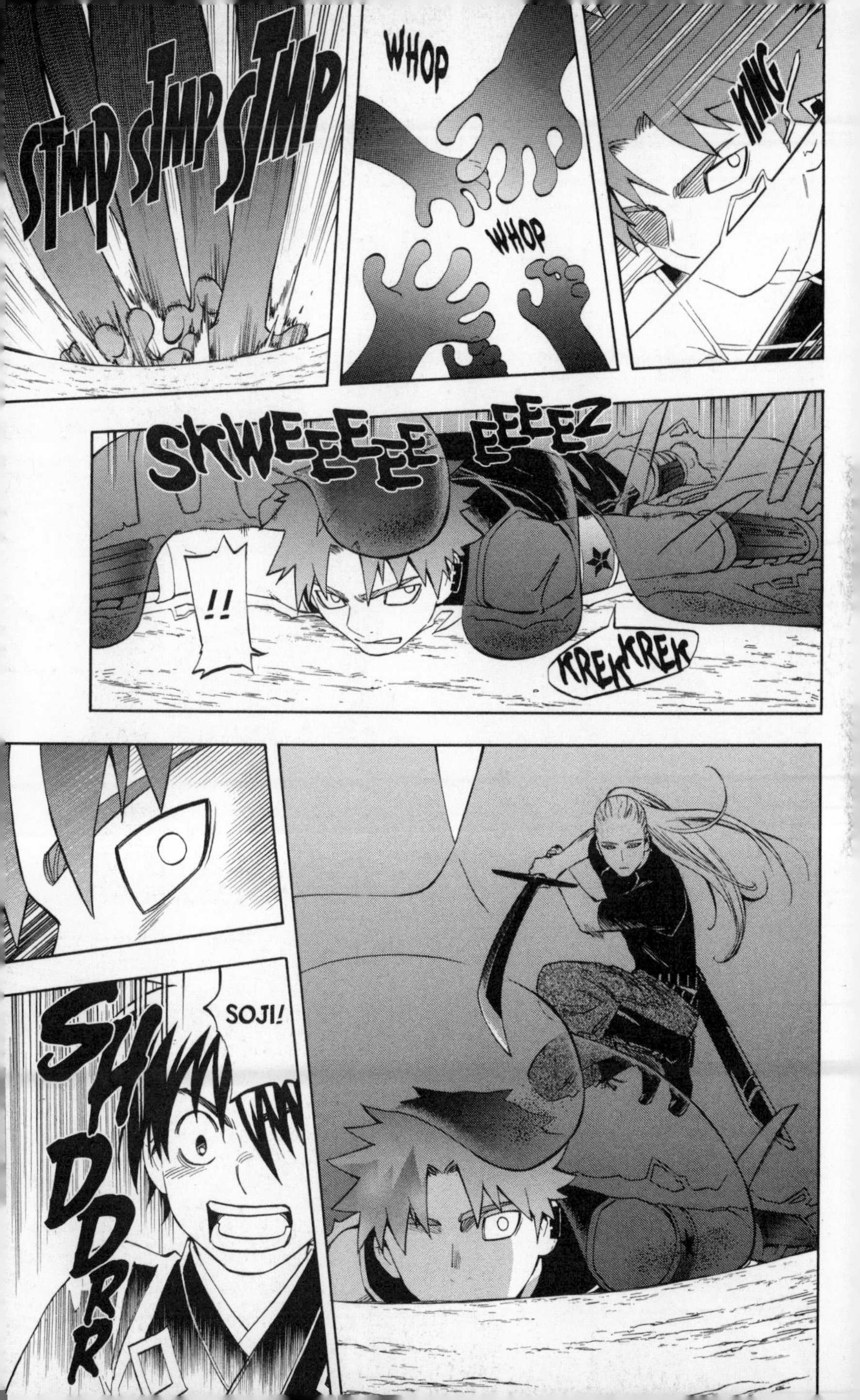
KING
WHOP
WHOP
STMP STMP STMP
SKWEEEEEEEEEZ
KREK KREK
!!
SOJI!
SHDDRR

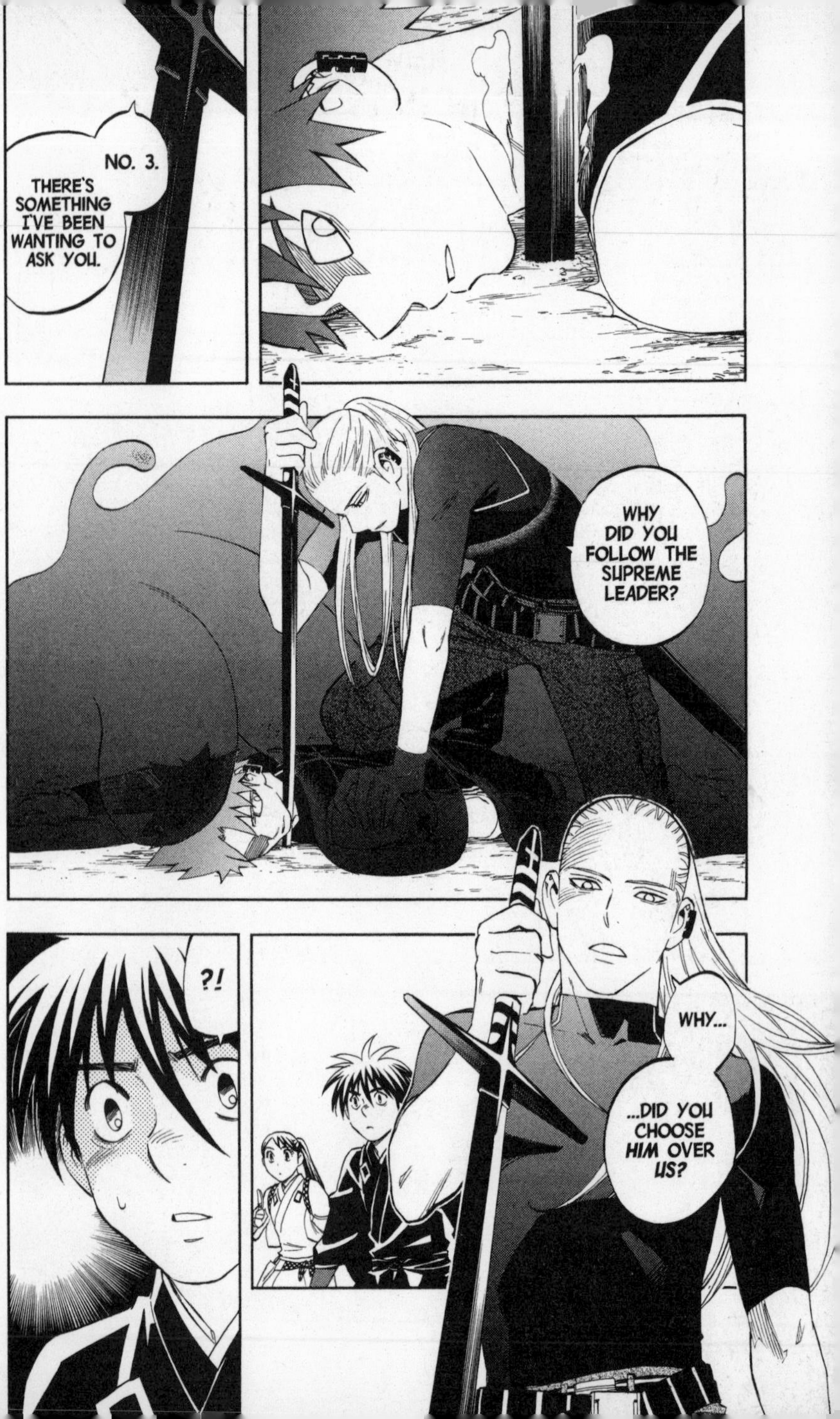
NO. 3.
THERE'S SOMETHING I'VE BEEN WANTING TO ASK YOU.
WHY DID YOU FOLLOW THE SUPREME LEADER?
WHY...
...DID YOU CHOOSE HIM OVER US?
?!

Chapter 260: COMBATANTS

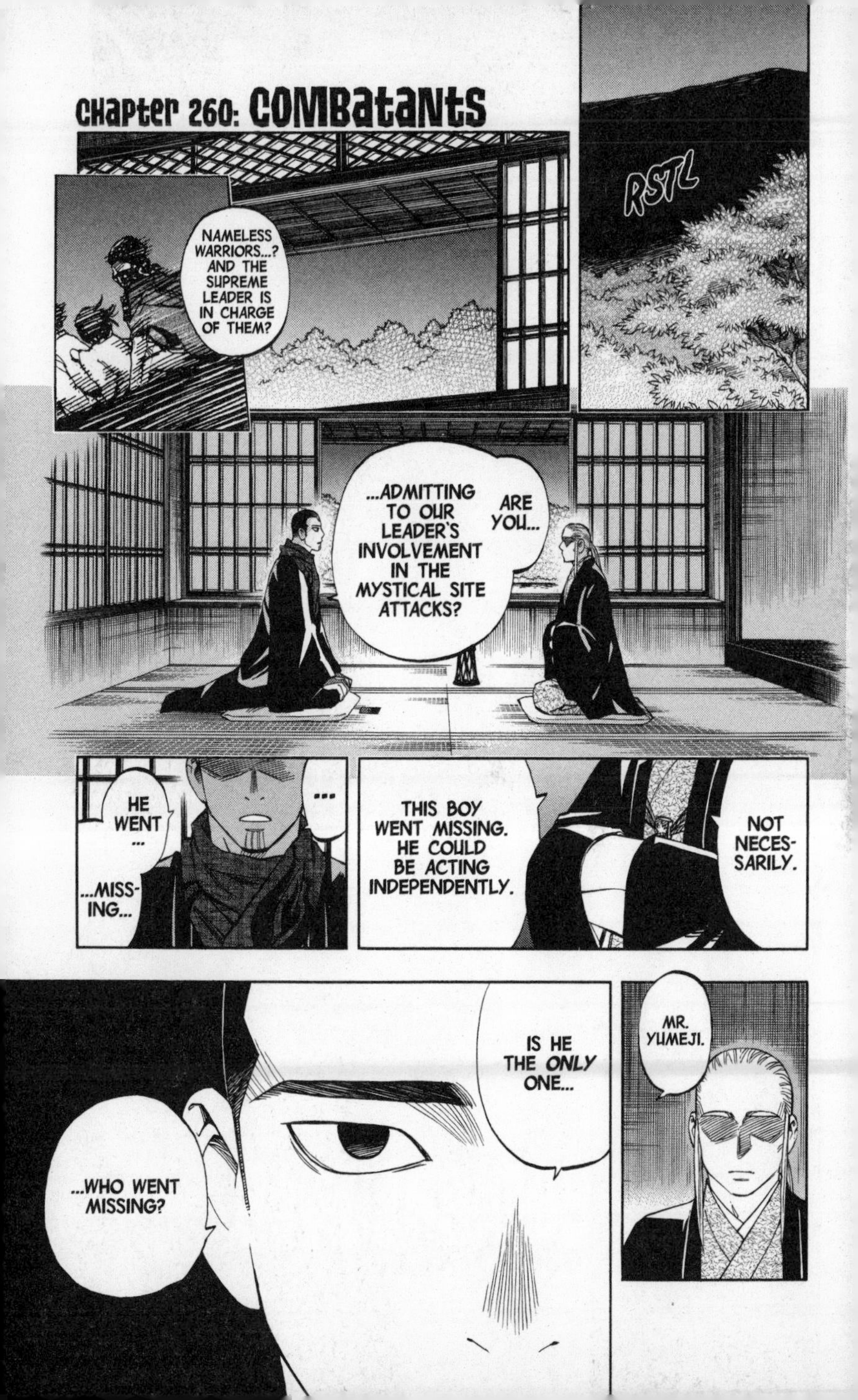
RSTL
NAMELESS WARRIORS...? AND THE SUPREME LEADER IS IN CHARGE OF THEM?
ARE YOU...
...ADMITTING TO OUR LEADER'S INVOLVEMENT IN THE MYSTICAL SITE ATTACKS?
NOT NECES-SARILY.
THIS BOY WENT MISSING. HE COULD BE ACTING INDEPENDENTLY.
...
HE WENT ...
...MISS-ING...
MR. YUMEJI.
IS HE THE *ONLY* ONE...
...WHO WENT MISSING?

Chapter 260:

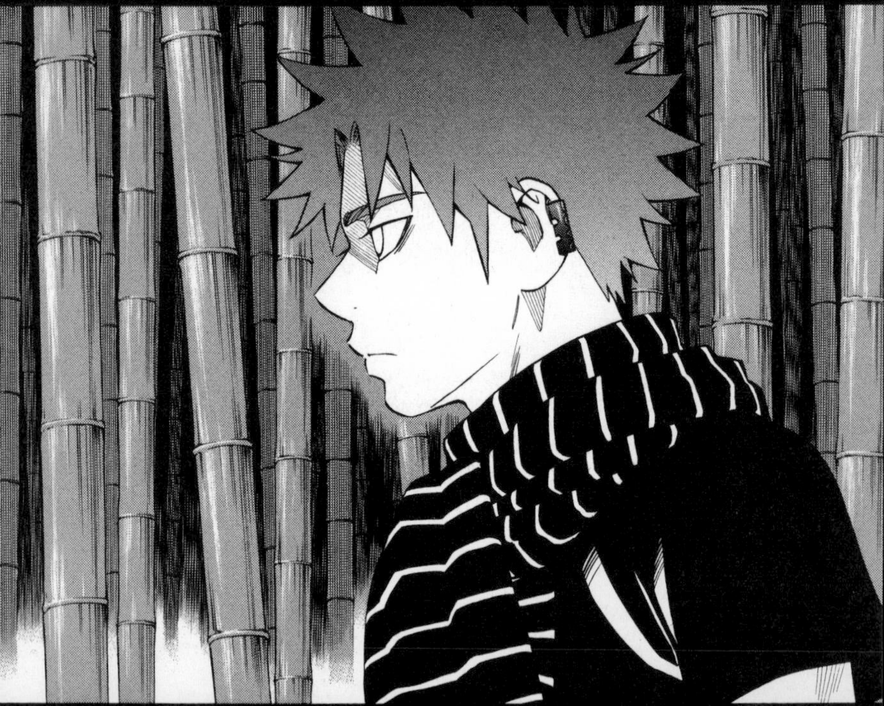

Combatants

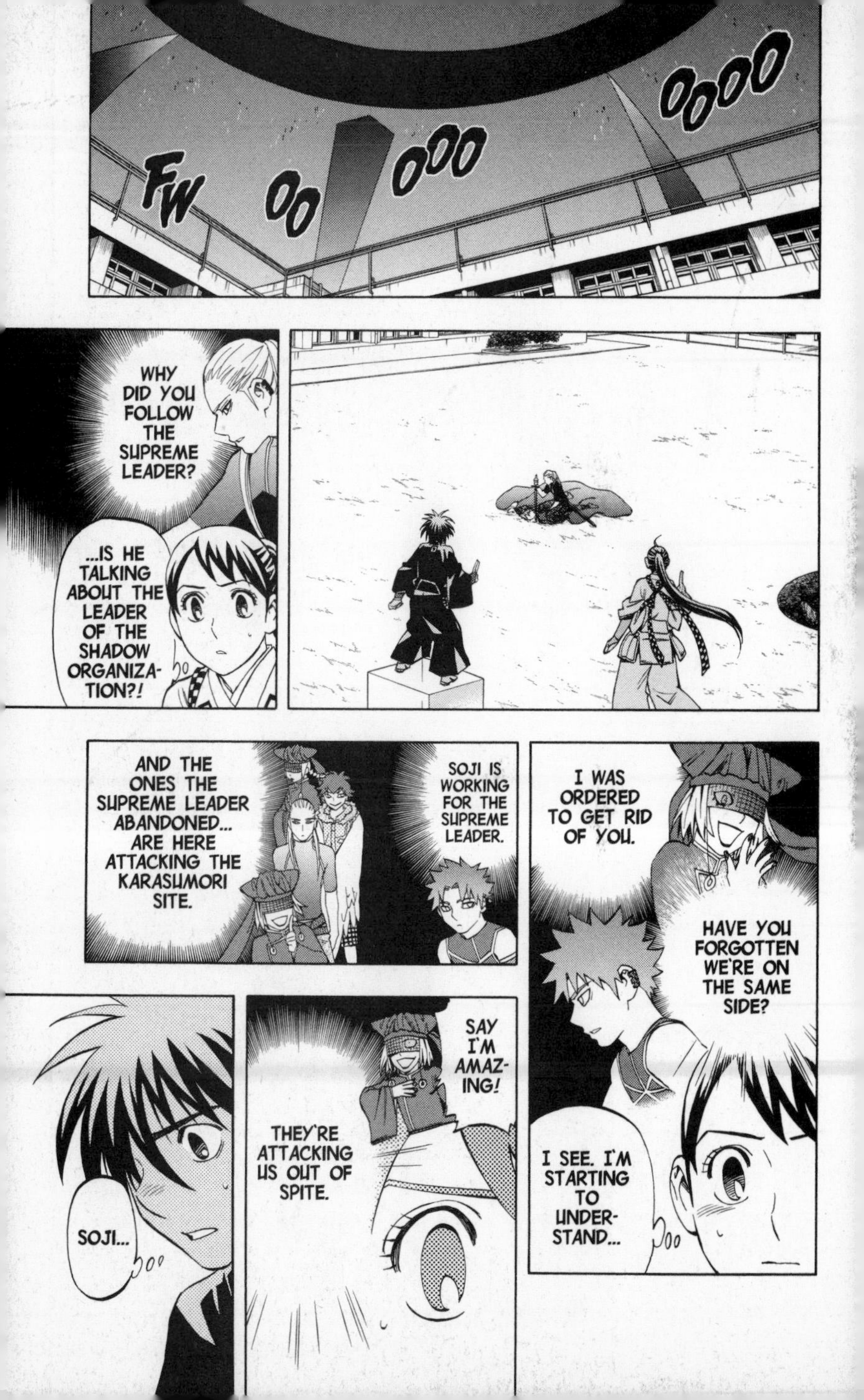

FWOOOOOOOOO
WHY DID YOU FOLLOW THE SUPREME LEADER?
...IS HE TALKING ABOUT THE LEADER OF THE SHADOW ORGANIZATION?!
I WAS ORDERED TO GET RID OF YOU.
HAVE YOU FORGOTTEN WE'RE ON THE SAME SIDE?
I SEE. I'M STARTING TO UNDERSTAND...
SOJI IS WORKING FOR THE SUPREME LEADER.
AND THE ONES THE SUPREME LEADER ABANDONED... ARE HERE ATTACKING THE KARASUMORI SITE.
SAY I'M AMAZING!
THEY'RE ATTACKING US OUT OF SPITE.
SOJI...

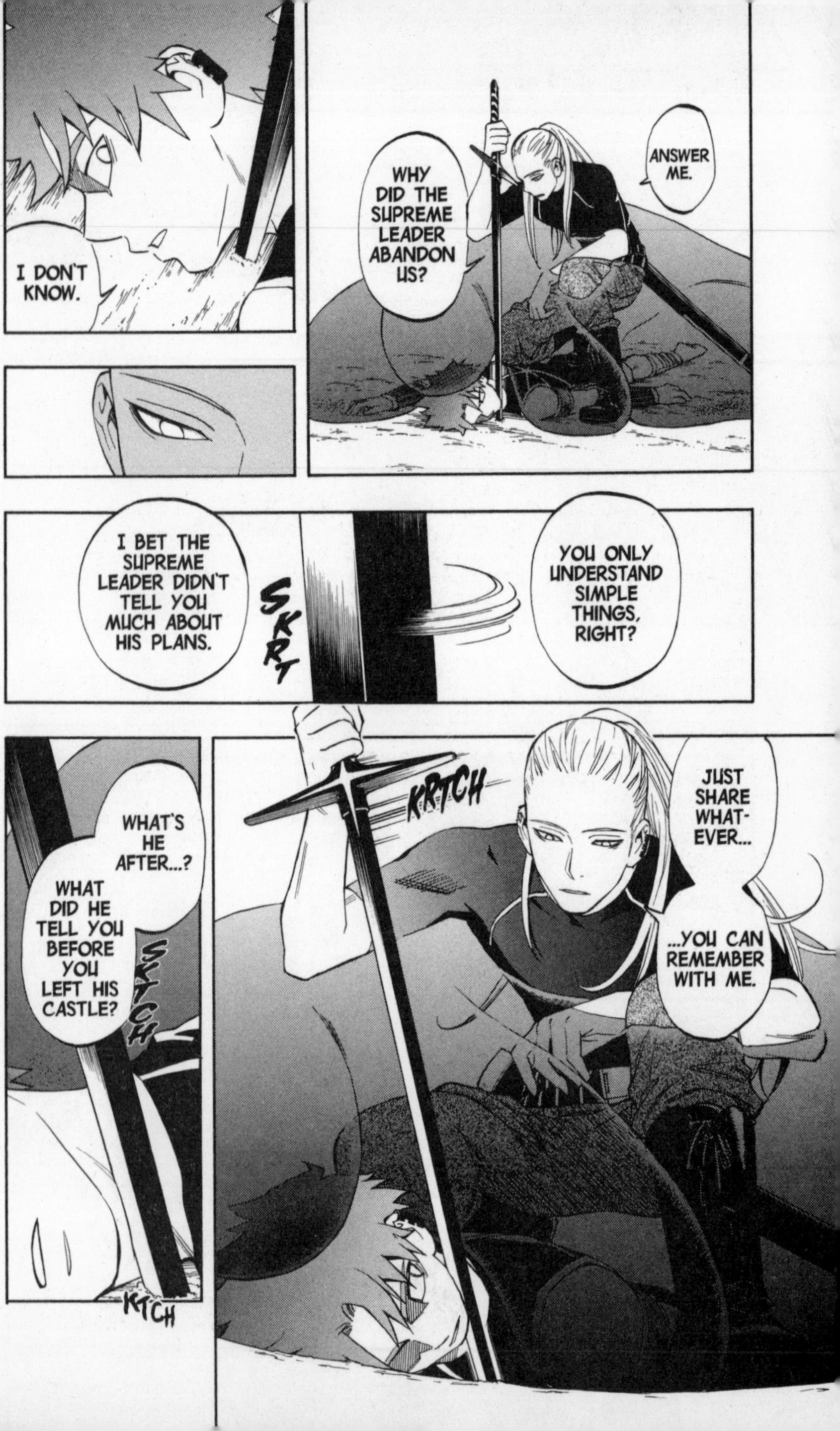
ANSWER ME.
WHY DID THE SUPREME LEADER ABANDON US?
I DON'T KNOW.
YOU ONLY UNDERSTAND SIMPLE THINGS, RIGHT?
SKRT
I BET THE SUPREME LEADER DIDN'T TELL YOU MUCH ABOUT HIS PLANS.
JUST SHARE WHAT-EVER...
KRTCH
...YOU CAN REMEMBER WITH ME.
WHAT'S HE AFTER...?
WHAT DID HE TELL YOU BEFORE YOU LEFT HIS CASTLE?
SKTCH
KTCH

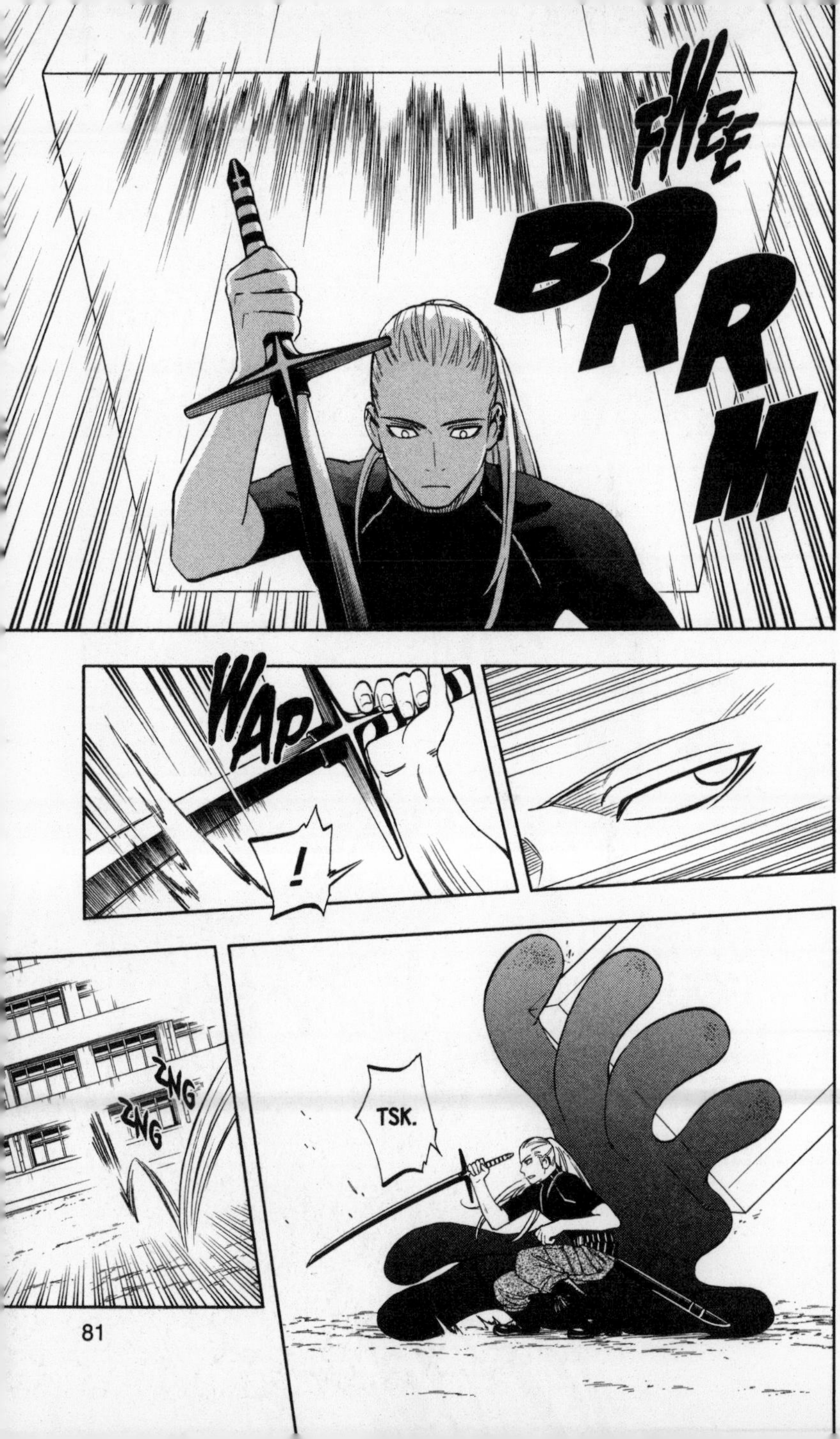
FWEE
BRRRM
WAP
!
TSK.
ZNG
ZNG

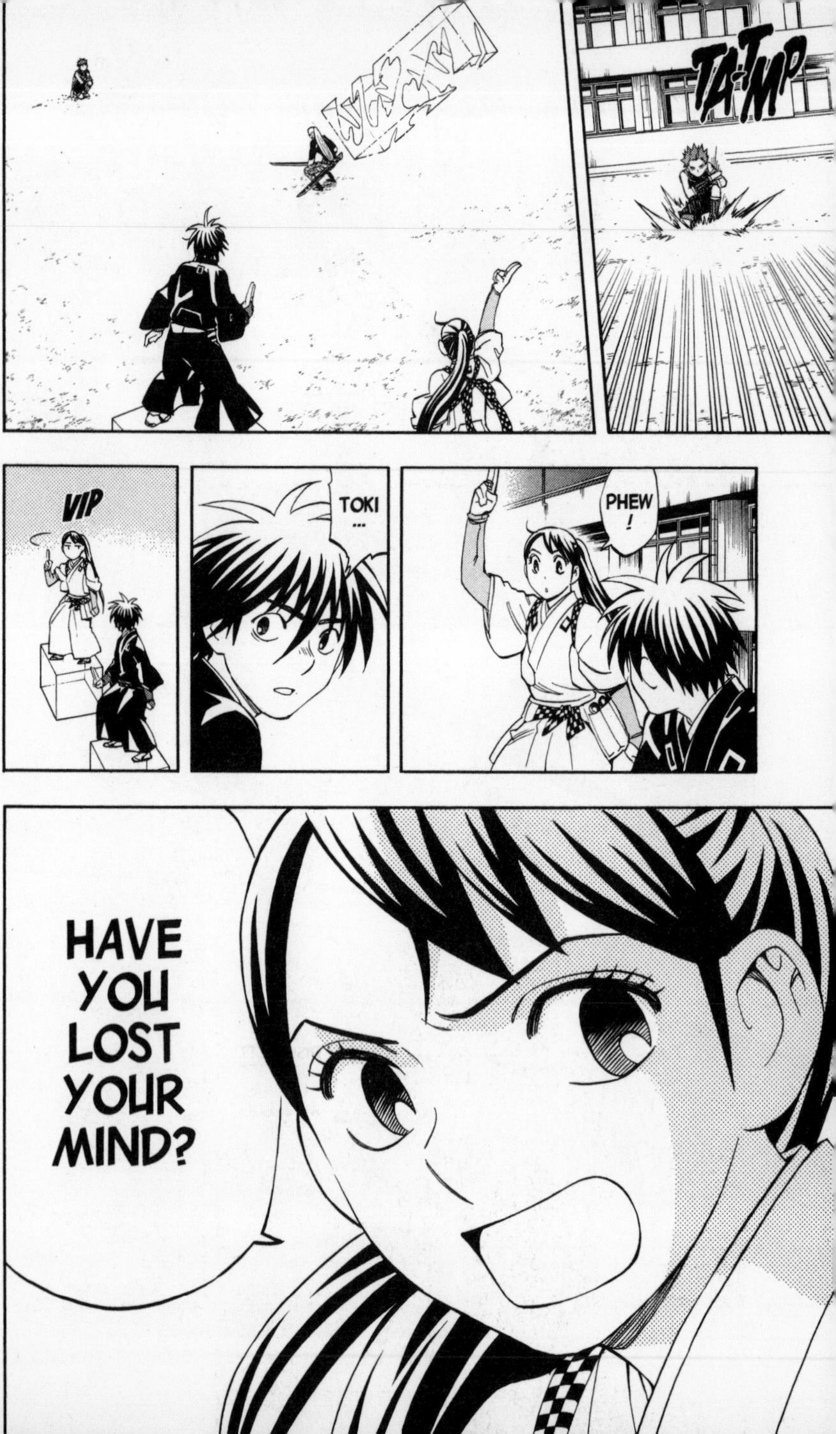
TA-TMP
PHEW!
TOKI...
VIP
HAVE YOU LOST YOUR MIND?

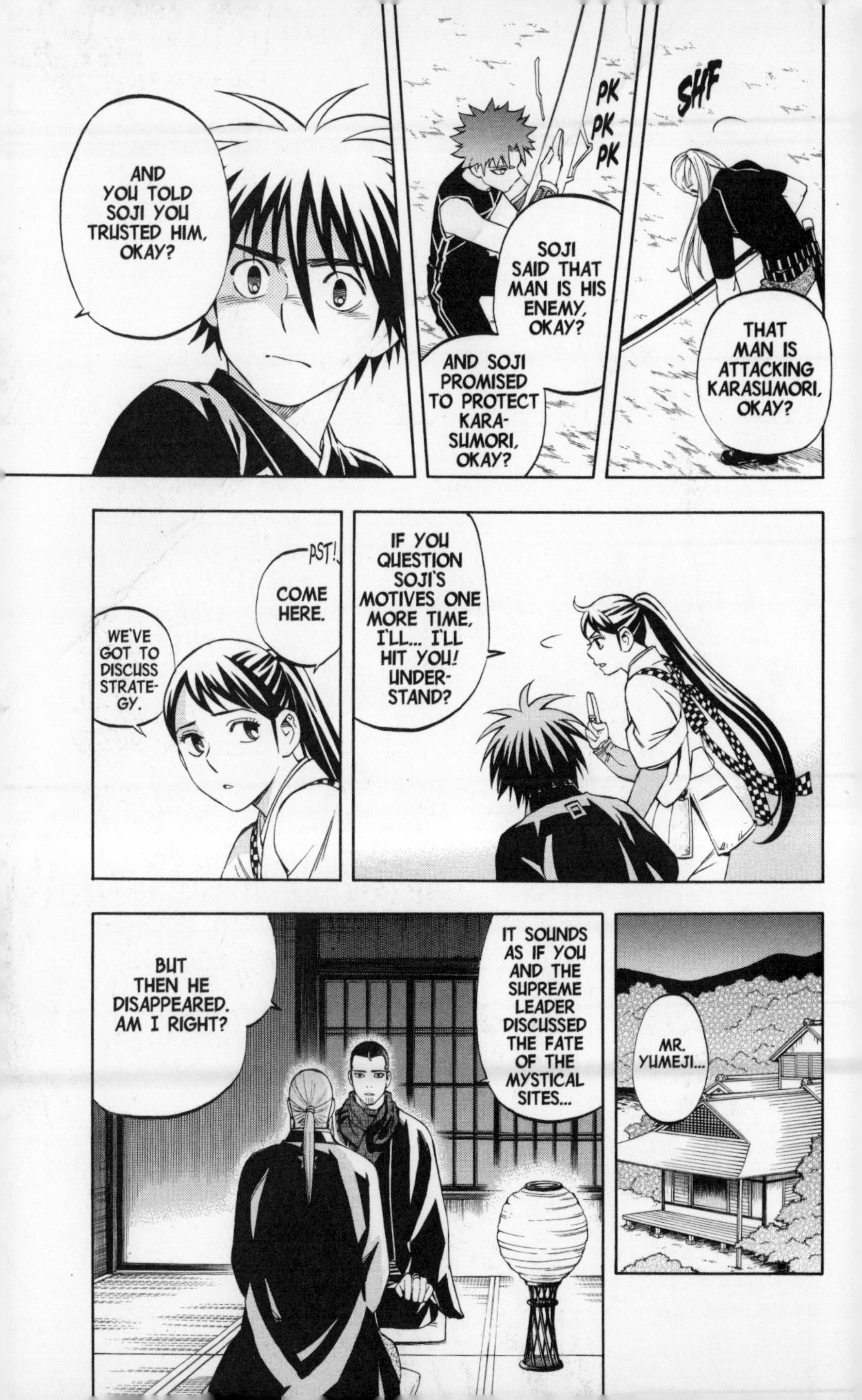
SHF
THAT MAN IS ATTACKING KARASUMORI, OKAY?
PK PK PK
SOJI SAID THAT MAN IS HIS ENEMY, OKAY?
AND SOJI PROMISED TO PROTECT KARA-SUMORI, OKAY?
AND YOU TOLD SOJI YOU TRUSTED HIM, OKAY?
IF YOU QUESTION SOJI'S MOTIVES ONE MORE TIME, I'LL... I'LL HIT YOU! UNDER-STAND?
PST!
COME HERE.
WE'VE GOT TO DISCUSS STRATE-GY.
MR. YUMEJI...
IT SOUNDS AS IF YOU AND THE SUPREME LEADER DISCUSSED THE FATE OF THE MYSTICAL SITES...
BUT THEN HE DISAPPEARED. AM I RIGHT?

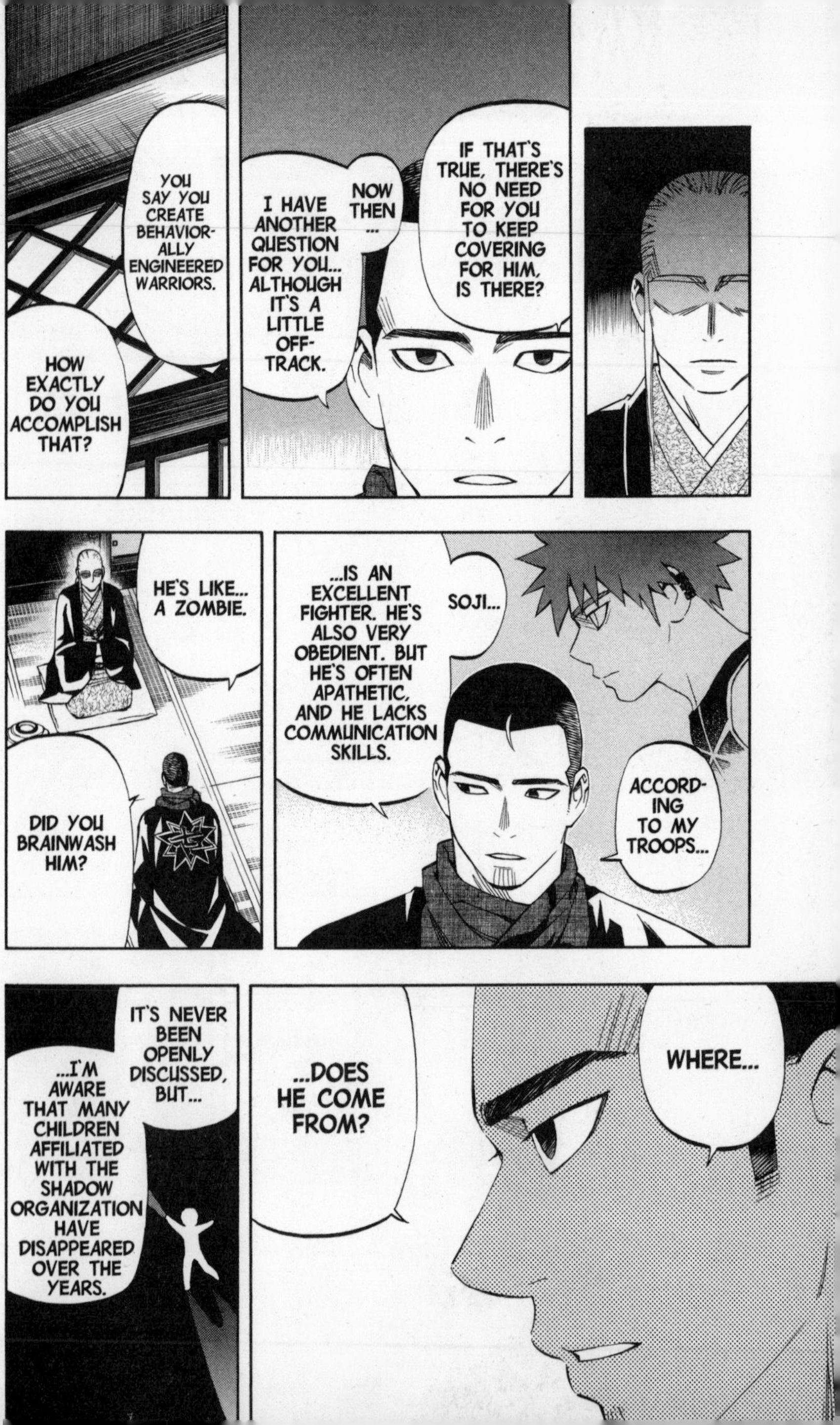
IF THAT'S TRUE, THERE'S NO NEED FOR YOU TO KEEP COVERING FOR HIM, IS THERE?
NOW THEN ...
I HAVE ANOTHER QUESTION FOR YOU... ALTHOUGH IT'S A LITTLE OFF-TRACK.
YOU SAY YOU CREATE BEHAVIORALLY ENGINEERED WARRIORS.
HOW EXACTLY DO YOU ACCOMPLISH THAT?
SOJI...
...IS AN EXCELLENT FIGHTER. HE'S ALSO VERY OBEDIENT. BUT HE'S OFTEN APATHETIC, AND HE LACKS COMMUNICATION SKILLS.
ACCORDING TO MY TROOPS...
HE'S LIKE... A ZOMBIE.
DID YOU BRAINWASH HIM?
WHERE...
...DOES HE COME FROM?
IT'S NEVER BEEN OPENLY DISCUSSED, BUT...
...I'M AWARE THAT MANY CHILDREN AFFILIATED WITH THE SHADOW ORGANIZATION HAVE DISAPPEARED OVER THE YEARS.

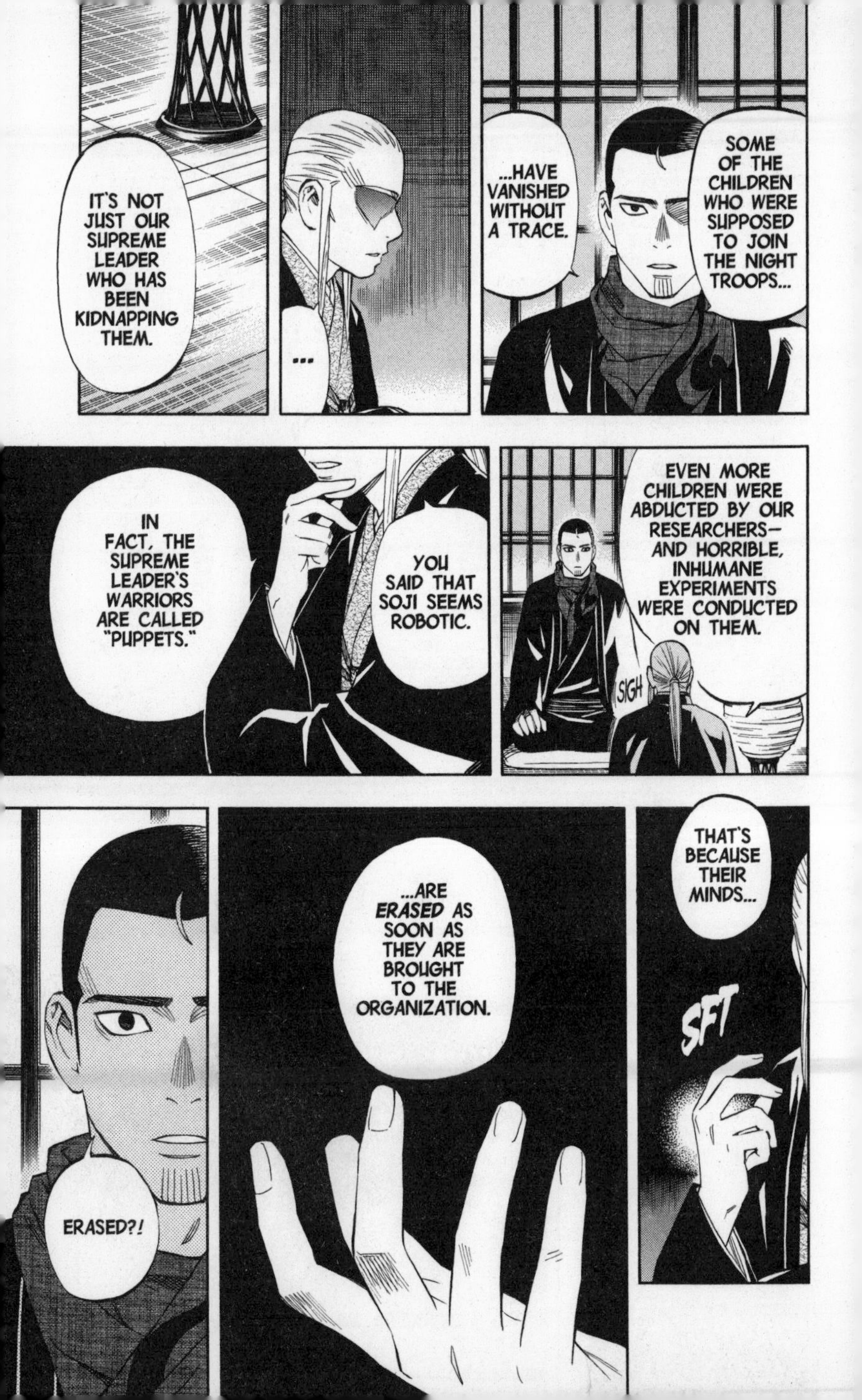
SOME OF THE CHILDREN WHO WERE SUPPOSED TO JOIN THE NIGHT TROOPS...
...HAVE VANISHED WITHOUT A TRACE.
...
IT'S NOT JUST OUR SUPREME LEADER WHO HAS BEEN KIDNAPPING THEM.
EVEN MORE CHILDREN WERE ABDUCTED BY OUR RESEARCHERS— AND HORRIBLE, INHUMANE EXPERIMENTS WERE CONDUCTED ON THEM.
SIGH
YOU SAID THAT SOJI SEEMS ROBOTIC.
IN FACT, THE SUPREME LEADER'S WARRIORS ARE CALLED "PUPPETS."
THAT'S BECAUSE THEIR MINDS...
SFT
...ARE ERASED AS SOON AS THEY ARE BROUGHT TO THE ORGANIZATION.
ERASED?!

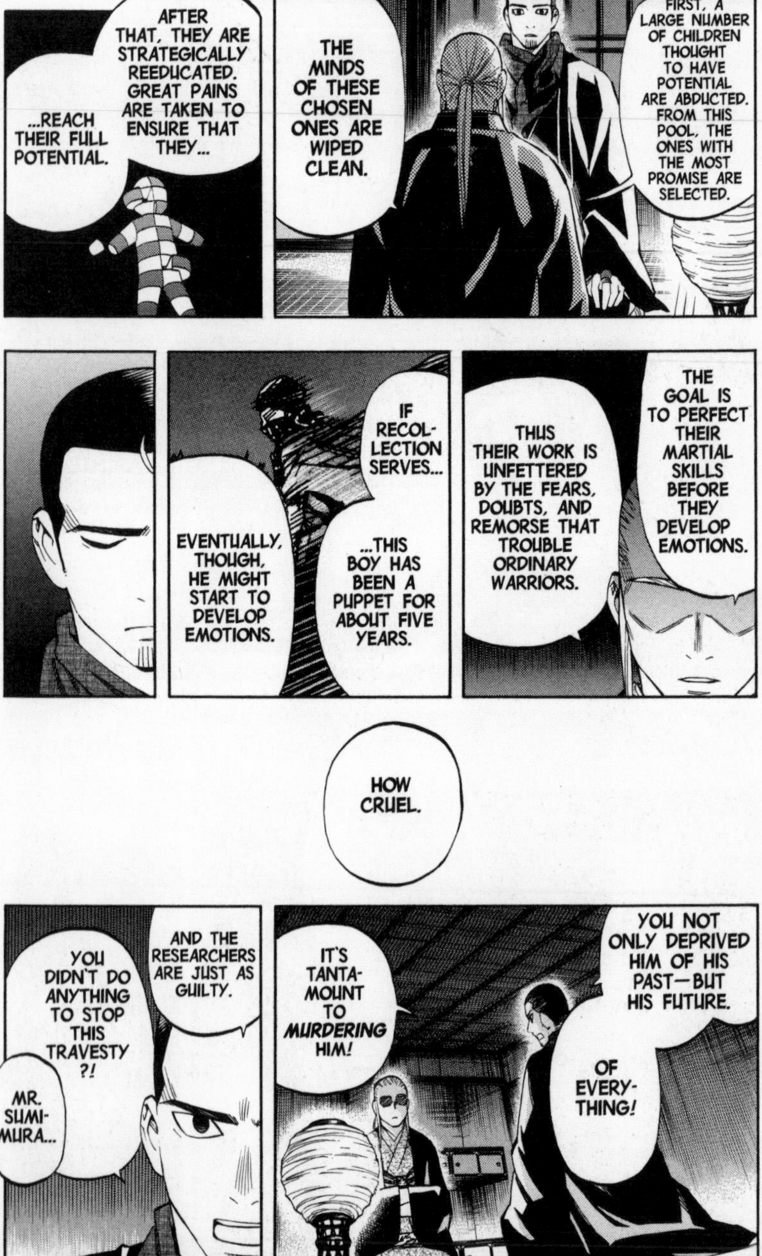
FIRST, A LARGE NUMBER OF CHILDREN THOUGHT TO HAVE POTENTIAL ARE ABDUCTED. FROM THIS POOL, THE ONES WITH THE MOST PROMISE ARE SELECTED.
THE MINDS OF THESE CHOSEN ONES ARE WIPED CLEAN.
AFTER THAT, THEY ARE STRATEGICALLY REEDUCATED. GREAT PAINS ARE TAKEN TO ENSURE THAT THEY...
...REACH THEIR FULL POTENTIAL.
THE GOAL IS TO PERFECT THEIR MARTIAL SKILLS BEFORE THEY DEVELOP EMOTIONS.
THUS THEIR WORK IS UNFETTERED BY THE FEARS, DOUBTS, AND REMORSE THAT TROUBLE ORDINARY WARRIORS.
IF RECOL-LECTION SERVES...
...THIS BOY HAS BEEN A PUPPET FOR ABOUT FIVE YEARS.
EVENTUALLY, THOUGH, HE MIGHT START TO DEVELOP EMOTIONS.
HOW CRUEL.
YOU NOT ONLY DEPRIVED HIM OF HIS PAST—BUT HIS FUTURE.
OF EVERY-THING!
IT'S TANTA-MOUNT TO *MURDERING* HIM!
AND THE RESEARCHERS ARE JUST AS GUILTY.
YOU DIDN'T DO ANYTHING TO STOP THIS TRAVESTY ?!
MR. SUMI-MURA...

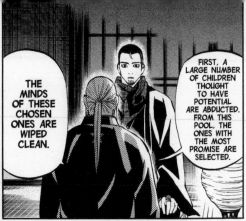

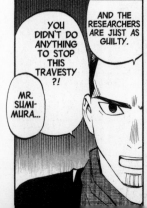

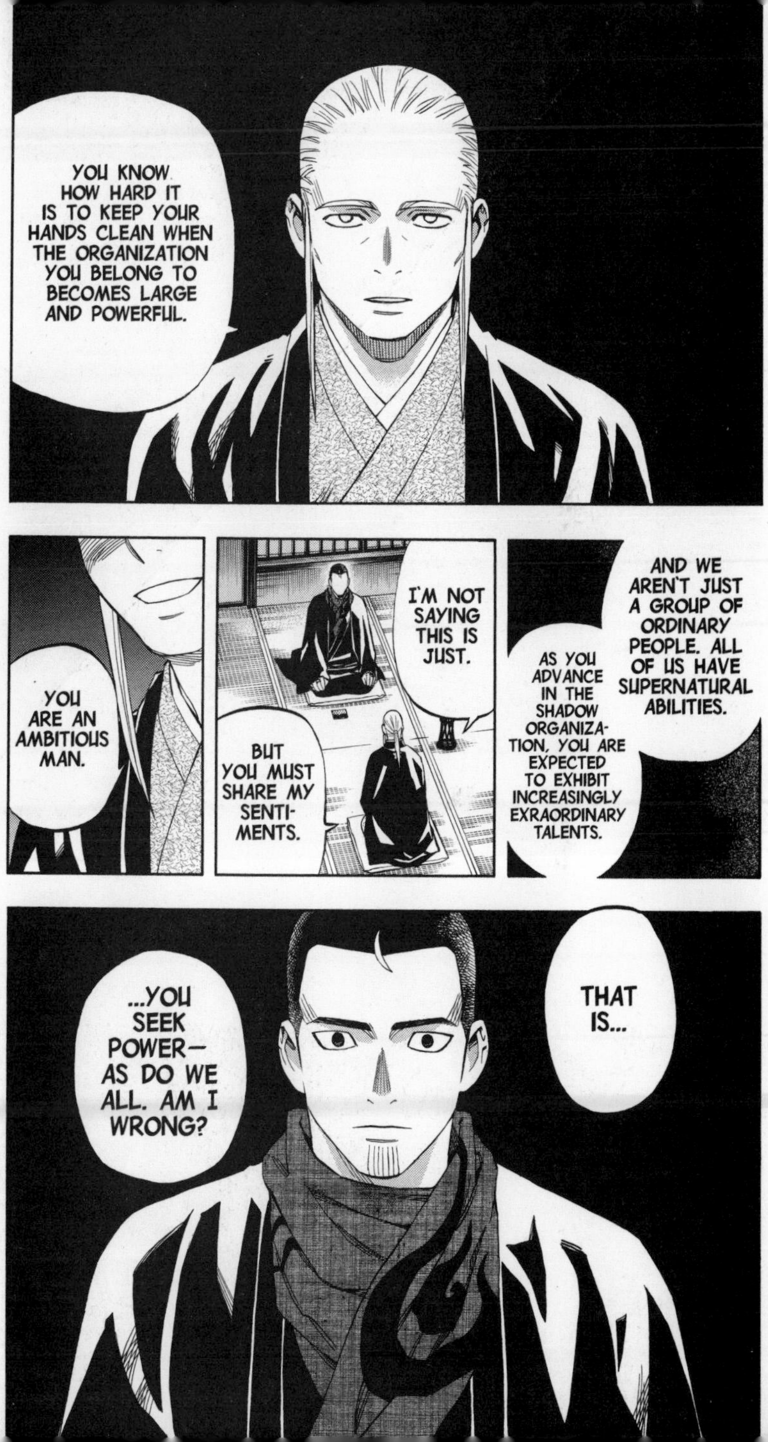
YOU KNOW HOW HARD IT IS TO KEEP YOUR HANDS CLEAN WHEN THE ORGANIZATION YOU BELONG TO BECOMES LARGE AND POWERFUL.
AND WE AREN'T JUST A GROUP OF ORDINARY PEOPLE. ALL OF US HAVE SUPERNATURAL ABILITIES.
AS YOU ADVANCE IN THE SHADOW ORGANIZA-TION, YOU ARE EXPECTED TO EXHIBIT INCREASINGLY EXRAORDINARY TALENTS.
I'M NOT SAYING THIS IS JUST.
BUT YOU MUST SHARE MY SENTI-MENTS.
YOU ARE AN AMBITIOUS MAN.
THAT IS...
...YOU SEEK POWER— AS DO WE ALL. AM I WRONG?

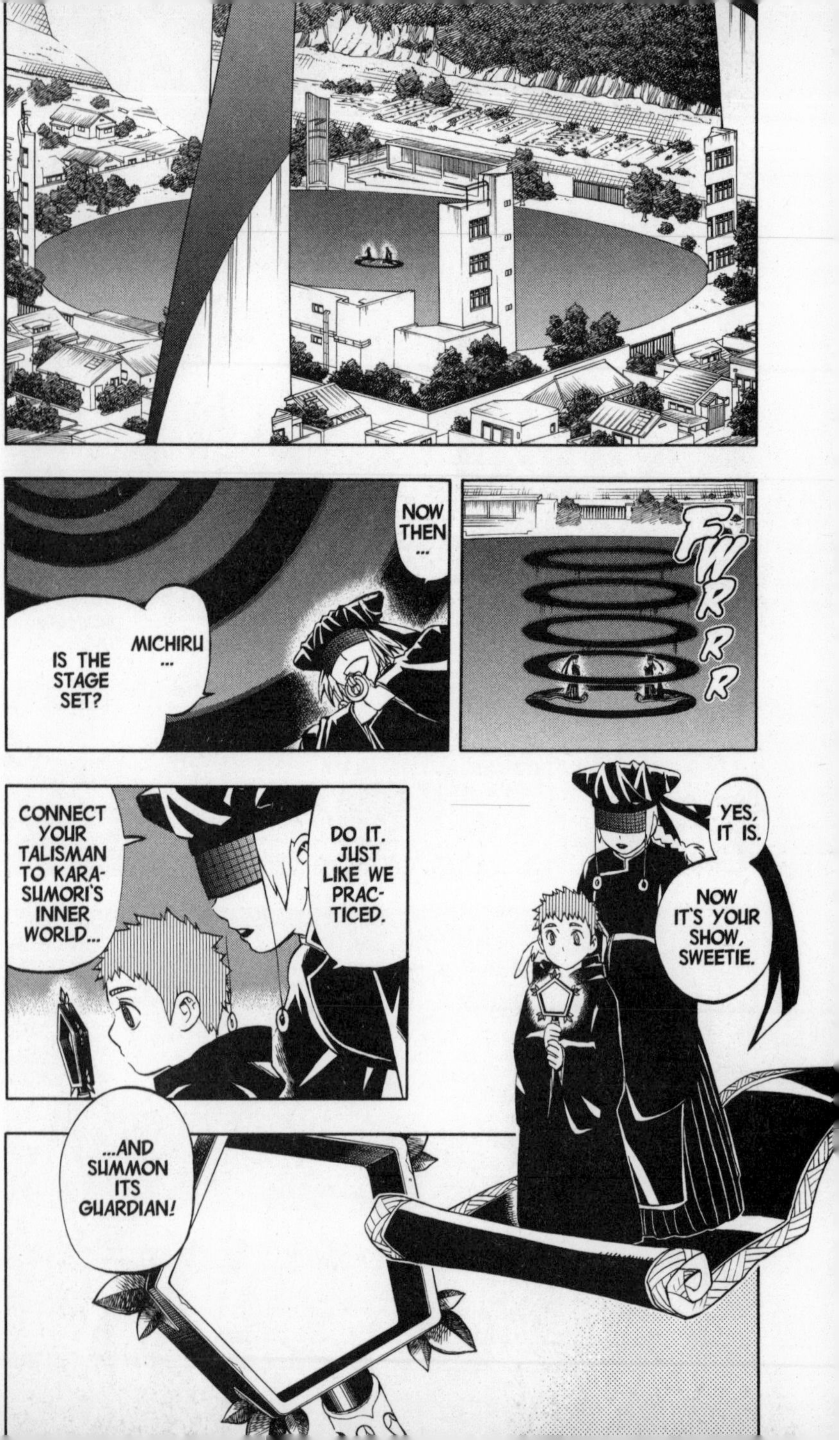
FWRRR
NOW THEN ...
MICHIRU ... IS THE STAGE SET?
YES, IT IS.
NOW IT'S YOUR SHOW, SWEETIE.
DO IT. JUST LIKE WE PRAC-TICED.
CONNECT YOUR TALISMAN TO KARA-SUMORI'S INNER WORLD...
...AND SUMMON ITS GUARDIAN!

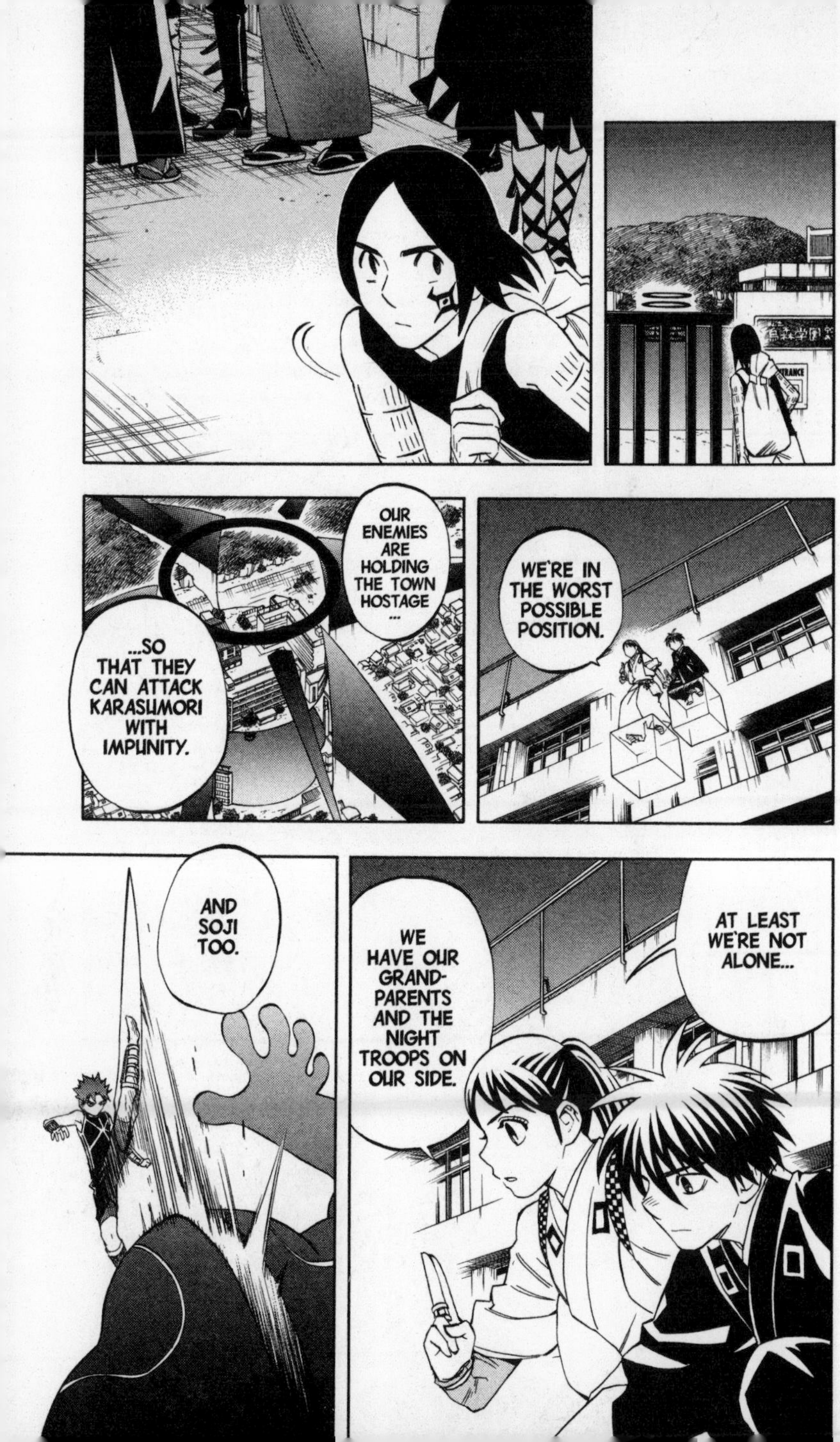
WE'RE IN THE WORST POSSIBLE POSITION.
OUR ENEMIES ARE HOLDING THE TOWN HOSTAGE...
...SO THAT THEY CAN ATTACK KARASUMORI WITH IMPUNITY.
AT LEAST WE'RE NOT ALONE...
WE HAVE OUR GRAND-PARENTS AND THE NIGHT TROOPS ON OUR SIDE.
AND SOJI TOO.

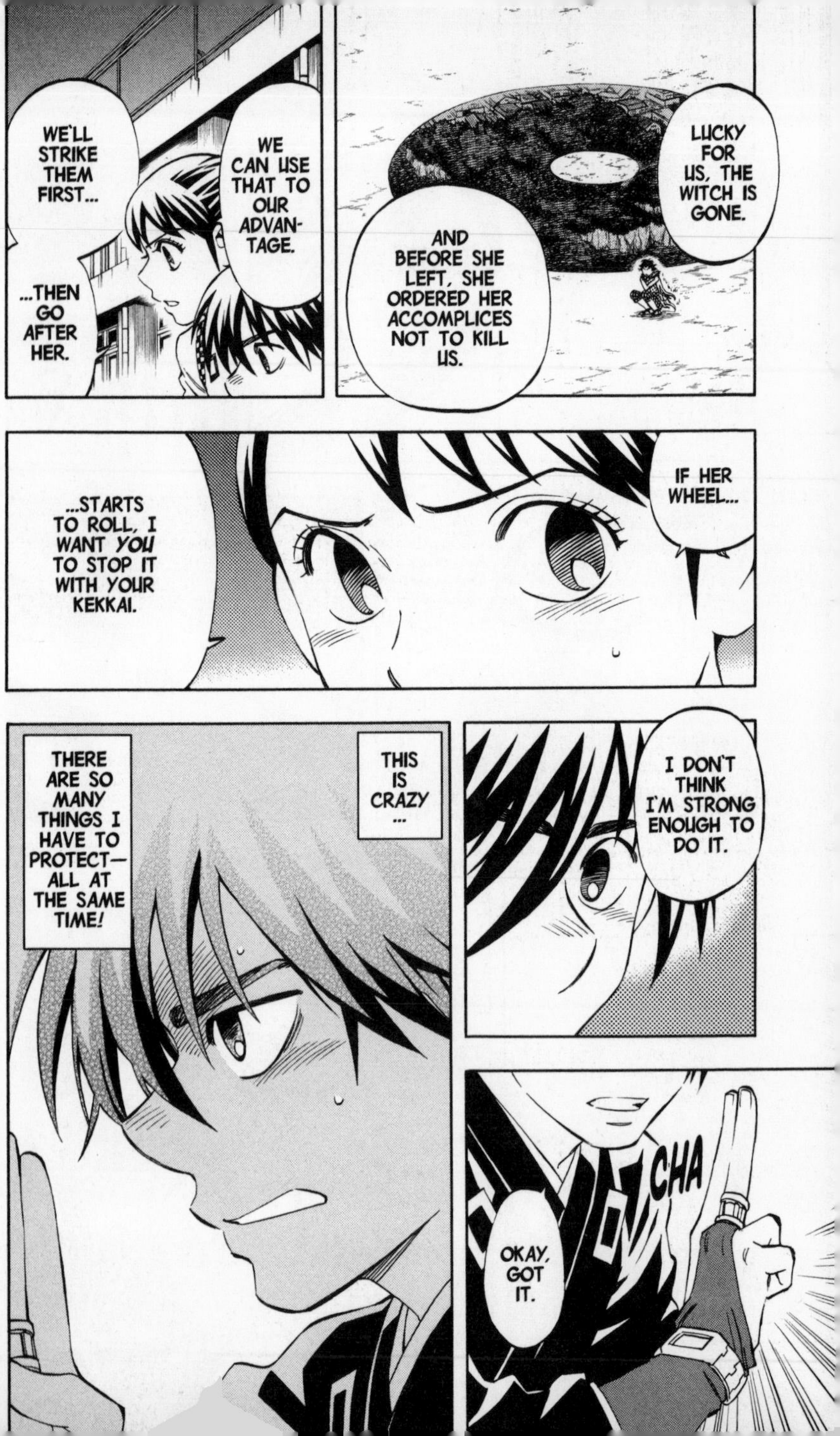
LUCKY FOR US, THE WITCH IS GONE.
AND BEFORE SHE LEFT, SHE ORDERED HER ACCOMPLICES NOT TO KILL US.
WE CAN USE THAT TO OUR ADVANTAGE.
WE'LL STRIKE THEM FIRST...
...THEN GO AFTER HER.
IF HER WHEEL...
...STARTS TO ROLL, I WANT *YOU* TO STOP IT WITH YOUR KEKKAI.
I DON'T THINK I'M STRONG ENOUGH TO DO IT.
CHA
OKAY, GOT IT.
THIS IS CRAZY...
THERE ARE SO *MANY* THINGS I HAVE TO PROTECT—ALL AT THE SAME TIME!

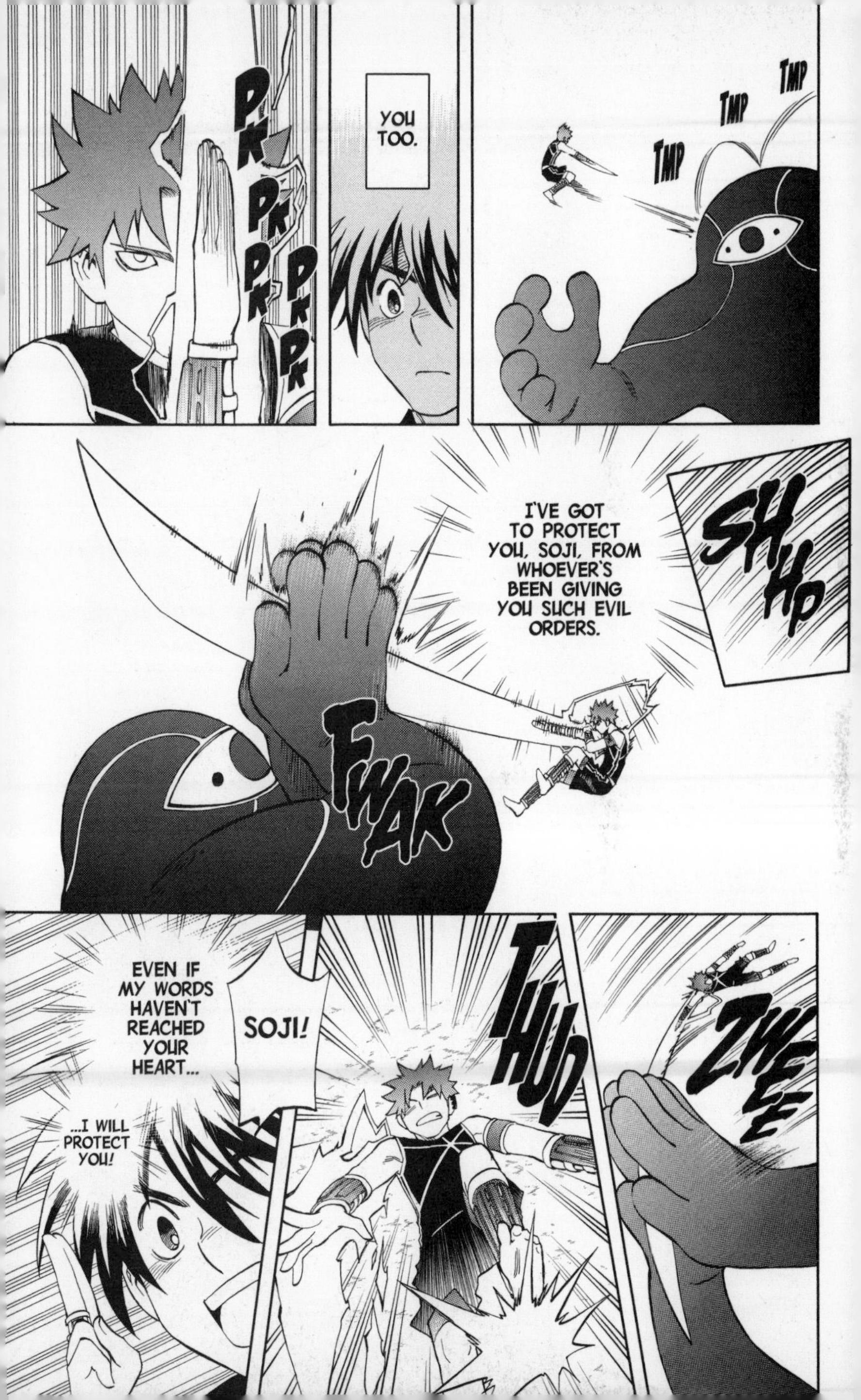
TMP
TMP
TMP
YOU TOO.
PK PK PK PK PK PK
SHHP
I'VE GOT TO PROTECT YOU, SOJI, FROM WHOEVER'S BEEN GIVING YOU SUCH EVIL ORDERS.
FWAK
ZWEE
THUD
SOJI!
EVEN IF MY WORDS HAVEN'T REACHED YOUR HEART...
...I WILL PROTECT YOU!

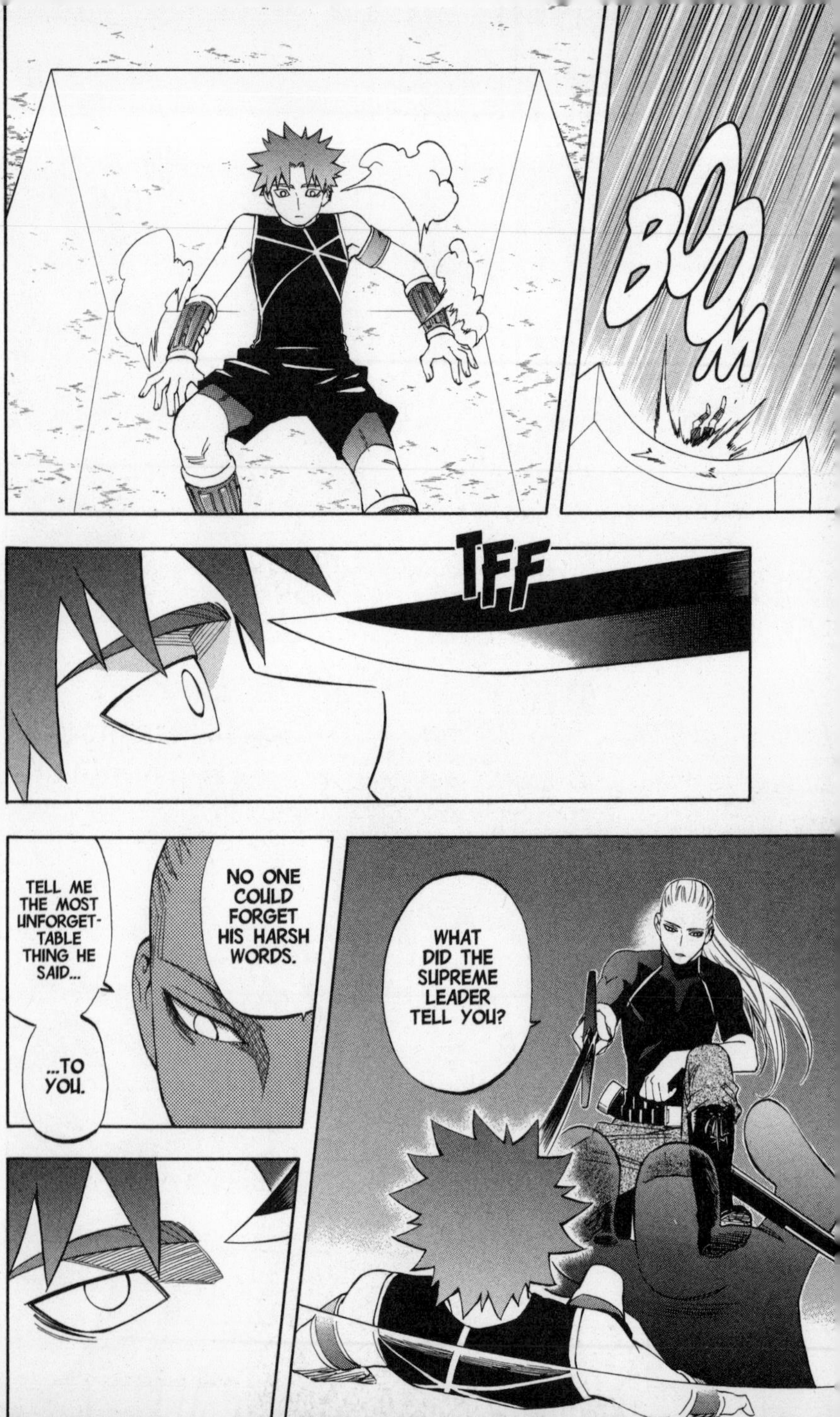
BOOM
TFF
WHAT DID THE SUPREME LEADER TELL YOU?
NO ONE COULD FORGET HIS HARSH WORDS.
TELL ME THE MOST UNFORGET-TABLE THING HE SAID...
...TO YOU.

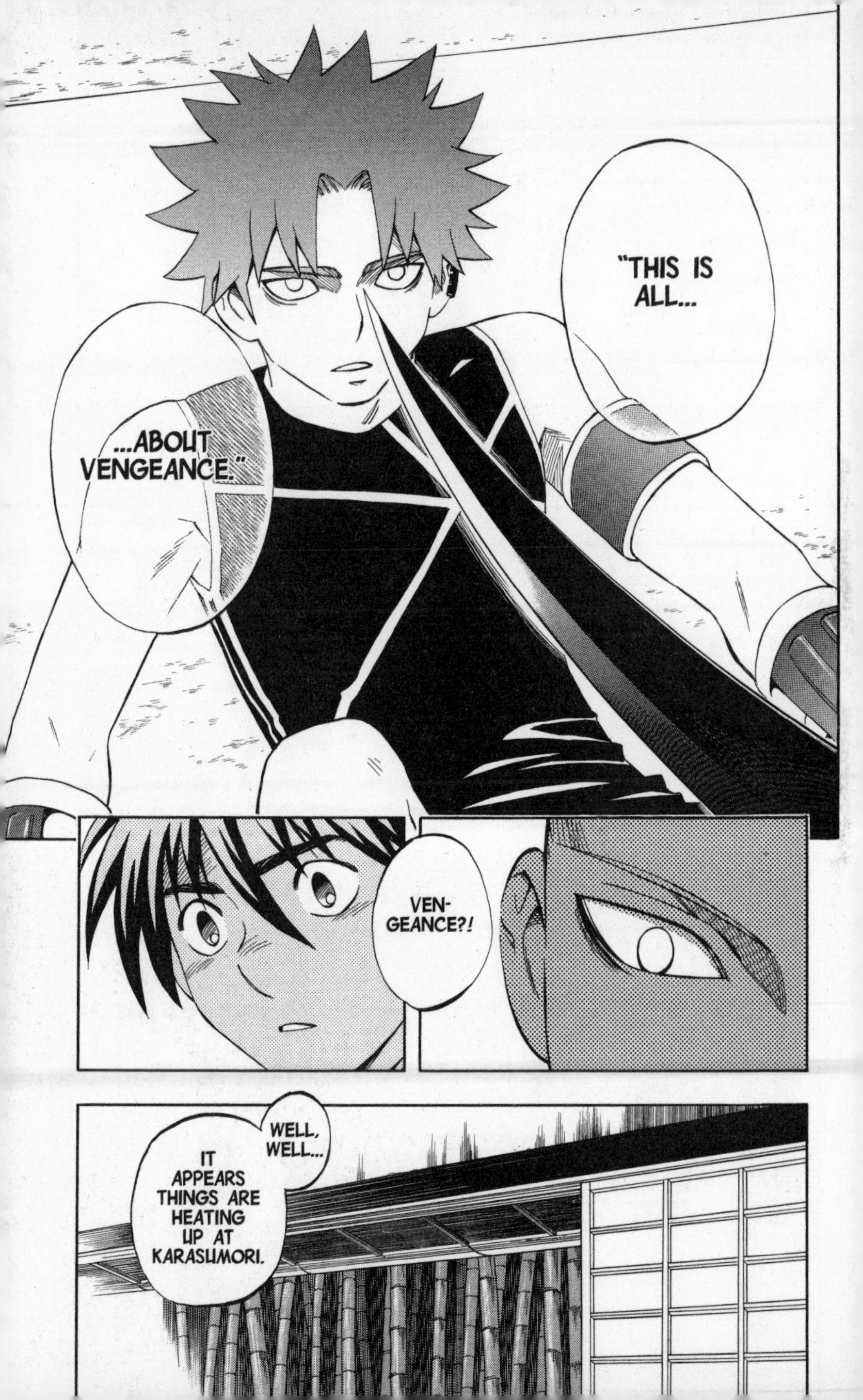
"THIS IS ALL...
...ABOUT VENGEANCE."
VEN-GEANCE?!
WELL, WELL...
IT APPEARS THINGS ARE HEATING UP AT KARASUMORI.

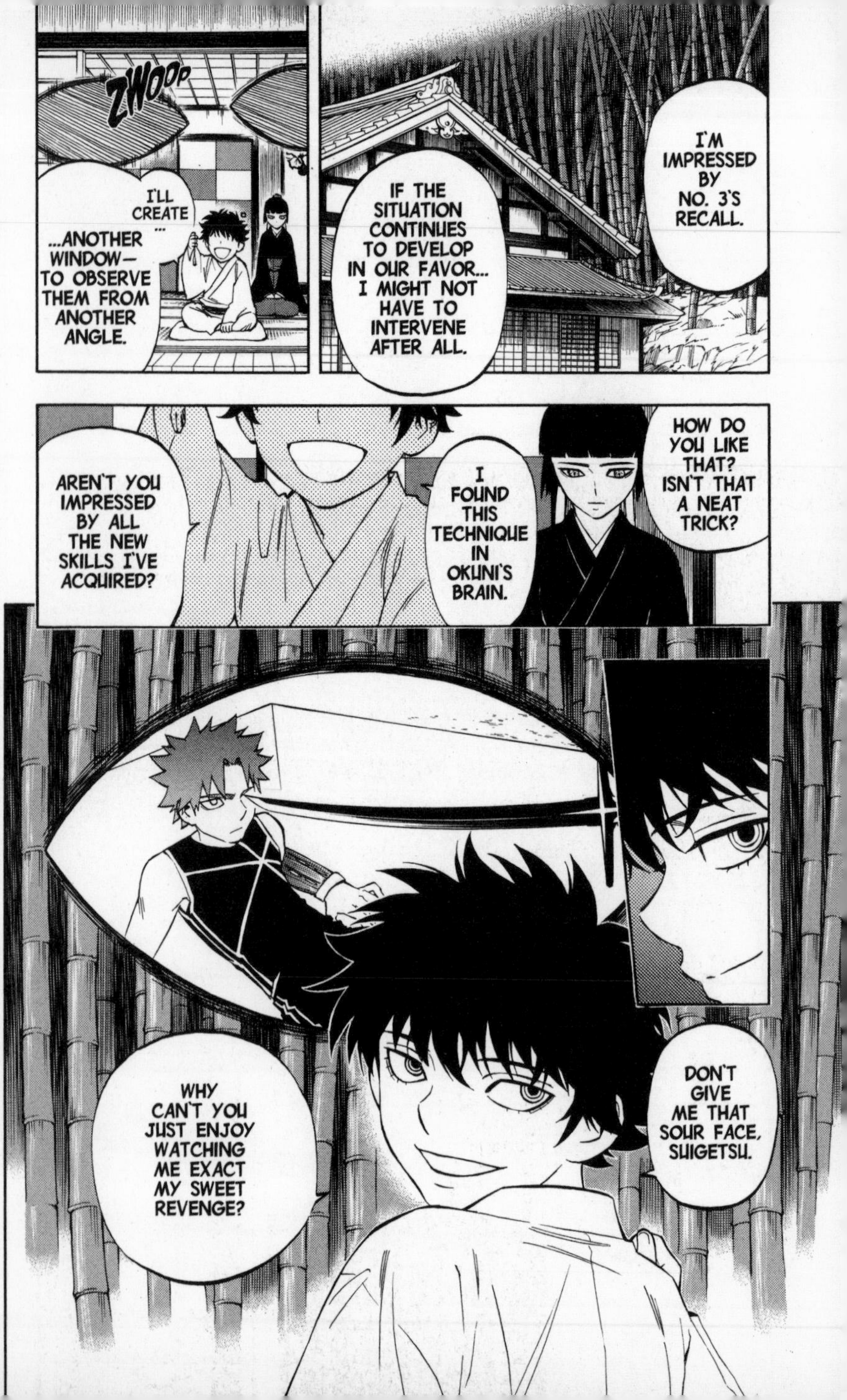
I'M IMPRESSED BY NO. 3'S RECALL.
IF THE SITUATION CONTINUES TO DEVELOP IN OUR FAVOR... I MIGHT NOT HAVE TO INTERVENE AFTER ALL.
ZWOOP
I'LL CREATE ...
...ANOTHER WINDOW— TO OBSERVE THEM FROM ANOTHER ANGLE.
HOW DO YOU LIKE THAT? ISN'T THAT A NEAT TRICK?
I FOUND THIS TECHNIQUE IN OKUNI'S BRAIN.
AREN'T YOU IMPRESSED BY ALL THE NEW SKILLS I'VE ACQUIRED?
DON'T GIVE ME THAT SOUR FACE, SUIGETSU.
WHY CAN'T YOU JUST ENJOY WATCHING ME EXACT MY SWEET REVENGE?

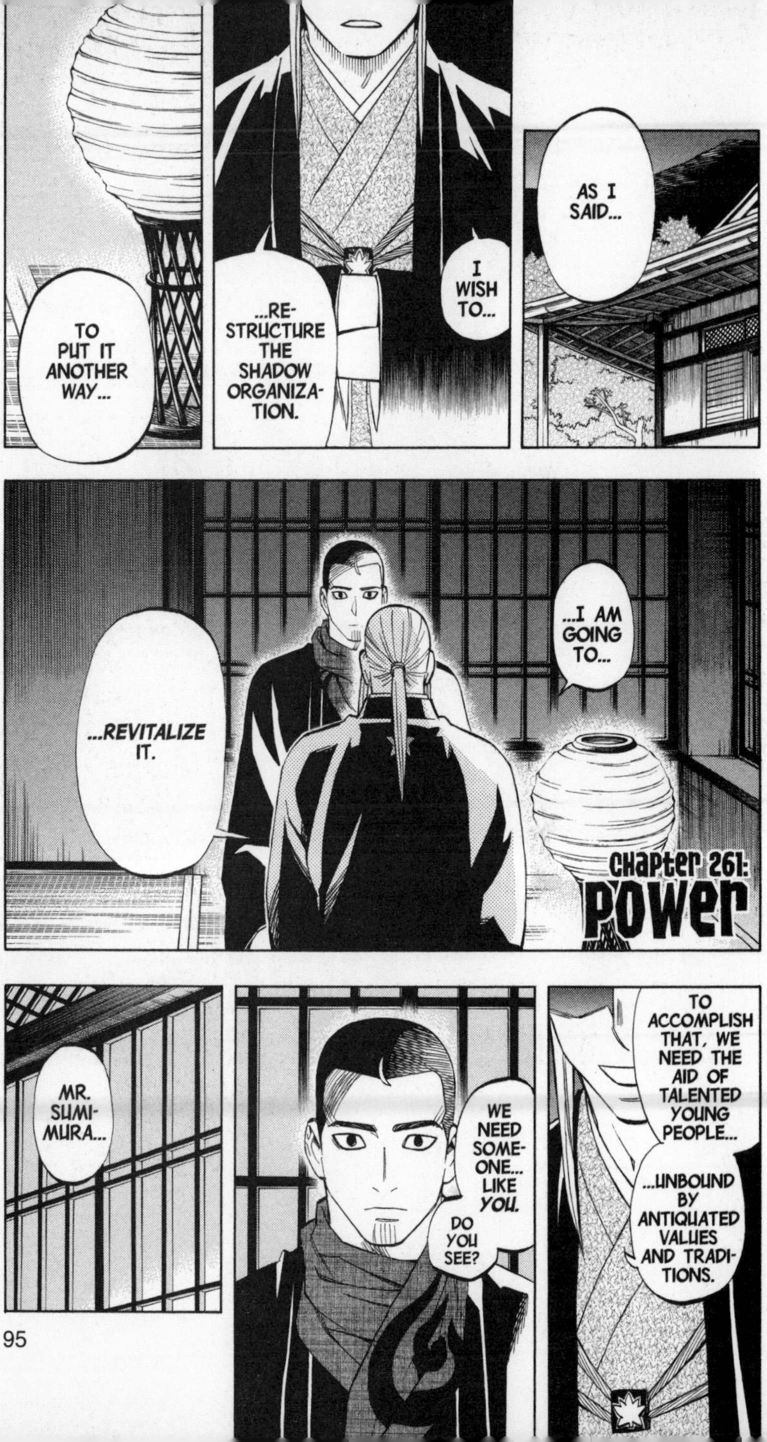
AS I SAID...
I WISH TO...
...RE-STRUCTURE THE SHADOW ORGANIZATION.
TO PUT IT ANOTHER WAY...
...I AM GOING TO...
...REVITALIZE IT.
Chapter 261:
Power
TO ACCOMPLISH THAT, WE NEED THE AID OF TALENTED YOUNG PEOPLE...
...UNBOUND BY ANTIQUATED VALUES AND TRADITIONS.
WE NEED SOMEONE... LIKE *YOU.*
DO YOU SEE?
MR. SUMIMURA...

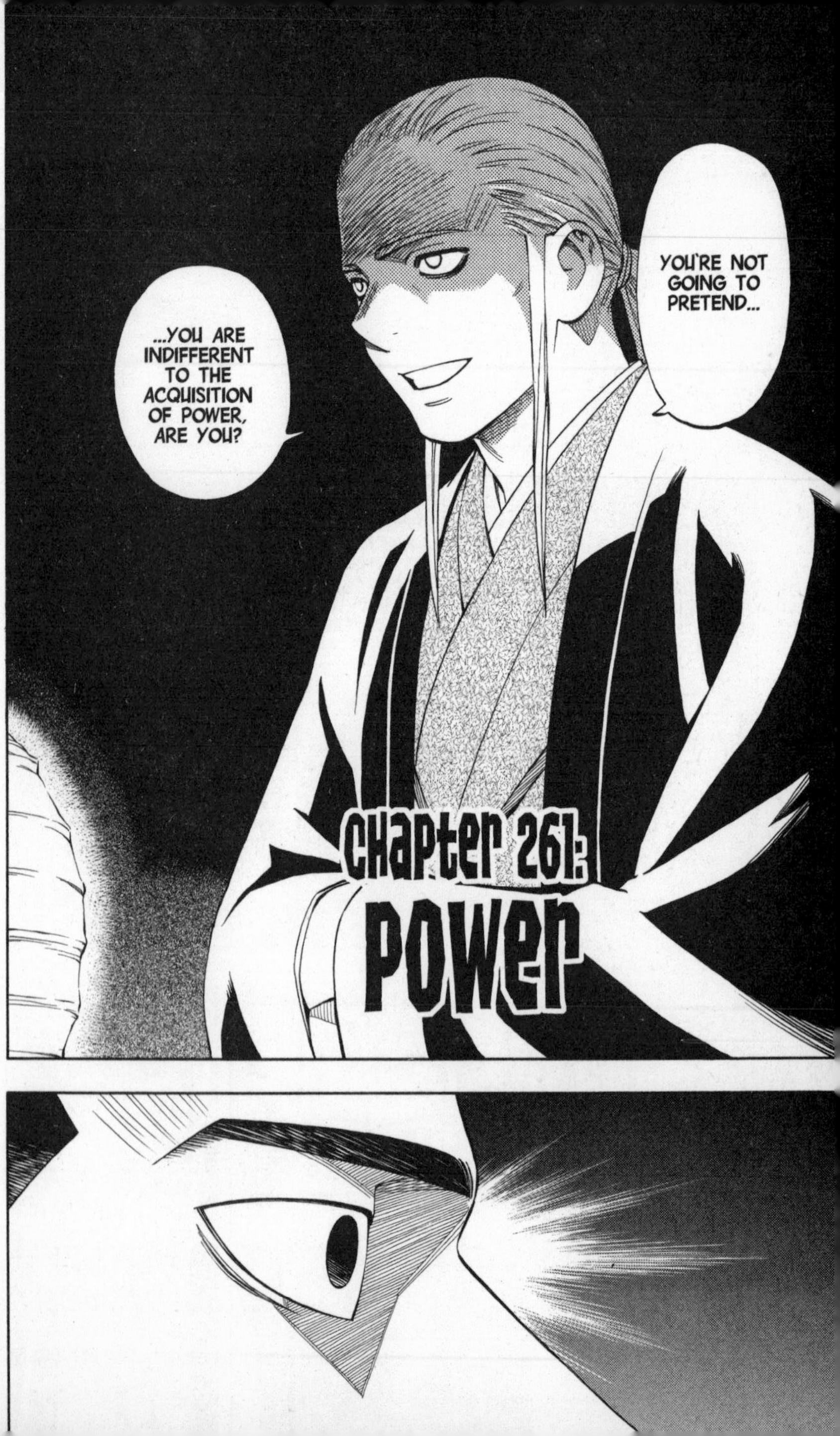
YOU'RE NOT GOING TO PRETEND...
...YOU ARE INDIFFERENT TO THE ACQUISITION OF POWER, ARE YOU?
CHAPTER 261: POWER

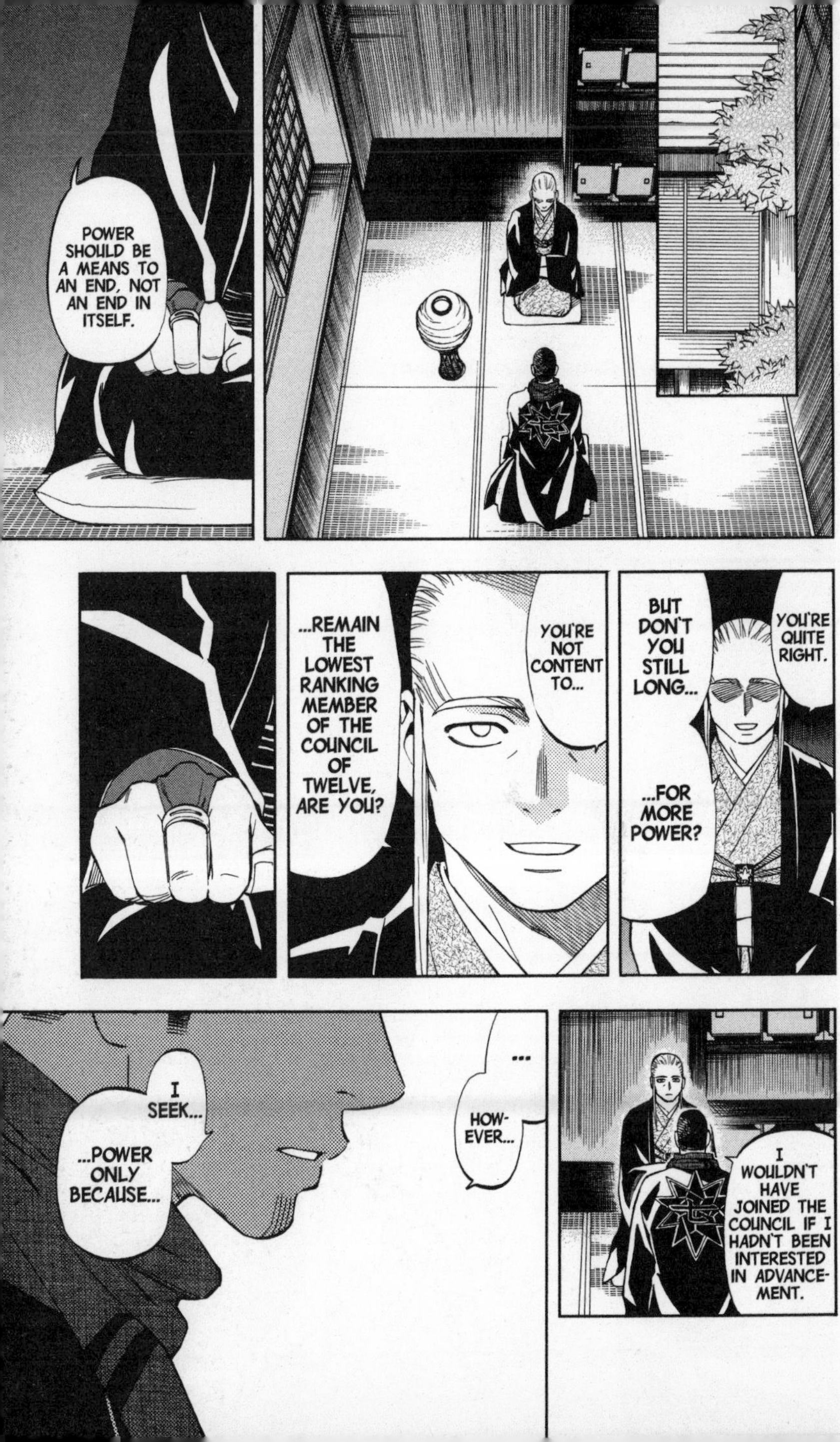
POWER SHOULD BE A MEANS TO AN END, NOT AN END IN ITSELF.
YOU'RE QUITE RIGHT.
BUT DON'T YOU STILL LONG...
...FOR MORE POWER?
YOU'RE NOT CONTENT TO...
...REMAIN THE LOWEST RANKING MEMBER OF THE COUNCIL OF TWELVE, ARE YOU?
I WOULDN'T HAVE JOINED THE COUNCIL IF I HADN'T BEEN INTERESTED IN ADVANCEMENT.
...
HOW-EVER...
I SEEK...
...POWER ONLY BECAUSE...

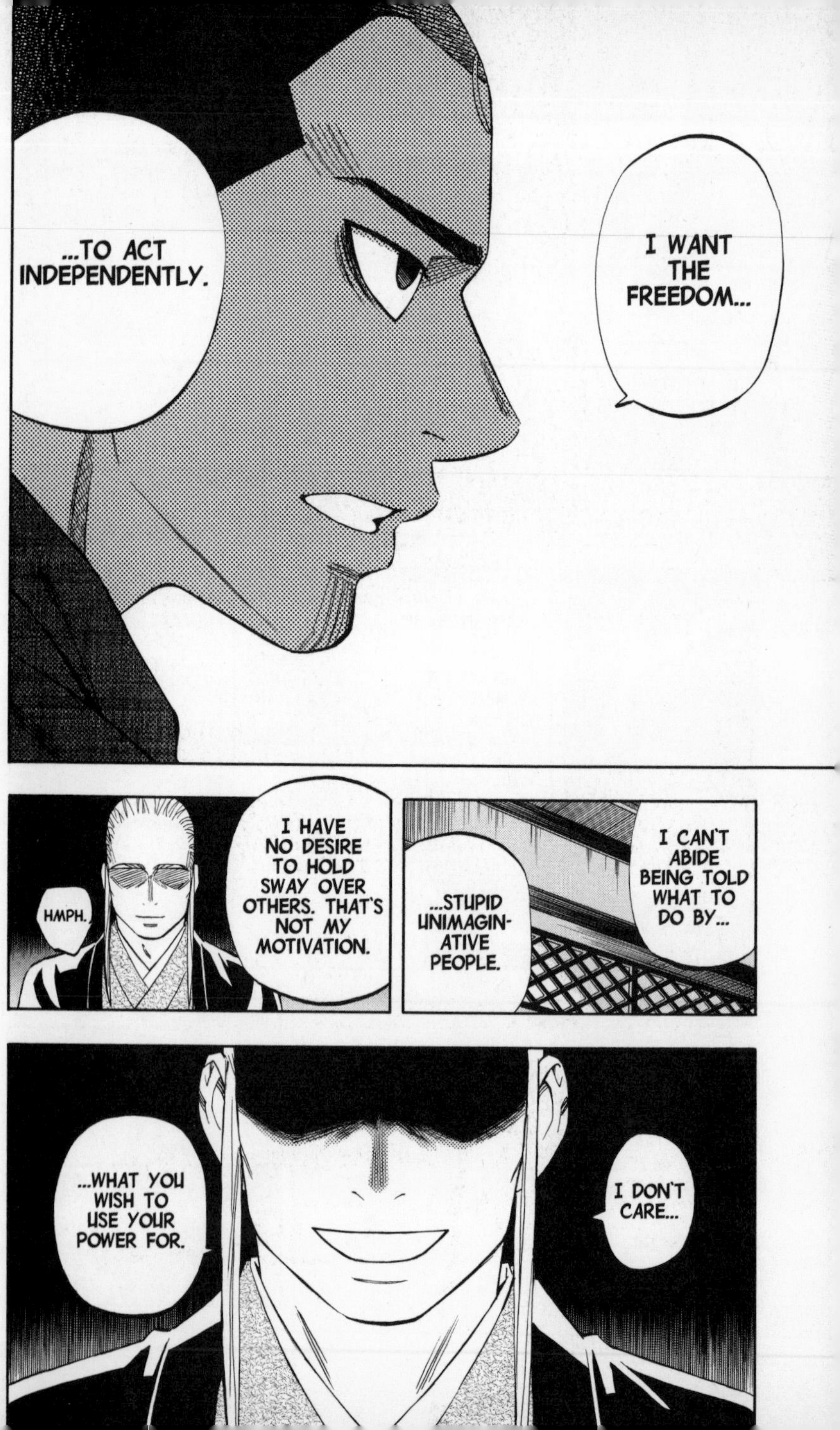
I WANT THE FREEDOM...
...TO ACT INDEPENDENTLY.
I CAN'T ABIDE BEING TOLD WHAT TO DO BY...
...STUPID UNIMAGINATIVE PEOPLE.
I HAVE NO DESIRE TO HOLD SWAY OVER OTHERS. THAT'S NOT MY MOTIVATION.
HMPH.
I DON'T CARE...
...WHAT YOU WISH TO USE YOUR POWER FOR.

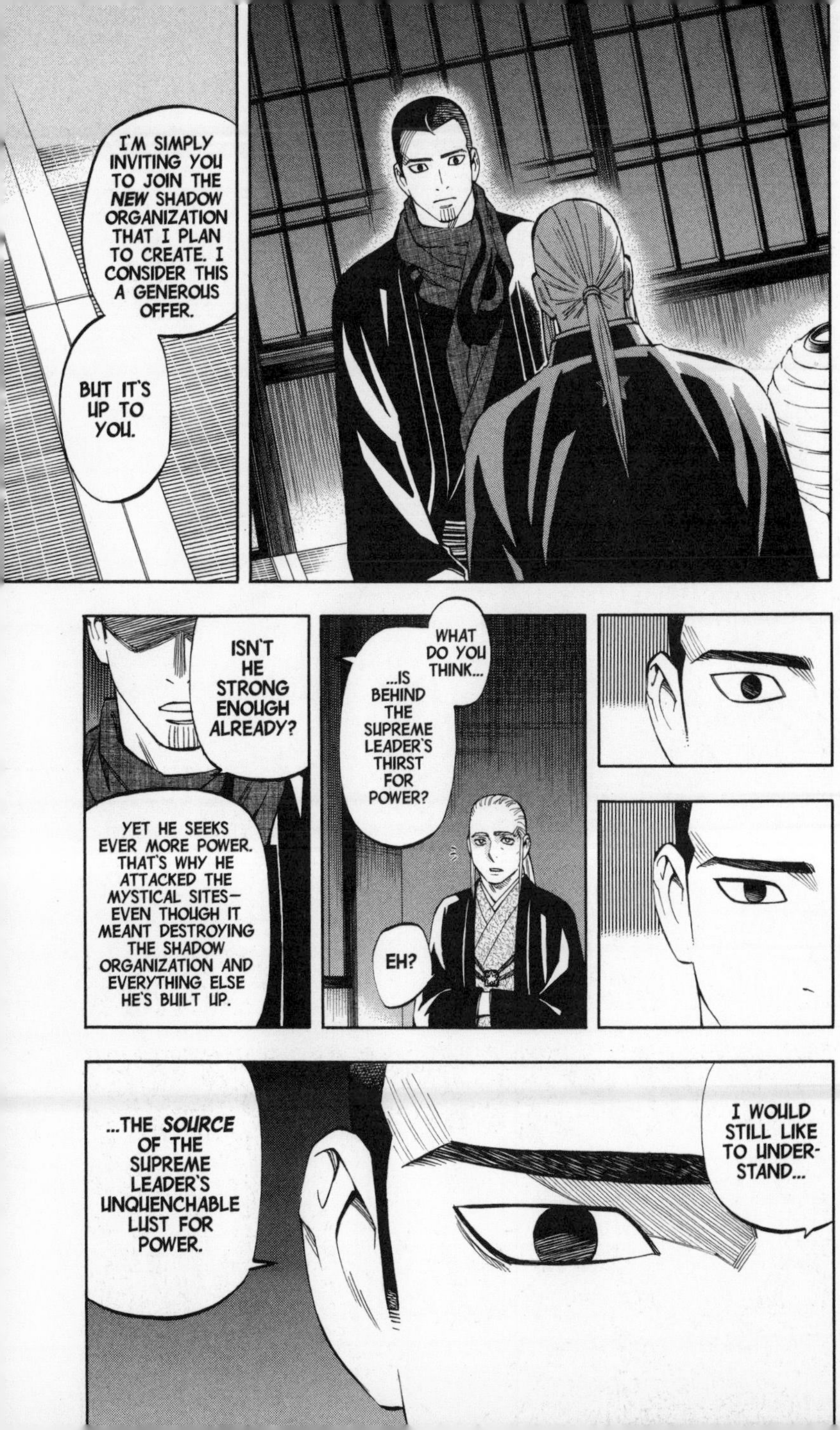
I'M SIMPLY INVITING YOU TO JOIN THE *NEW* SHADOW ORGANIZATION THAT I PLAN TO CREATE. I CONSIDER THIS A GENEROUS OFFER.
BUT IT'S UP TO YOU.
WHAT DO YOU THINK...
...IS BEHIND THE SUPREME LEADER'S THIRST FOR POWER?
EH?
ISN'T HE STRONG ENOUGH ALREADY?
YET HE SEEKS EVER MORE POWER. THAT'S WHY HE ATTACKED THE MYSTICAL SITES—EVEN THOUGH IT MEANT DESTROYING THE SHADOW ORGANIZATION AND EVERYTHING ELSE HE'S BUILT UP.
I WOULD STILL LIKE TO UNDER-STAND...
...THE *SOURCE* OF THE SUPREME LEADER'S UNQUENCHABLE LUST FOR POWER.

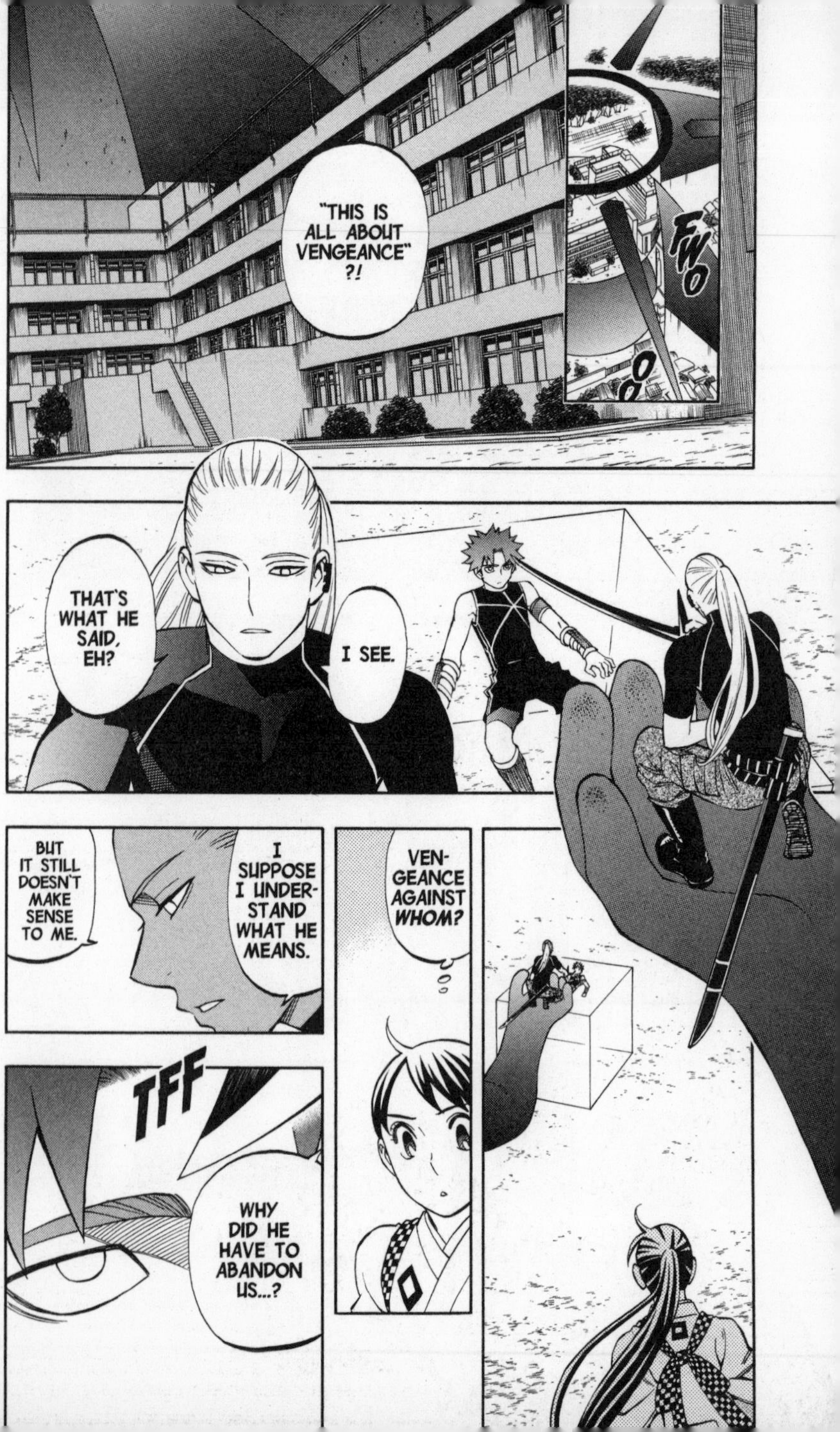
FWOOO
"THIS IS ALL ABOUT VENGEANCE"?!
THAT'S WHAT HE SAID, EH?
I SEE.
VEN-GEANCE AGAINST WHOM?
I SUPPOSE I UNDER-STAND WHAT HE MEANS.
BUT IT STILL DOESN'T MAKE SENSE TO ME.
TFF
WHY DID HE HAVE TO ABANDON US...?

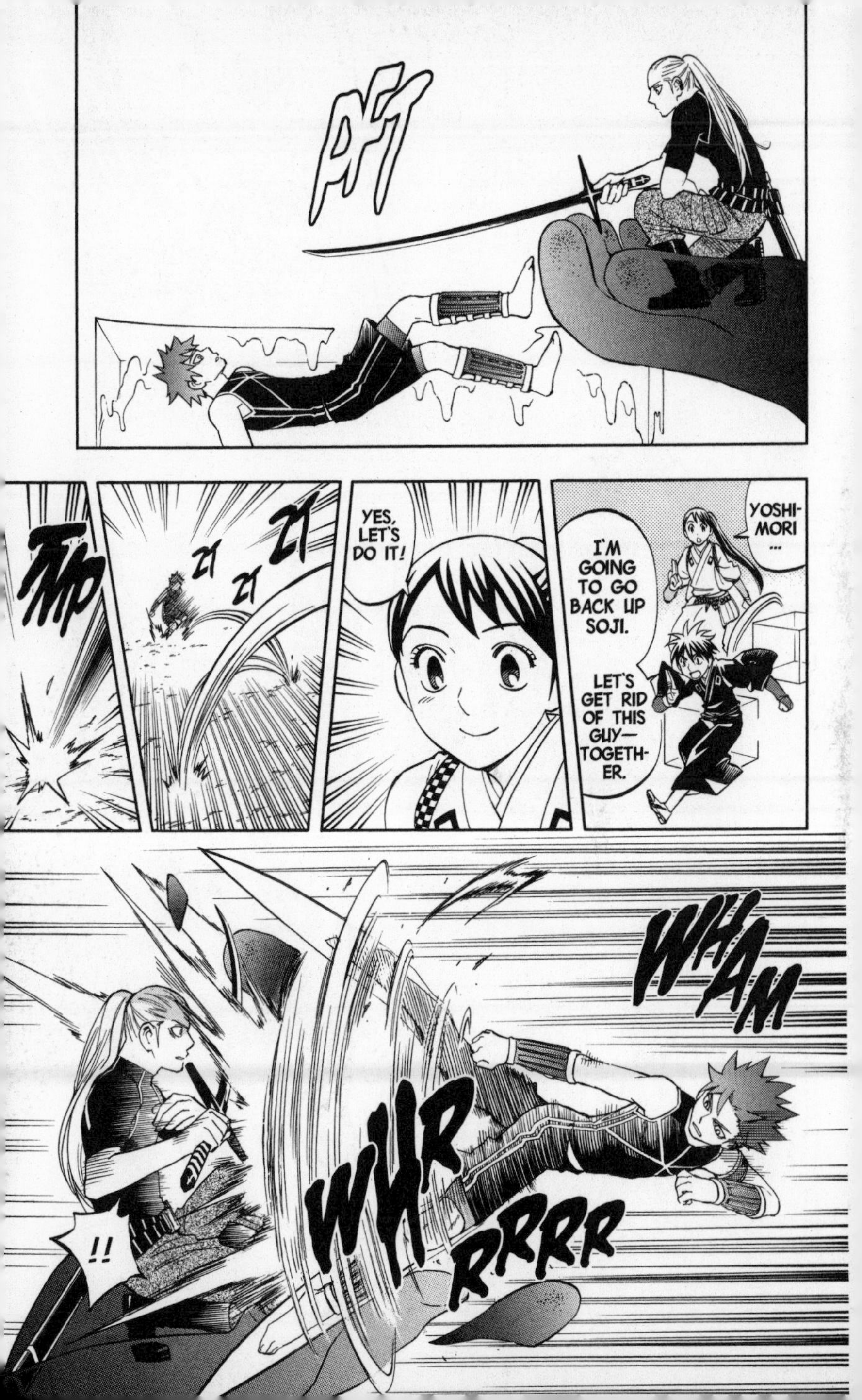
PFT
YOSHI-MORI...
I'M GOING TO GO BACK UP SOJI.
LET'S GET RID OF THIS GUY—TOGETH-ER.
YES, LET'S DO IT!
ZT
ZT
ZT
TMP
WHAM
!!
WHR RRRR

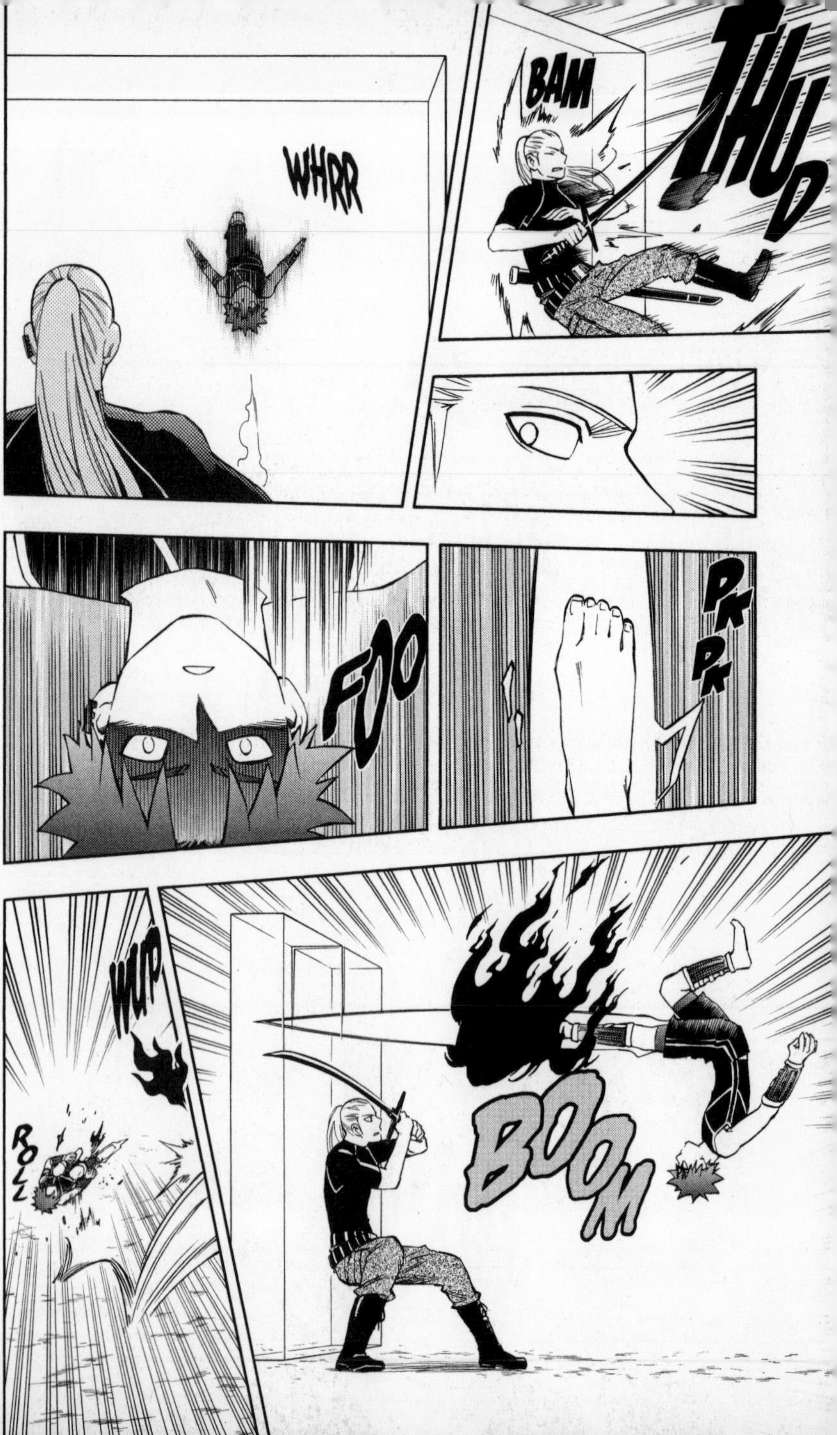
THUD
BAM
WHRR
PK PK PK
FOO
BOOM
WUP
ROLL

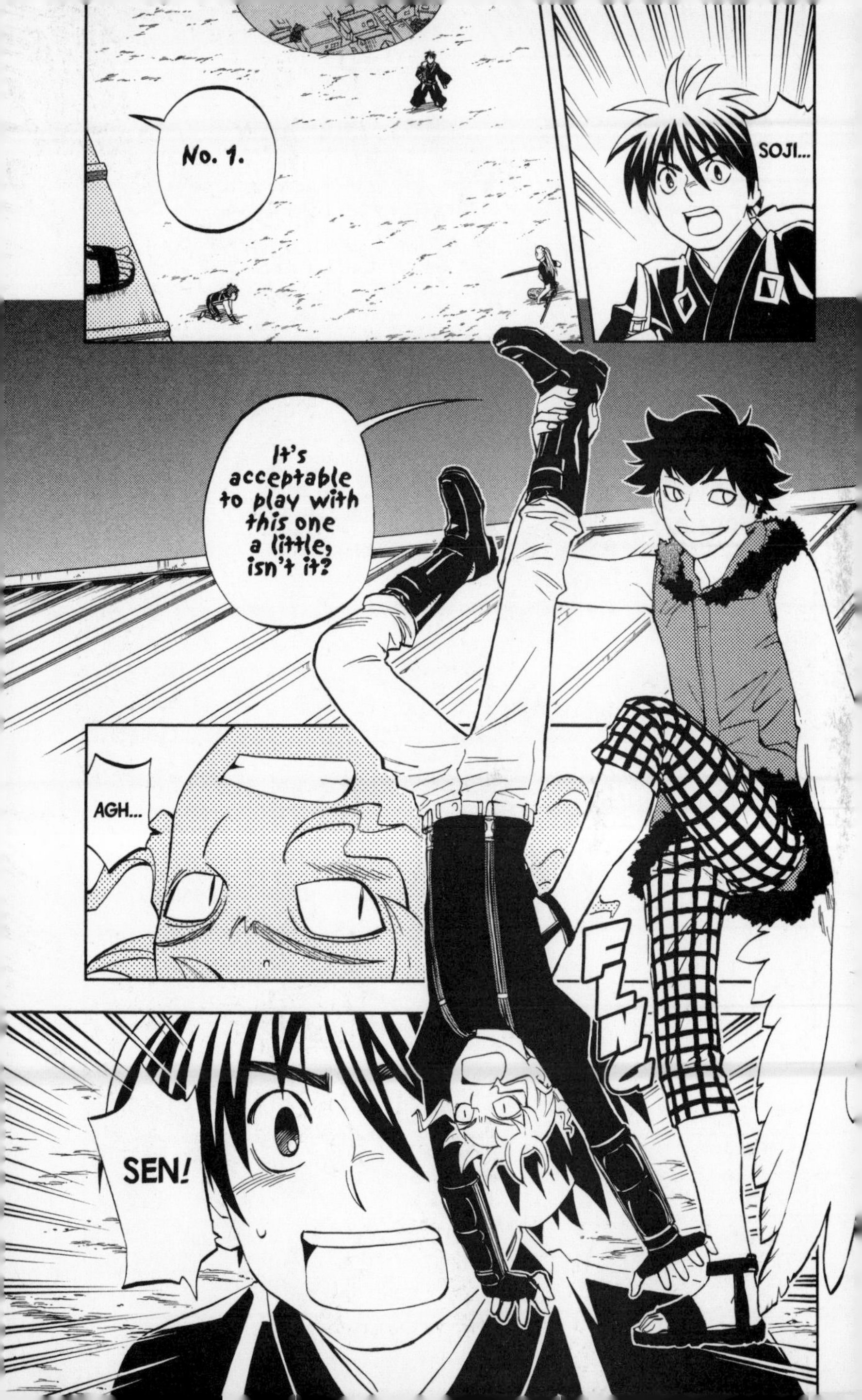
SOJI...
No. 1.
It's acceptable to play with this one a little, isn't it?
FLNG
AGH...
SEN!

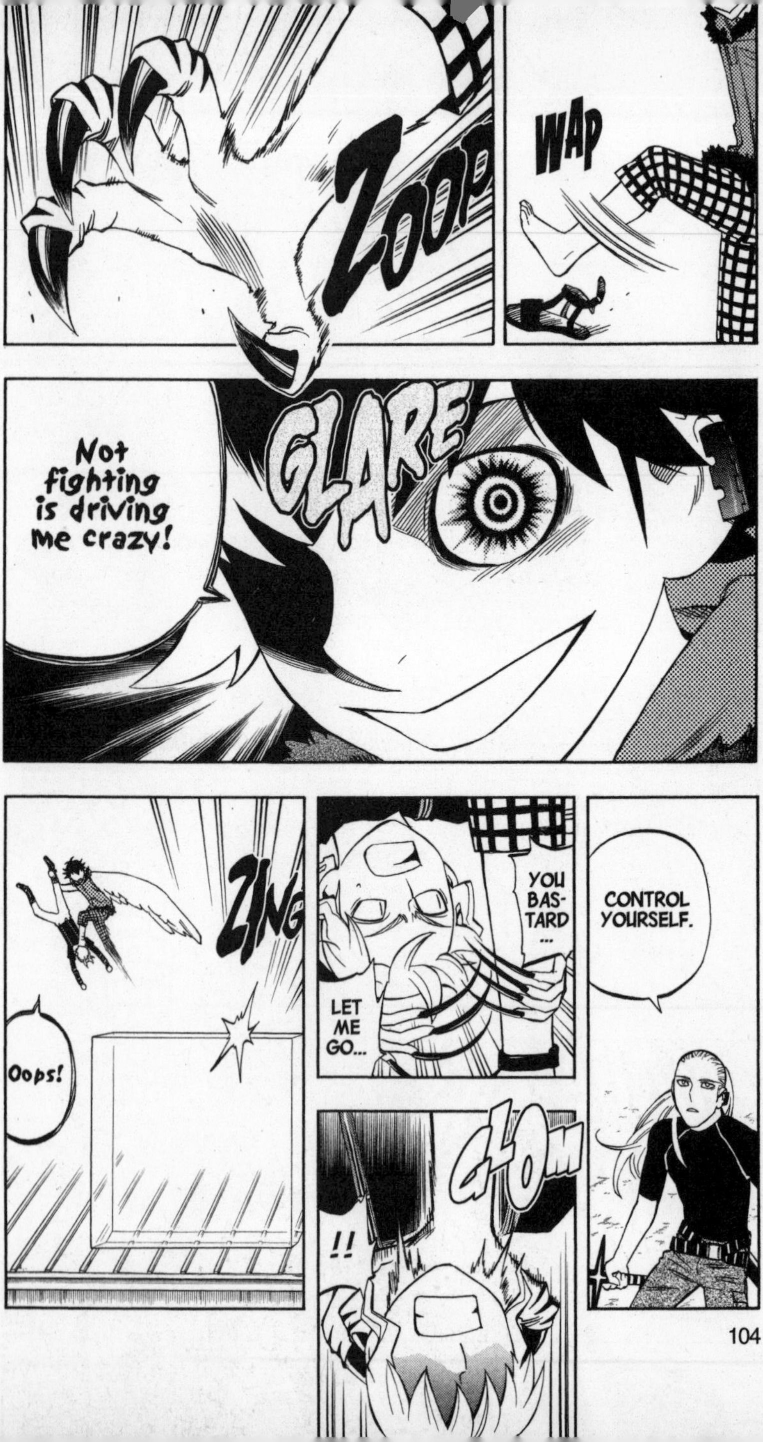

WAP
ZOOP
GLARE
Not fighting is driving me crazy!
CONTROL YOURSELF.
YOU BASTARD...
LET ME GO...
GLOM
!!
ZING
Oops!

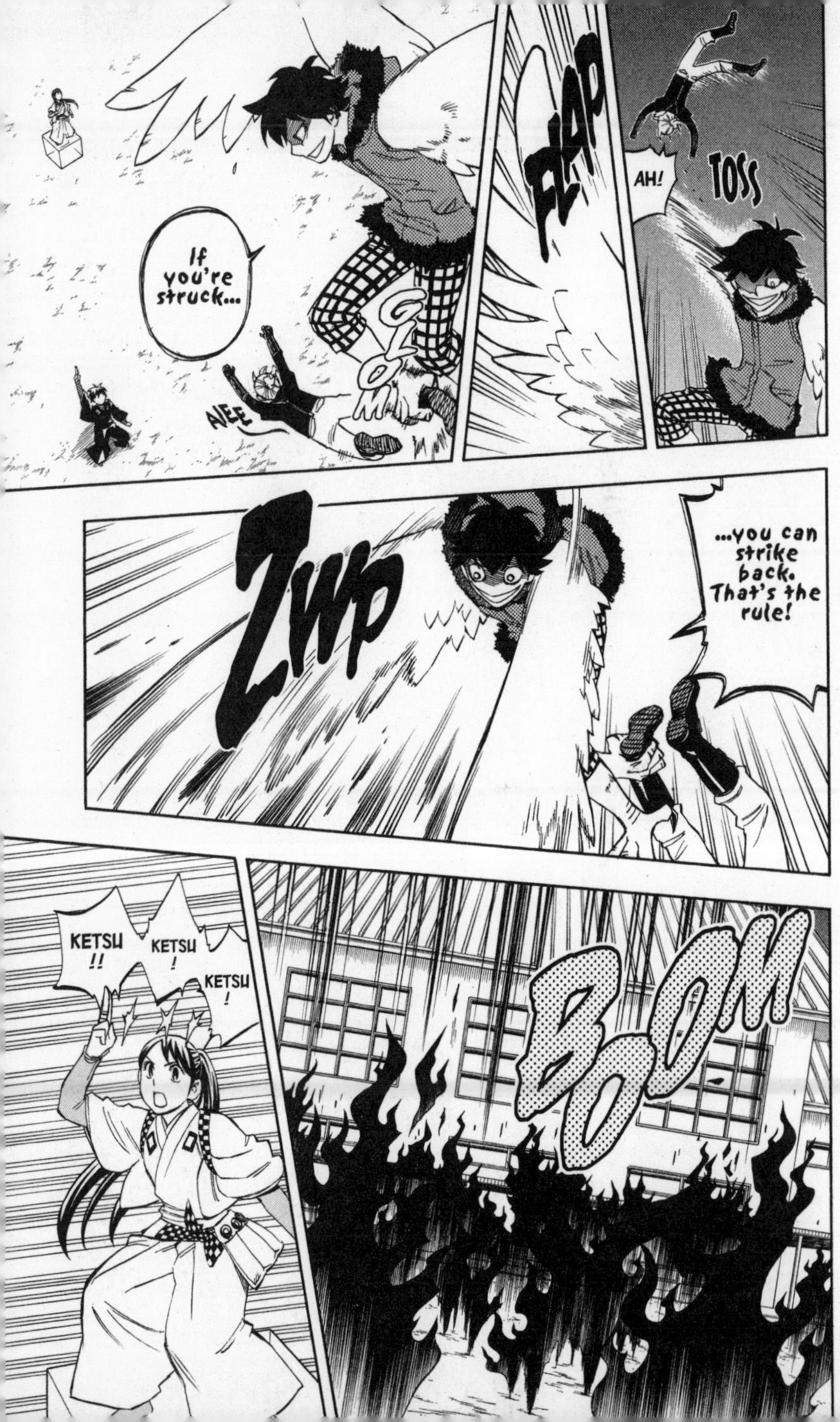
TOSS
AH!
FLAP
If you're struck...
GLOM
AIEE
...you can strike back. That's the rule!
ZWP
BOOM
KETSU!!
KETSU!
KETSU!

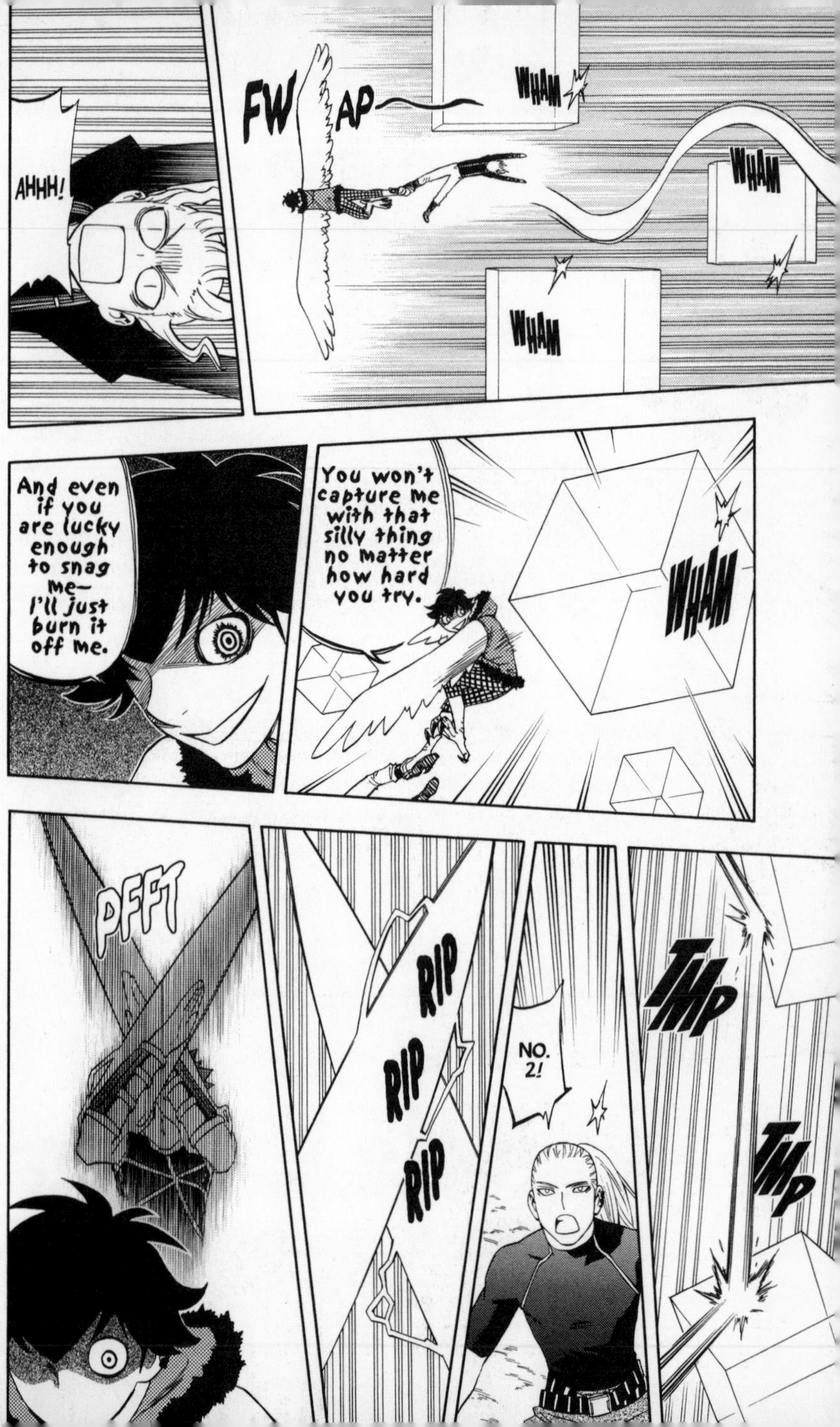
WHAM
WHAM
FW AP
WHAM
AHHH!
WHAM
You won't capture me with that silly thing no matter how hard you try.
And even if you are lucky enough to snag me— I'll just burn it off me.
TMP
TMP
NO. 2!
RIP
RIP
RIP
PFFT

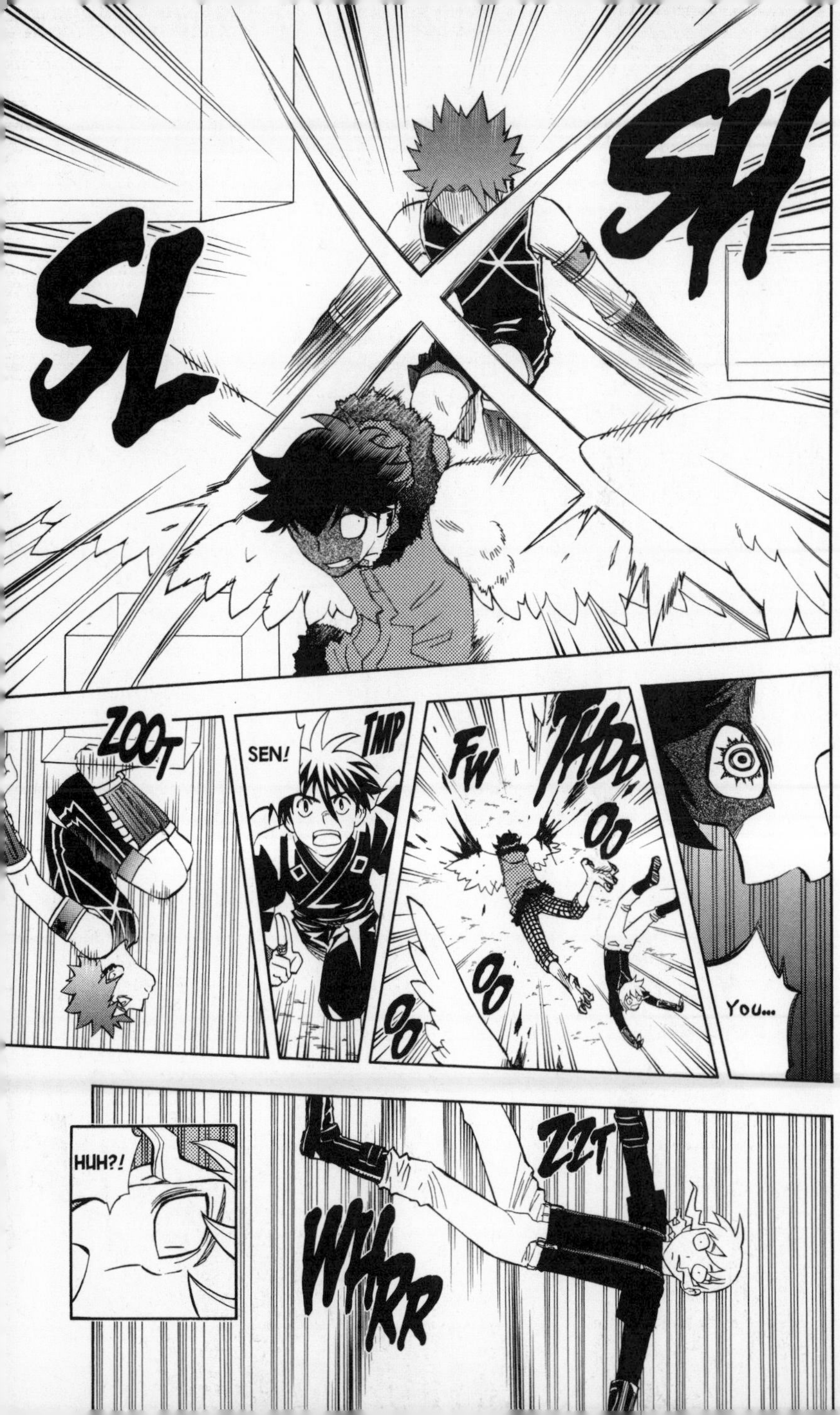
SL
SH
YOU...
FW
THOOOOOO
TMP
SEN!
ZOOT
ZZT
WHRR
HUH?!

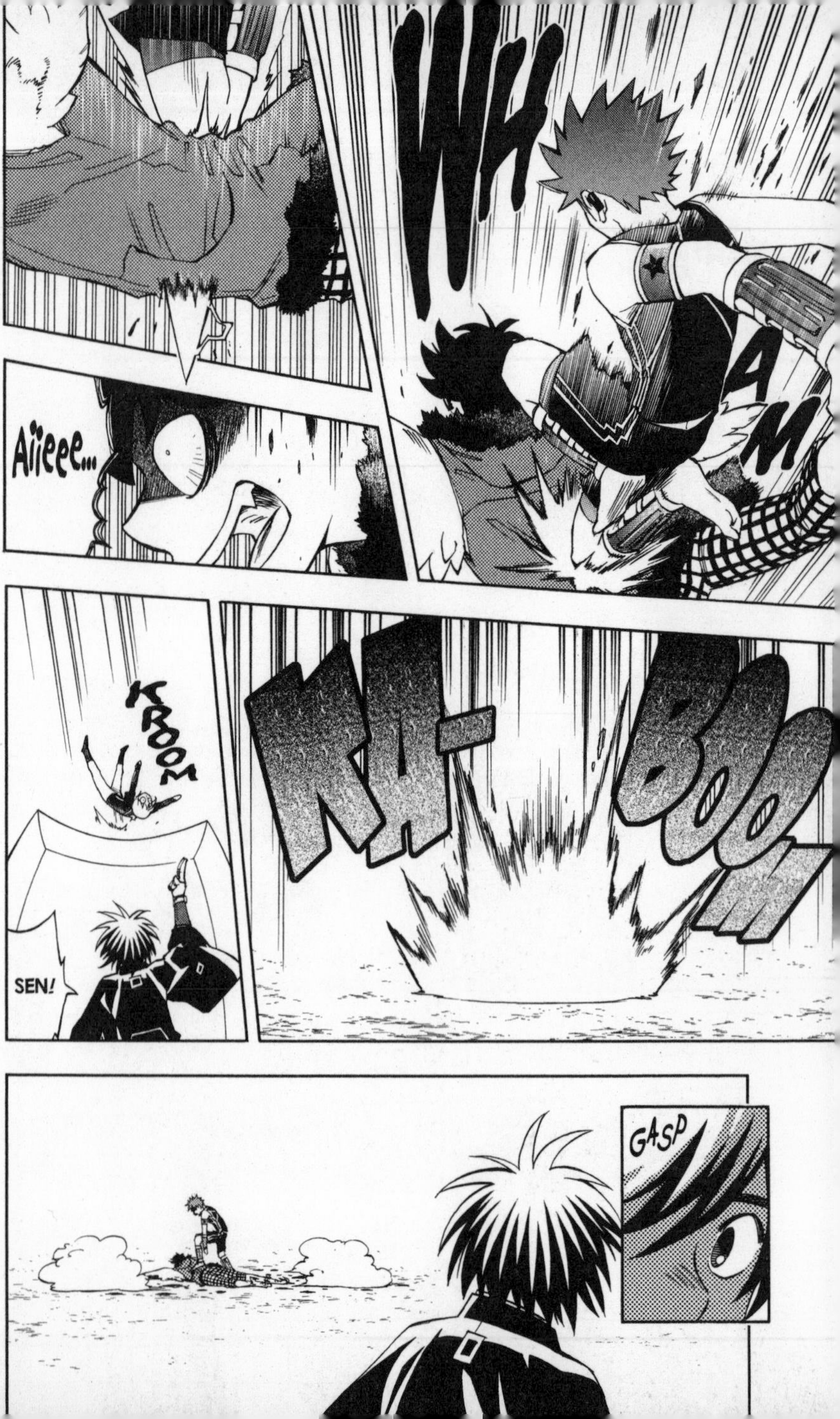
WHAM
Aiieee...
KA-BOOM
KROOM
SEN!
GASP

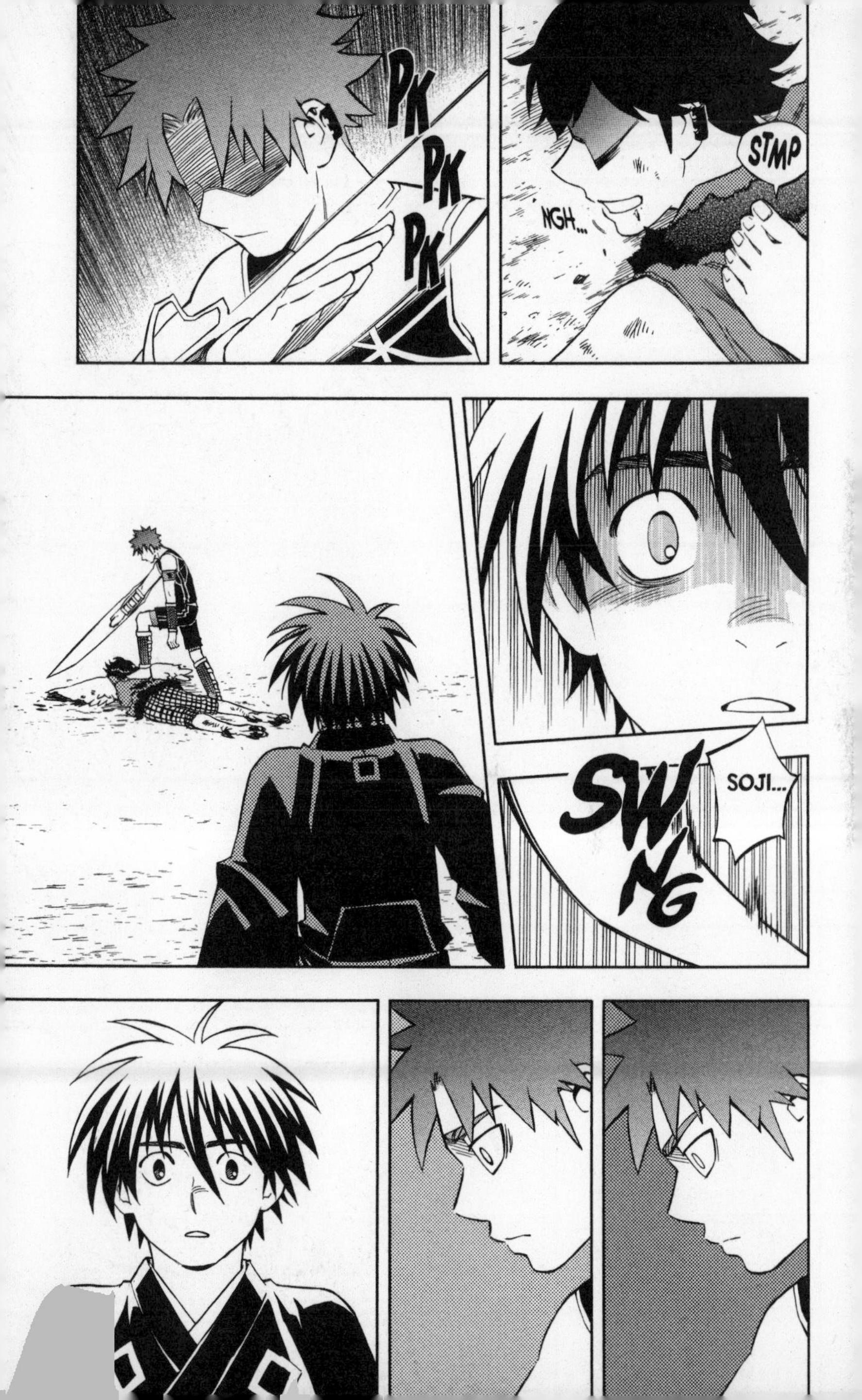
STMP
NGH...
PK PK PK
SOJI...
SWING

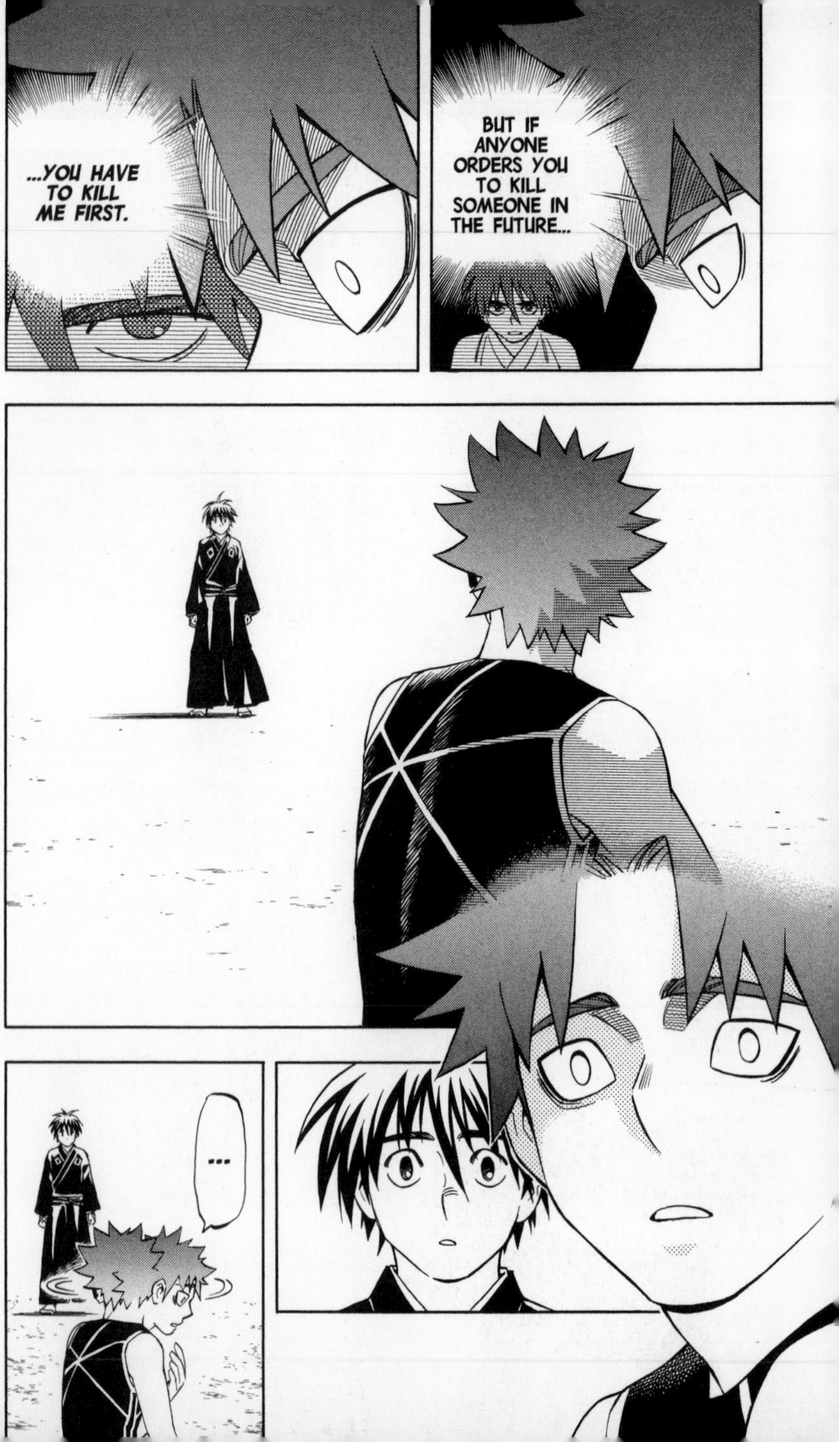
BUT IF ANYONE ORDERS YOU TO KILL SOMEONE IN THE FUTURE...
...YOU HAVE TO KILL ME FIRST.
...

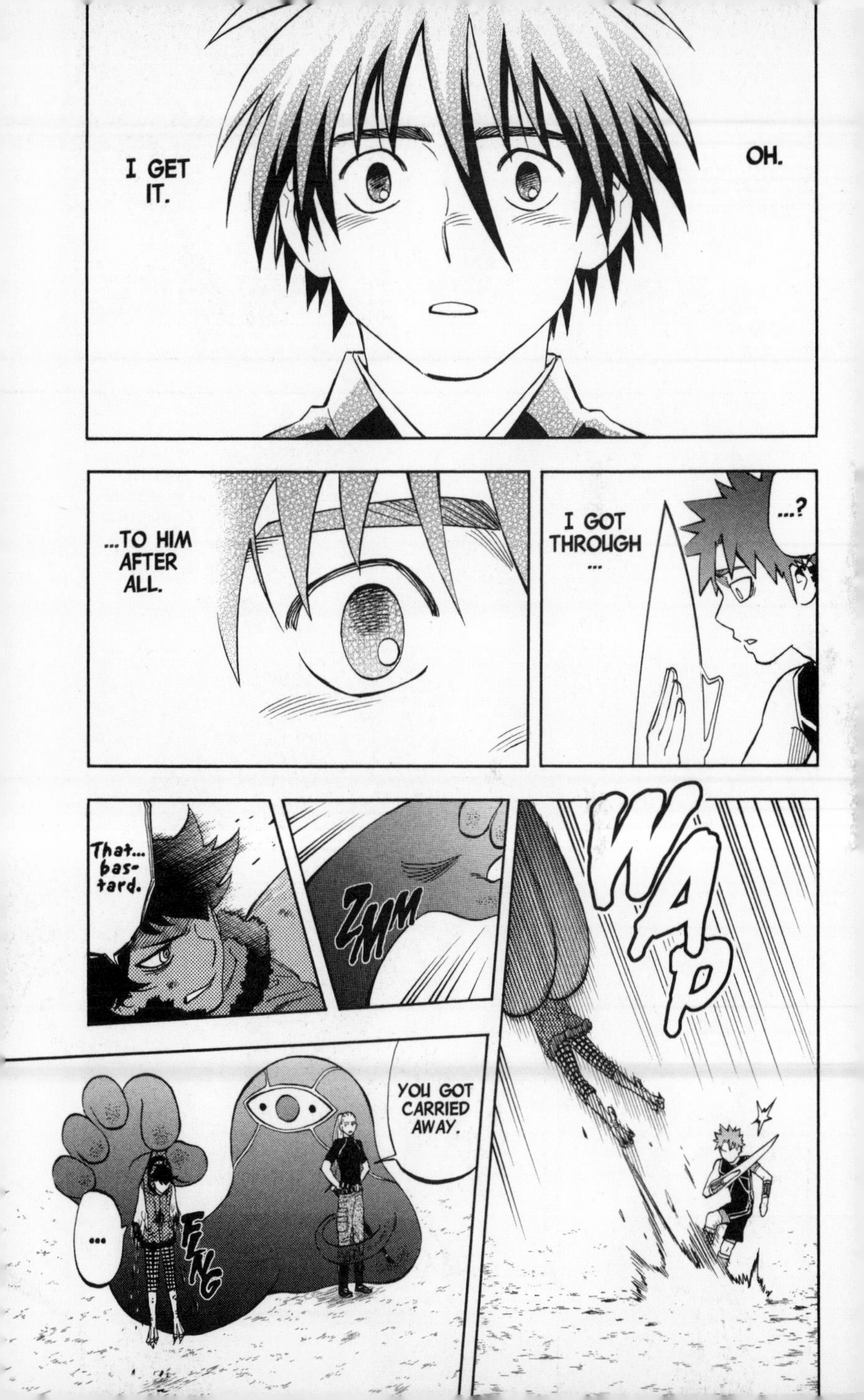
OH.
I GET IT.
...?
I GOT THROUGH ...
...TO HIM AFTER ALL.
WAP
ZMM
That... bas-tard.
YOU GOT CARRIED AWAY.
FLING
...

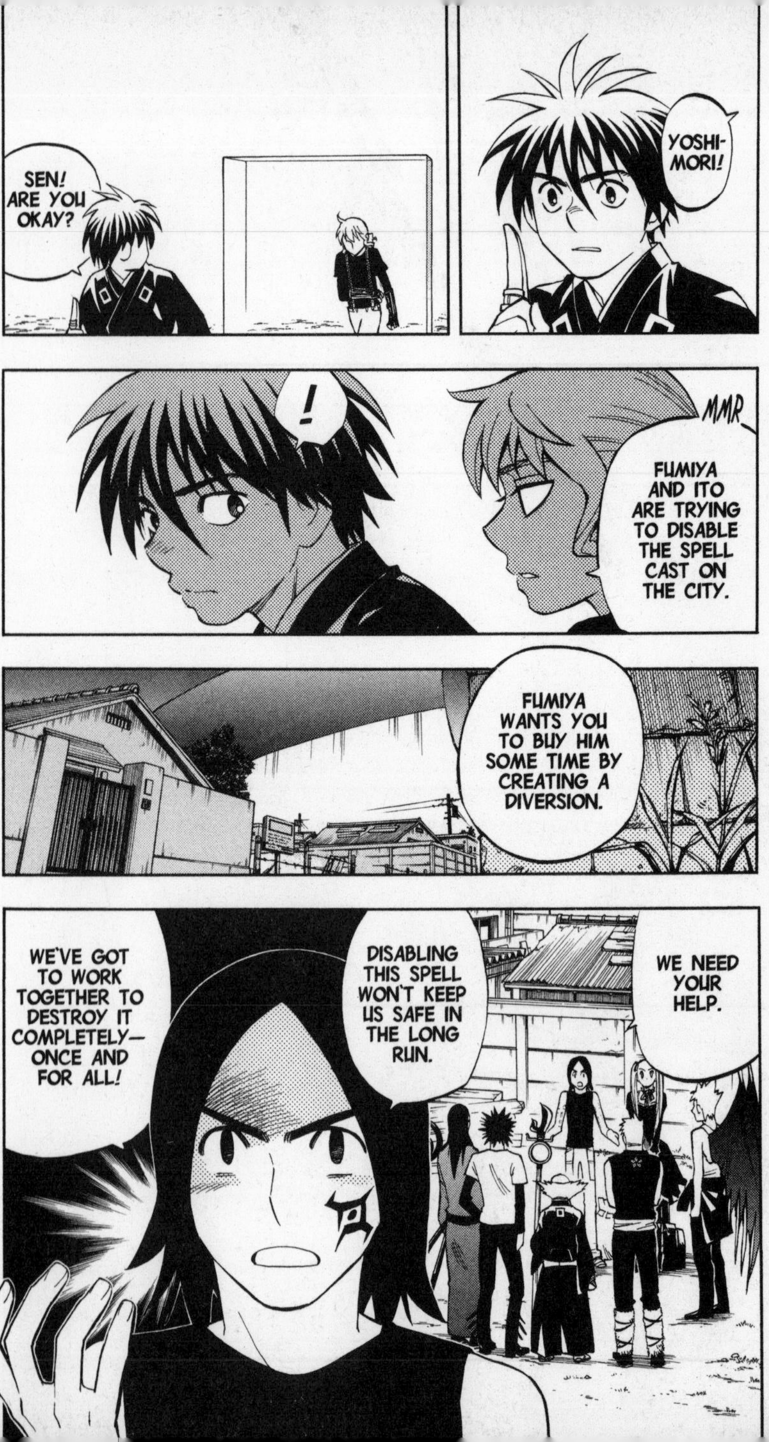
YOSHI-MORI!
SEN! ARE YOU OKAY?
MMR
FUMIYA AND ITO ARE TRYING TO DISABLE THE SPELL CAST ON THE CITY.
!
FUMIYA WANTS YOU TO BUY HIM SOME TIME BY CREATING A DIVERSION.
WE NEED YOUR HELP.
DISABLING THIS SPELL WON'T KEEP US SAFE IN THE LONG RUN.
WE'VE GOT TO WORK TOGETHER TO DESTROY IT COMPLETELY—ONCE AND FOR ALL!

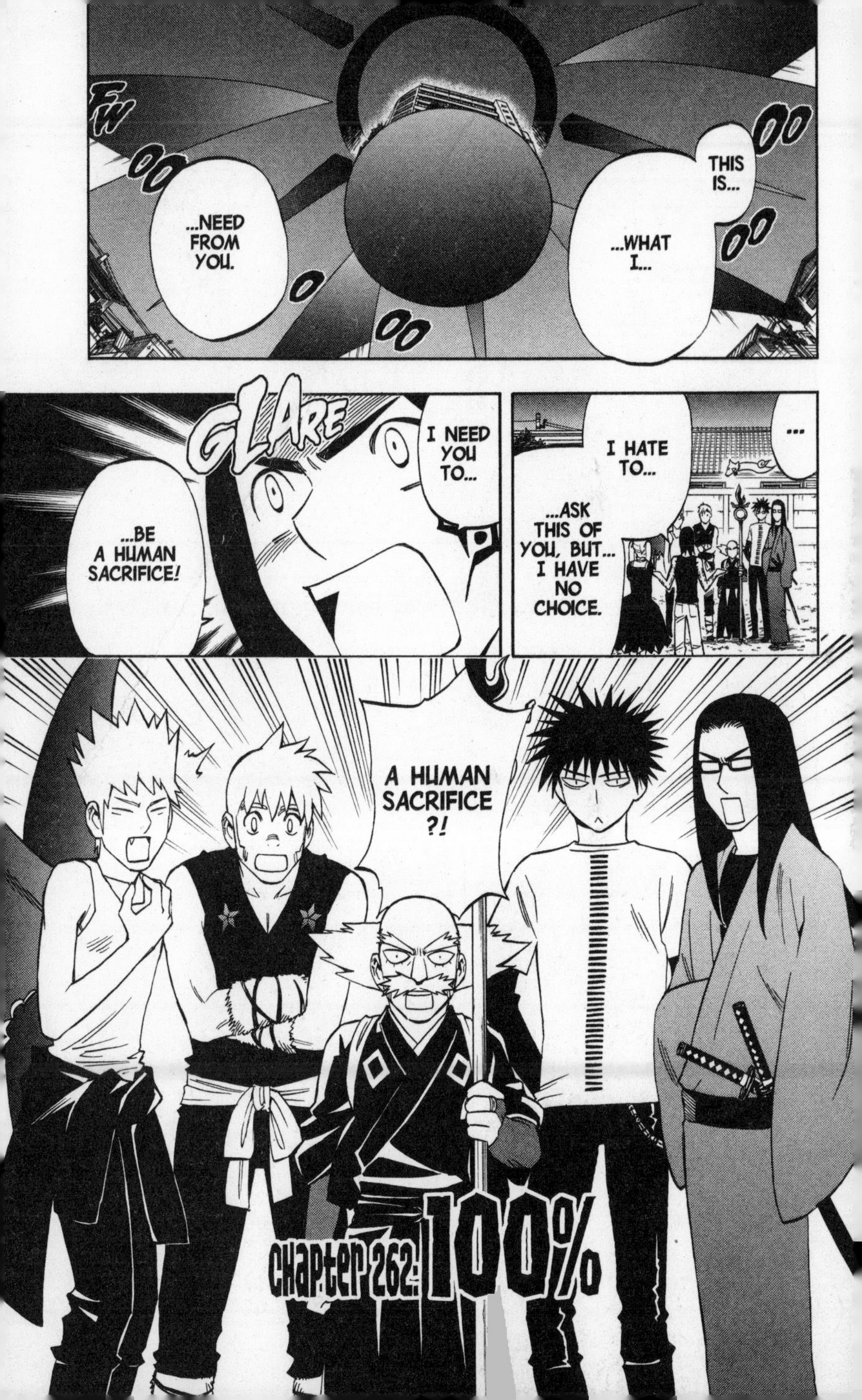
FW
OO
THIS IS...
...WHAT I...
...NEED FROM YOU.
...
I HATE TO...
...ASK THIS OF YOU, BUT... I HAVE NO CHOICE.
I NEED YOU TO...
GLARE
...BE A HUMAN SACRIFICE!
A HUMAN SACRIFICE ?!
CHAPTER 262: 100%

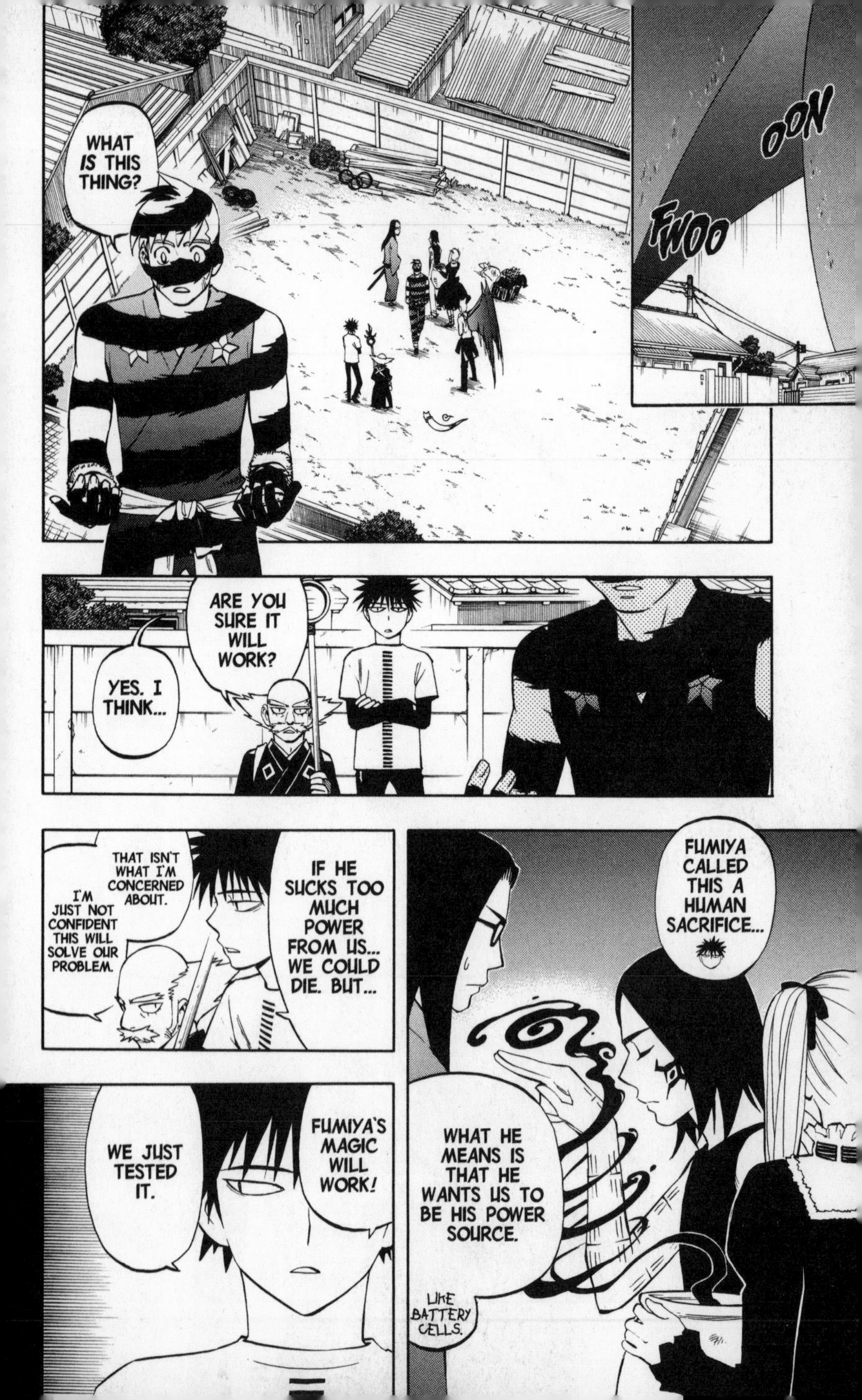
FWOO
OON
WHAT IS THIS THING?
ARE YOU SURE IT WILL WORK?
YES. I THINK...
FUMIYA CALLED THIS A HUMAN SACRIFICE...
WHAT HE MEANS IS THAT HE WANTS US TO BE HIS POWER SOURCE.
LIKE BATTERY CELLS.
IF HE SUCKS TOO MUCH POWER FROM US... WE COULD DIE. BUT...
THAT ISN'T WHAT I'M CONCERNED ABOUT.
I'M JUST NOT CONFIDENT THIS WILL SOLVE OUR PROBLEM.
FUMIYA'S MAGIC WILL WORK!
WE JUST TESTED IT.

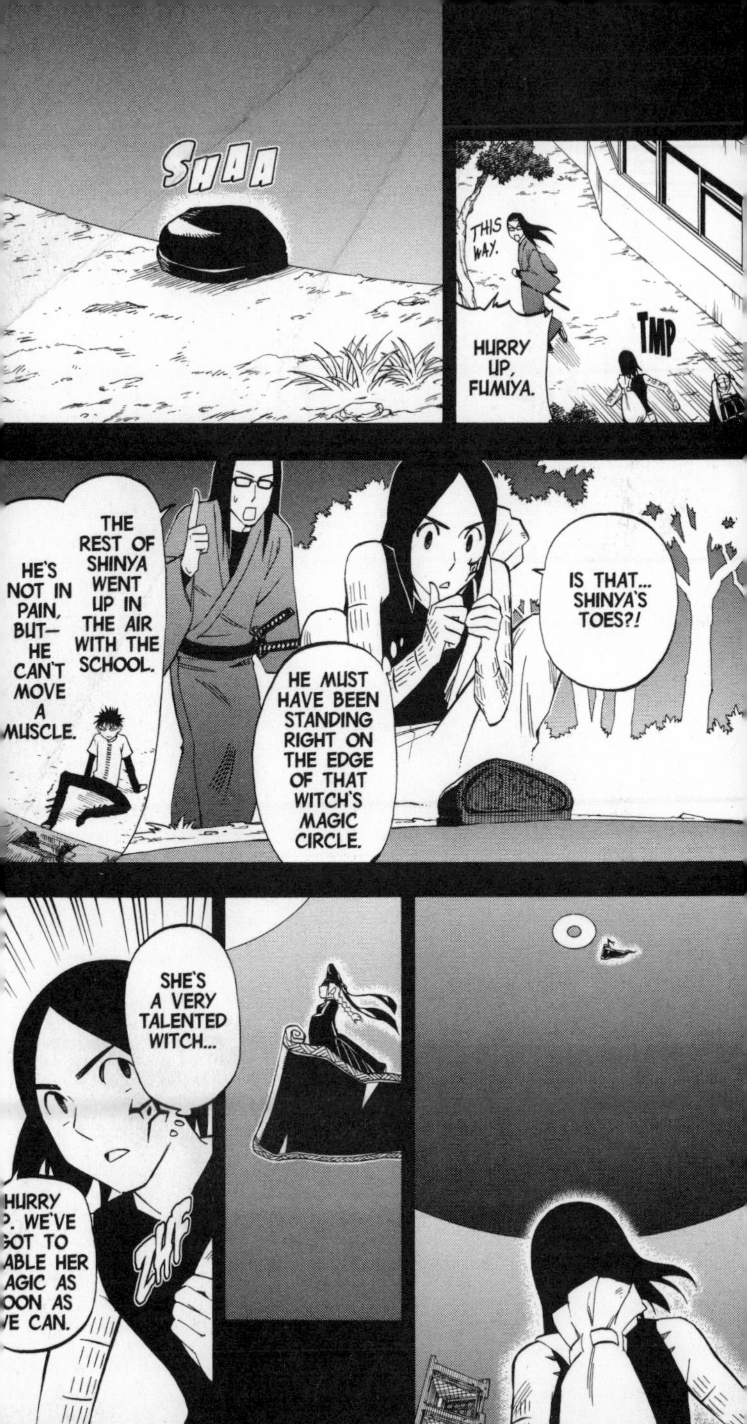
THIS WAY.
HURRY UP, FUMIYA.
TMP
SHAA
IS THAT... SHINYA'S TOES?!
HE MUST HAVE BEEN STANDING RIGHT ON THE EDGE OF THAT WITCH'S MAGIC CIRCLE.
THE REST OF SHINYA WENT UP IN THE AIR WITH THE SCHOOL.
HE'S NOT IN PAIN, BUT— HE CAN'T MOVE A MUSCLE.
SHE'S A VERY TALENTED WITCH...
ZHF
HURRY P. WE'VE GOT TO ABLE HER AGIC AS OON AS E CAN.

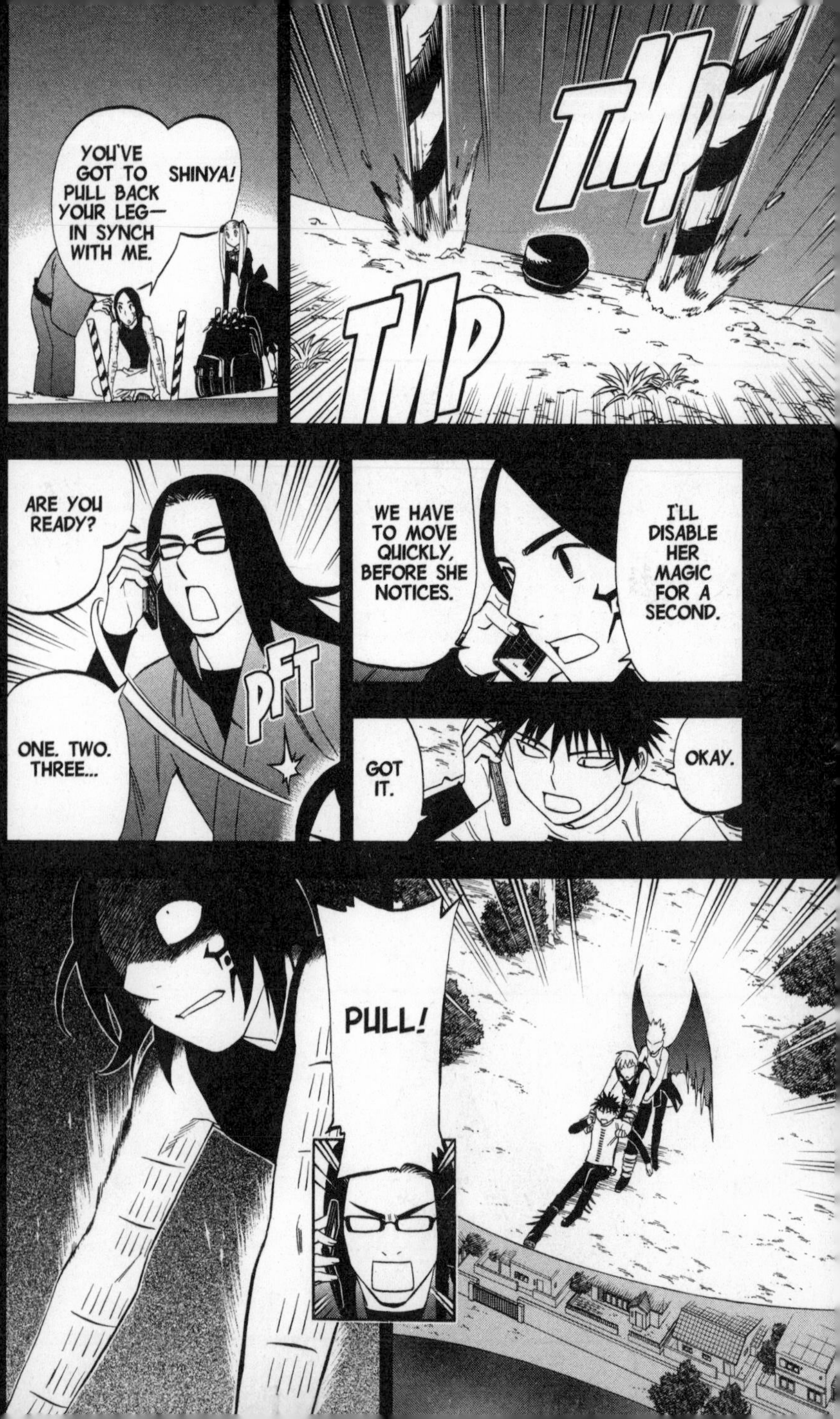
TMP
TMP
SHINYA!
YOU'VE GOT TO PULL BACK YOUR LEG—IN SYNCH WITH ME.
I'LL DISABLE HER MAGIC FOR A SECOND.
WE HAVE TO MOVE QUICKLY, BEFORE SHE NOTICES.
OKAY.
GOT IT.
ARE YOU READY?
PFT
ONE. TWO. THREE...
PULL!

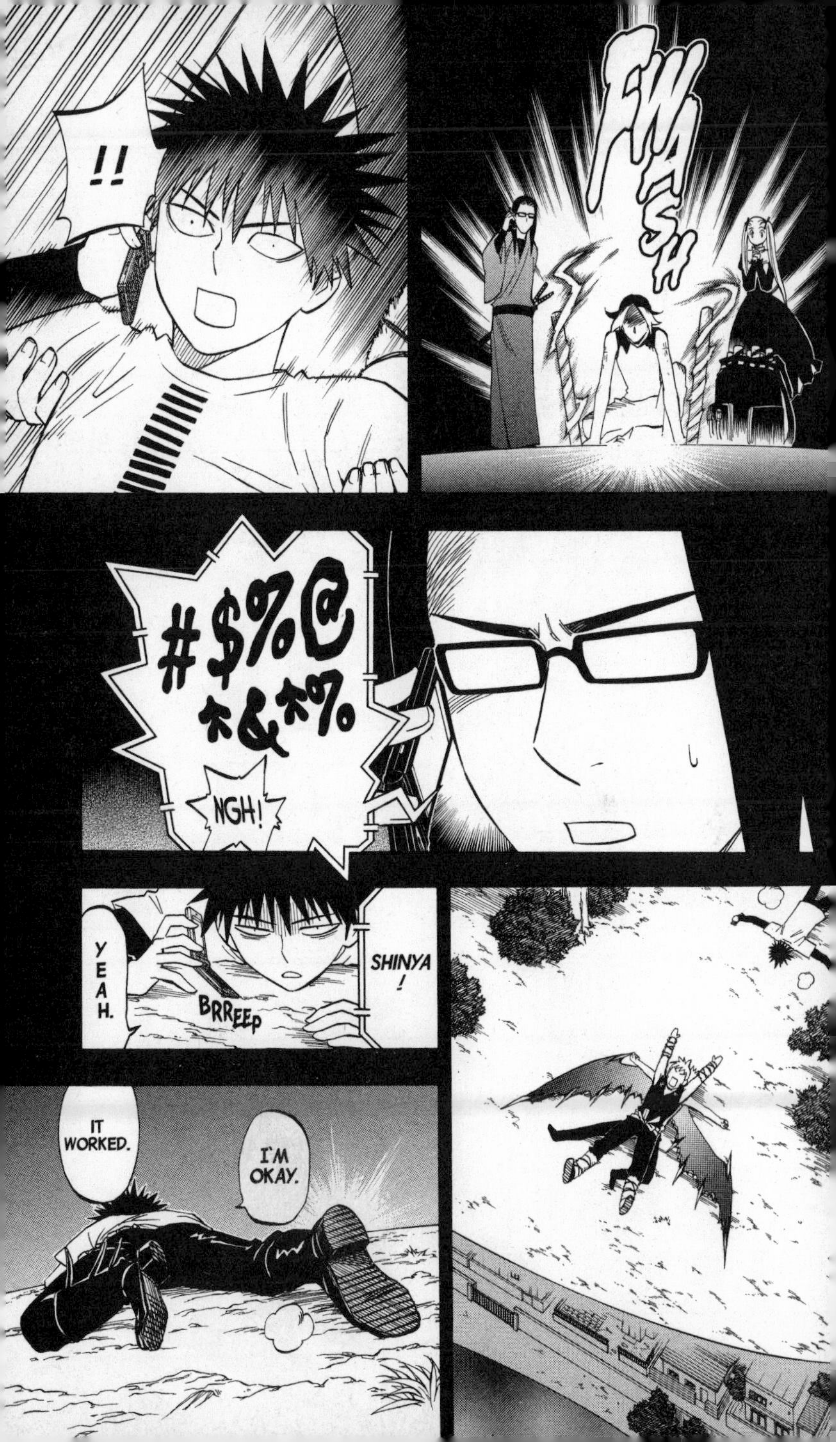
FWASH
!!
#$%@ *&*%
NGH!
SHINYA!
BRRREEP
YEAH.
I'M OKAY.
IT WORKED.

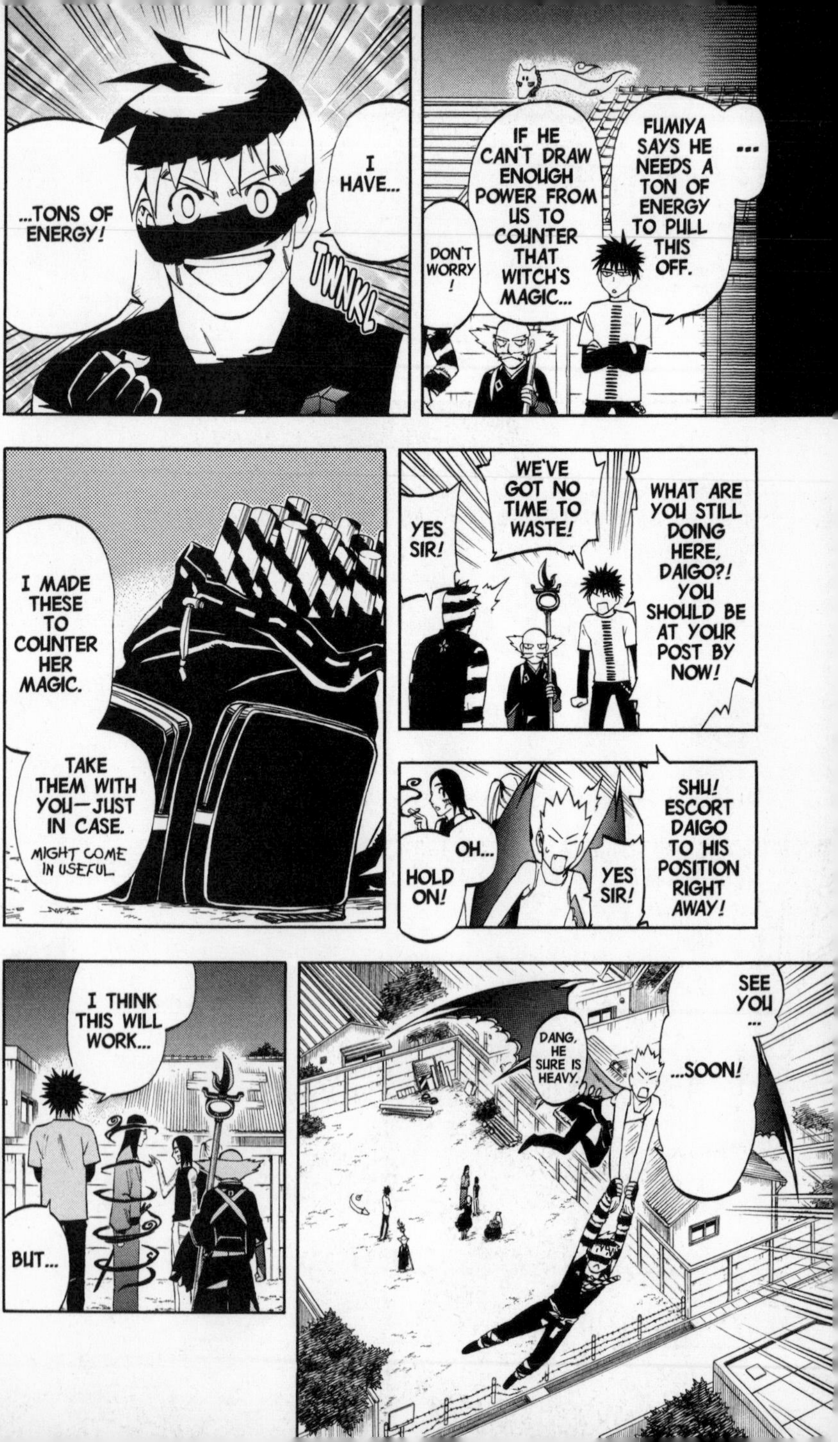
FUMIYA SAYS HE NEEDS A TON OF ENERGY TO PULL THIS OFF.
...
IF HE CAN'T DRAW ENOUGH POWER FROM US TO COUNTER THAT WITCH'S MAGIC...
DON'T WORRY!
I HAVE...
TWNKL
...TONS OF ENERGY!
WHAT ARE YOU STILL DOING HERE, DAIGO?! YOU SHOULD BE AT YOUR POST BY NOW!
WE'VE GOT NO TIME TO WASTE!
YES SIR!
SHU! ESCORT DAIGO TO HIS POSITION RIGHT AWAY!
YES SIR!
OH...
HOLD ON!
I MADE THESE TO COUNTER HER MAGIC.
TAKE THEM WITH YOU—JUST IN CASE.
MIGHT COME IN USEFUL
SEE YOU...
...SOON!
DANG, HE SURE IS HEAVY.
I THINK THIS WILL WORK...
BUT...

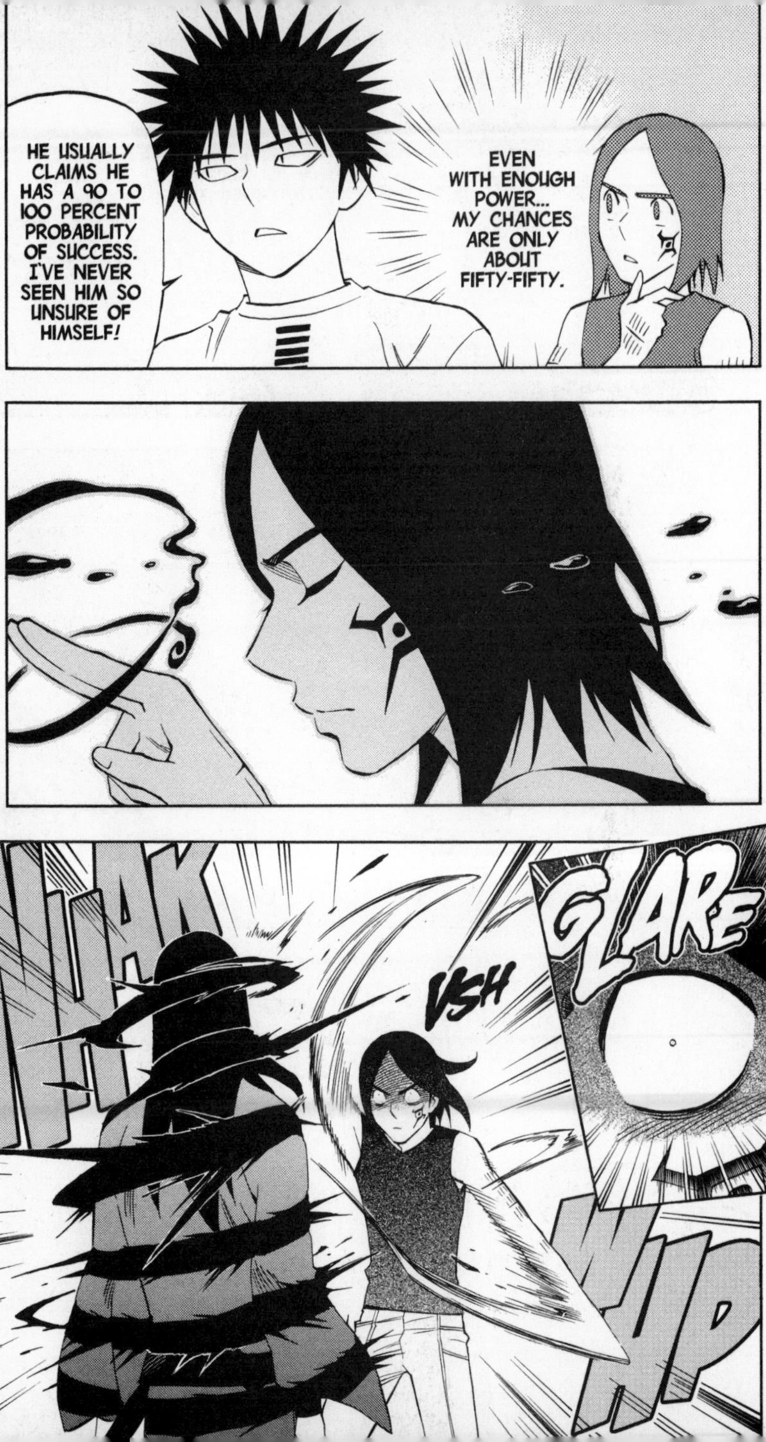
EVEN WITH ENOUGH POWER... MY CHANCES ARE ONLY ABOUT FIFTY-FIFTY.
HE USUALLY CLAIMS HE HAS A 90 TO 100 PERCENT PROBABILITY OF SUCCESS. I'VE NEVER SEEN HIM SO UNSURE OF HIMSELF!
GLARE
WHIP
VSH
WHAK

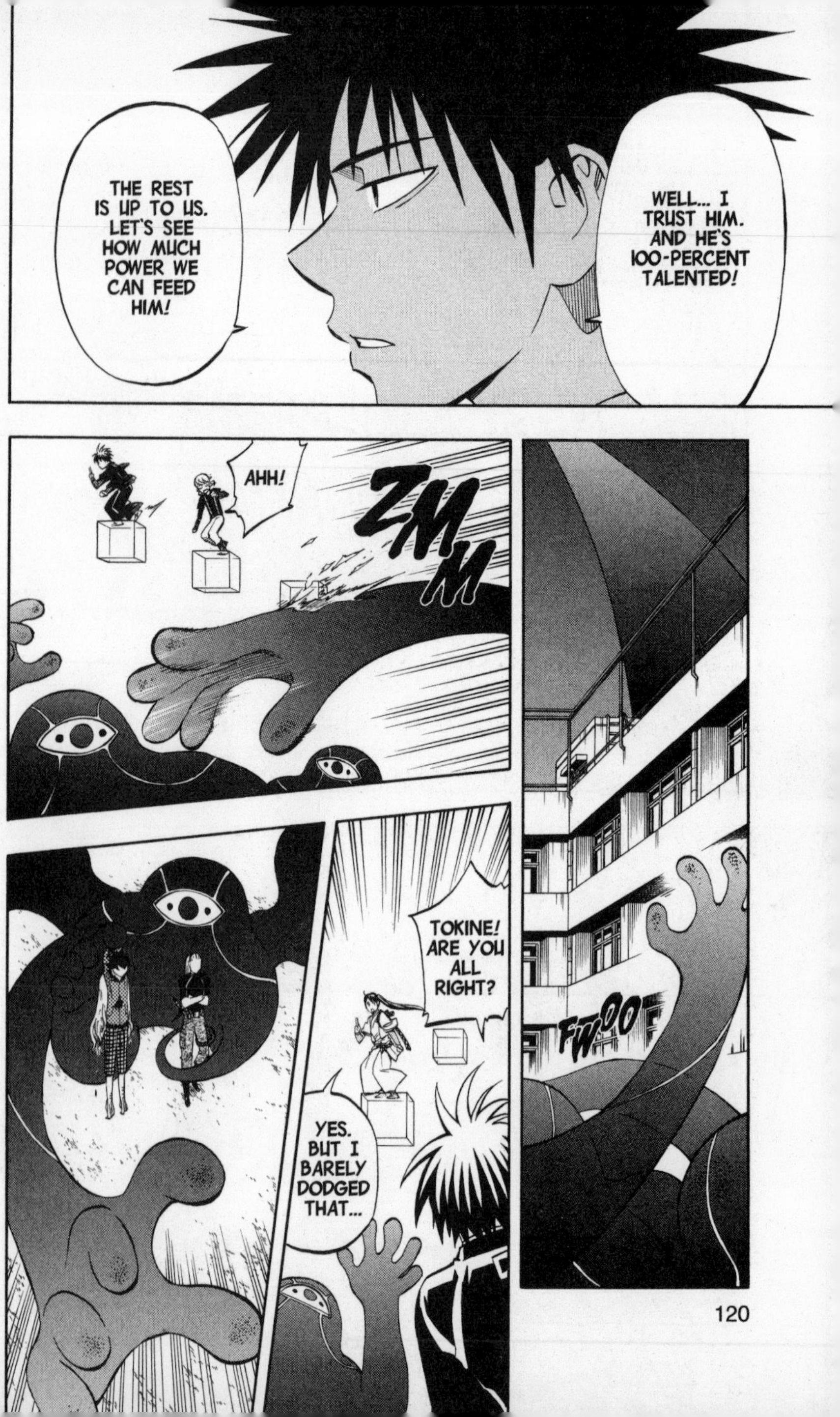
WELL... I TRUST HIM. AND HE'S 100-PERCENT TALENTED!
THE REST IS UP TO US. LET'S SEE HOW MUCH POWER WE CAN FEED HIM!
FWOO
AHH!
ZMM
TOKINE! ARE YOU ALL RIGHT?
YES. BUT I BARELY DODGED THAT...

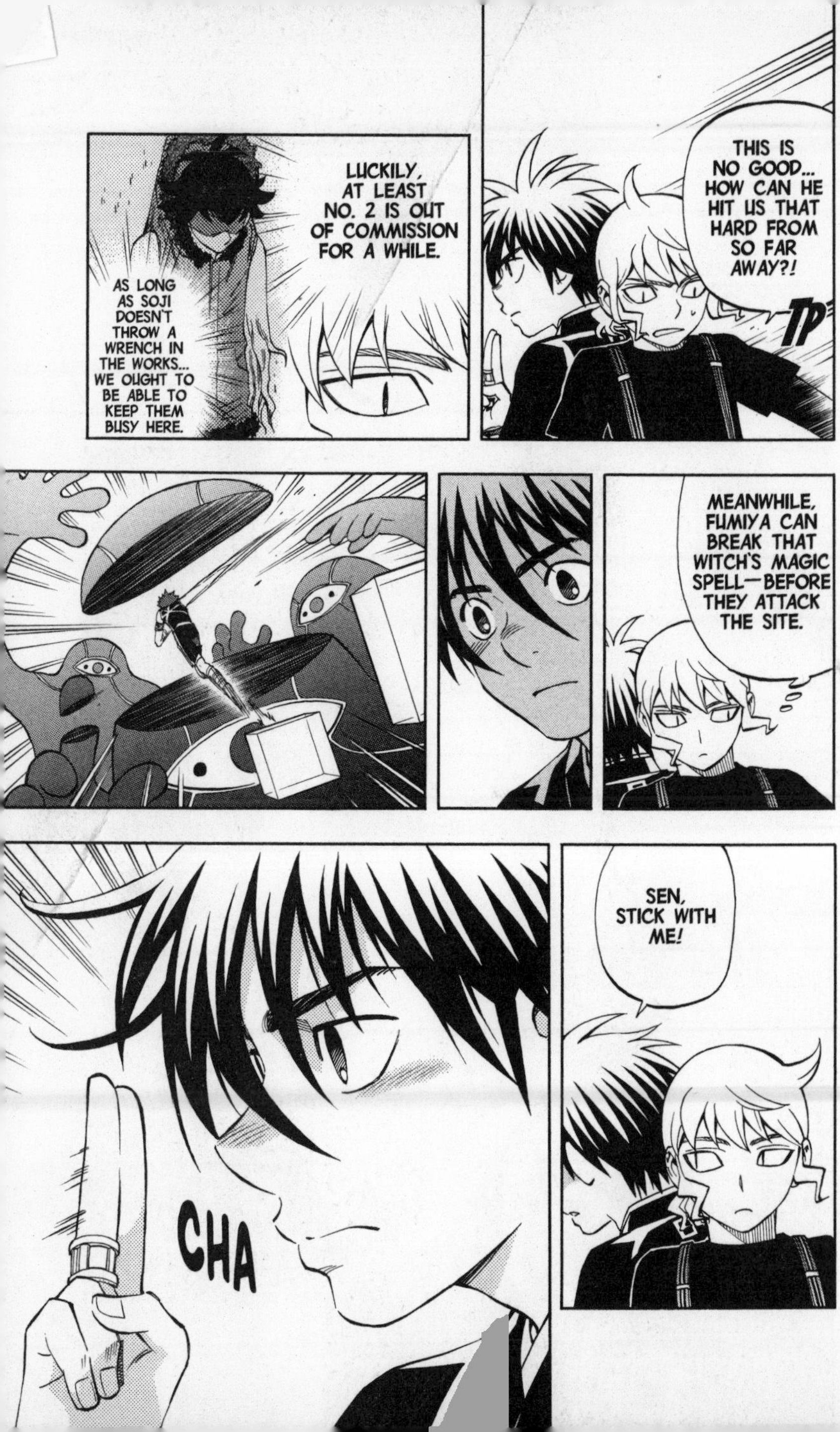
THIS IS NO GOOD... HOW CAN HE HIT US THAT HARD FROM SO FAR AWAY?!
TP
LUCKILY, AT LEAST NO. 2 IS OUT OF COMMISSION FOR A WHILE.
AS LONG AS SOJI DOESN'T THROW A WRENCH IN THE WORKS... WE OUGHT TO BE ABLE TO KEEP THEM BUSY HERE.
MEANWHILE, FUMIYA CAN BREAK THAT WITCH'S MAGIC SPELL—BEFORE THEY ATTACK THE SITE.
SEN, STICK WITH ME!
CHA

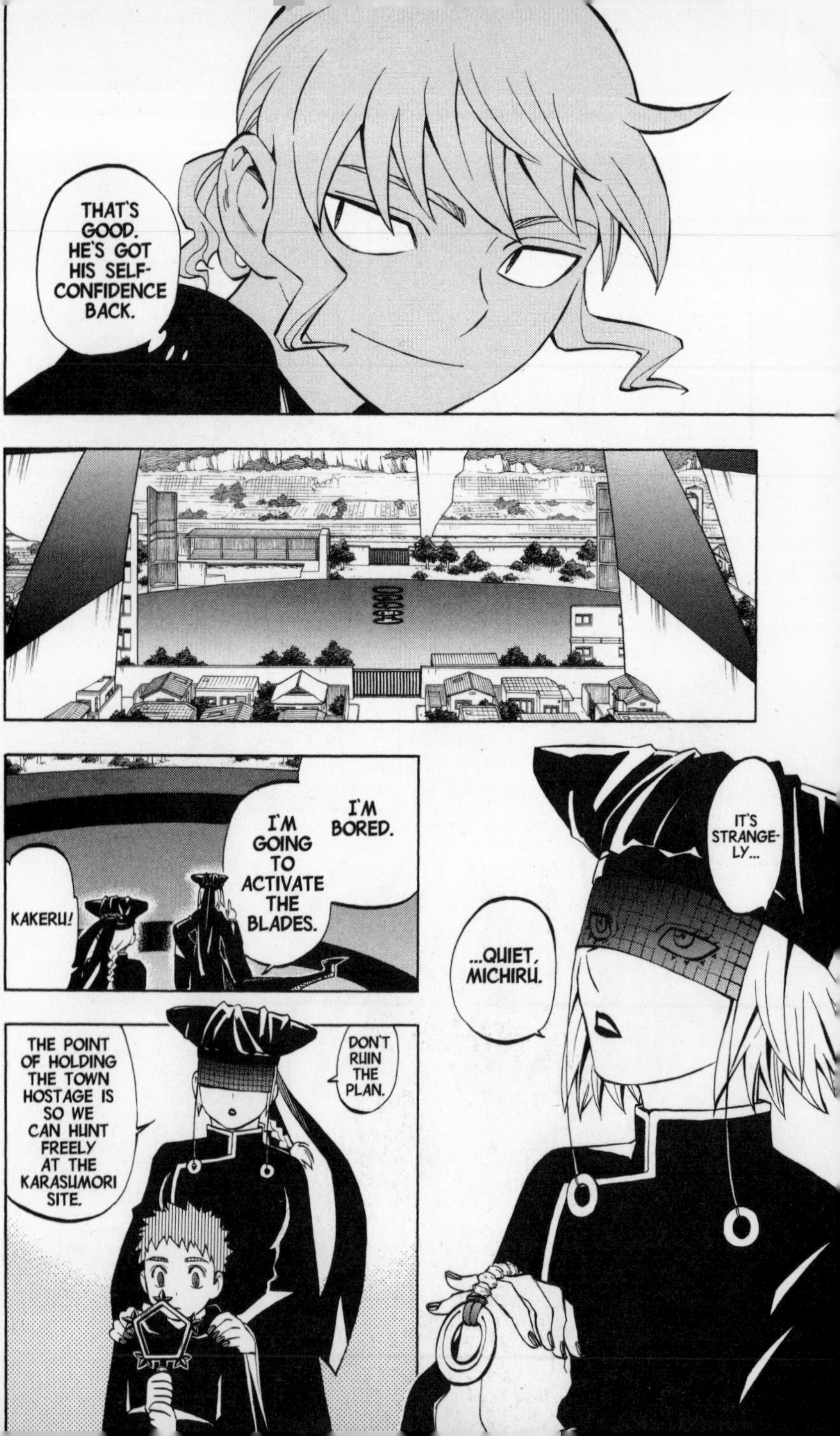
THAT'S GOOD. HE'S GOT HIS SELF-CONFIDENCE BACK.
IT'S STRANGELY...
...QUIET, MICHIRU.
I'M BORED.
I'M GOING TO ACTIVATE THE BLADES.
KAKERU!
DON'T RUIN THE PLAN.
THE POINT OF HOLDING THE TOWN HOSTAGE IS SO WE CAN HUNT FREELY AT THE KARASUMORI SITE.

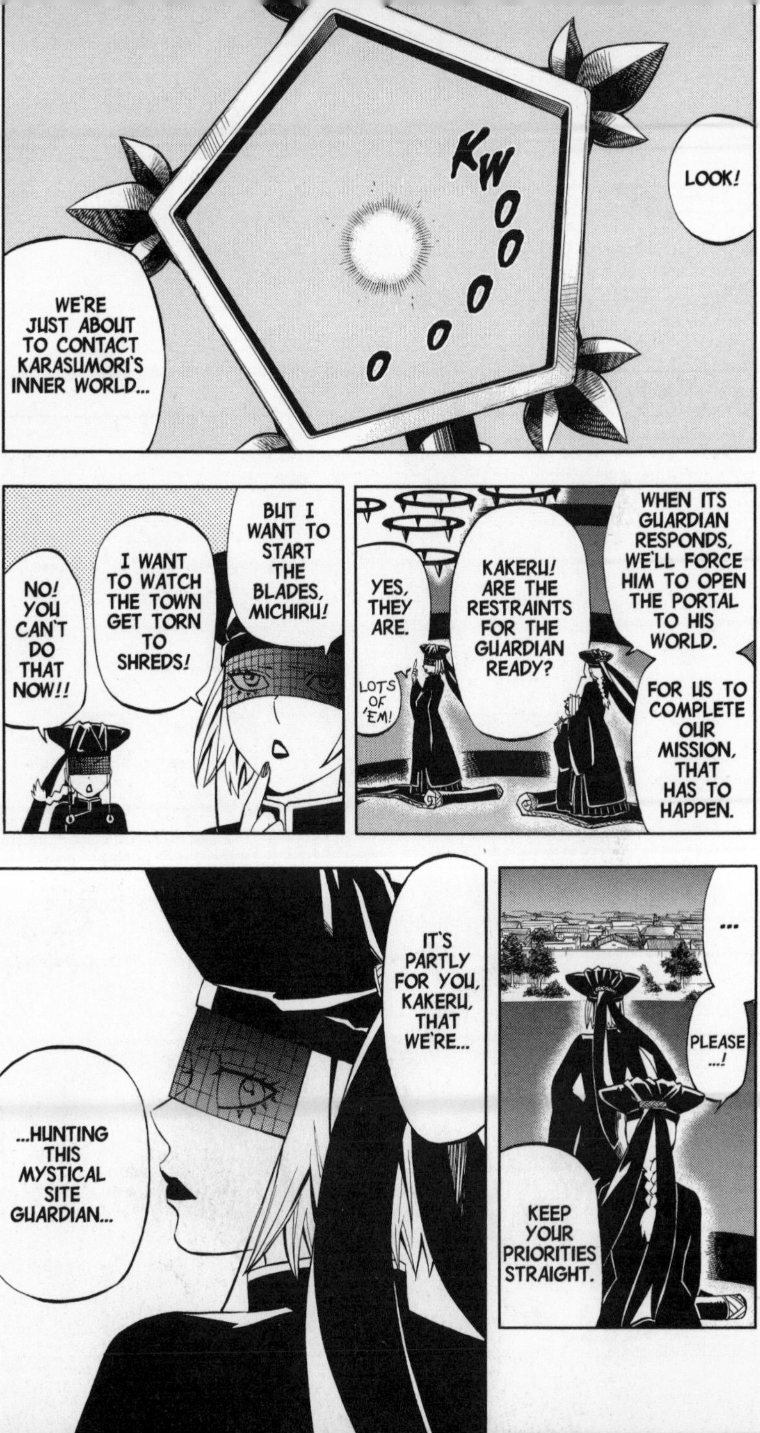
LOOK!
KWOOOOOO
WE'RE JUST ABOUT TO CONTACT KARASUMORI'S INNER WORLD...
WHEN ITS GUARDIAN RESPONDS, WE'LL FORCE HIM TO OPEN THE PORTAL TO HIS WORLD.
FOR US TO COMPLETE OUR MISSION, THAT HAS TO HAPPEN.
KAKERU! ARE THE RESTRAINTS FOR THE GUARDIAN READY?
YES, THEY ARE.
LOTS OF 'EM!
BUT I WANT TO START THE BLADES, MICHIRU!
I WANT TO WATCH THE TOWN GET TORN TO SHREDS!
NO! YOU CAN'T DO THAT NOW!!
...
PLEASE ...!
KEEP YOUR PRIORITIES STRAIGHT.
IT'S PARTLY FOR YOU, KAKERU, THAT WE'RE...
...HUNTING THIS MYSTICAL SITE GUARDIAN...

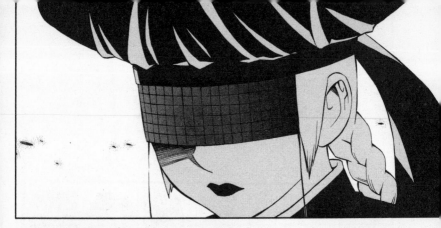

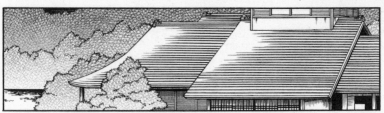

BEING A PART OF THE RESTRUCTURING OF OUR ORGANIZATION...
...IS AN ATTRACTIVE PROSPECT.
HOWEVER, I'D LIKE TO HEAR...
...YOUR ANSWER TO MY THIRD QUESTION BEFORE I RESPOND.
BUT FIRST, PERMIT ME TO STRAY FROM THE TOPIC..
...FOR A MOMENT. TELL ME, MR. YUMEJI...
...DO YOU KNOW HOW TO HUNT MYSTICAL SITES?

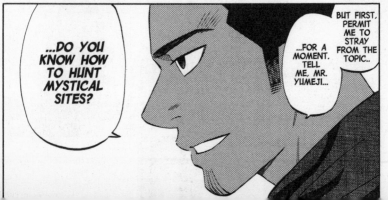

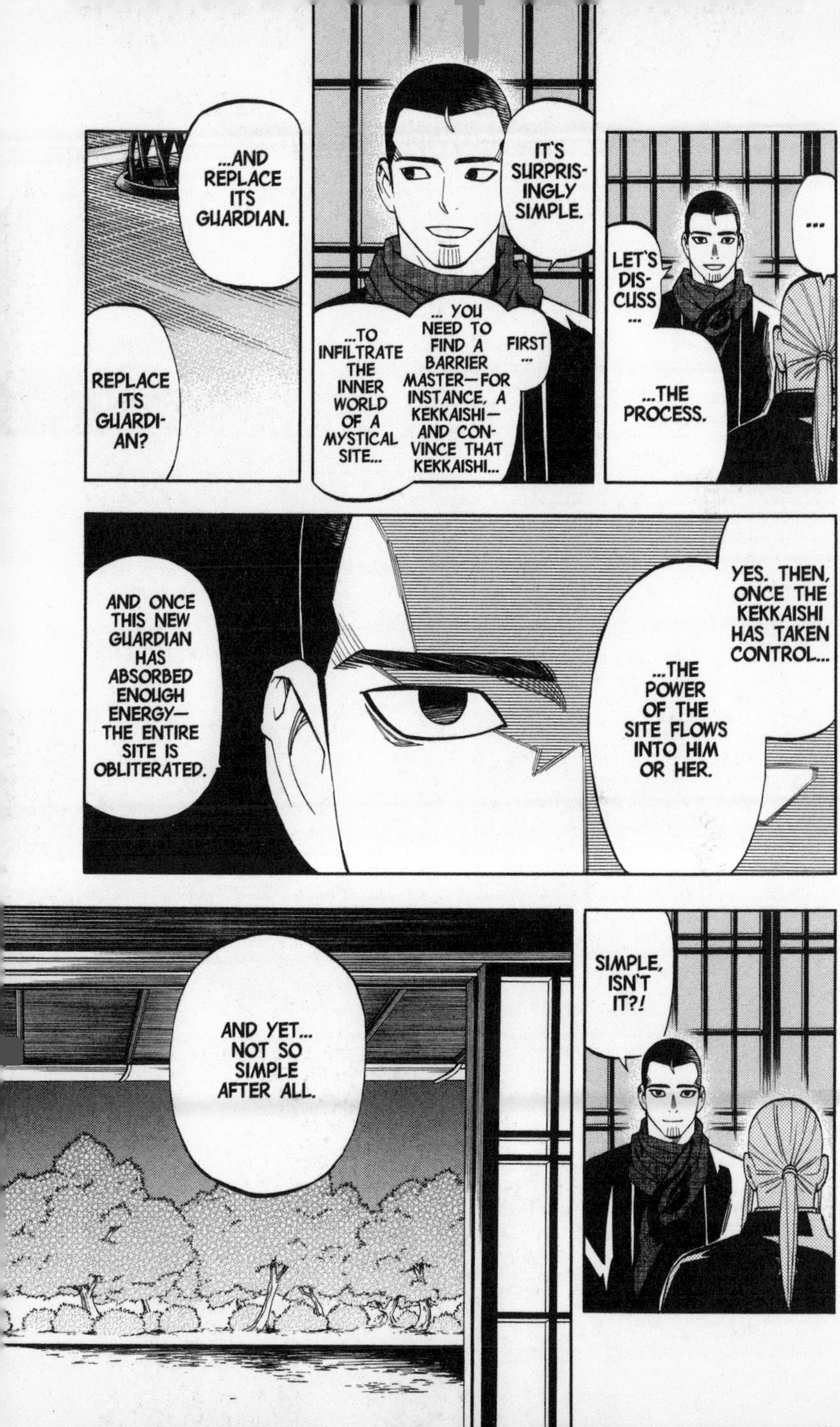
...
LET'S DISCUSS...
...THE PROCESS.
IT'S SURPRISINGLY SIMPLE.
FIRST...
... YOU NEED TO FIND A BARRIER MASTER—FOR INSTANCE, A KEKKAISHI—AND CONVINCE THAT KEKKAISHI...
...TO INFILTRATE THE INNER WORLD OF A MYSTICAL SITE...
...AND REPLACE ITS GUARDIAN.
REPLACE ITS GUARDIAN?
YES. THEN, ONCE THE KEKKAISHI HAS TAKEN CONTROL...
...THE POWER OF THE SITE FLOWS INTO HIM OR HER.
AND ONCE THIS NEW GUARDIAN HAS ABSORBED ENOUGH ENERGY—THE ENTIRE SITE IS OBLITERATED.
SIMPLE, ISN'T IT?!
AND YET... NOT SO SIMPLE AFTER ALL.

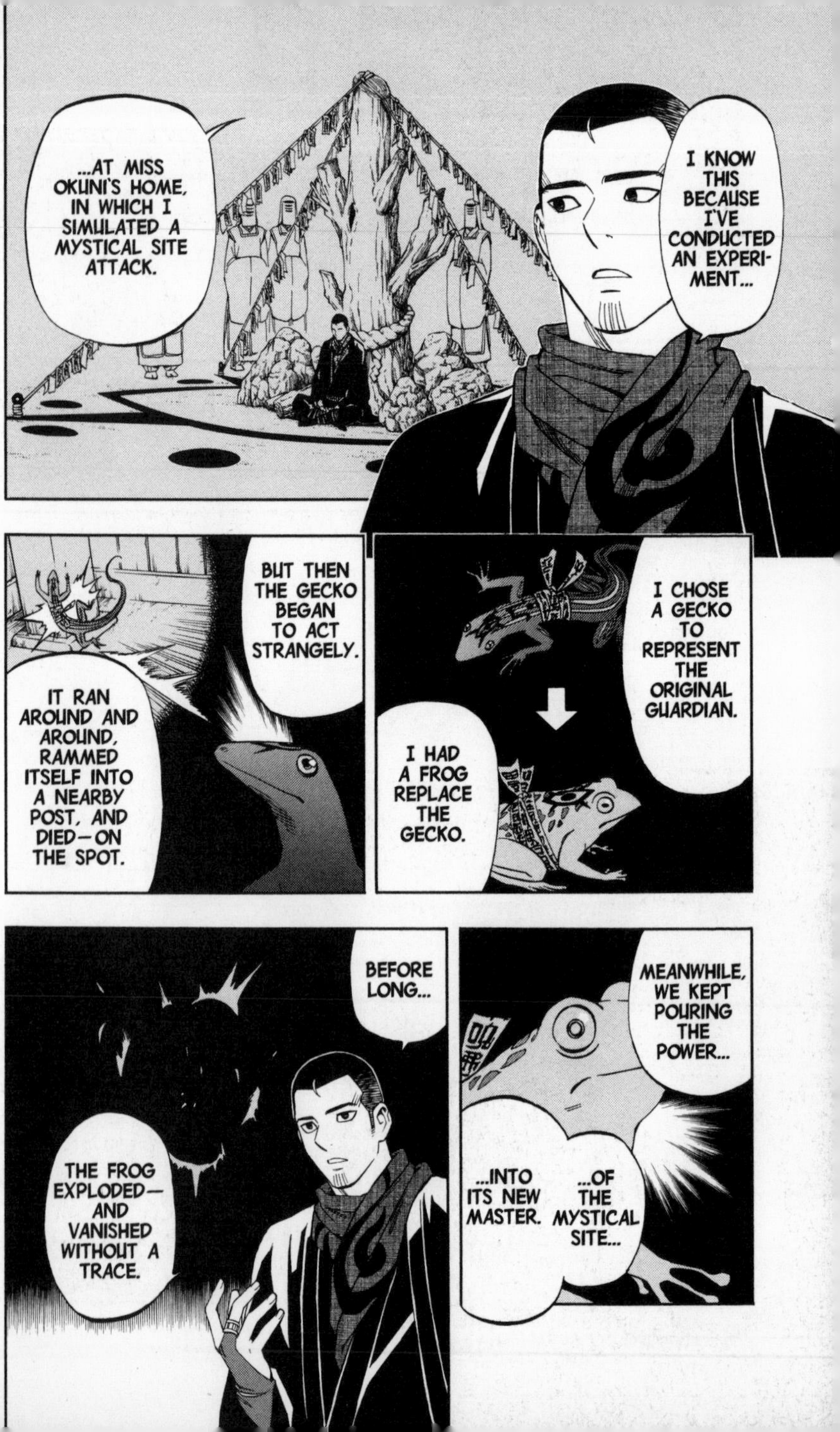
I KNOW THIS BECAUSE I'VE CONDUCTED AN EXPERIMENT...
...AT MISS OKUNI'S HOME, IN WHICH I SIMULATED A MYSTICAL SITE ATTACK.
I CHOSE A GECKO TO REPRESENT THE ORIGINAL GUARDIAN.
I HAD A FROG REPLACE THE GECKO.
BUT THEN THE GECKO BEGAN TO ACT STRANGELY.
IT RAN AROUND AND AROUND, RAMMED ITSELF INTO A NEARBY POST, AND DIED—ON THE SPOT.
MEANWHILE, WE KEPT POURING THE POWER...
...OF THE MYSTICAL SITE...
...INTO ITS NEW MASTER.
BEFORE LONG...
THE FROG EXPLODED—AND VANISHED WITHOUT A TRACE.

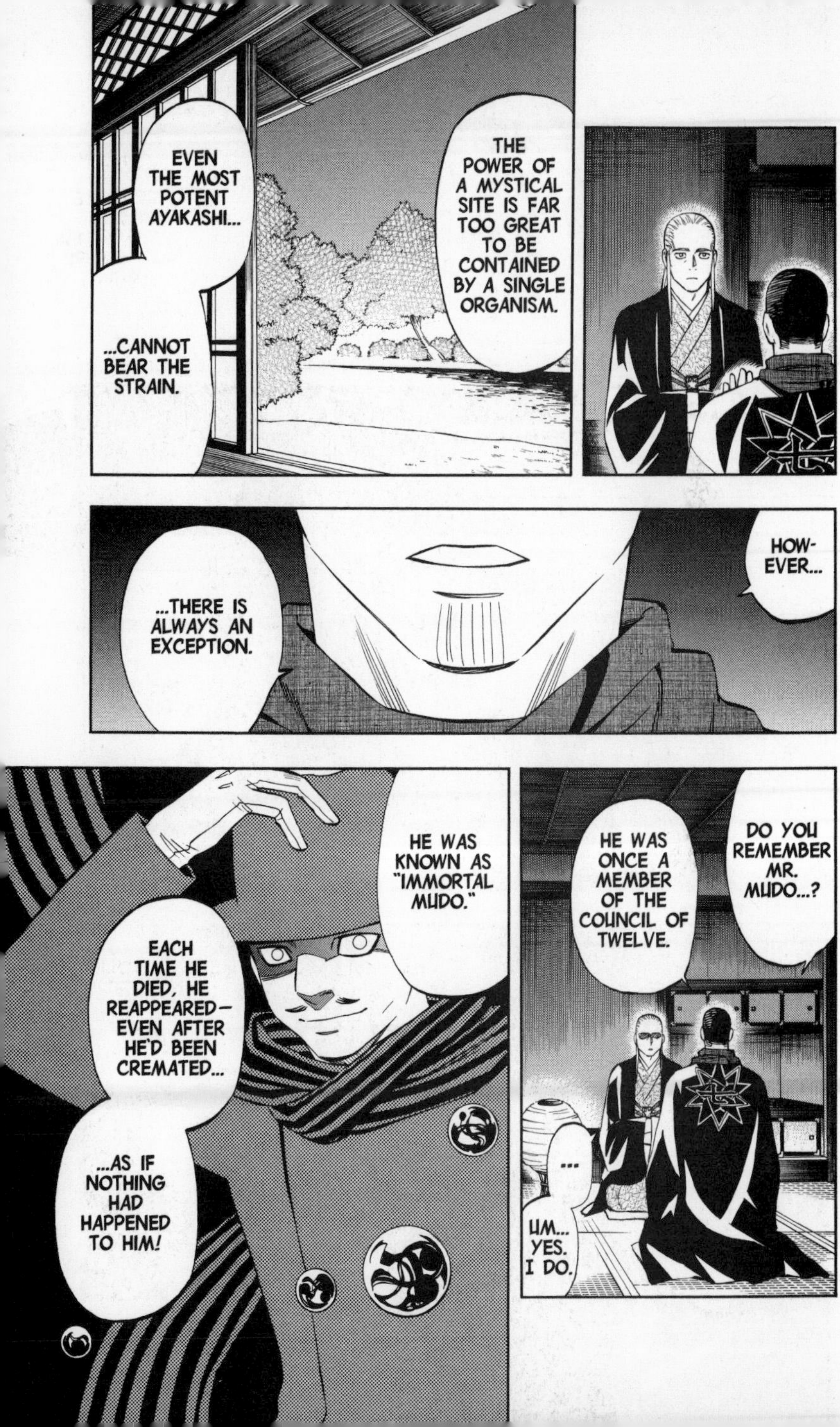
THE POWER OF A MYSTICAL SITE IS FAR TOO GREAT TO BE CONTAINED BY A SINGLE ORGANISM.
EVEN THE MOST POTENT AYAKASHI...
...CANNOT BEAR THE STRAIN.
HOW-EVER...
...THERE IS ALWAYS AN EXCEPTION.
DO YOU REMEMBER MR. MUDO...?
HE WAS ONCE A MEMBER OF THE COUNCIL OF TWELVE.
...
UM... YES. I DO.
HE WAS KNOWN AS "IMMORTAL MUDO."
EACH TIME HE DIED, HE REAPPEARED—EVEN AFTER HE'D BEEN CREMATED...
...AS IF NOTHING HAD HAPPENED TO HIM!

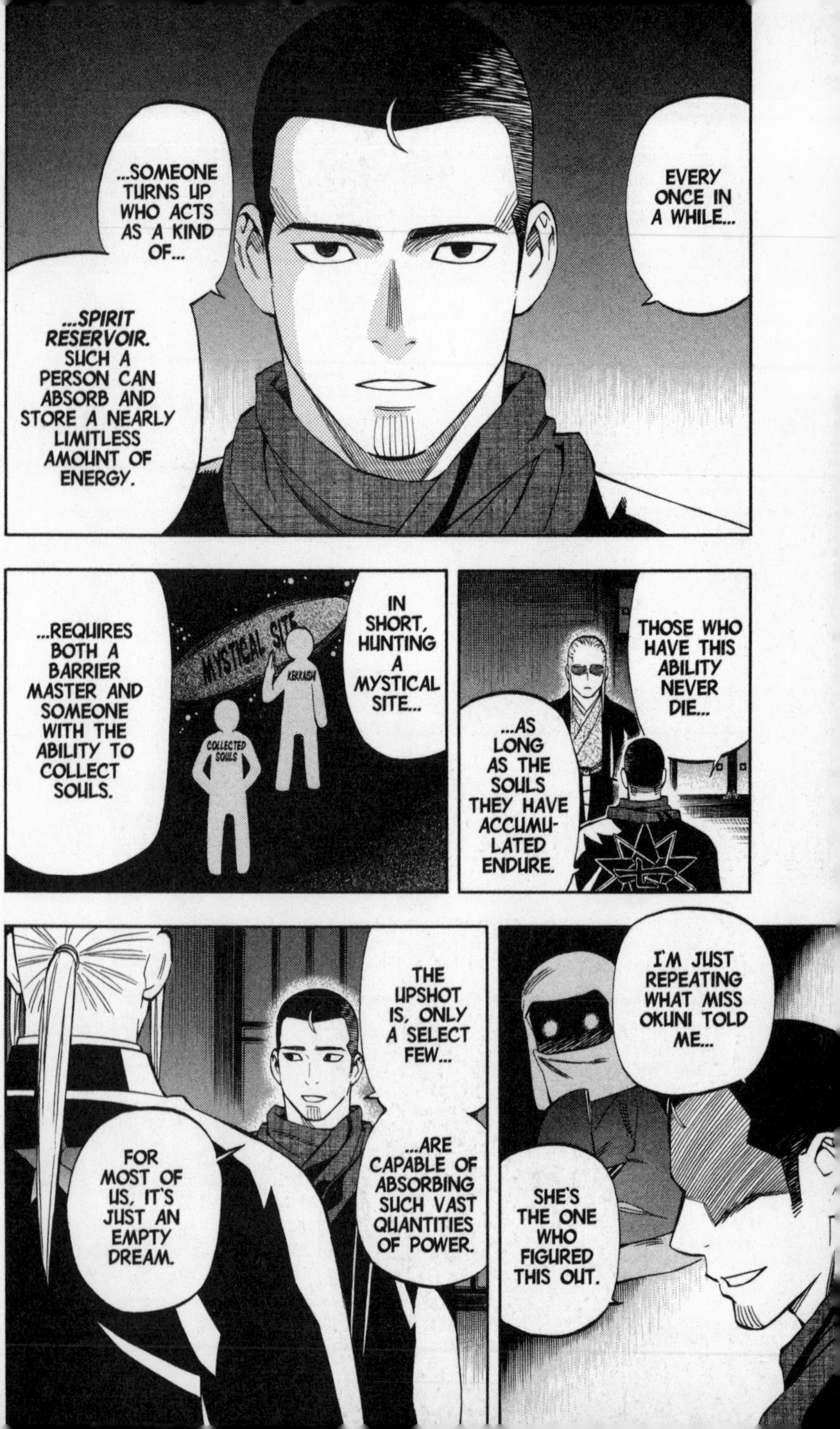
EVERY ONCE IN A WHILE...
...SOMEONE TURNS UP WHO ACTS AS A KIND OF...
...SPIRIT RESERVOIR. SUCH A PERSON CAN ABSORB AND STORE A NEARLY LIMITLESS AMOUNT OF ENERGY.
THOSE WHO HAVE THIS ABILITY NEVER DIE...
...AS LONG AS THE SOULS THEY HAVE ACCUMULATED ENDURE.
IN SHORT, HUNTING A MYSTICAL SITE...
MYSTICAL SITE
KEKKAISHI
COLLECTED SOULS
...REQUIRES BOTH A BARRIER MASTER AND SOMEONE WITH THE ABILITY TO COLLECT SOULS.
I'M JUST REPEATING WHAT MISS OKUNI TOLD ME...
SHE'S THE ONE WHO FIGURED THIS OUT.
THE UPSHOT IS, ONLY A SELECT FEW...
...ARE CAPABLE OF ABSORBING SUCH VAST QUANTITIES OF POWER.
FOR MOST OF US, IT'S JUST AN EMPTY DREAM.

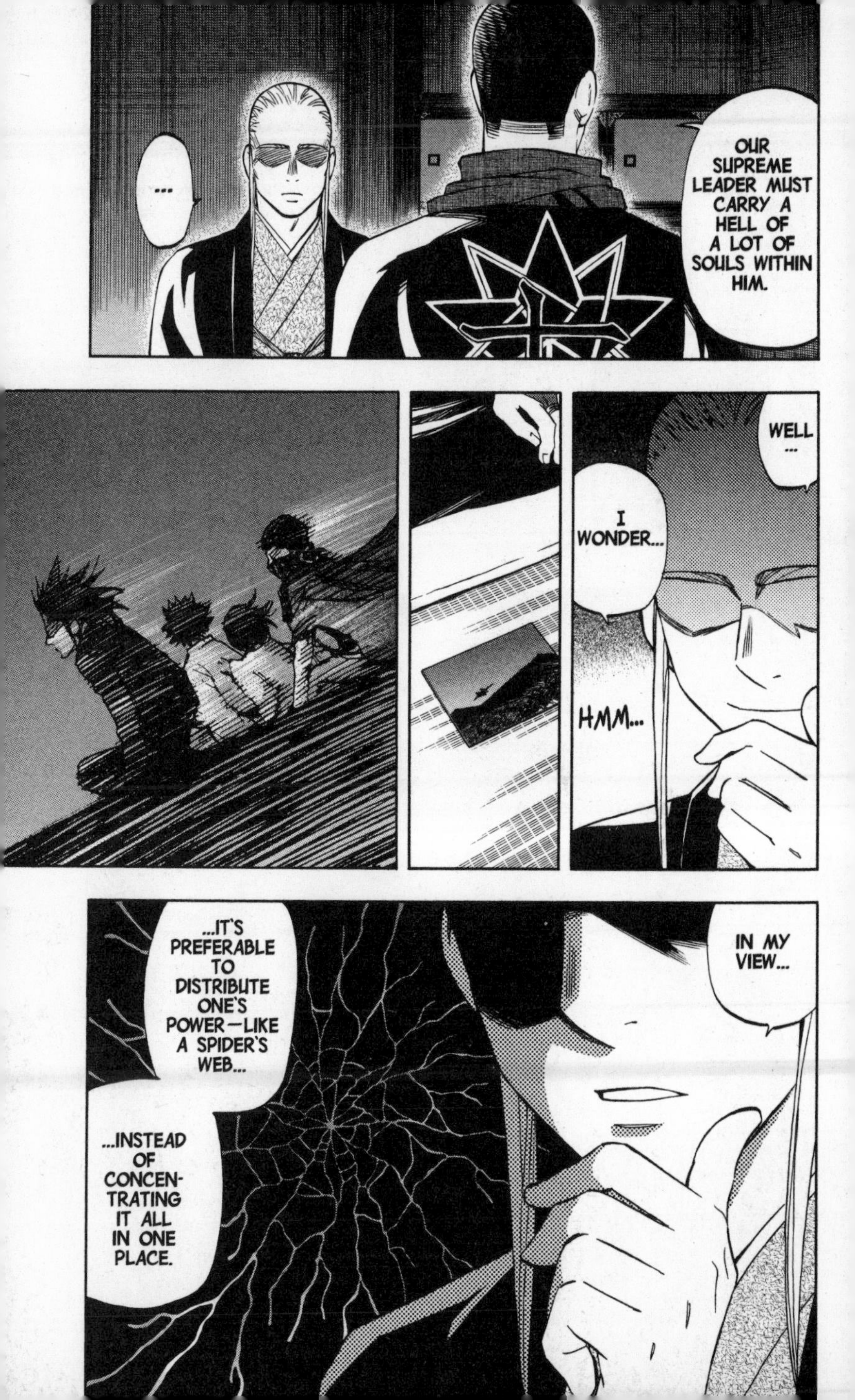
OUR SUPREME LEADER MUST CARRY A HELL OF A LOT OF SOULS WITHIN HIM.
...
WELL...
I WONDER...
HMM...
IN MY VIEW...
...IT'S PREFERABLE TO DISTRIBUTE ONE'S POWER—LIKE A SPIDER'S WEB...
...INSTEAD OF CONCEN-TRATING IT ALL IN ONE PLACE.

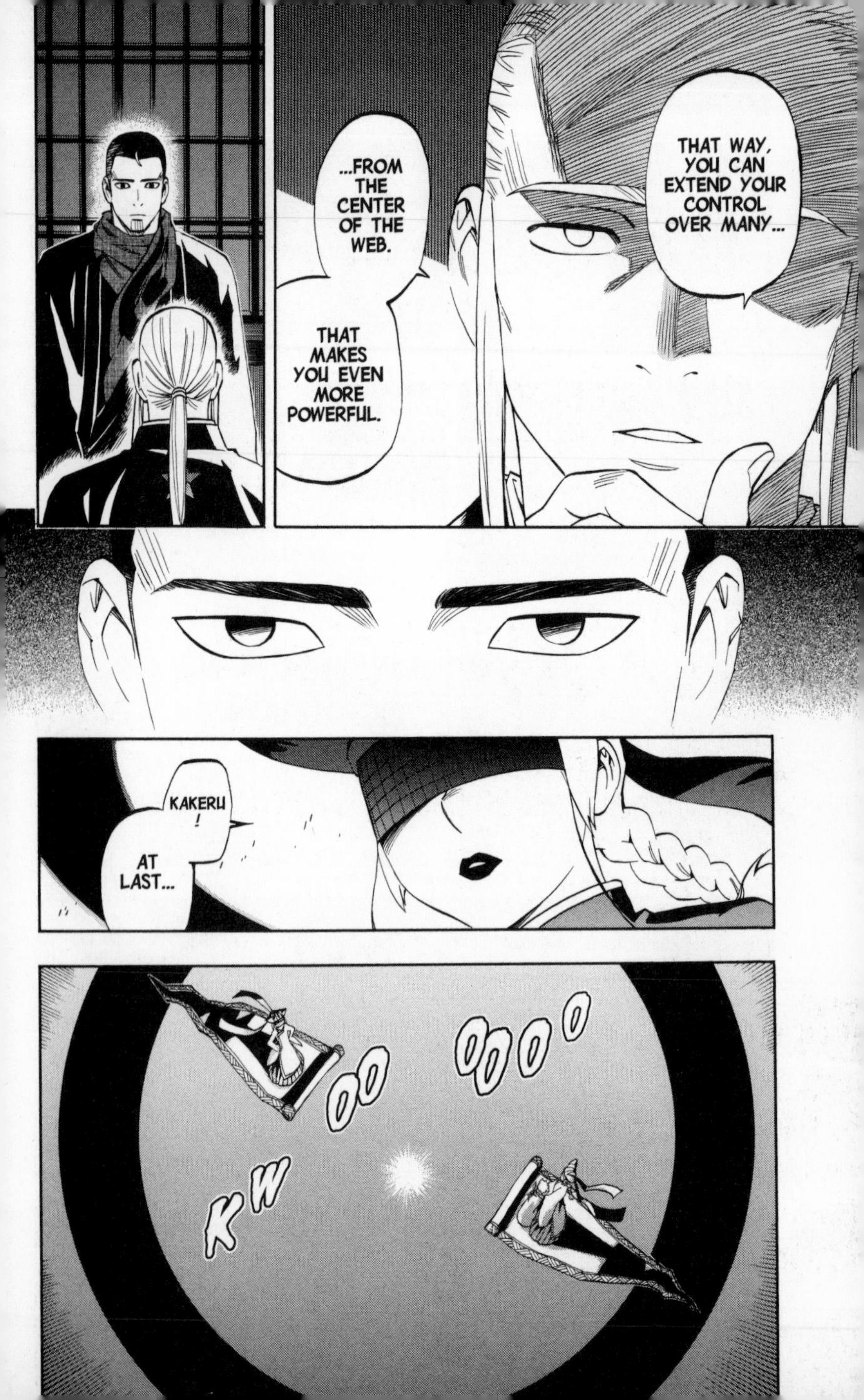
THAT WAY, YOU CAN EXTEND YOUR CONTROL OVER MANY...
...FROM THE CENTER OF THE WEB.
THAT MAKES YOU EVEN MORE POWERFUL.
KAKERU!
AT LAST...
KWOOOOOOOO

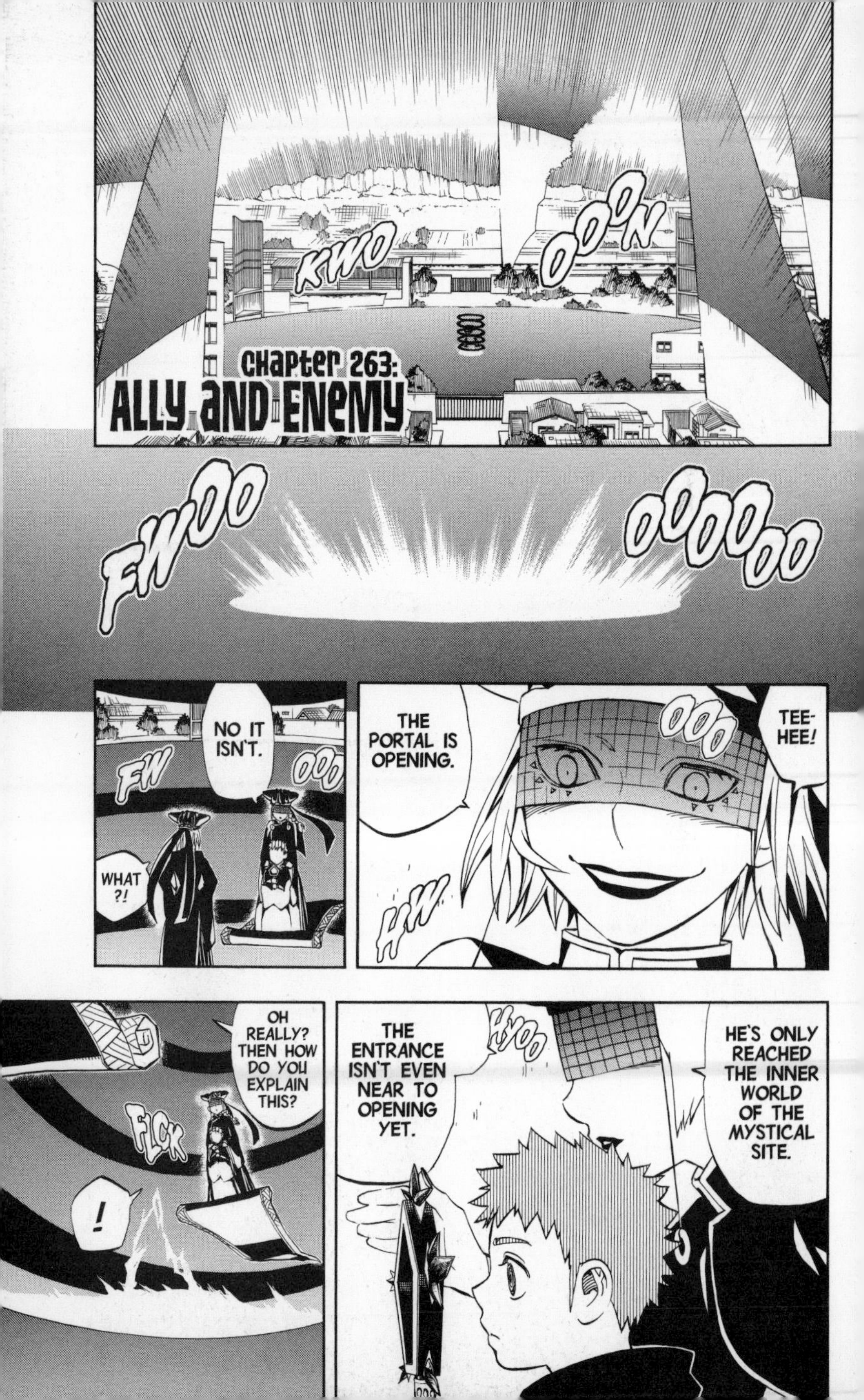
KWO
OOON
Chapter 263:
ALLY AND ENEMY
FWOO
OOOOOO
TEE-HEE!
OOO
THE PORTAL IS OPENING.
HW
NO IT ISN'T.
OOO
FW
WHAT?!
HE'S ONLY REACHED THE INNER WORLD OF THE MYSTICAL SITE.
HYOO
THE ENTRANCE ISN'T EVEN NEAR TO OPENING YET.
OH REALLY? THEN HOW DO YOU EXPLAIN THIS?
FLCK
!

FWOO

OOO

CHAPTER 263:
ALLY AND ENEMY

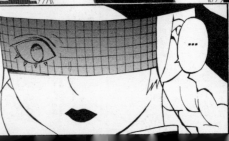

THAT'S
THE...

...

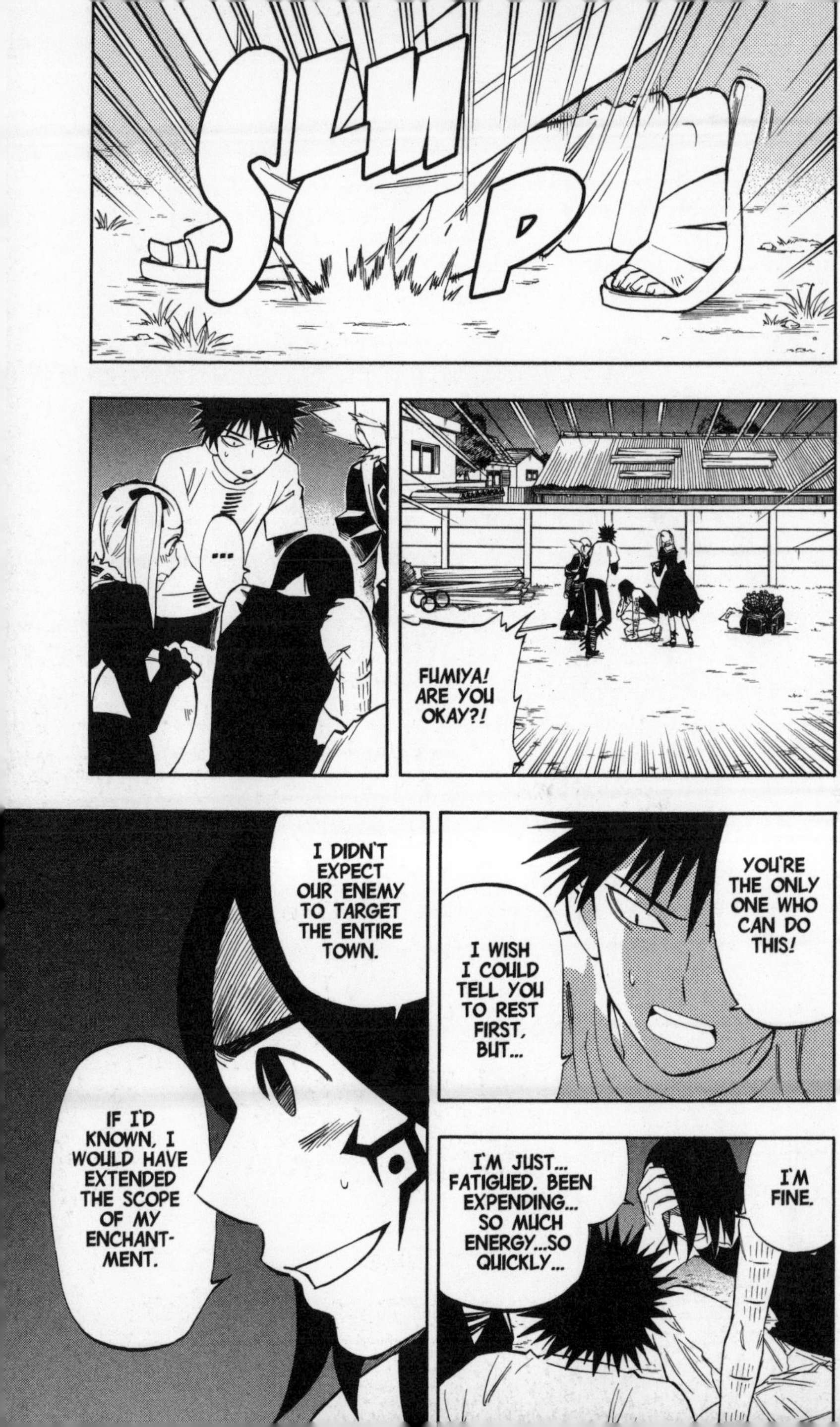
SLMP
FUMIYA! ARE YOU OKAY?!
...
YOU'RE THE ONLY ONE WHO CAN DO THIS!
I WISH I COULD TELL YOU TO REST FIRST, BUT...
I'M FINE.
I'M JUST... FATIGUED. BEEN EXPENDING... SO MUCH ENERGY...SO QUICKLY...
I DIDN'T EXPECT OUR ENEMY TO TARGET THE ENTIRE TOWN.
IF I'D KNOWN, I WOULD HAVE EXTENDED THE SCOPE OF MY ENCHANT-MENT.

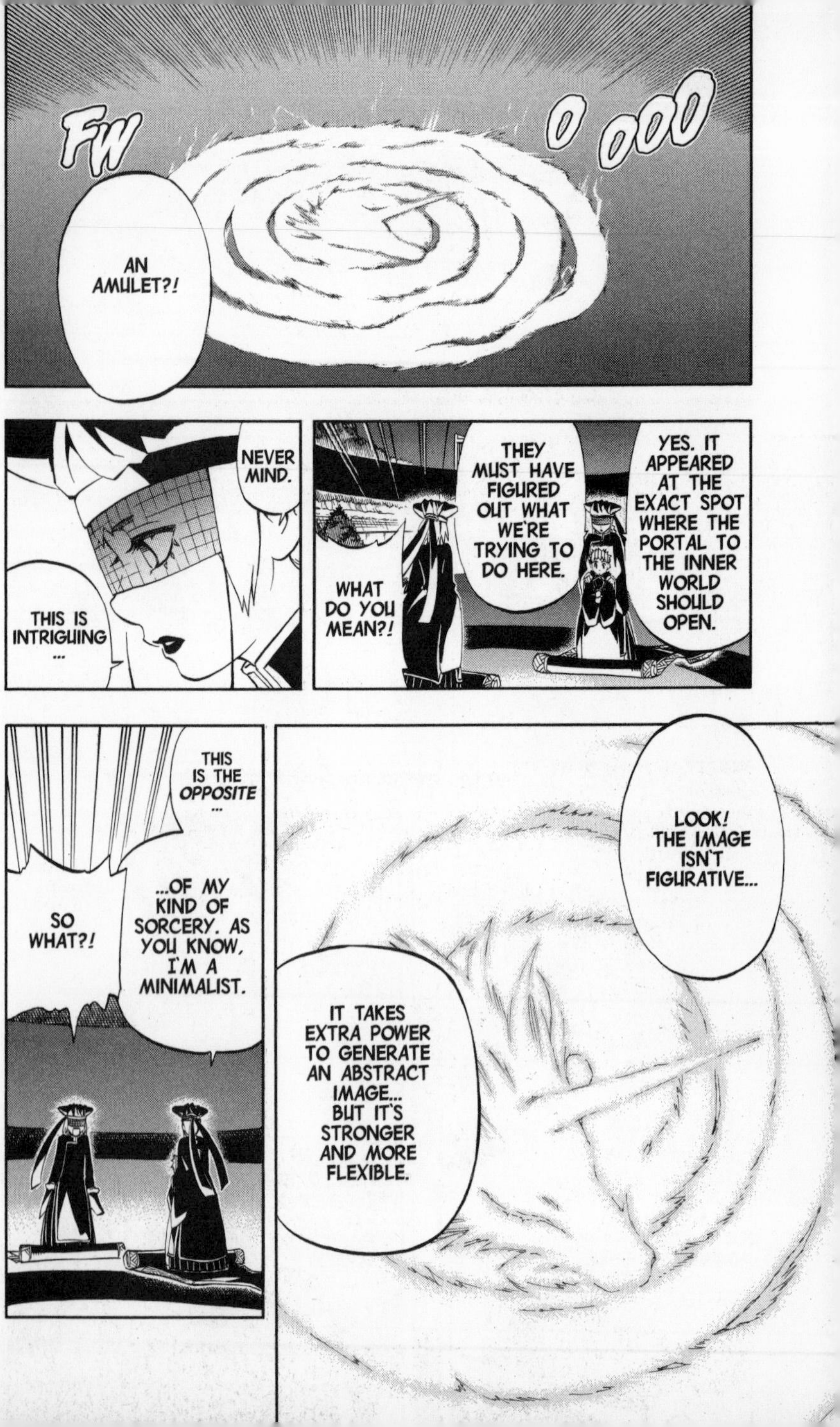

FW
O OOO
AN AMULET?!
YES. IT APPEARED AT THE EXACT SPOT WHERE THE PORTAL TO THE INNER WORLD SHOULD OPEN.
THEY MUST HAVE FIGURED OUT WHAT WE'RE TRYING TO DO HERE.
WHAT DO YOU MEAN?!
NEVER MIND.
THIS IS INTRIGUING ...
LOOK! THE IMAGE ISN'T FIGURATIVE...
IT TAKES EXTRA POWER TO GENERATE AN ABSTRACT IMAGE... BUT IT'S STRONGER AND MORE FLEXIBLE.
THIS IS THE *OPPOSITE* ...
...OF MY KIND OF SORCERY. AS YOU KNOW, I'M A MINIMALIST.
SO WHAT?!

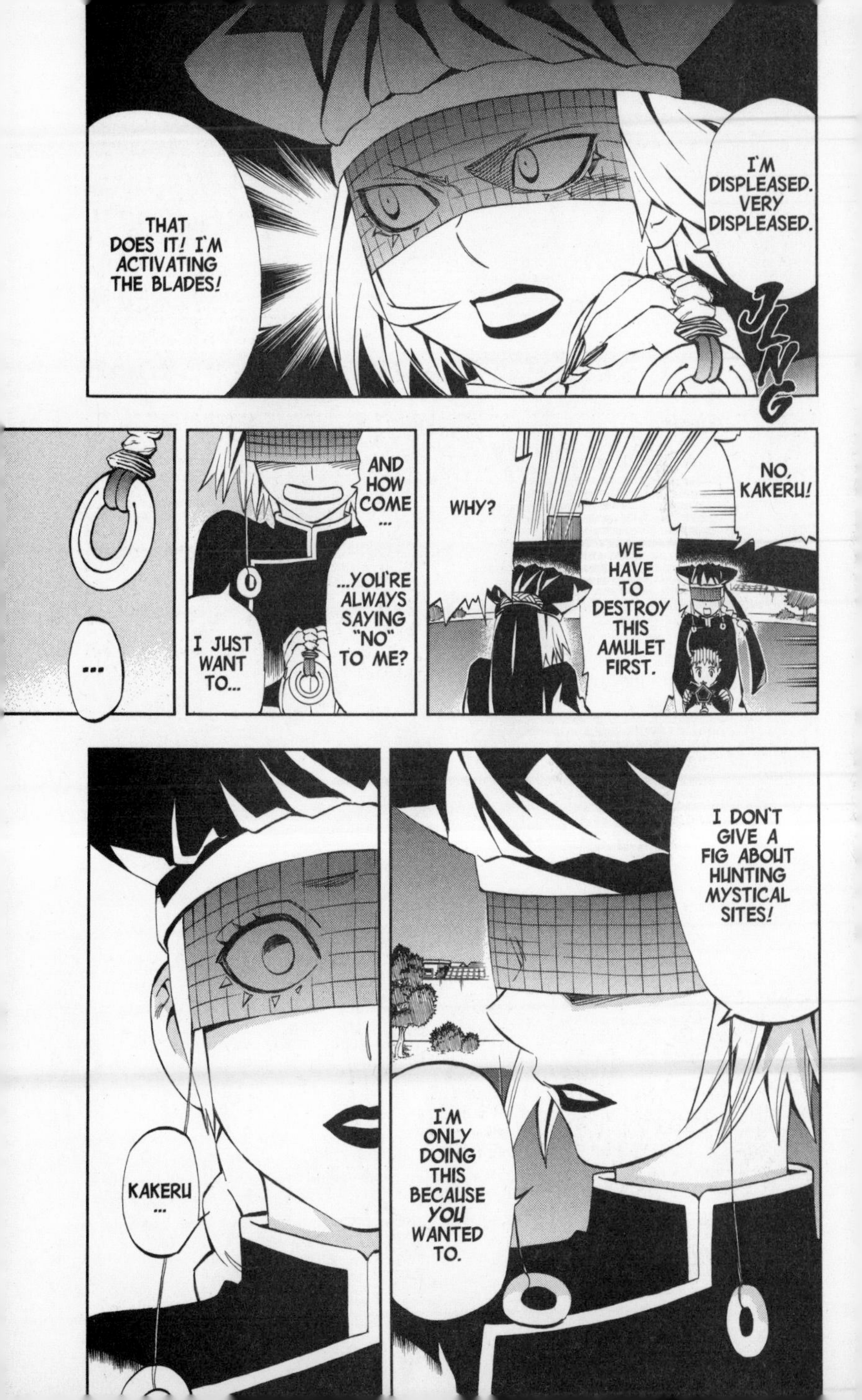
I'M DISPLEASED. VERY DISPLEASED.
JING
THAT DOES IT! I'M ACTIVATING THE BLADES!
NO, KAKERU!
WHY?
WE HAVE TO DESTROY THIS AMULET FIRST.
AND HOW COME ...
...YOU'RE ALWAYS SAYING "NO" TO ME?
I JUST WANT TO...
...
I DON'T GIVE A FIG ABOUT HUNTING MYSTICAL SITES!
I'M ONLY DOING THIS BECAUSE *YOU* WANTED TO.
KAKERU ...

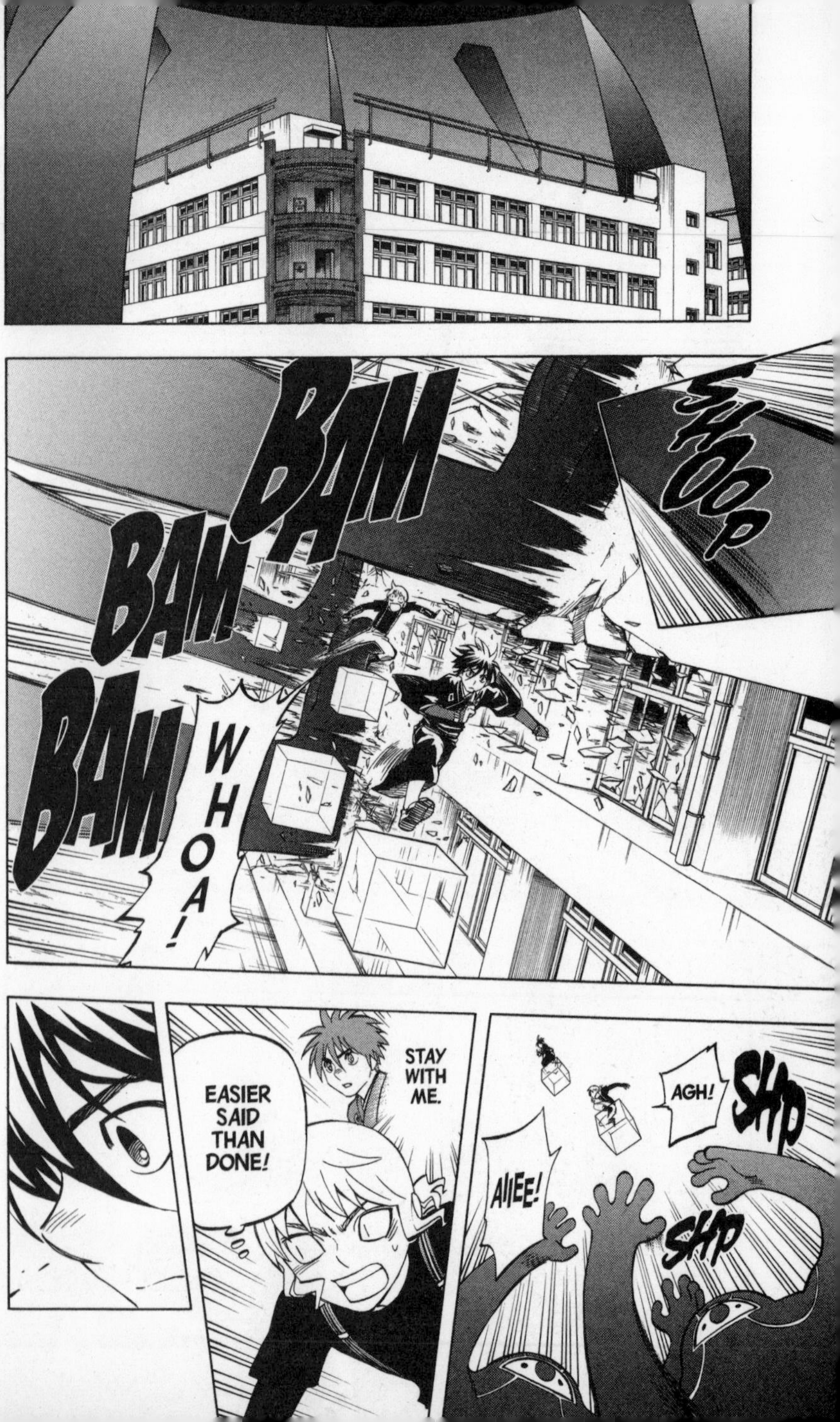
SHOOP
BAM
BAM
BAM
WHOA!
SHP
AGH!
AIIEE!
SHP
STAY WITH ME.
EASIER SAID THAN DONE!

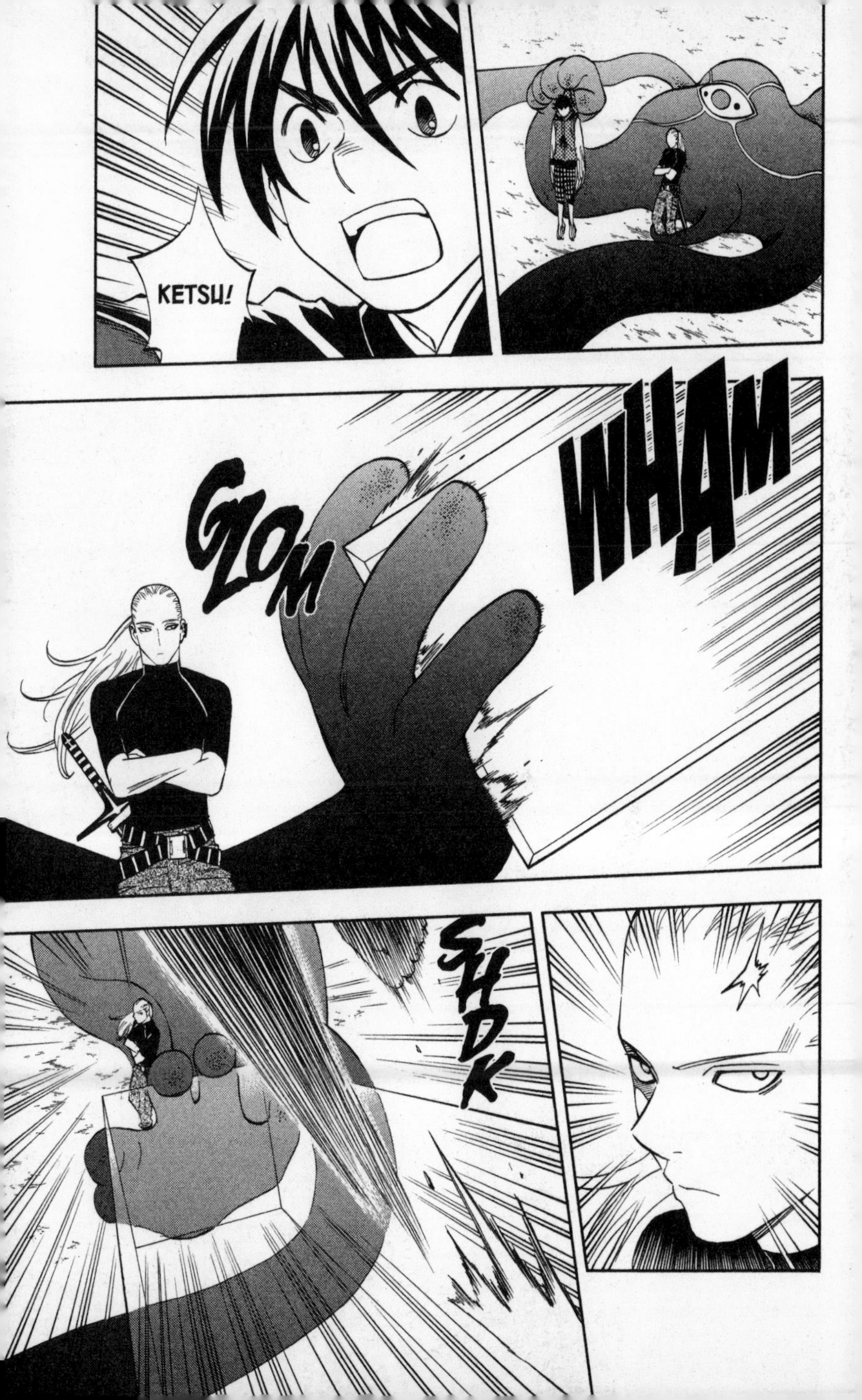
KETSU!
WHAM
GZOM
SHDK

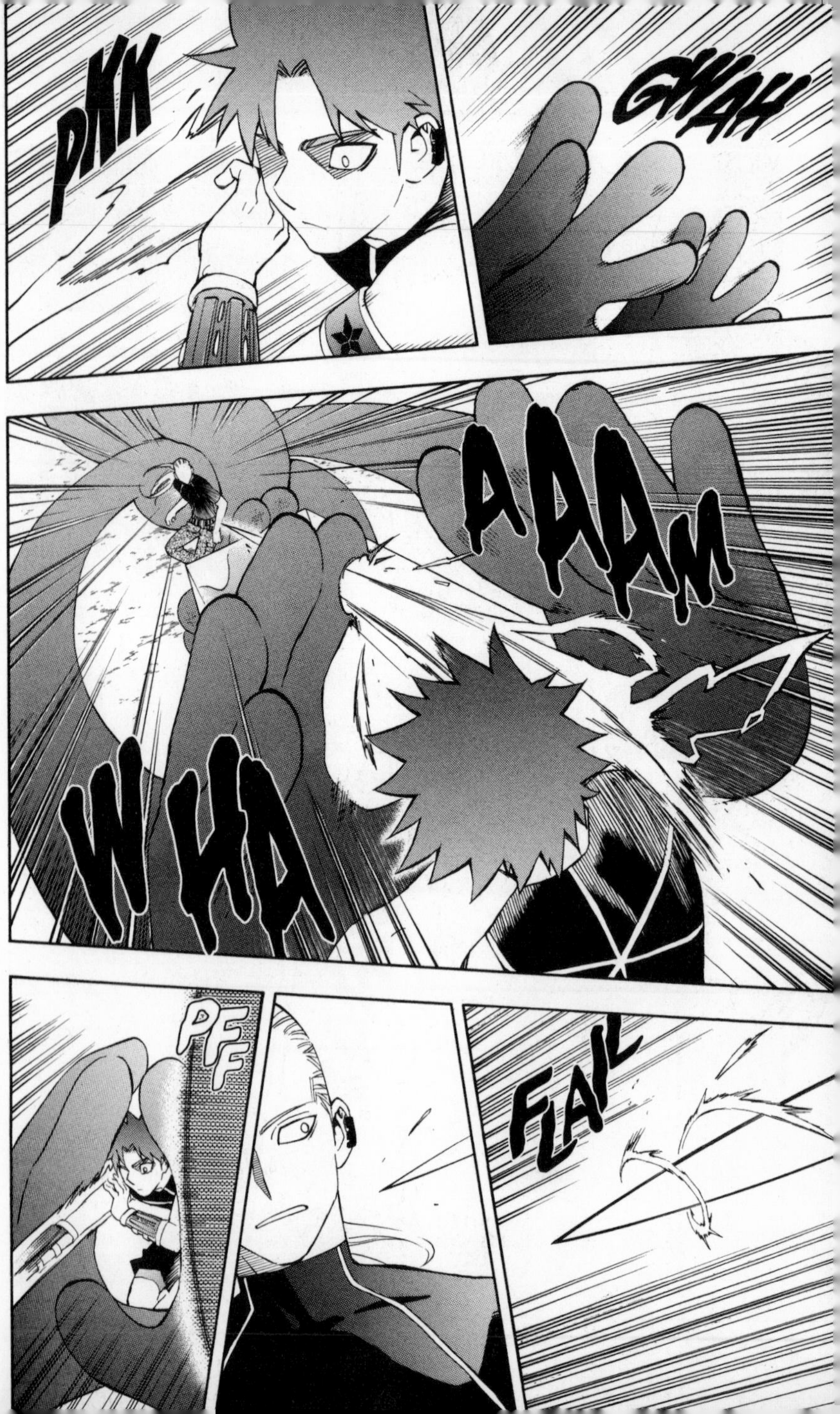
GWAH
PKK
AAAM
WHA
FLAIL
PFF

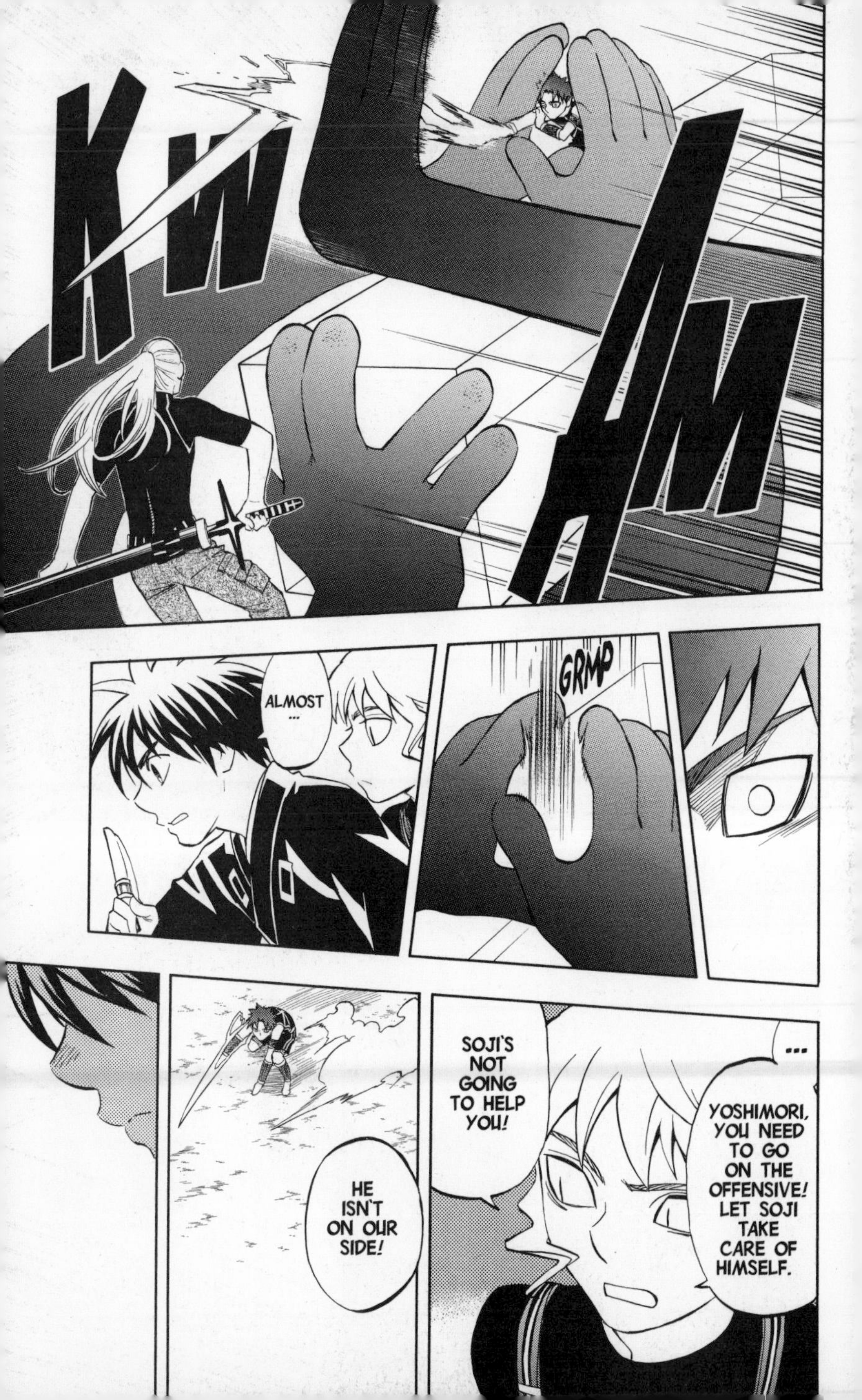
KWAM
GRMP
ALMOST ...
...
YOSHIMORI, YOU NEED TO GO ON THE OFFENSIVE! LET SOJI TAKE CARE OF HIMSELF.
SOJI'S NOT GOING TO HELP YOU!
HE ISN'T ON OUR SIDE!

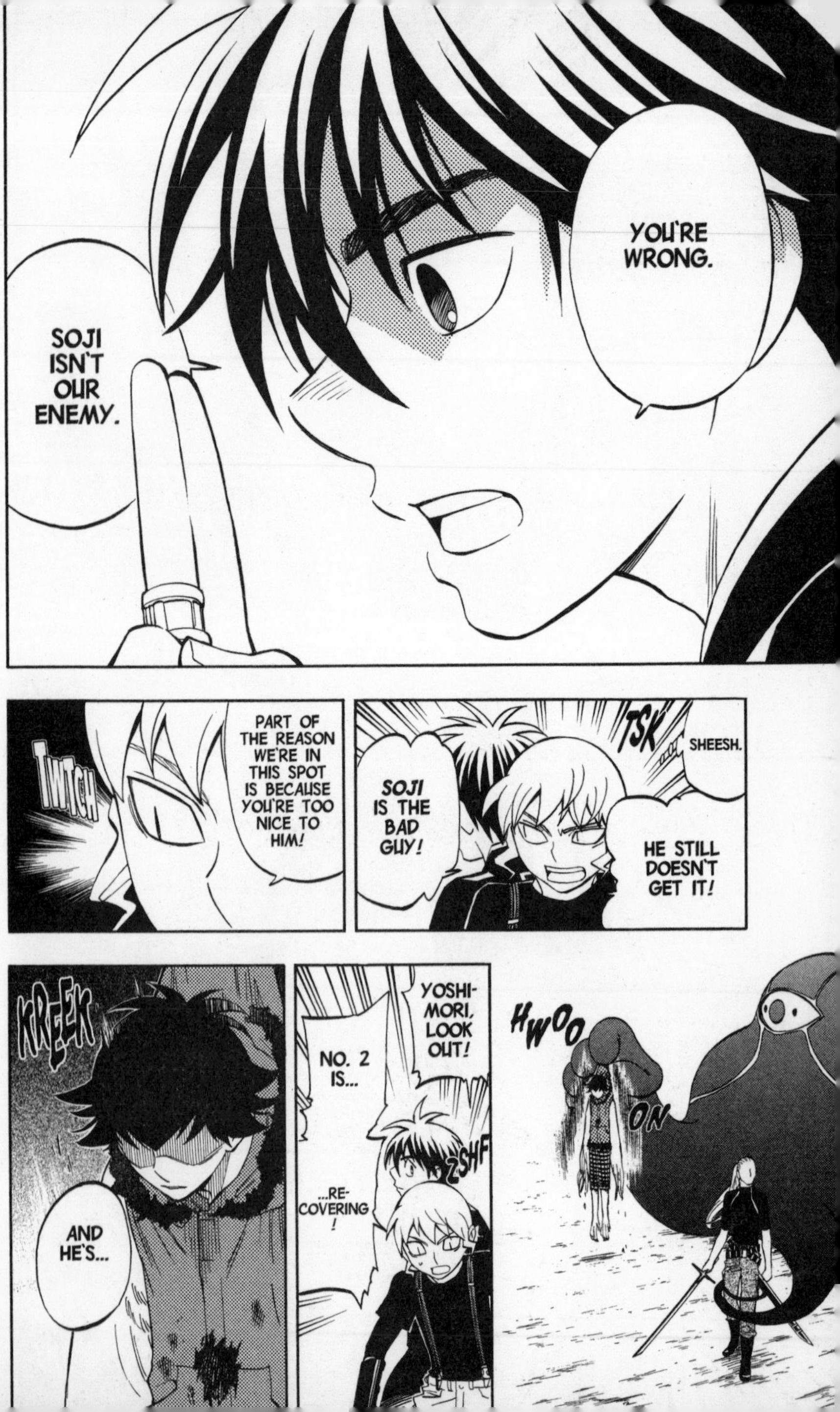
YOU'RE WRONG.
SOJI ISN'T OUR ENEMY.
TSK
SHEESH.
SOJI IS THE BAD GUY!
HE STILL DOESN'T GET IT!
TWITCH
PART OF THE REASON WE'RE IN THIS SPOT IS BECAUSE YOU'RE TOO NICE TO HIM!
HWOO
ON
YOSHIMORI, LOOK OUT!
NO. 2 IS...
ZSHF
...RECOVERING!
KREEK
AND HE'S...

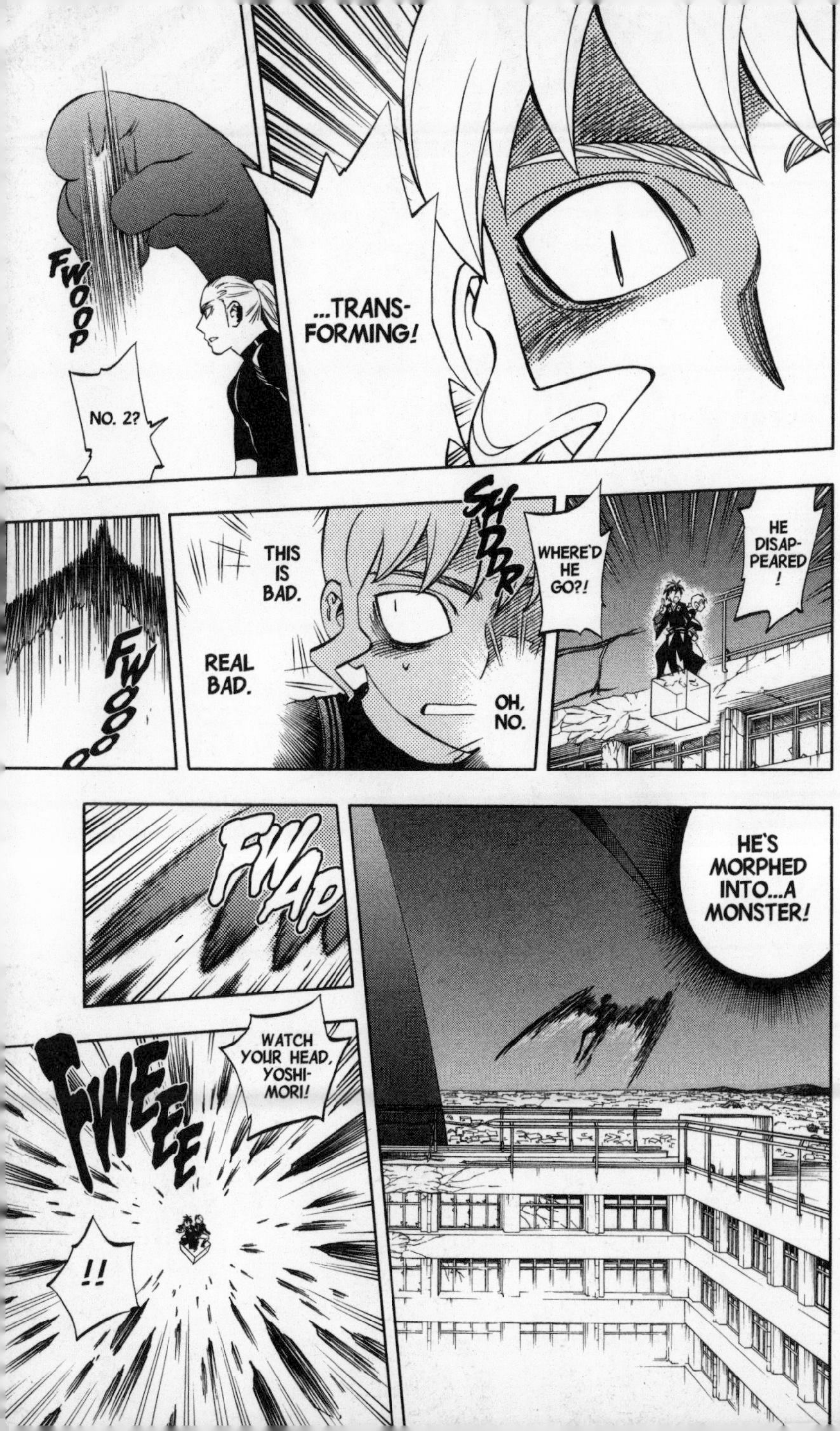
...TRANS-FORMING!
FWOOOP
NO. 2?
HE DISAP-PEARED!
WHERE'D HE GO?!
SHDDR
THIS IS BAD.
REAL BAD.
OH, NO.
FWOOOO
HE'S MORPHED INTO...A MONSTER!
FWAP
WATCH YOUR HEAD, YOSHI-MORI!
FWEEE
!!

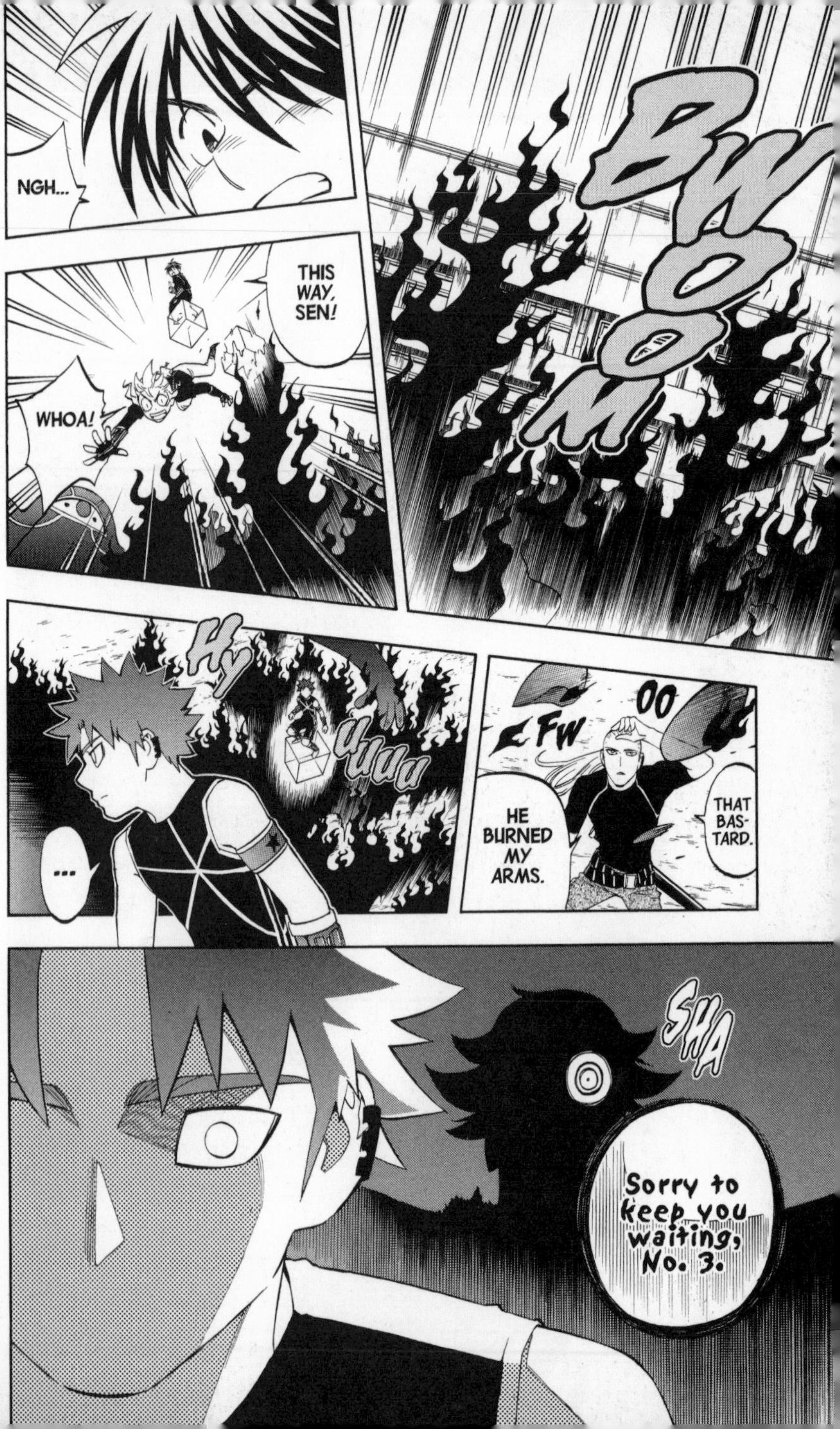
BWOOM
NGH...
THIS WAY, SEN!
WHOA!
FWOO
THAT BASTARD.
HE BURNED MY ARMS.
Hyuuuu
...
SHA
Sorry to keep you waiting, No. 3.

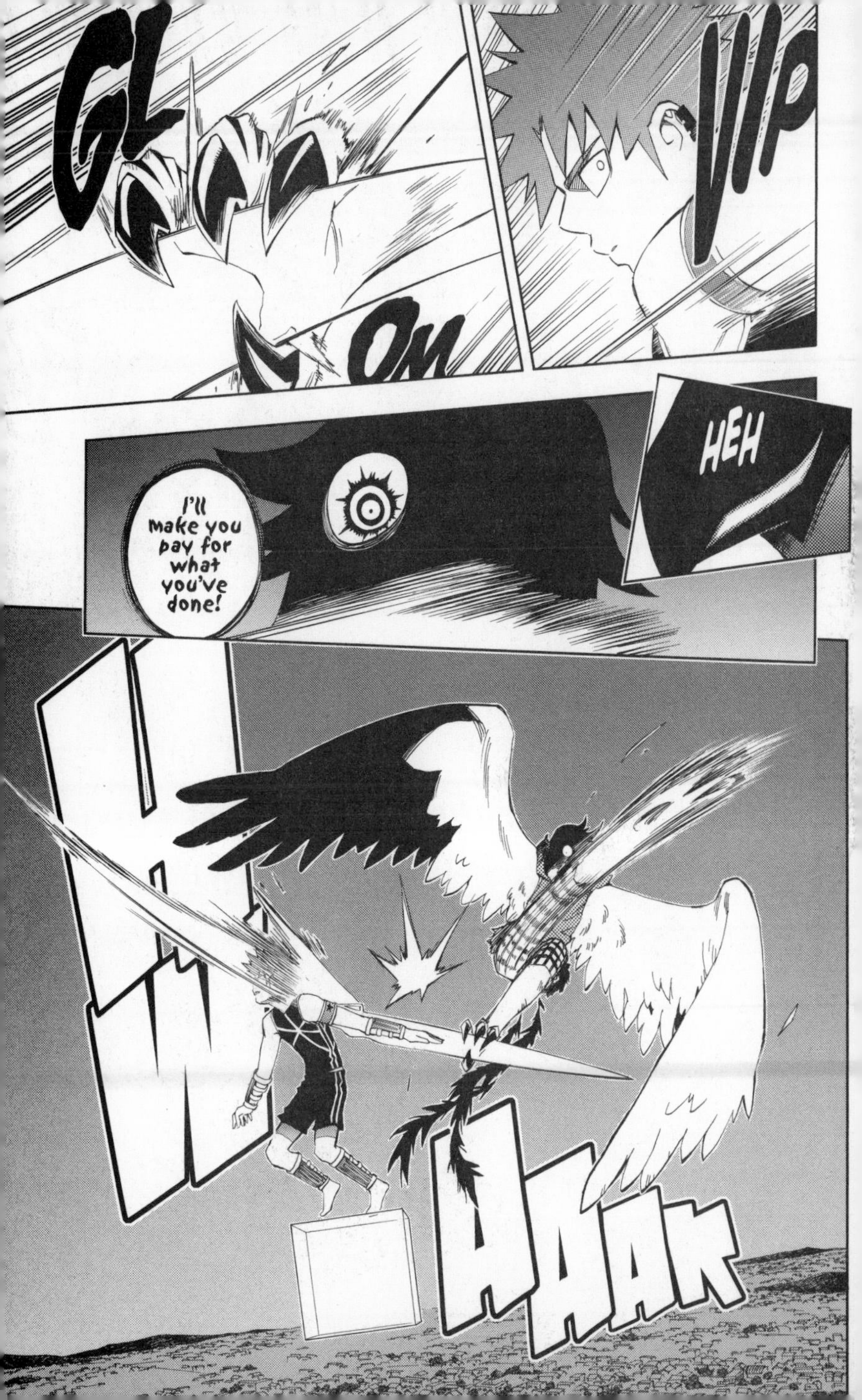
VIP
GL
OM
HEH
I'll make you pay for what you've done!
HAAK

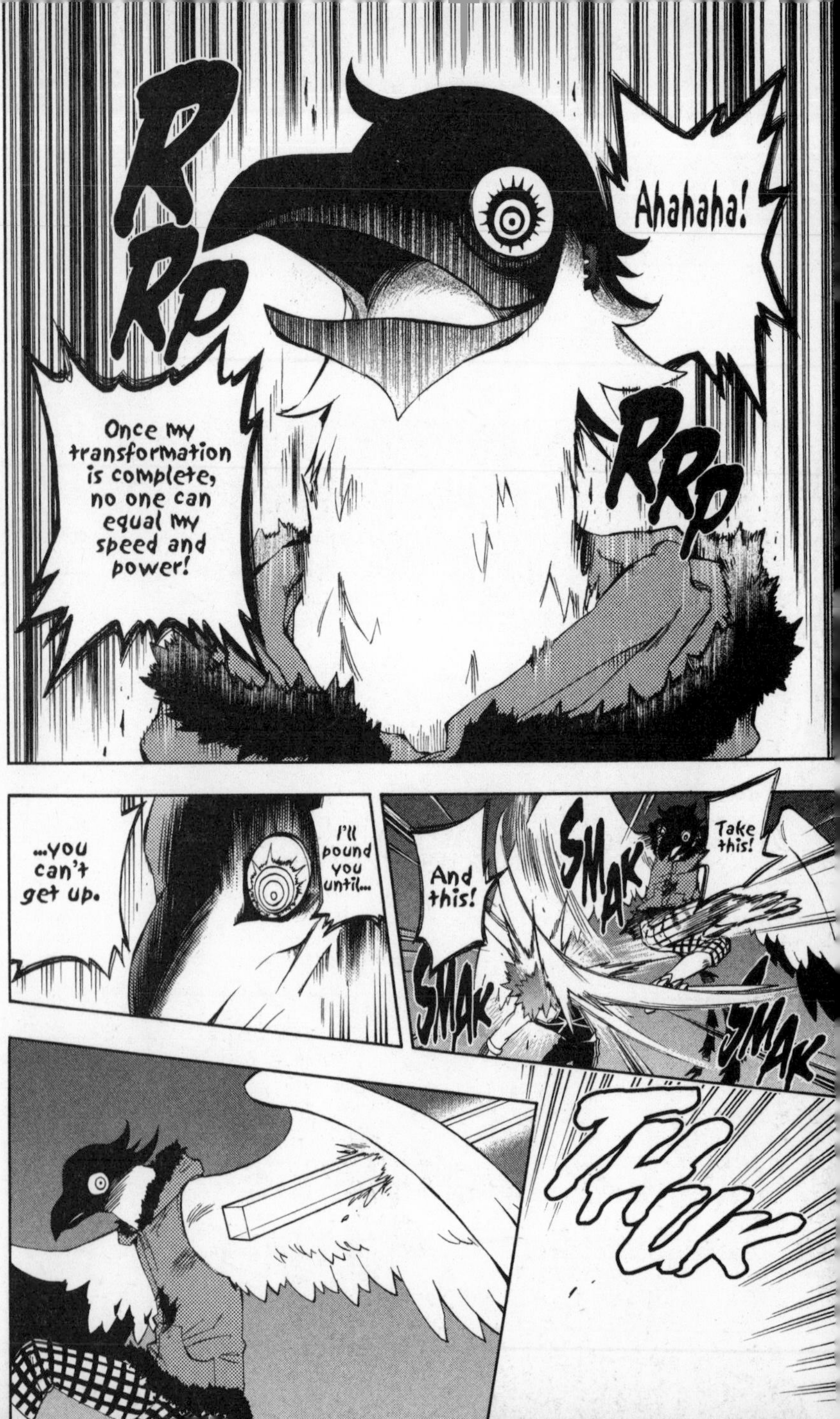
Ahahaha!
RRP
Once my transformation is complete, no one can equal my speed and power!
RRP
Take this!
SMAK
And this!
SMAK
SMAK
I'll pound you until...
...you can't get up.
THUK

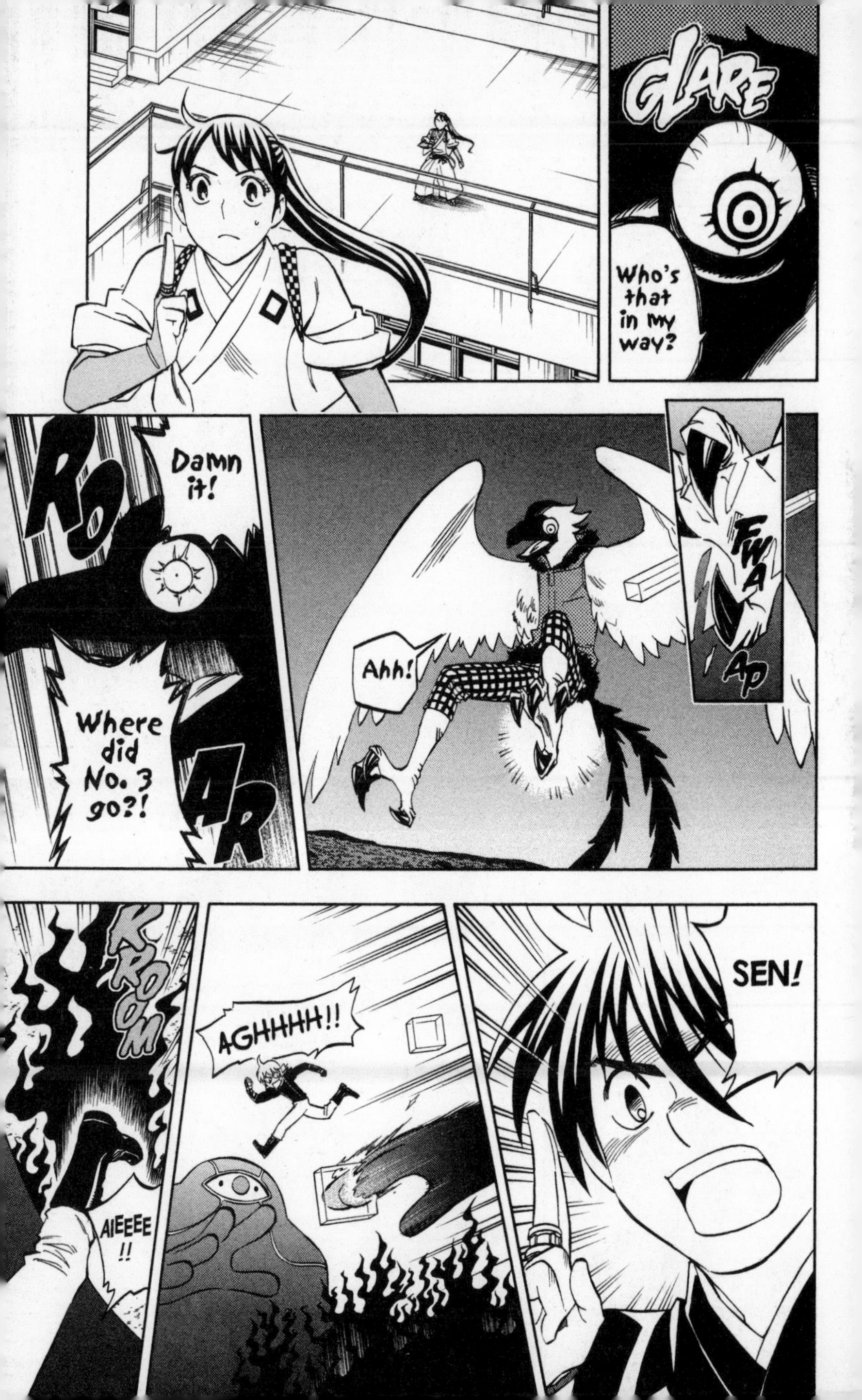
GLARE
Who's that in my way?
FWAAP
Ahh!
ROAR
Damn it!
Where did No. 3 go?!
SEN!
AGHHHH!!
KROOM
AIEEEE!!

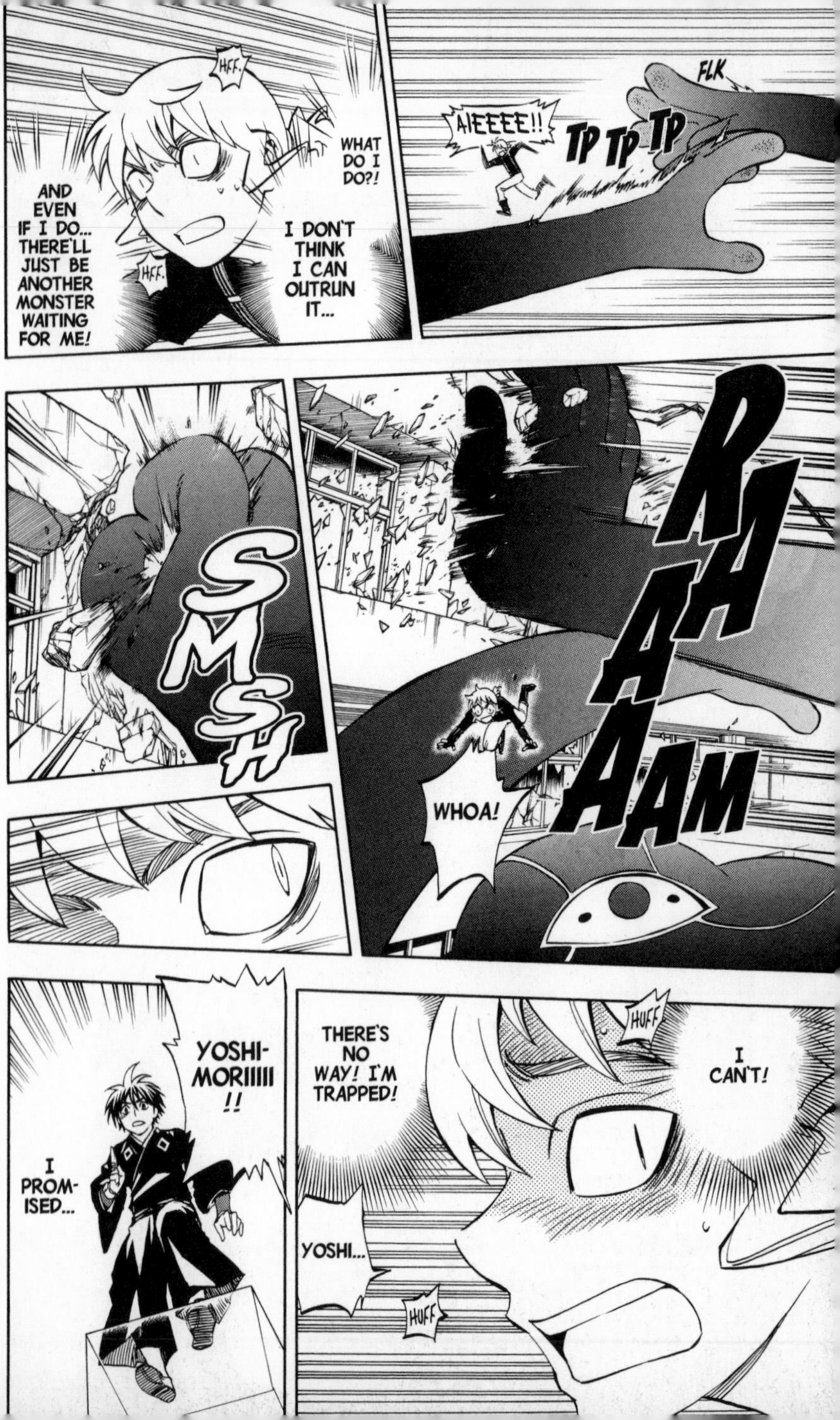
FLK
TP TP TP
AIEEEE!!
HFF.
WHAT DO I DO?!
I DON'T THINK I CAN OUTRUN IT...
AND EVEN IF I DO... THERE'LL JUST BE ANOTHER MONSTER WAITING FOR ME!
HFF.
RAAAAM
WHOA!
SMSH
HUFF
I CAN'T!
THERE'S NO WAY! I'M TRAPPED!
YOSHI...
HUFF
YOSHI-MORIIIIII!!
I PROM-ISED...

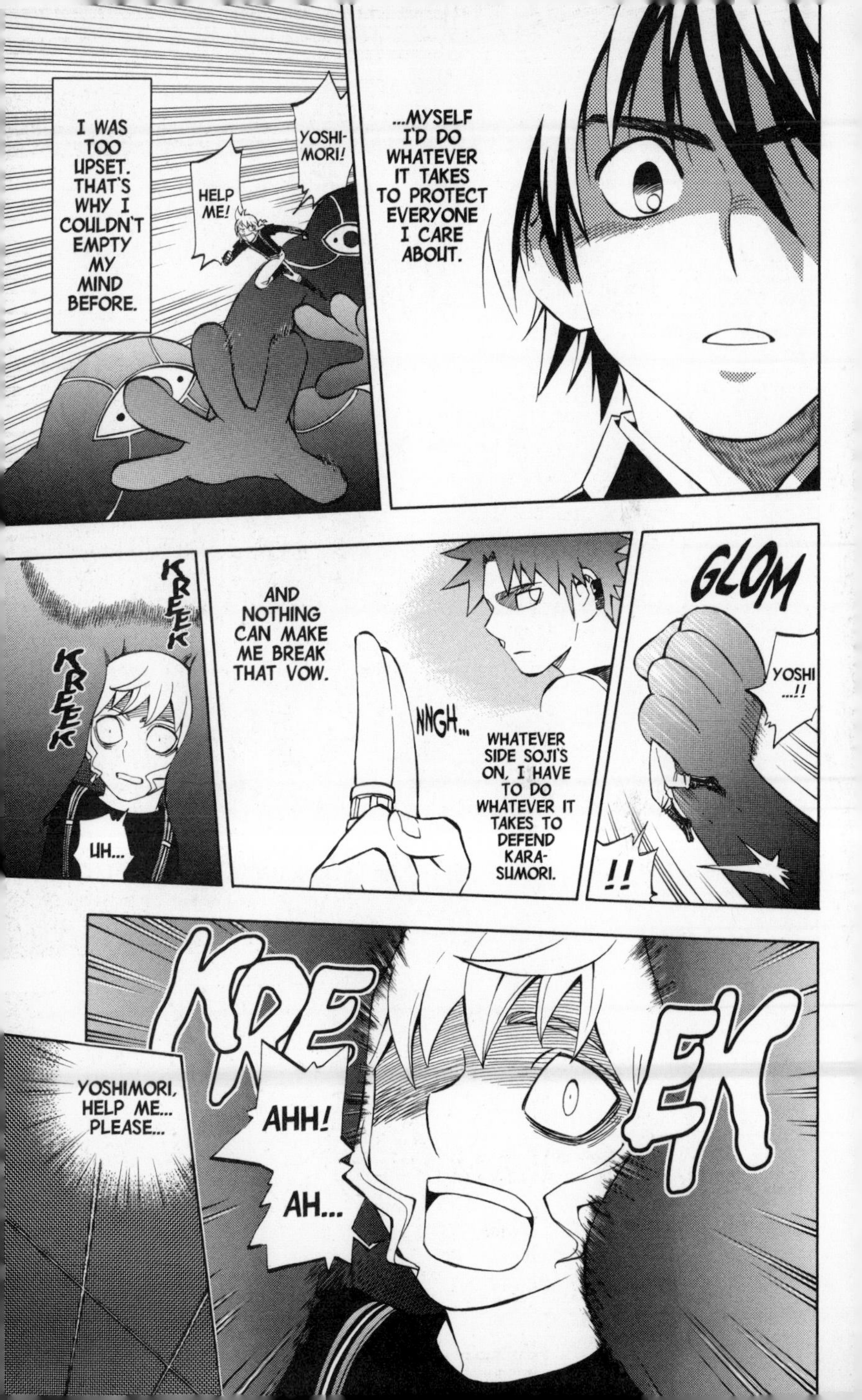
...MYSELF I'D DO WHATEVER IT TAKES TO PROTECT EVERYONE I CARE ABOUT.
YOSHI-MORI!
HELP ME!
I WAS TOO UPSET. THAT'S WHY I COULDN'T EMPTY MY MIND BEFORE.
GLOM
YOSHI ...!!
!!
AND NOTHING CAN MAKE ME BREAK THAT VOW.
NNGH...
WHATEVER SIDE SOJI'S ON, I HAVE TO DO WHATEVER IT TAKES TO DEFEND KARA-SUMORI.
KREEK
KREEK
UH...
KREEEK
AHH!
AH...
YOSHIMORI, HELP ME... PLEASE...

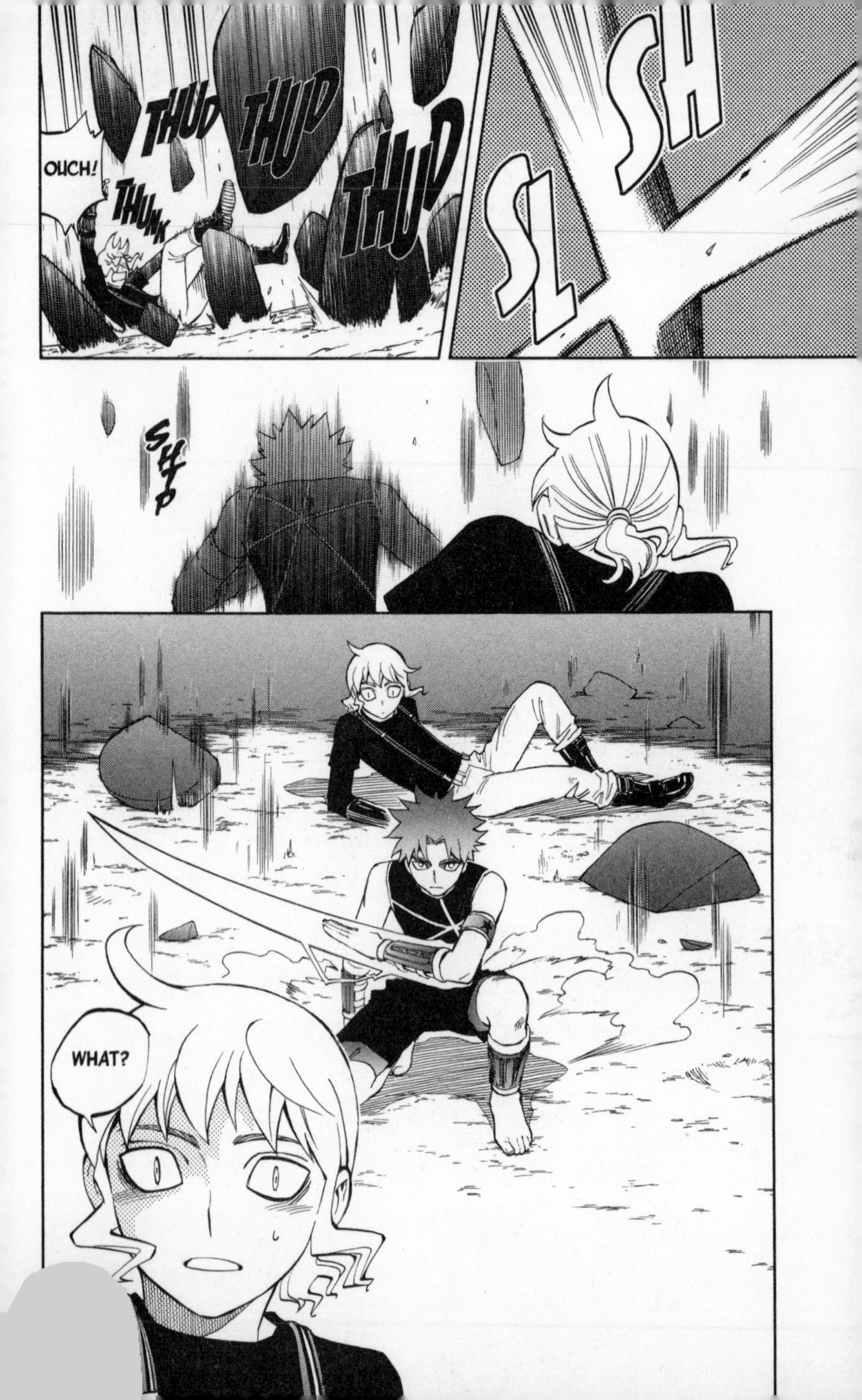
SLASH
THUD
THUD
THUD
THUNK
OUCH!
SHIP
WHAT?

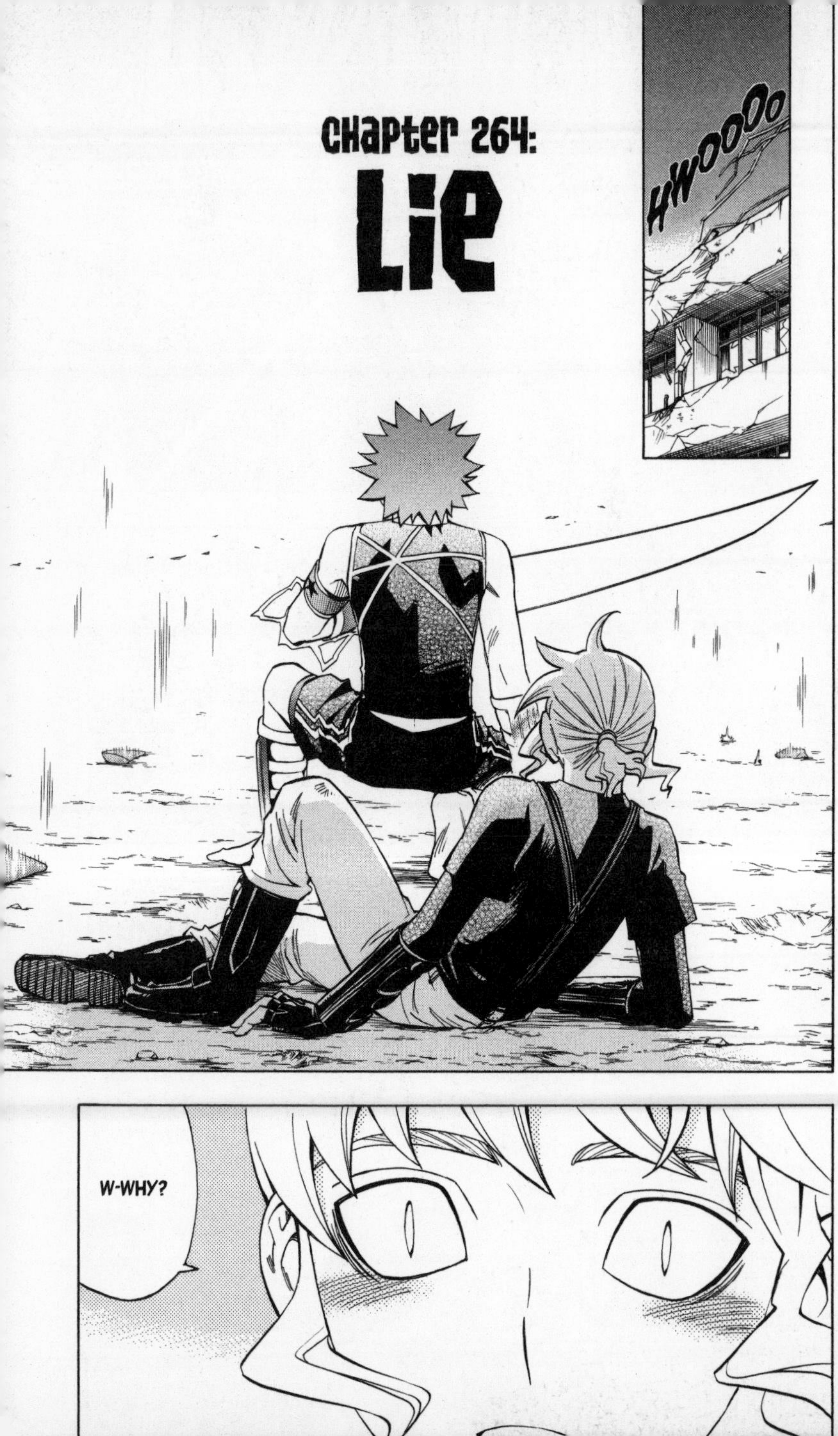
HWOOOO
Chapter 264:
Lie
W-WHY?

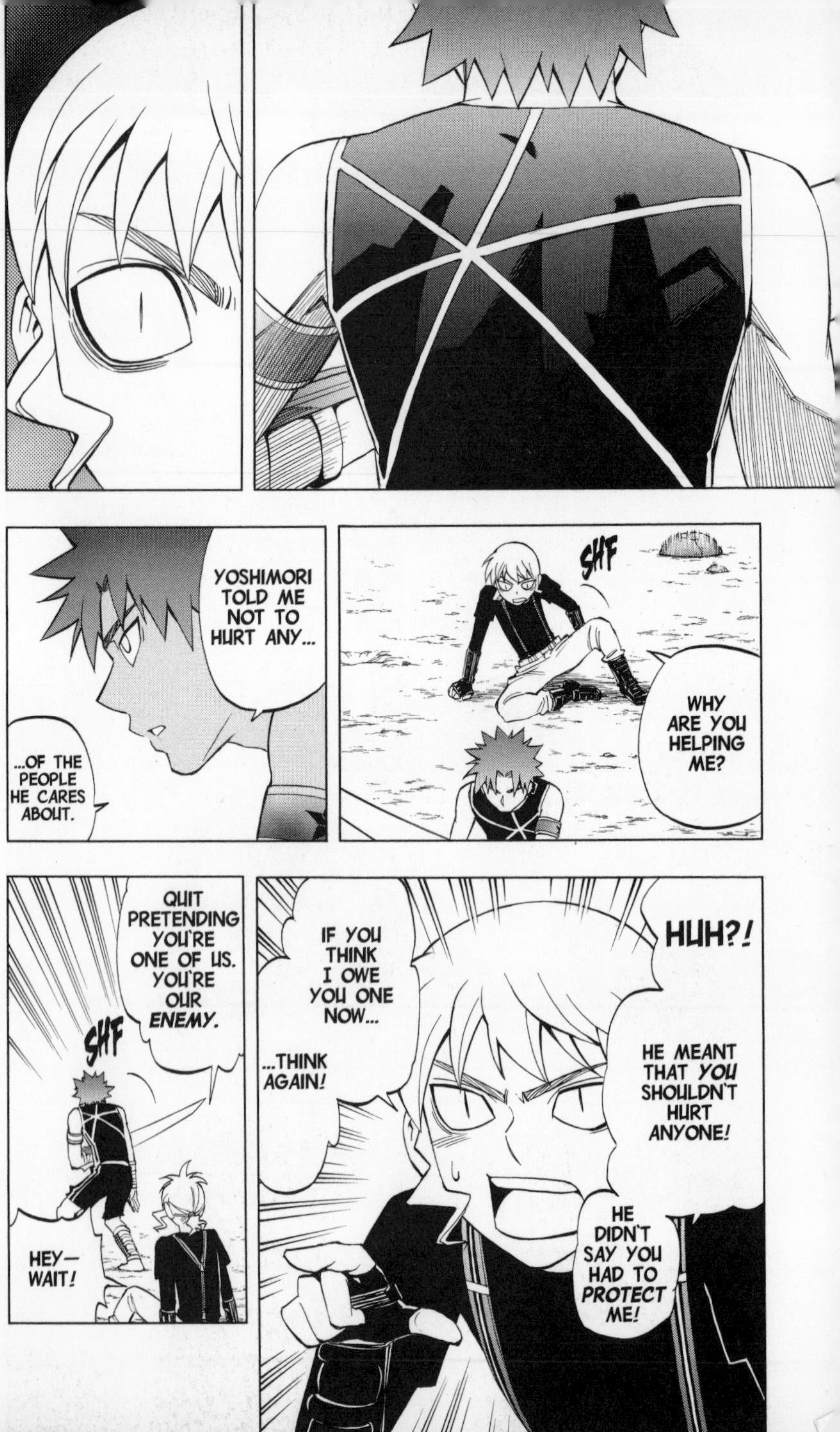
SHF
WHY ARE YOU HELPING ME?
YOSHIMORI TOLD ME NOT TO HURT ANY...
...OF THE PEOPLE HE CARES ABOUT.
HUH?!
HE MEANT THAT *YOU* SHOULDN'T HURT ANYONE!
HE DIDN'T SAY YOU HAD TO *PROTECT* ME!
IF YOU THINK I OWE YOU ONE NOW...
...THINK AGAIN!
QUIT PRETENDING YOU'RE ONE OF US. YOU'RE OUR *ENEMY*.
SHF
HEY— WAIT!

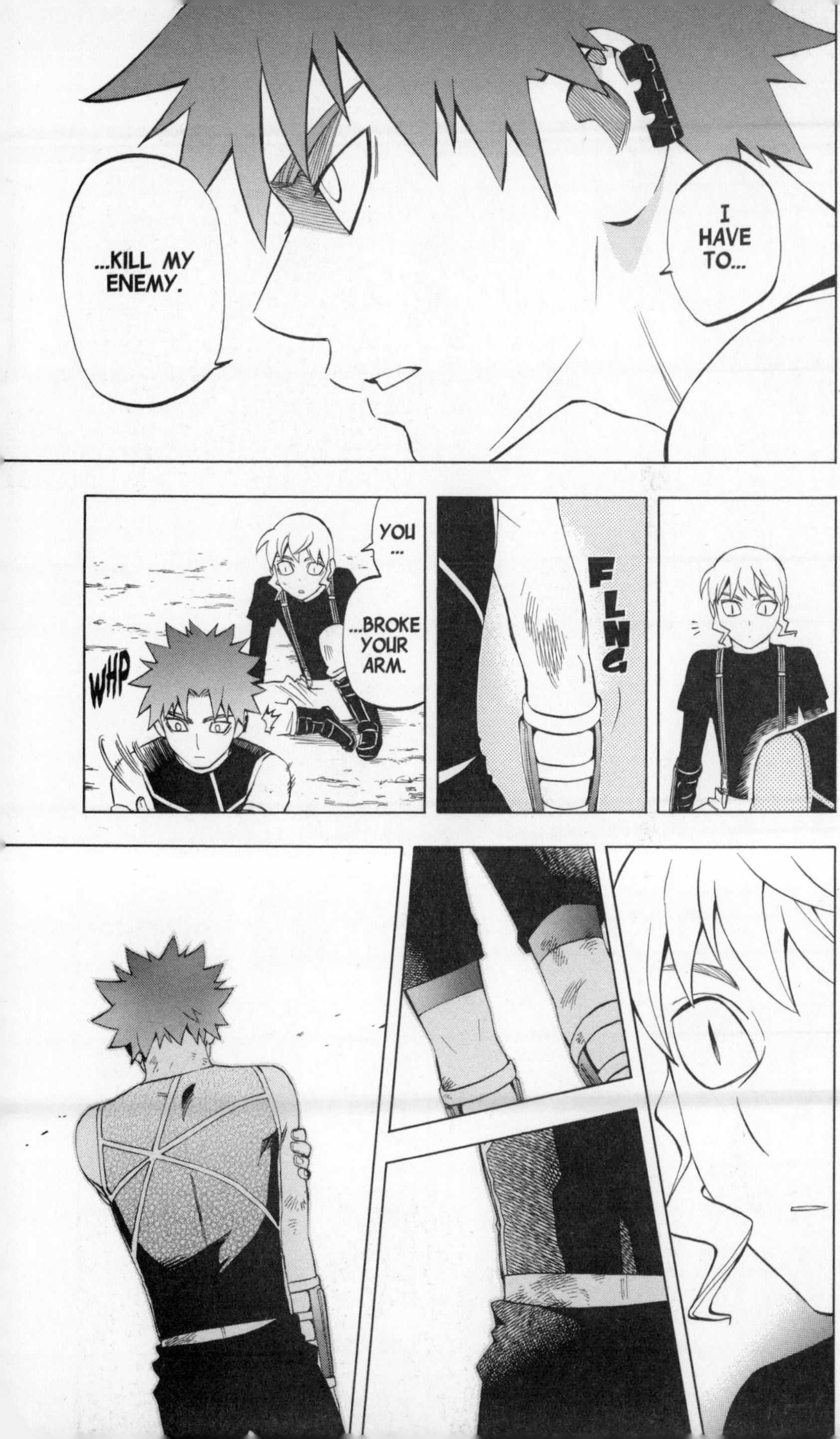
I HAVE TO...
...KILL MY ENEMY.
FLNG
YOU ...
...BROKE YOUR ARM.
WHP

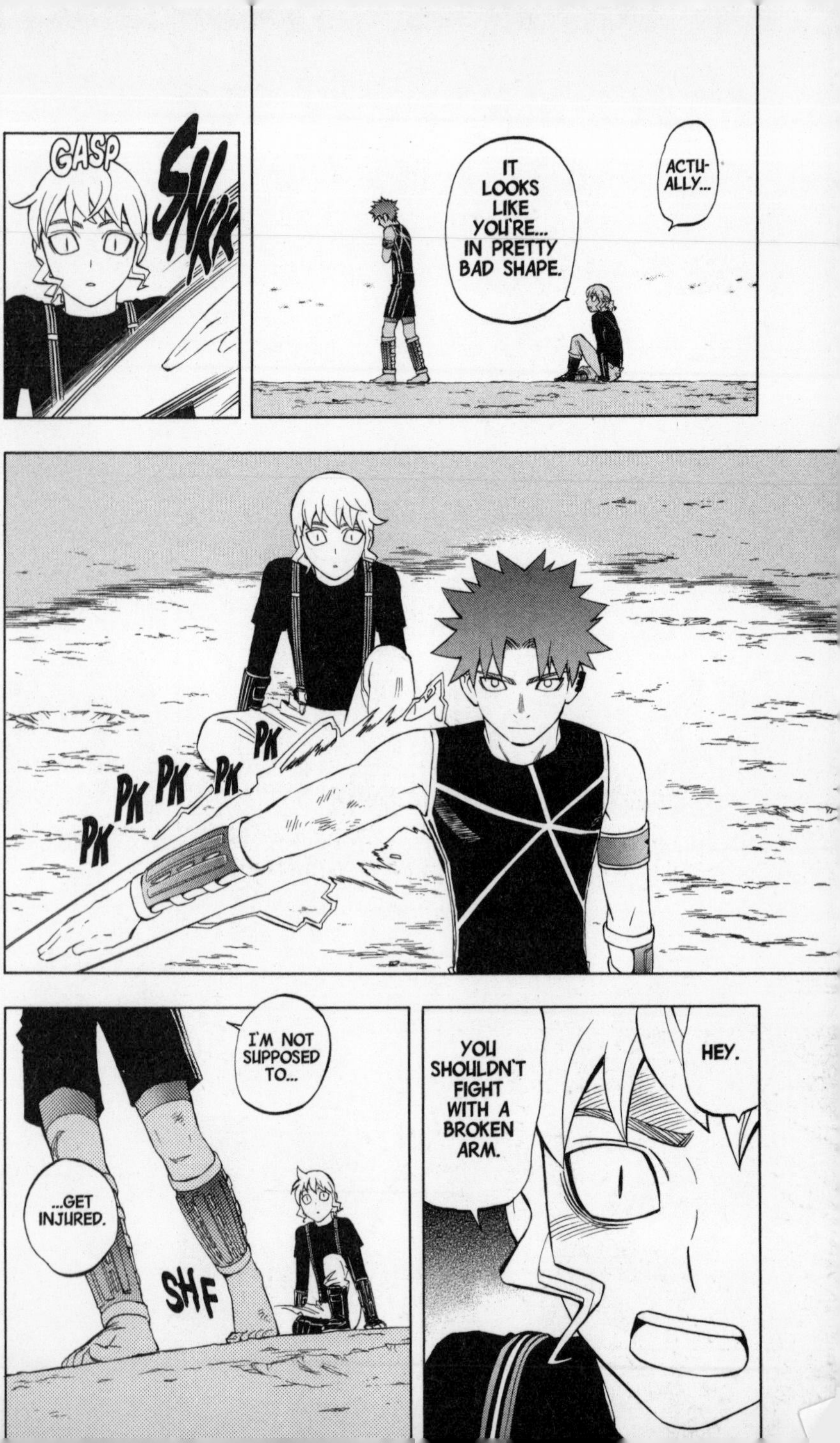
ACTU-ALLY...
IT LOOKS LIKE YOU'RE... IN PRETTY BAD SHAPE.
GASP
SNKK
PK
PK
PK
PK
PK
HEY.
YOU SHOULDN'T FIGHT WITH A BROKEN ARM.
I'M NOT SUPPOSED TO...
...GET INJURED.
SHF

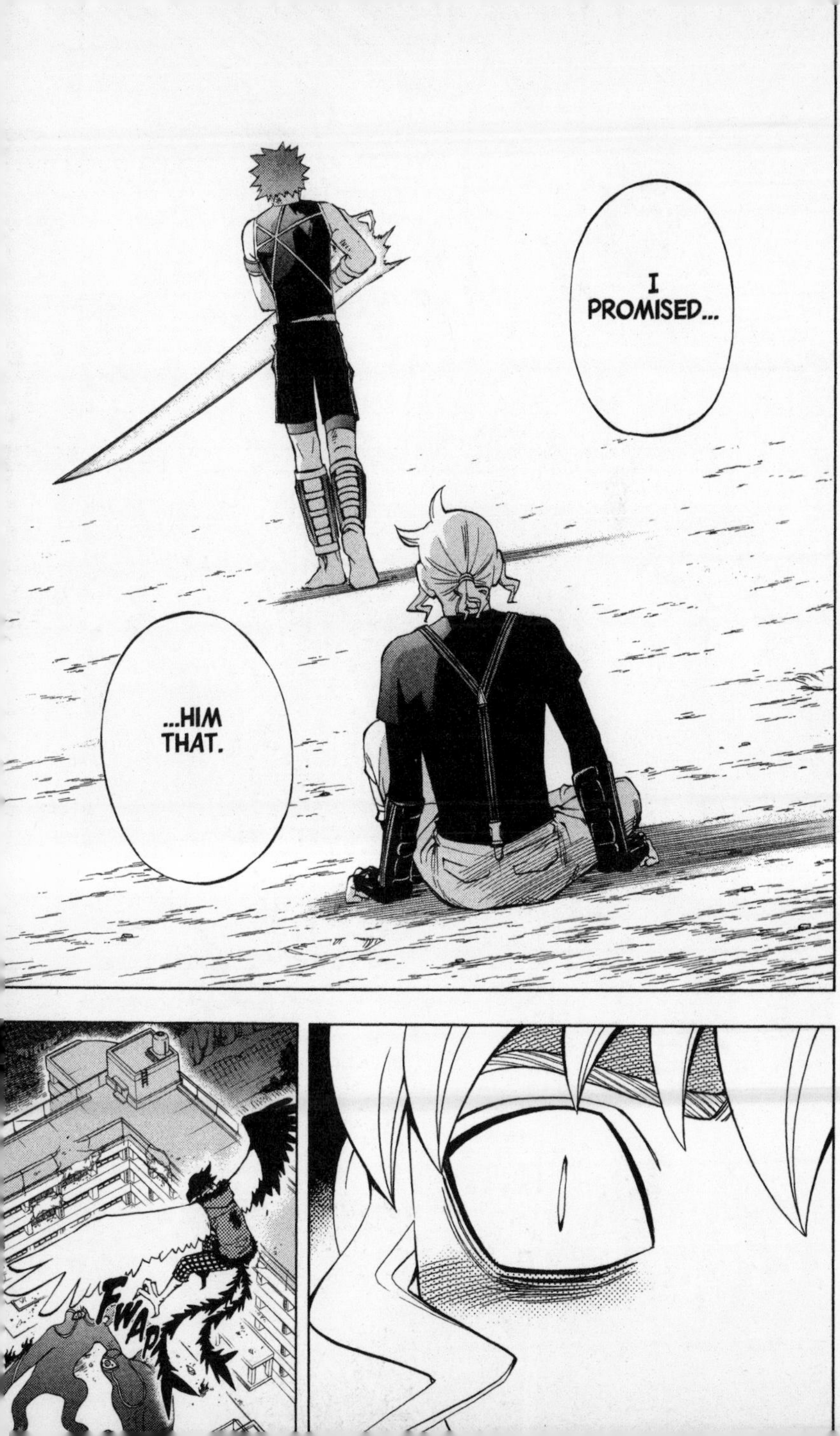
I PROMISED...
...HIM THAT.
FWAP

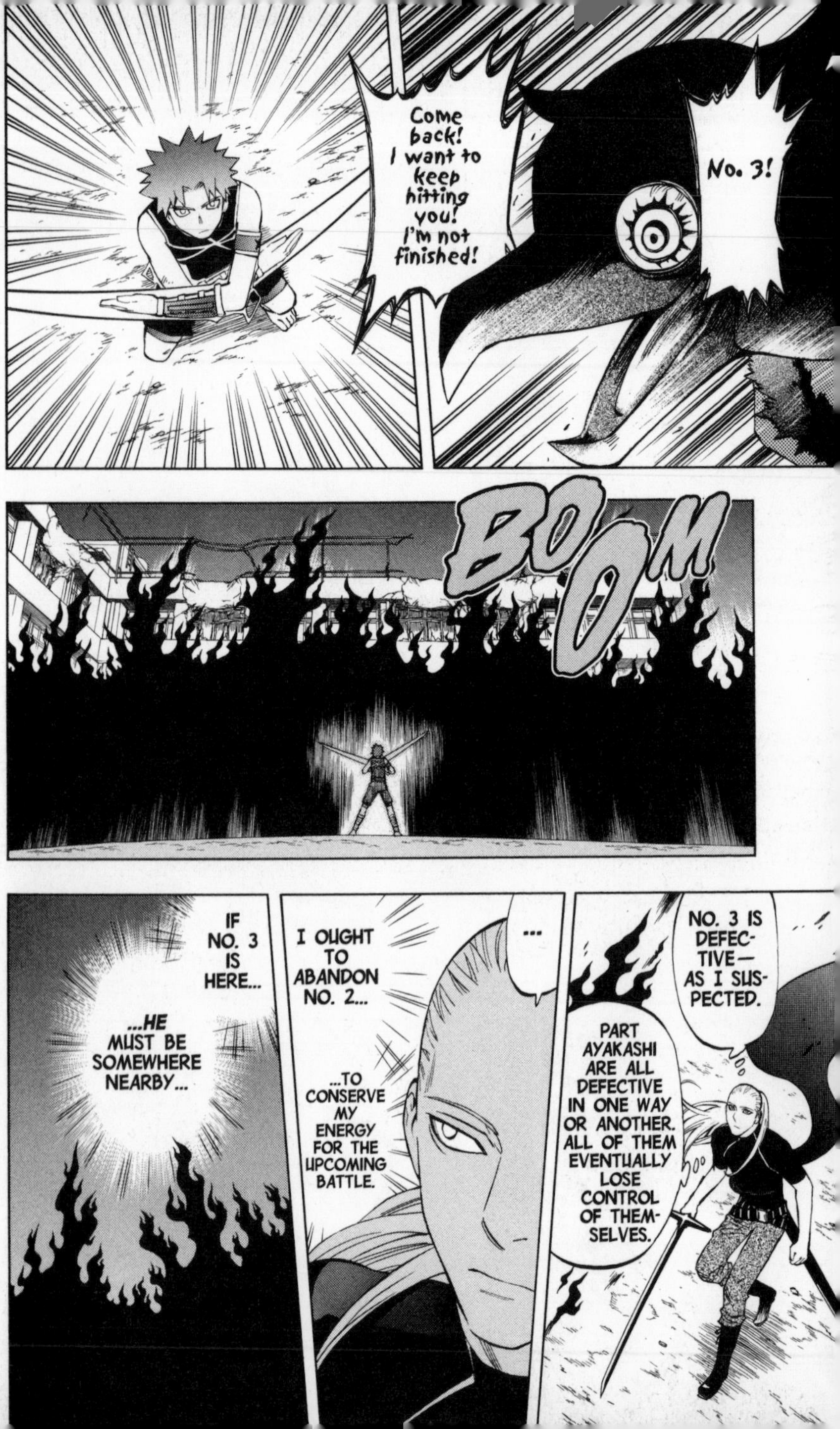
No. 3!
Come back! I want to keep hitting you! I'm not finished!
BOOM
NO. 3 IS DEFECTIVE—AS I SUSPECTED.
PART AYAKASHI ARE ALL DEFECTIVE IN ONE WAY OR ANOTHER. ALL OF THEM EVENTUALLY LOSE CONTROL OF THEMSELVES.
...
I OUGHT TO ABANDON NO. 2...
...TO CONSERVE MY ENERGY FOR THE UPCOMING BATTLE.
IF NO. 3 IS HERE...
...HE MUST BE SOMEWHERE NEARBY...

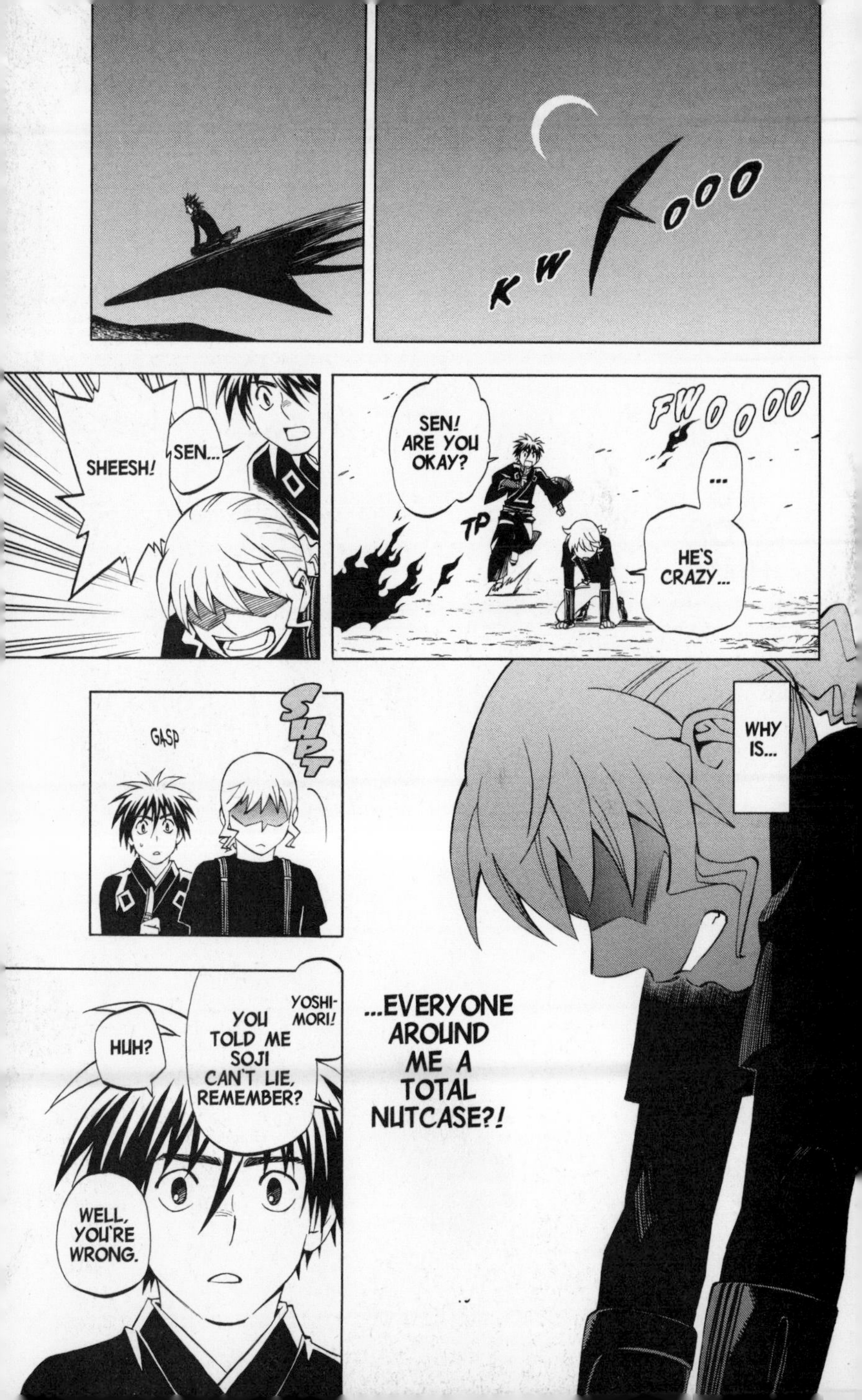
KWOOOO
FWOOOOO
...
SEN! ARE YOU OKAY?
HE'S CRAZY...
TP
SEN...
SHEESH!
WHY IS...
...EVERYONE AROUND ME A TOTAL NUTCASE?!
SHPT
GASP
YOSHIMORI!
YOU TOLD ME SOJI CAN'T LIE, REMEMBER?
HUH?
WELL, YOU'RE WRONG.

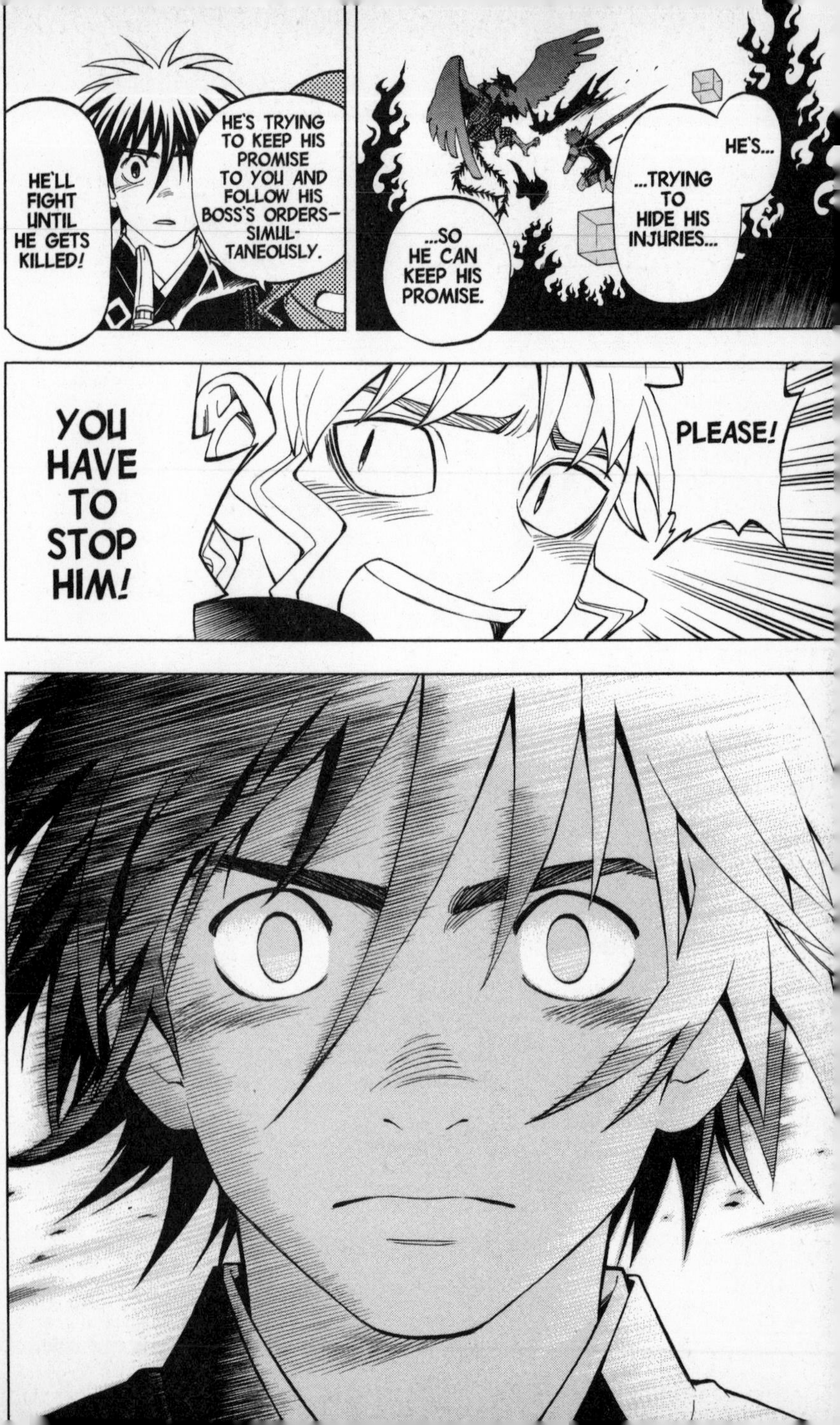
HE'S...
...TRYING TO HIDE HIS INJURIES...
...SO HE CAN KEEP HIS PROMISE.
HE'S TRYING TO KEEP HIS PROMISE TO YOU AND FOLLOW HIS BOSS'S ORDERS— SIMUL-TANEOUSLY.
HE'LL FIGHT UNTIL HE GETS KILLED!
PLEASE!
YOU HAVE TO STOP HIM!

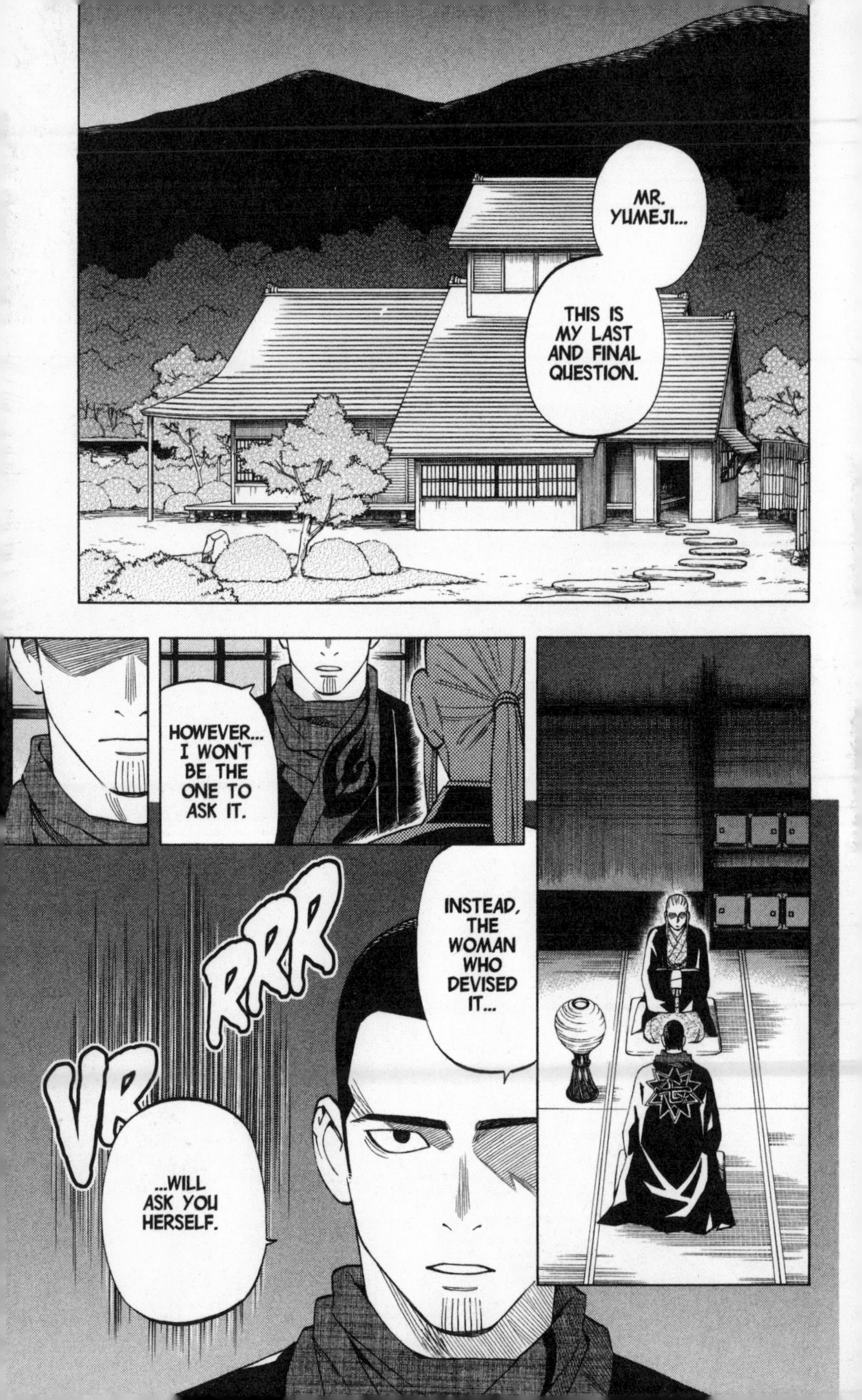
MR. YUMEJI...
THIS IS MY LAST AND FINAL QUESTION.
HOWEVER... I WON'T BE THE ONE TO ASK IT.
INSTEAD, THE WOMAN WHO DEVISED IT...
RRR
VR
...WILL ASK YOU HERSELF.

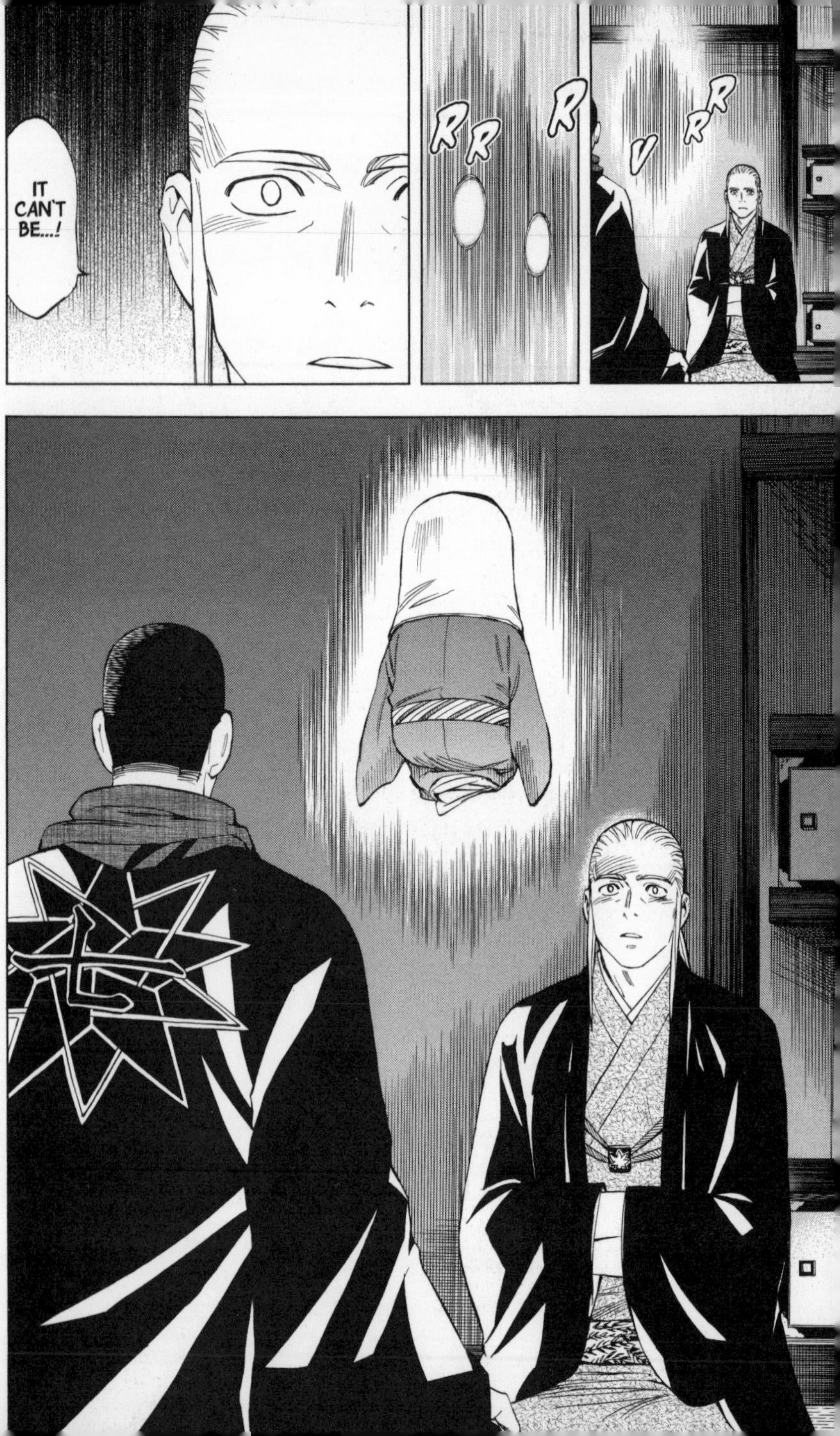
RRVR
RRR
IT CAN'T BE...!

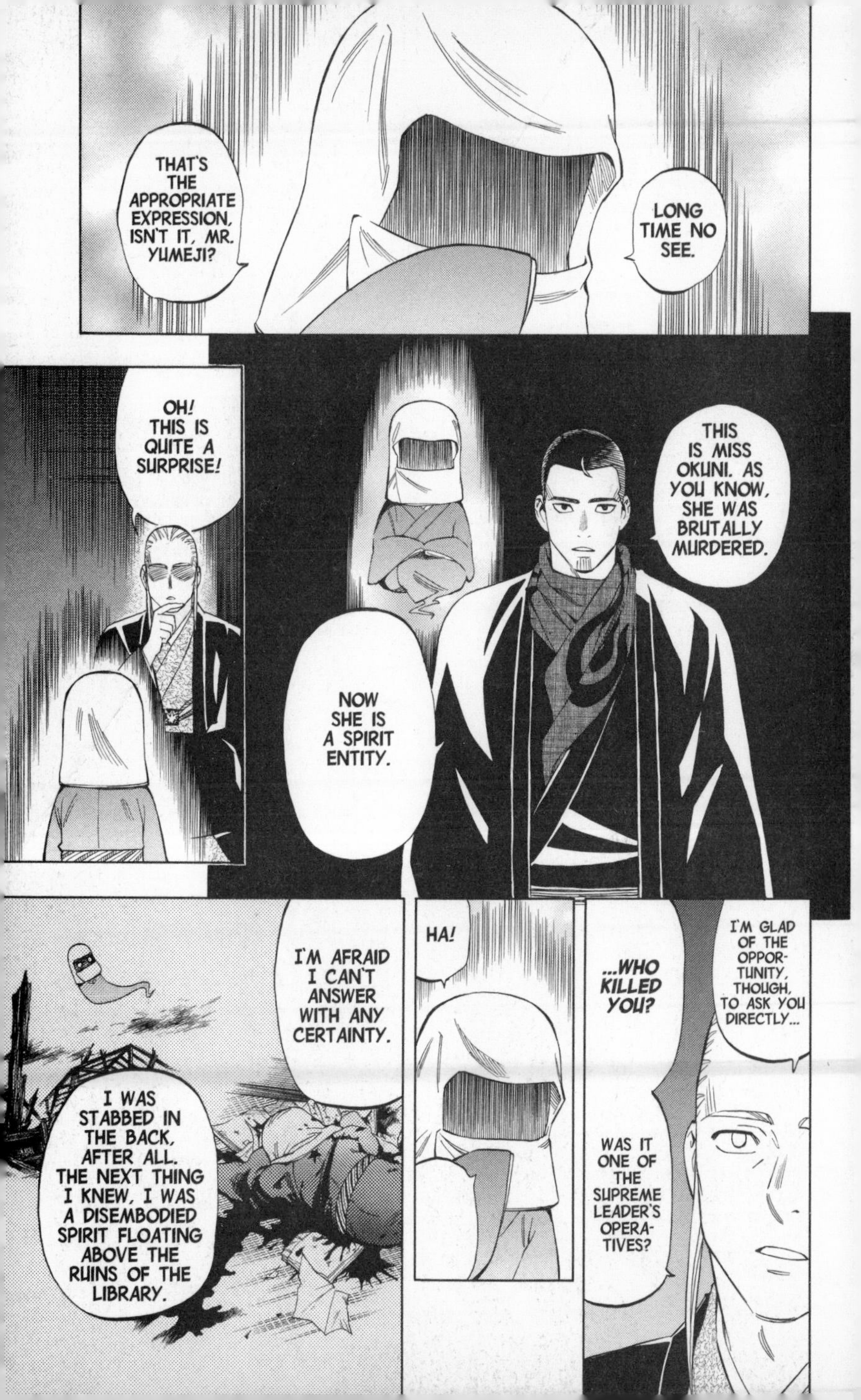
LONG TIME NO SEE.
THAT'S THE APPROPRIATE EXPRESSION, ISN'T IT, MR. YUMEJI?
THIS IS MISS OKUNI. AS YOU KNOW, SHE WAS BRUTALLY MURDERED.
NOW SHE IS A SPIRIT ENTITY.
OH! THIS IS QUITE A SURPRISE!
I'M GLAD OF THE OPPORTUNITY, THOUGH, TO ASK YOU DIRECTLY...
...WHO KILLED YOU?
WAS IT ONE OF THE SUPREME LEADER'S OPERATIVES?
HA!
I'M AFRAID I CAN'T ANSWER WITH ANY CERTAINTY.
I WAS STABBED IN THE BACK, AFTER ALL. THE NEXT THING I KNEW, I WAS A DISEMBODIED SPIRIT FLOATING ABOVE THE RUINS OF THE LIBRARY.

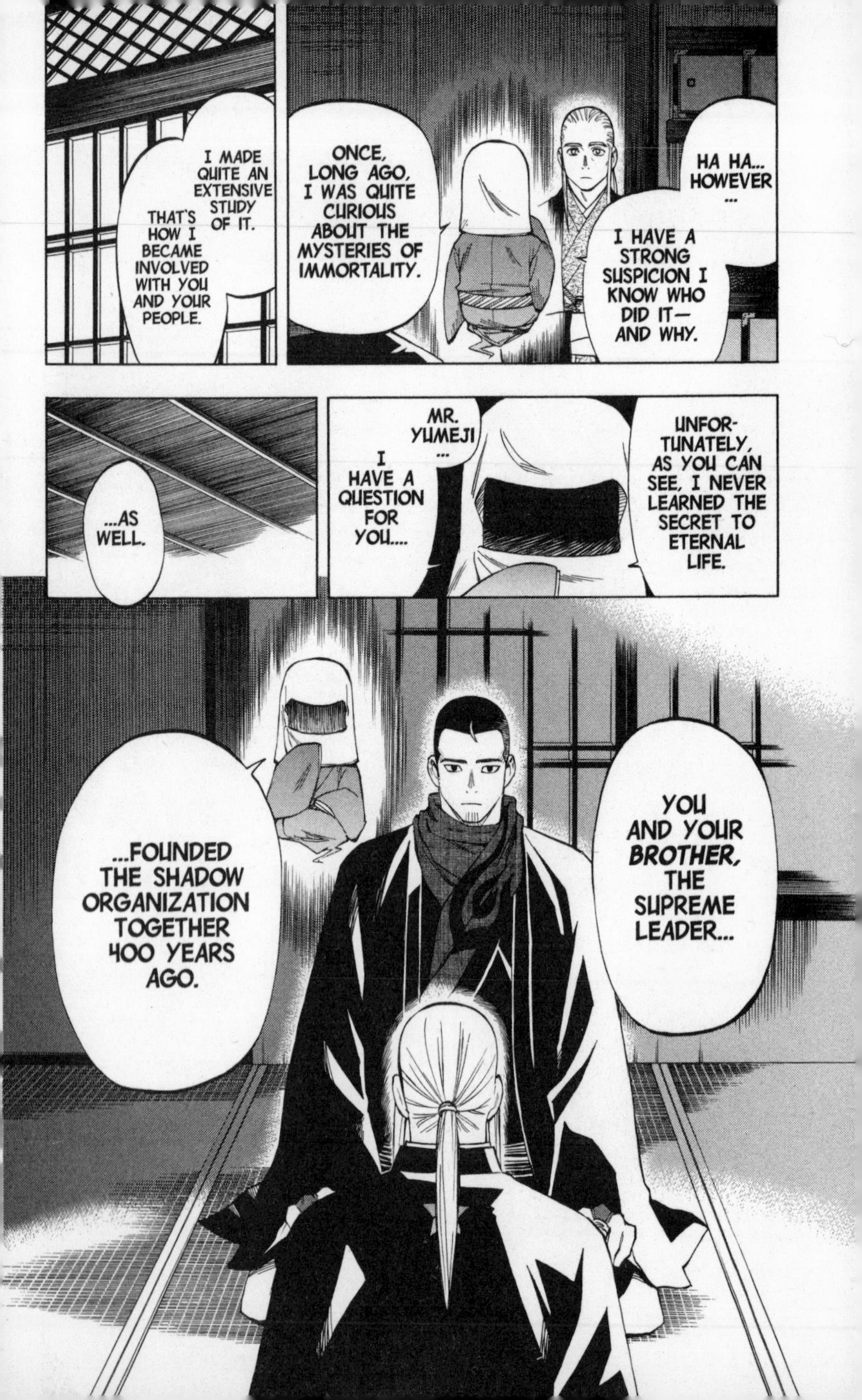
HA HA... HOWEVER ...
I HAVE A STRONG SUSPICION I KNOW WHO DID IT— AND WHY.
ONCE, LONG AGO, I WAS QUITE CURIOUS ABOUT THE MYSTERIES OF IMMORTALITY.
I MADE QUITE AN EXTENSIVE STUDY OF IT.
THAT'S HOW I BECAME INVOLVED WITH YOU AND YOUR PEOPLE.
UNFORTUNATELY, AS YOU CAN SEE, I NEVER LEARNED THE SECRET TO ETERNAL LIFE.
MR. YUMEJI ...
I HAVE A QUESTION FOR YOU....
...AS WELL.
YOU AND YOUR BROTHER, THE SUPREME LEADER...
...FOUNDED THE SHADOW ORGANIZATION TOGETHER 400 YEARS AGO.

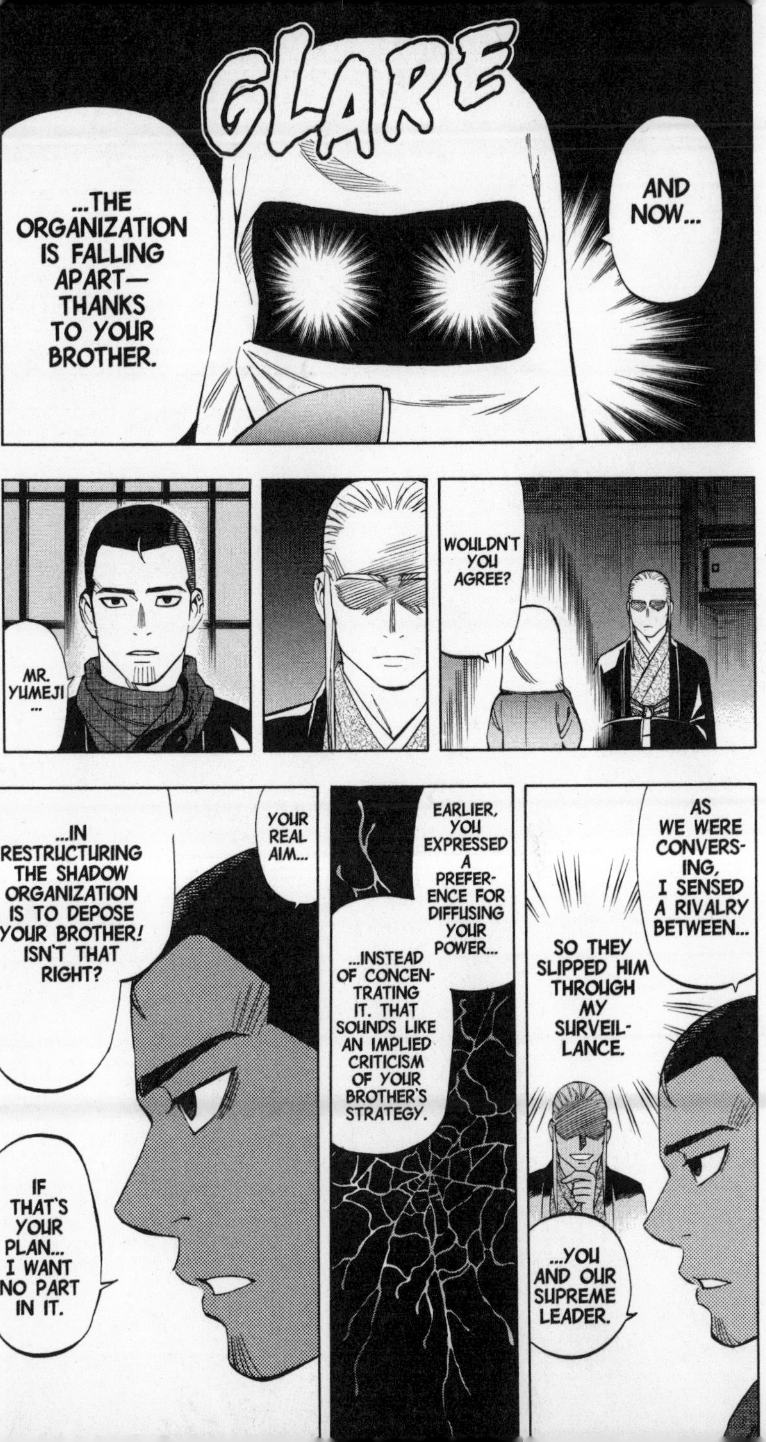
GLARE
AND NOW...
...THE ORGANIZATION IS FALLING APART—THANKS TO YOUR BROTHER.
WOULDN'T YOU AGREE?
MR. YUMEJI...
AS WE WERE CONVERSING, I SENSED A RIVALRY BETWEEN...
SO THEY SLIPPED HIM THROUGH MY SURVEILLANCE.
...YOU AND OUR SUPREME LEADER.
EARLIER, YOU EXPRESSED A PREFERENCE FOR DIFFUSING YOUR POWER...
...INSTEAD OF CONCENTRATING IT. THAT SOUNDS LIKE AN IMPLIED CRITICISM OF YOUR BROTHER'S STRATEGY.
YOUR REAL AIM...
...IN RESTRUCTURING THE SHADOW ORGANIZATION IS TO DEPOSE YOUR BROTHER! ISN'T THAT RIGHT?
IF THAT'S YOUR PLAN... I WANT NO PART IN IT.

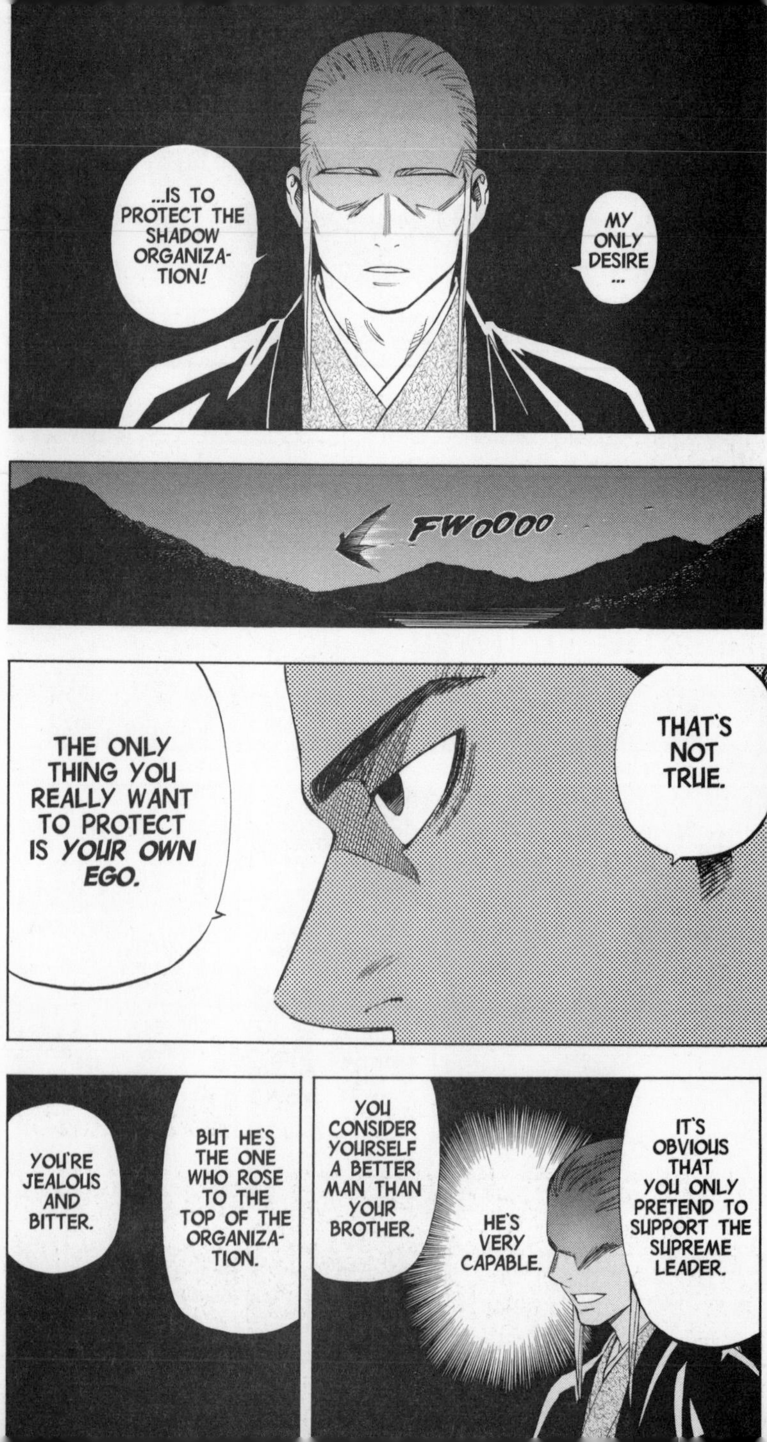
MY ONLY DESIRE ...
...IS TO PROTECT THE SHADOW ORGANIZATION!
FWOOOO
THAT'S NOT TRUE.
THE ONLY THING YOU REALLY WANT TO PROTECT IS *YOUR OWN EGO.*
IT'S OBVIOUS THAT YOU ONLY PRETEND TO SUPPORT THE SUPREME LEADER.
YOU CONSIDER YOURSELF A BETTER MAN THAN YOUR BROTHER.
HE'S VERY CAPABLE.
BUT HE'S THE ONE WHO ROSE TO THE TOP OF THE ORGANIZATION.
YOU'RE JEALOUS AND BITTER.

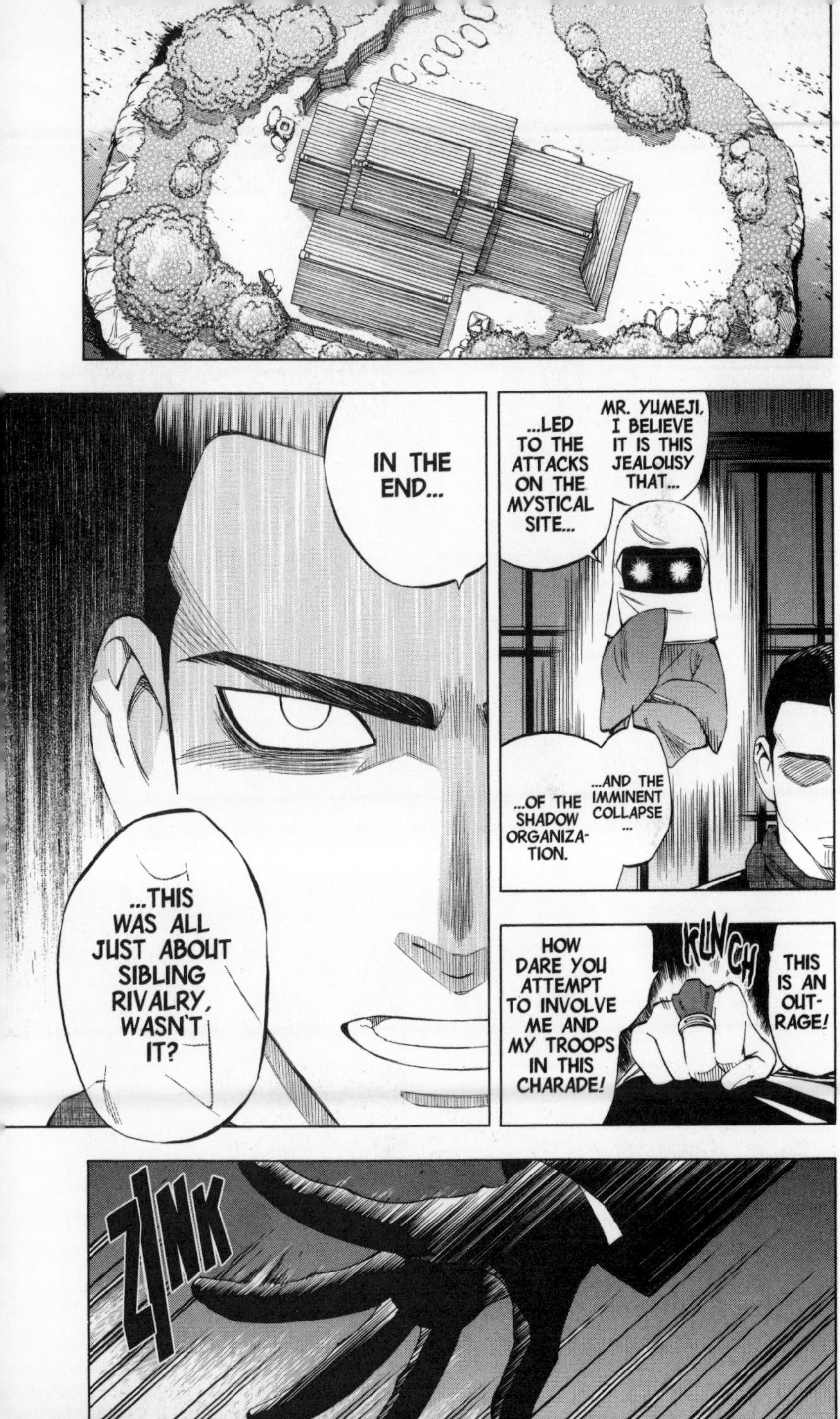
MR. YUMEJI, I BELIEVE IT IS THIS JEALOUSY THAT...
...LED TO THE ATTACKS ON THE MYSTICAL SITE...
...AND THE IMMINENT COLLAPSE...
...OF THE SHADOW ORGANIZATION.
THIS IS AN OUTRAGE!
KLUNCH
HOW DARE YOU ATTEMPT TO INVOLVE ME AND MY TROOPS IN THIS CHARADE!
IN THE END...
...THIS WAS ALL JUST ABOUT SIBLING RIVALRY, WASN'T IT?
ZINK

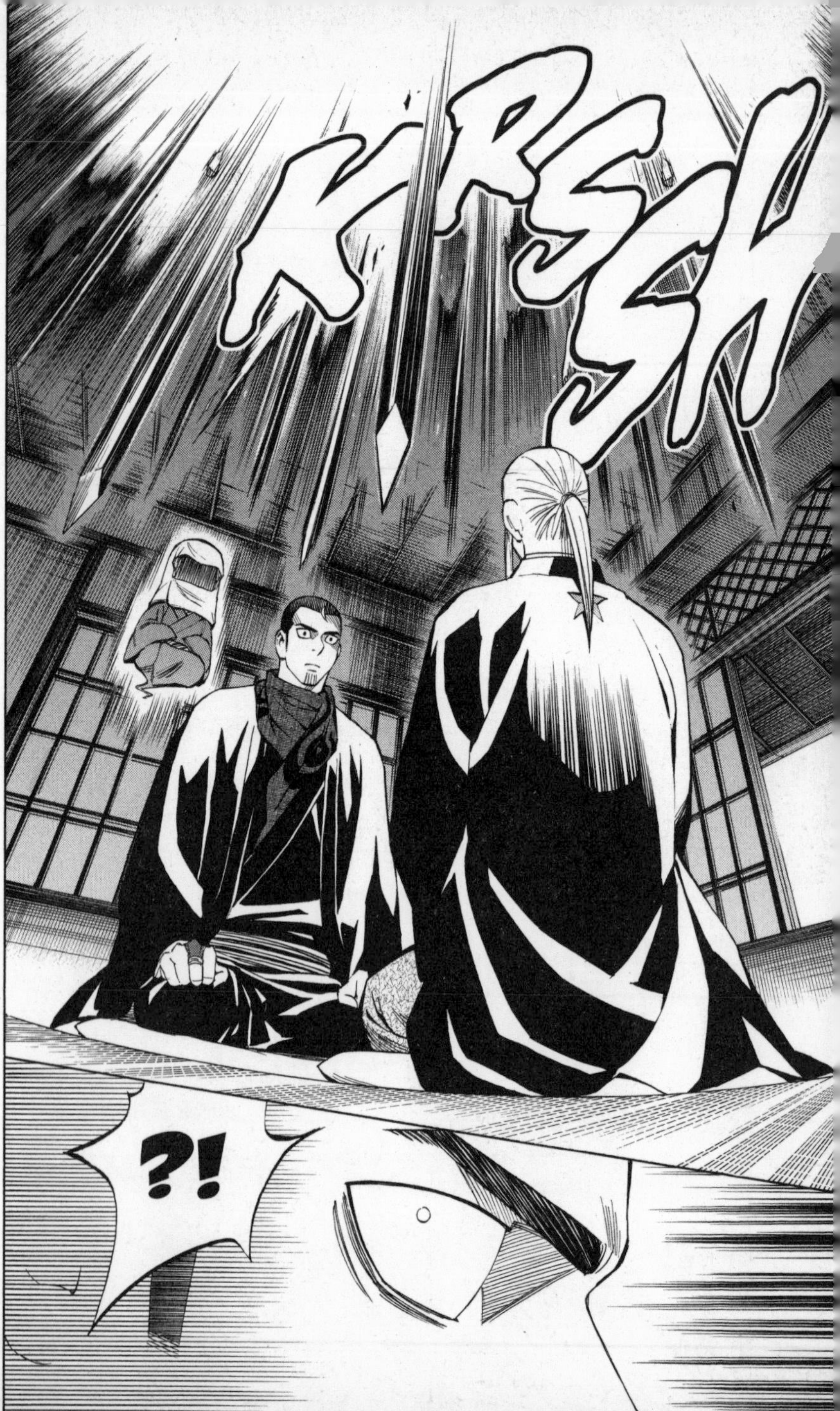
?!

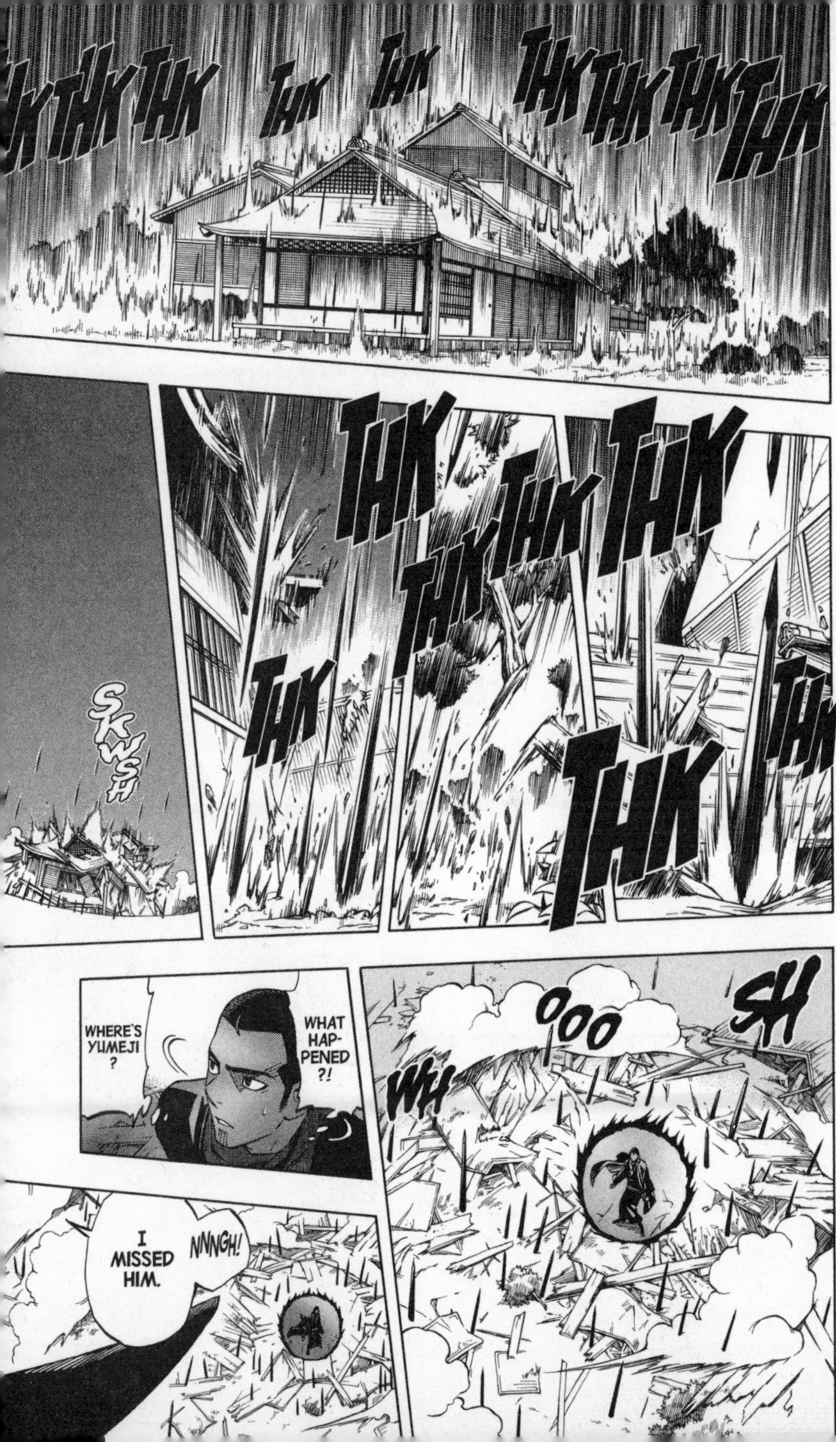
THK THK THK THK THK
THK
THK
THK THK
THK
THK THK
THK
THK
SKWSH
WH OOO SH
WHAT HAP-PENED ?!
WHERE'S YUMEJI ?
NNNGH!
I MISSED HIM.

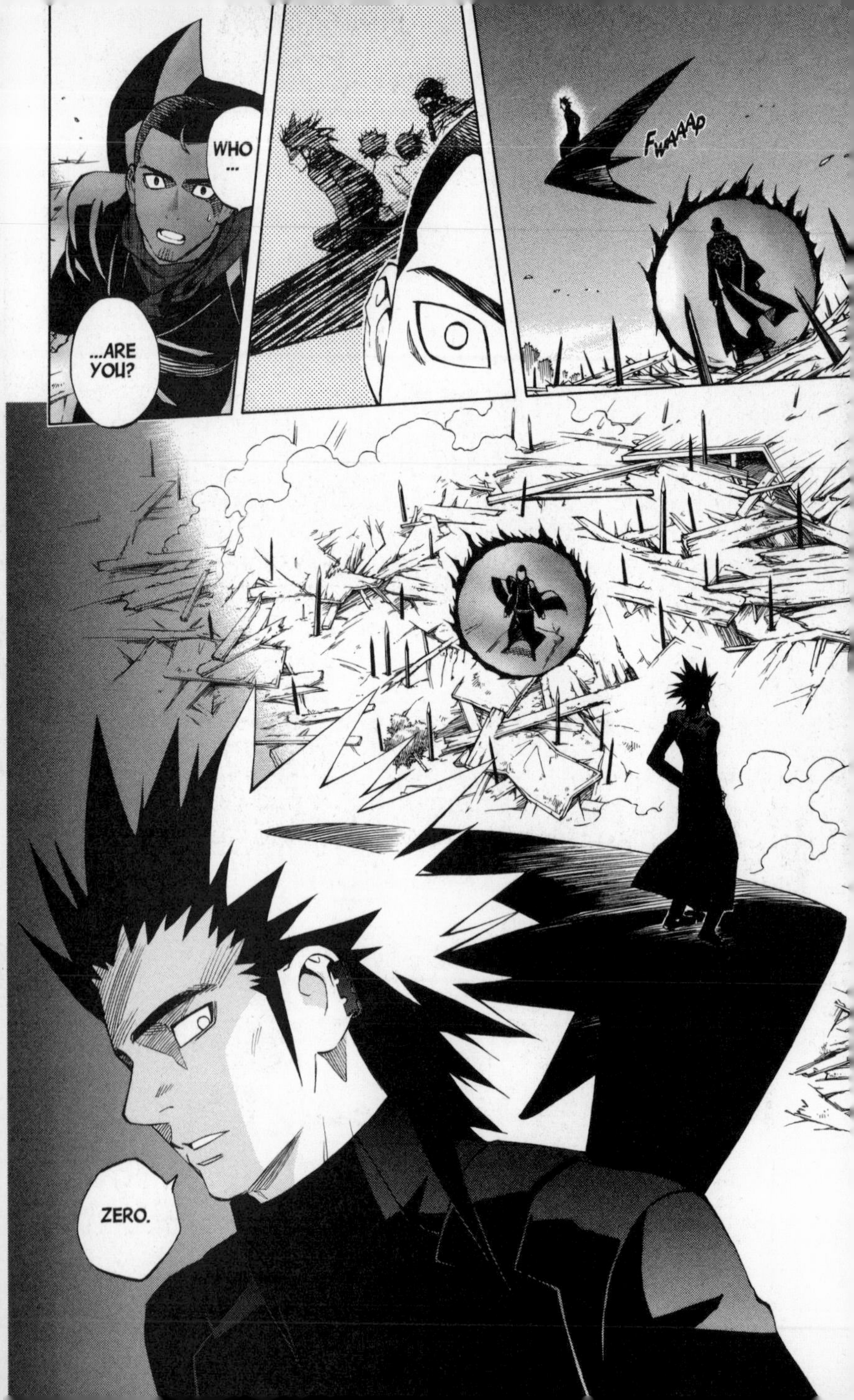
FWAAAP
WHO ...
...ARE YOU?
ZERO.

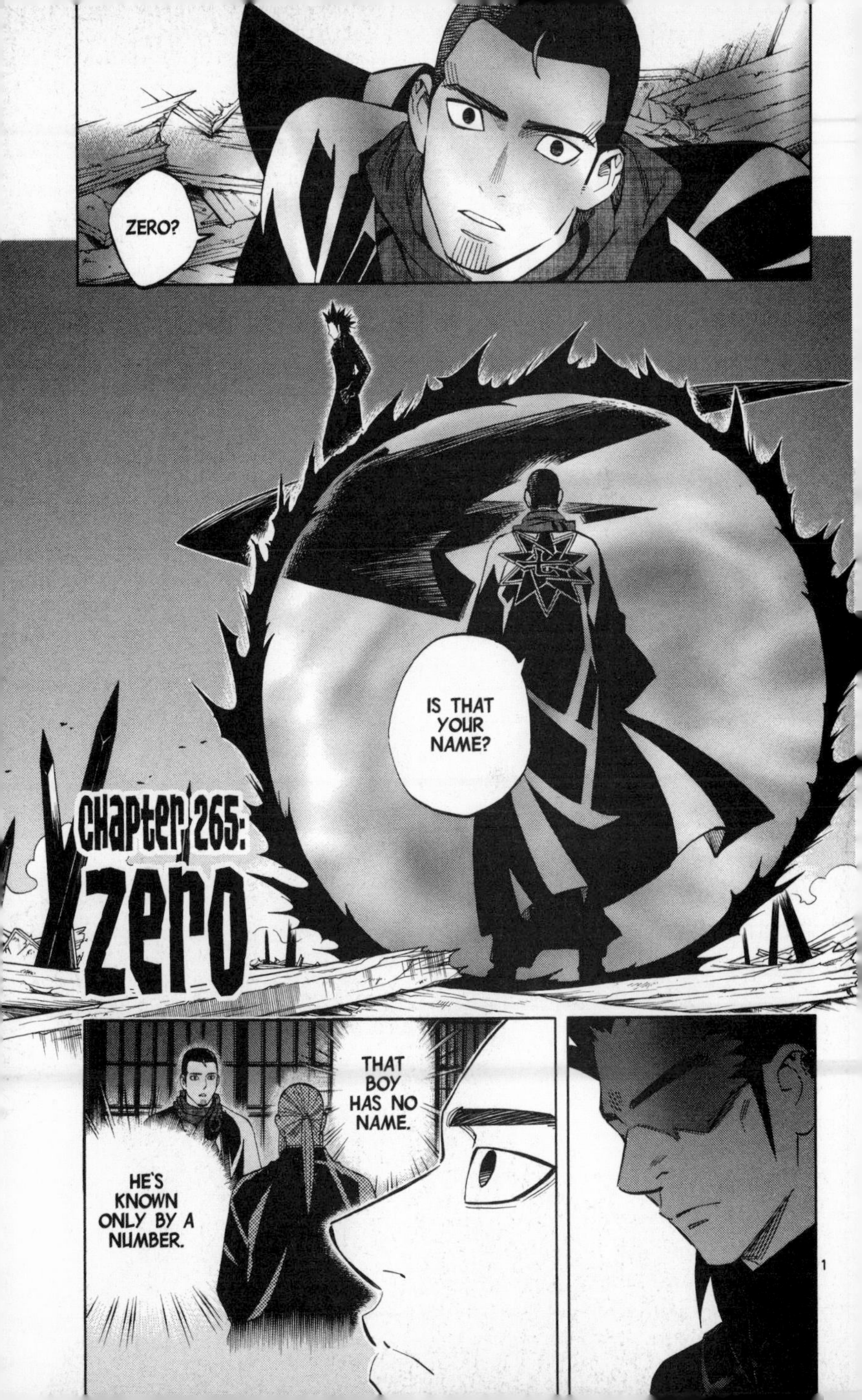
ZERO?
IS THAT YOUR NAME?
Chapter 265:
Zero
THAT BOY HAS NO NAME.
HE'S KNOWN ONLY BY A NUMBER.

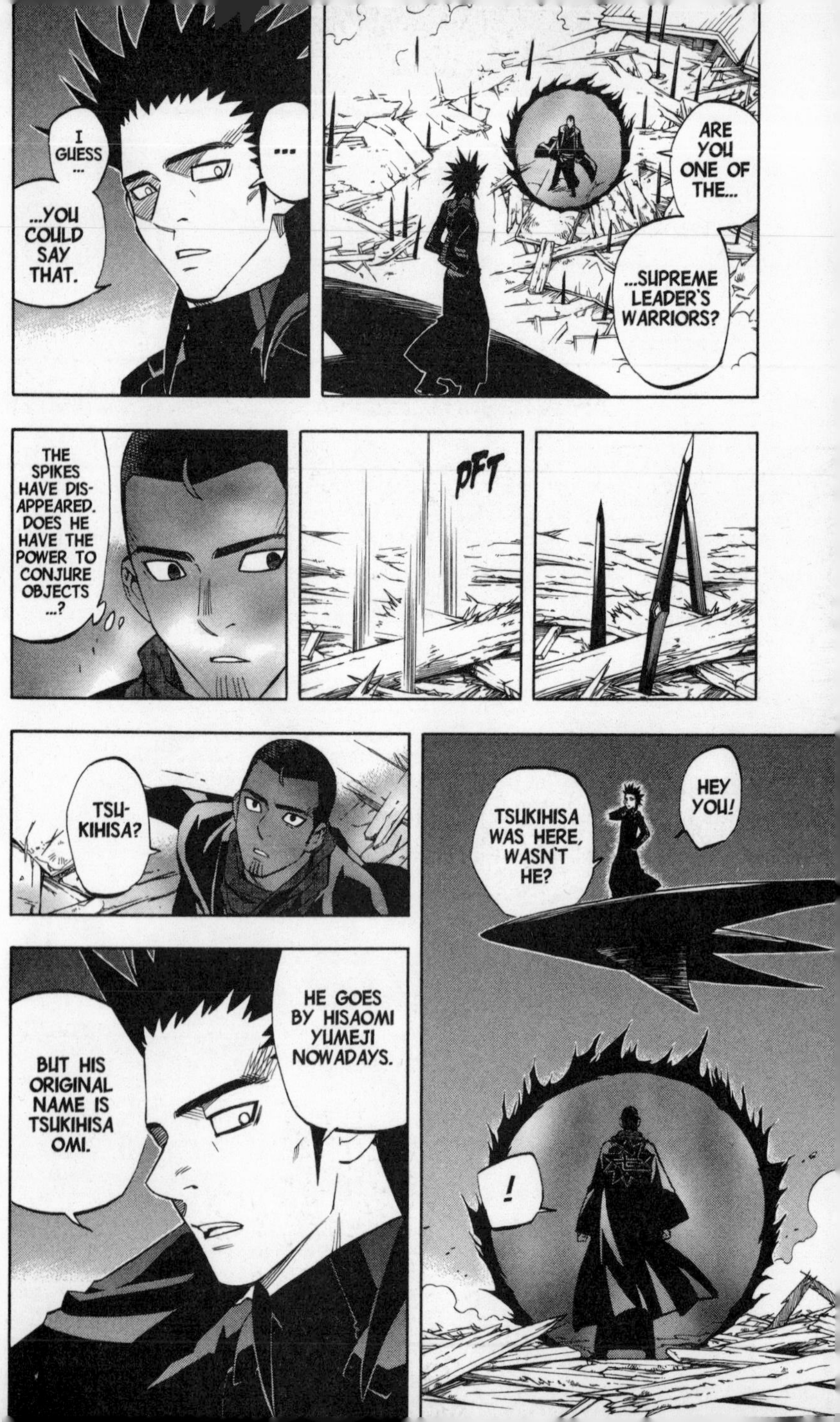
ARE YOU ONE OF THE...
...SUPREME LEADER'S WARRIORS?
...
I GUESS ...
...YOU COULD SAY THAT.
PFT
THE SPIKES HAVE DIS-APPEARED. DOES HE HAVE THE POWER TO CONJURE OBJECTS ...?
HEY YOU!
TSUKIHISA WAS HERE, WASN'T HE?
!
TSU-KIHISA?
HE GOES BY HISAOMI YUMEJI NOWADAYS.
BUT HIS ORIGINAL NAME IS TSUKIHISA OMI.

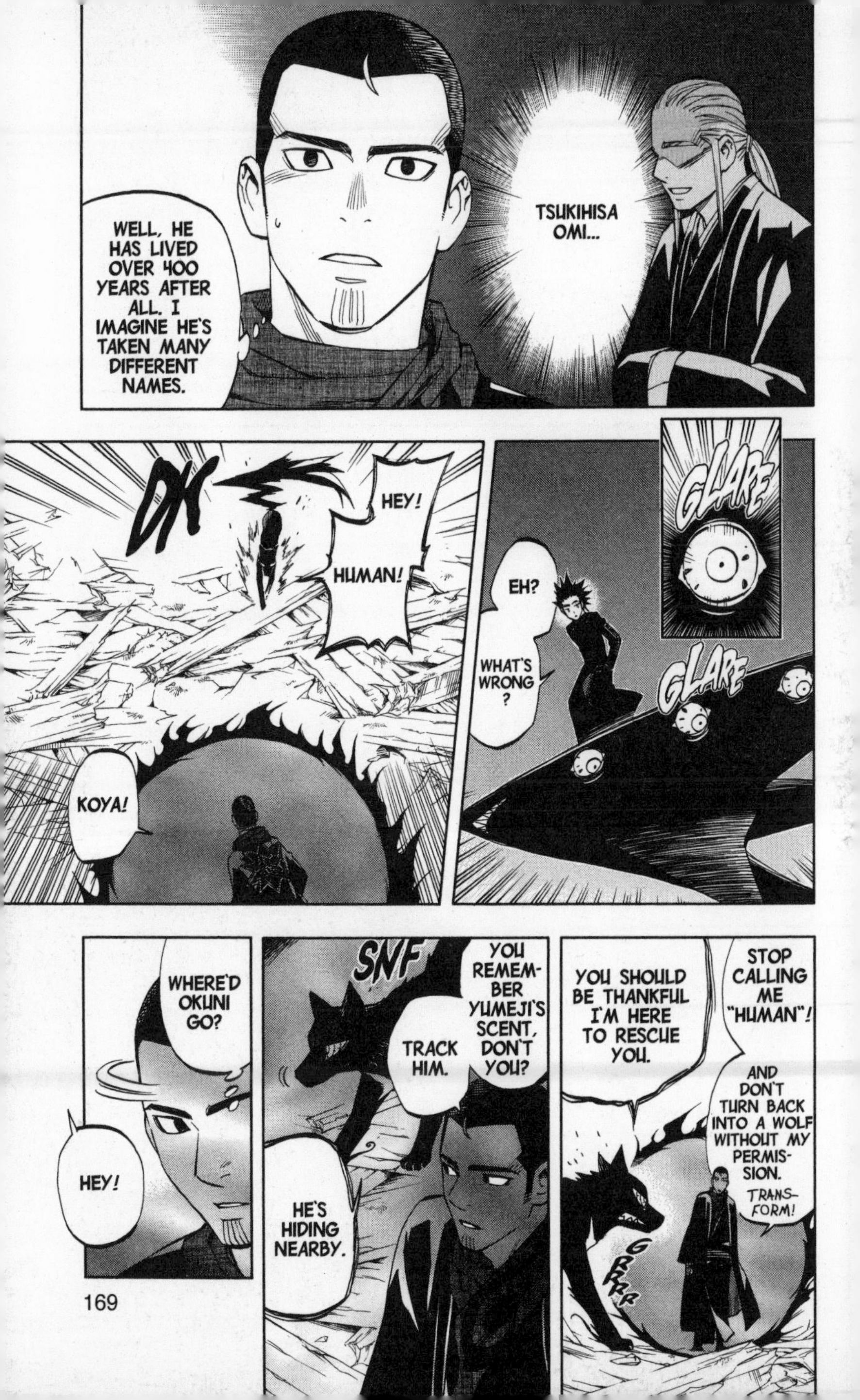

TSUKIHISA OMI...
WELL, HE HAS LIVED OVER 400 YEARS AFTER ALL. I IMAGINE HE'S TAKEN MANY DIFFERENT NAMES.
GLARE
EH?
WHAT'S WRONG?
GLARE
HEY!
HUMAN!
DK
KOYA!
STOP CALLING ME "HUMAN"!
YOU SHOULD BE THANKFUL I'M HERE TO RESCUE YOU.
AND DON'T TURN BACK INTO A WOLF WITHOUT MY PERMISSION.
TRANSFORM!
GRRRR
YOU REMEMBER YUMEJI'S SCENT, DON'T YOU?
SNF
TRACK HIM.
HE'S HIDING NEARBY.
WHERE'D OKUNI GO?
HEY!

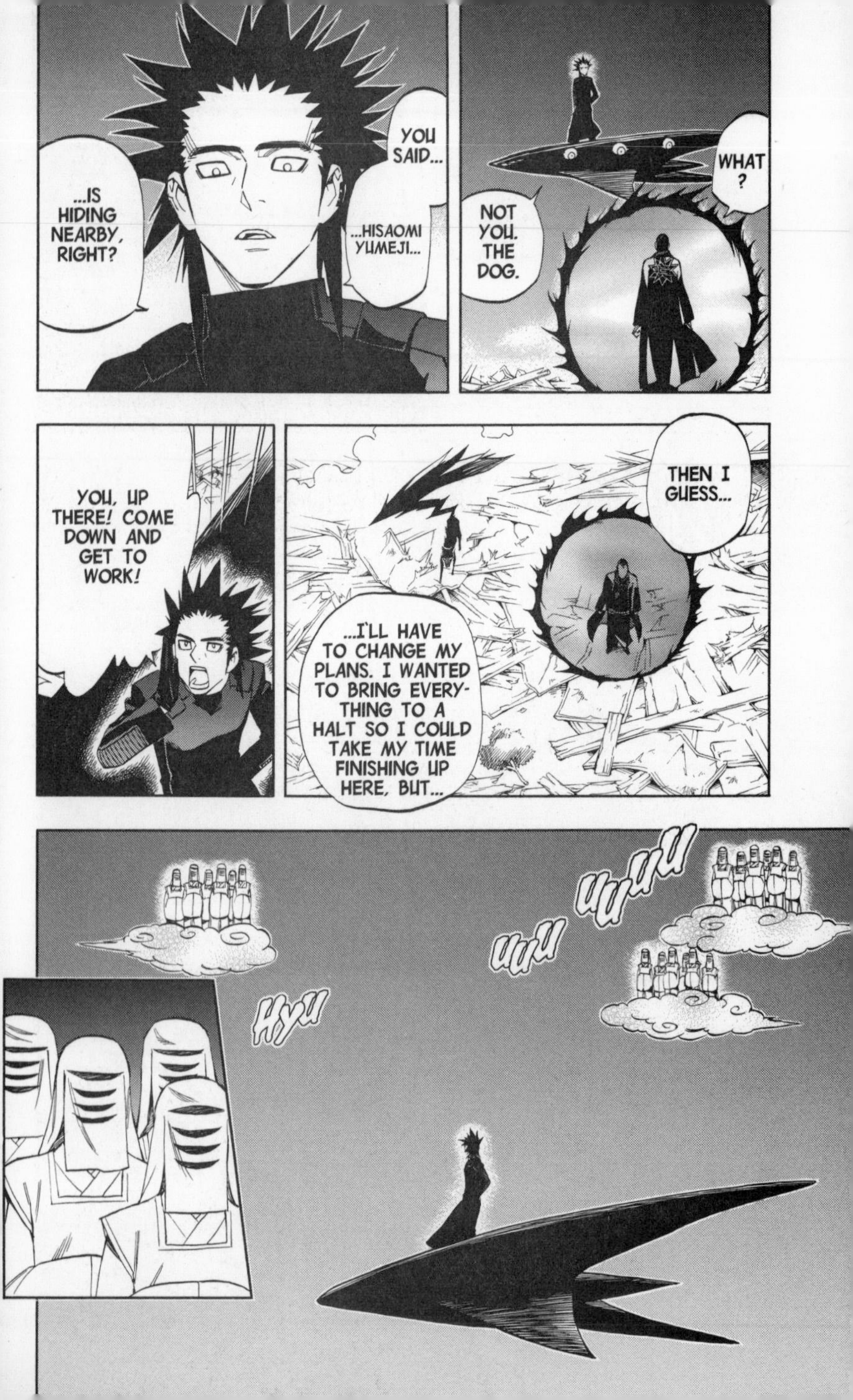
WHAT?
NOT YOU. THE DOG.
YOU SAID...
...HISAOMI YUMEJI...
...IS HIDING NEARBY, RIGHT?
THEN I GUESS...
...I'LL HAVE TO CHANGE MY PLANS. I WANTED TO BRING EVERY-THING TO A HALT SO I COULD TAKE MY TIME FINISHING UP HERE, BUT...
YOU, UP THERE! COME DOWN AND GET TO WORK!
UUUUU
UUU
HYU

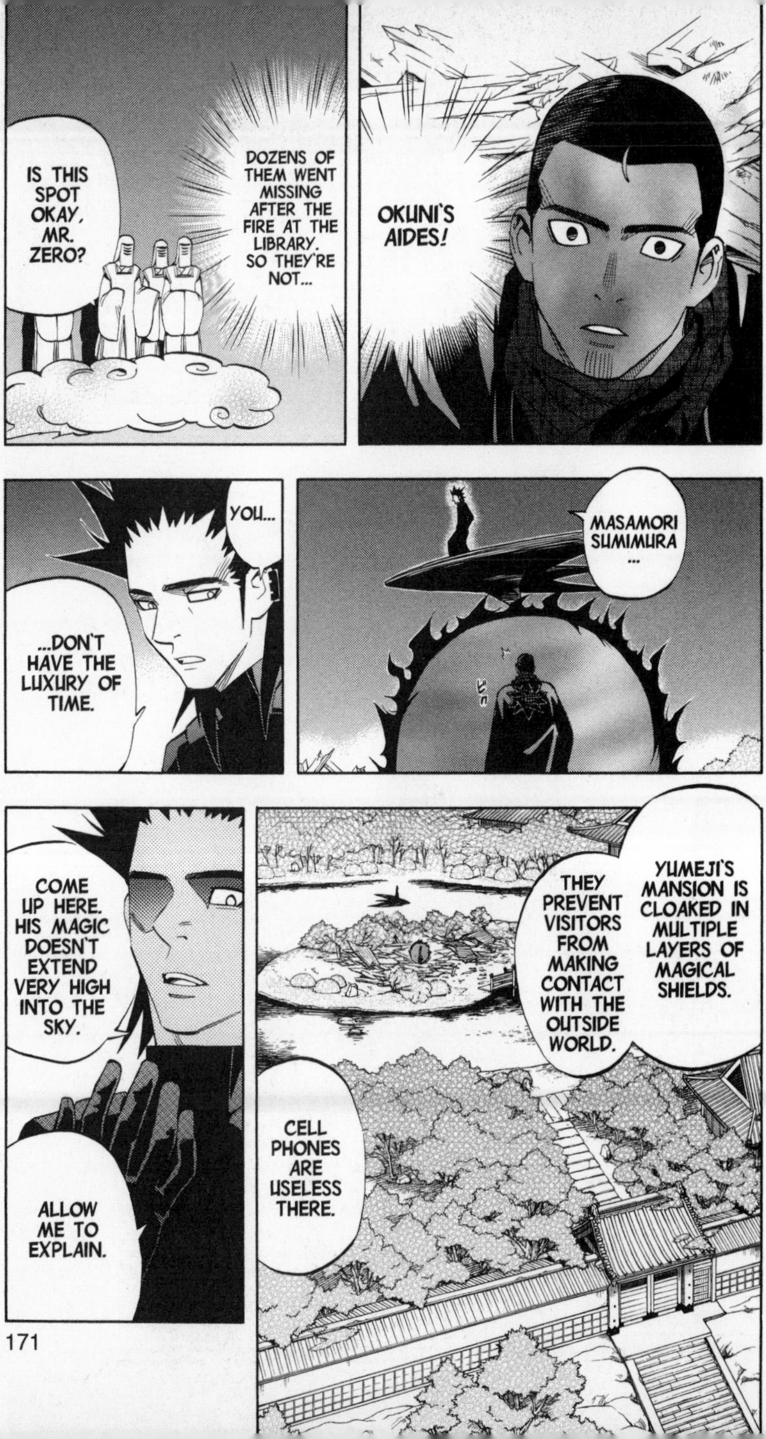
OKUNI'S AIDES!
DOZENS OF THEM WENT MISSING AFTER THE FIRE AT THE LIBRARY. SO THEY'RE NOT...
IS THIS SPOT OKAY, MR. ZERO?
MASAMORI SUMIMURA ...
YOU...
...DON'T HAVE THE LUXURY OF TIME.
YUMEJI'S MANSION IS CLOAKED IN MULTIPLE LAYERS OF MAGICAL SHIELDS.
THEY PREVENT VISITORS FROM MAKING CONTACT WITH THE OUTSIDE WORLD.
CELL PHONES ARE USELESS THERE.
COME UP HERE. HIS MAGIC DOESN'T EXTEND VERY HIGH INTO THE SKY.
ALLOW ME TO EXPLAIN.

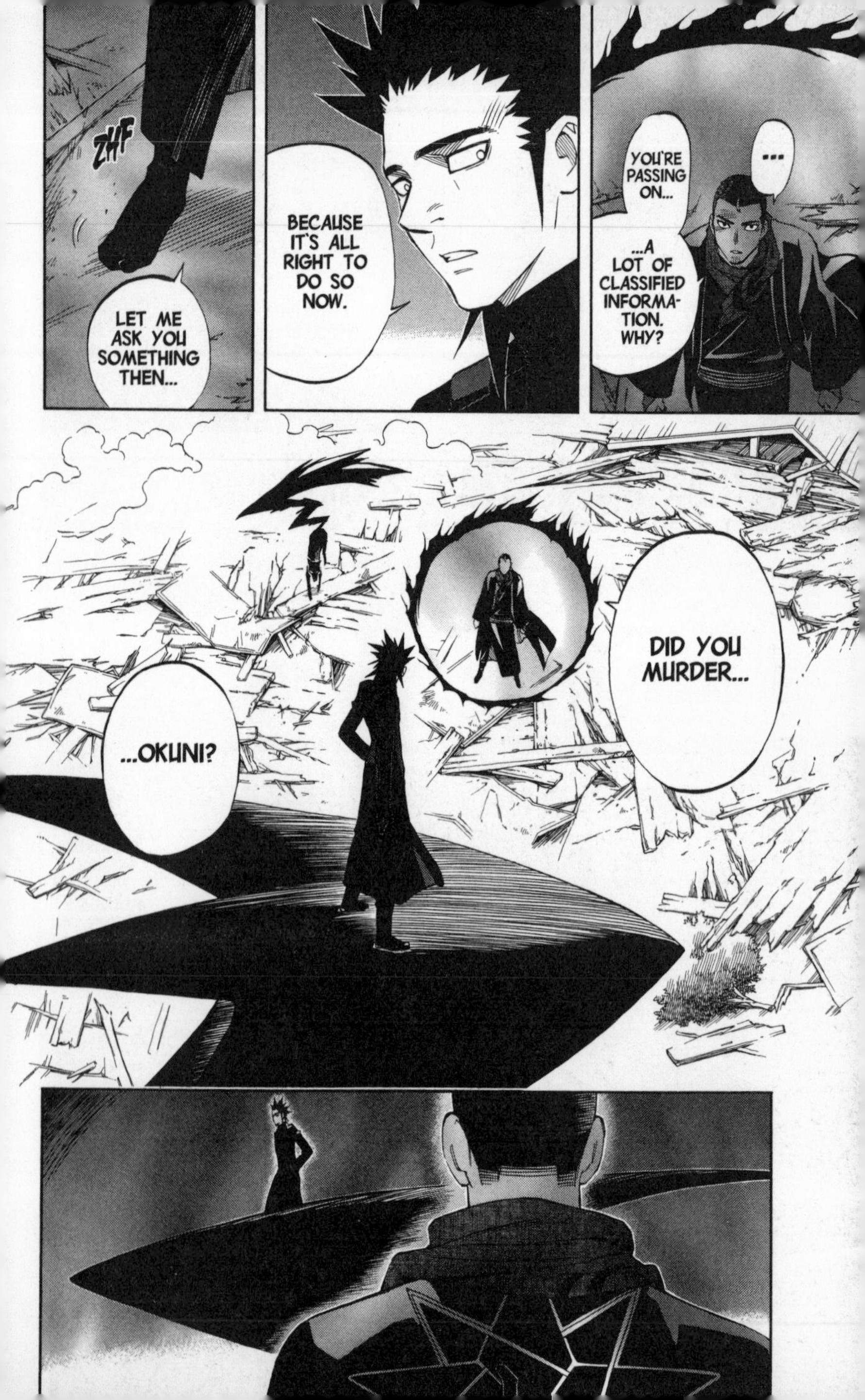
...
YOU'RE PASSING ON...
...A LOT OF CLASSIFIED INFORMATION. WHY?
BECAUSE IT'S ALL RIGHT TO DO SO NOW.
ZHF
LET ME ASK YOU SOMETHING THEN...
DID YOU MURDER...
...OKUNI?

YEP.

I KILLED HER.

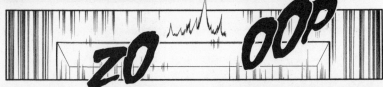

ZO OOP

TPF

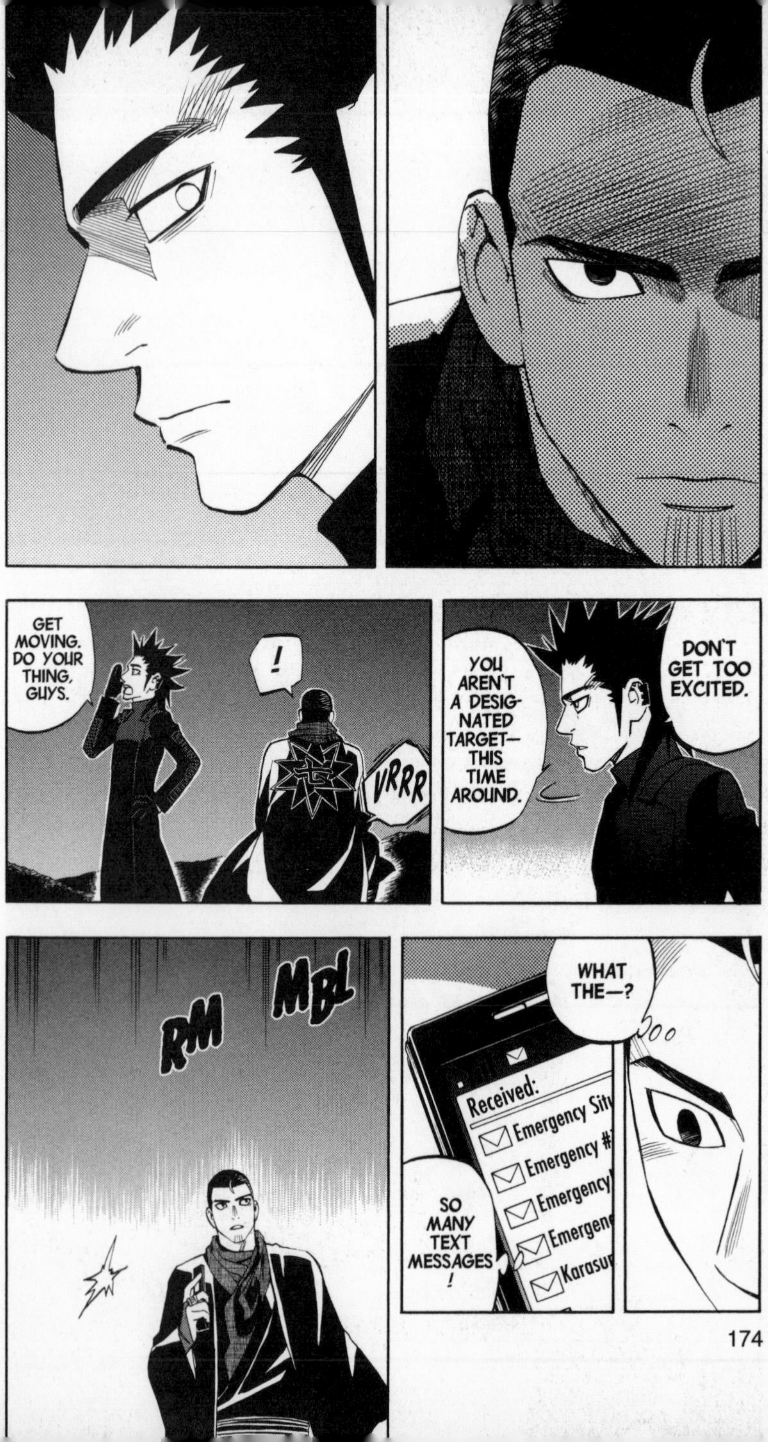
DON'T GET TOO EXCITED.
YOU AREN'T A DESIGNATED TARGET—THIS TIME AROUND.
GET MOVING. DO YOUR THING, GUYS.
!
VRRR
WHAT THE—?
Received:
Emergency Sit
Emergency #
Emergency
Emergenc
Karasu
SO MANY TEXT MESSAGES!
RM MBL

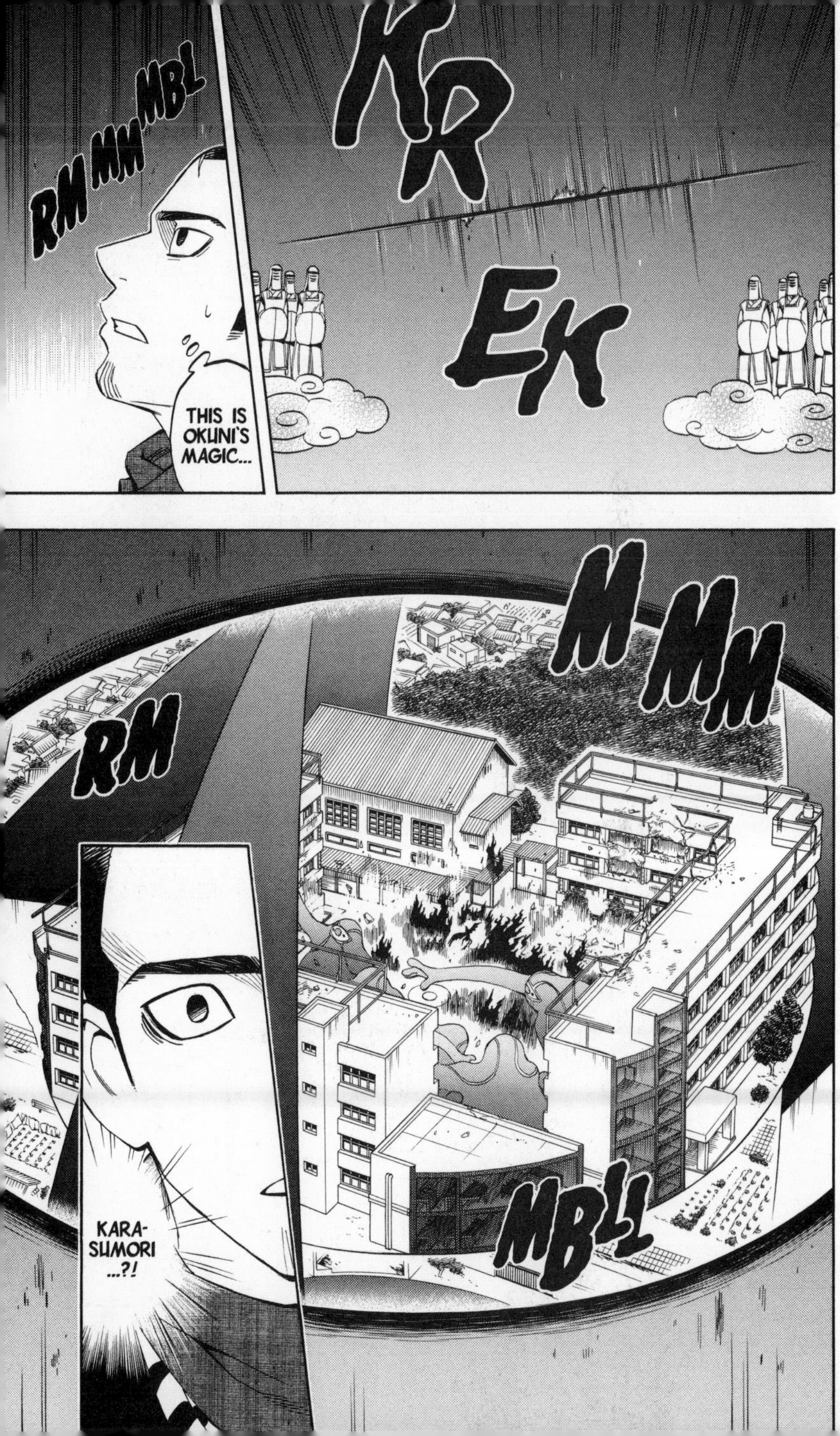
KR
EK
RM MM MBL
THIS IS OKUNI'S MAGIC...
M MM
RM
MBLL
KARA-SUMORI ...?!

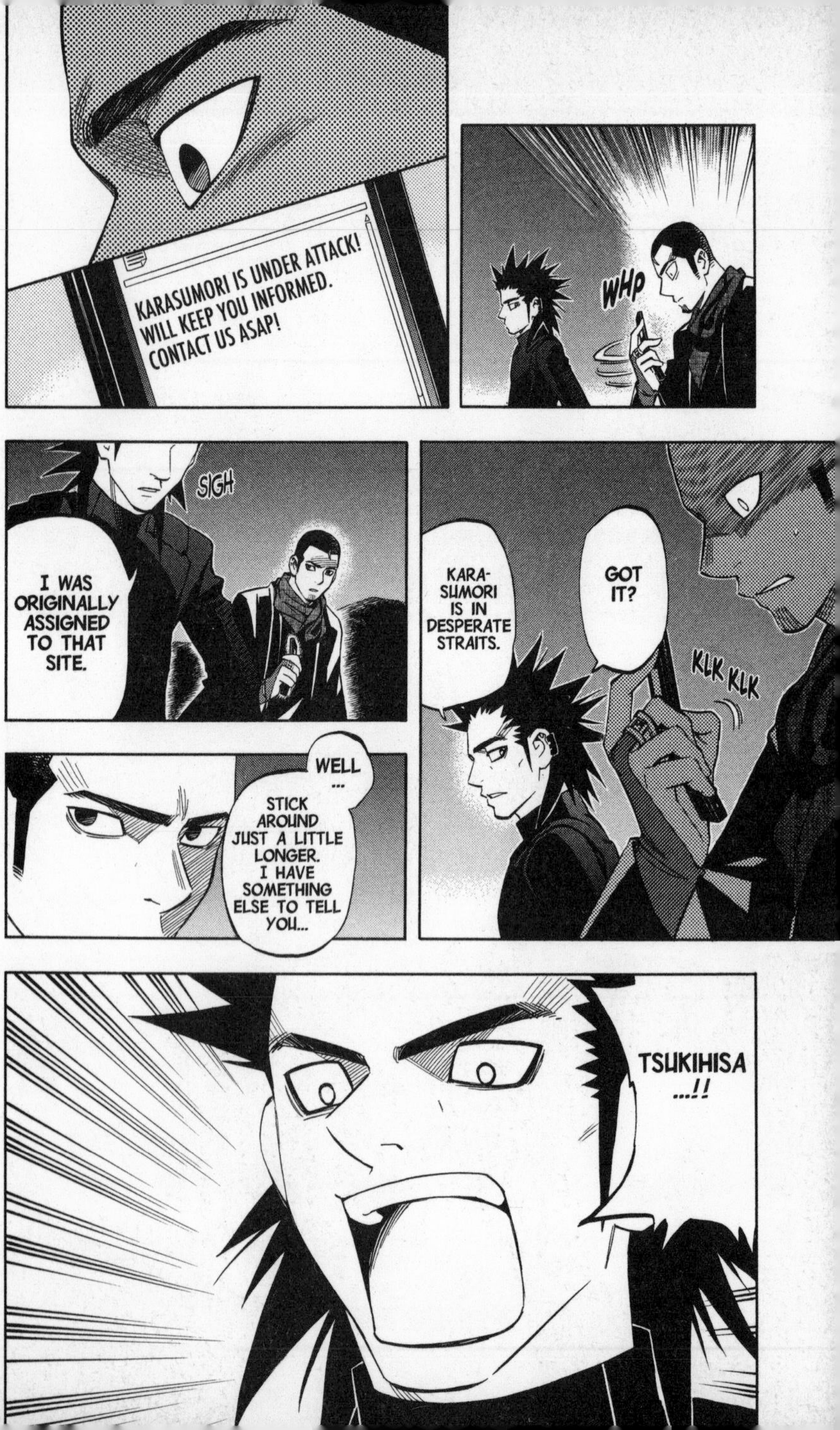
WHP
KARASUMORI IS UNDER ATTACK! WILL KEEP YOU INFORMED. CONTACT US ASAP!
GOT IT?
KARA-SUMORI IS IN DESPERATE STRAITS.
KLK KLK
SIGH
I WAS ORIGINALLY ASSIGNED TO THAT SITE.
WELL... STICK AROUND JUST A LITTLE LONGER. I HAVE SOMETHING ELSE TO TELL YOU...
TSUKIHISA...!!

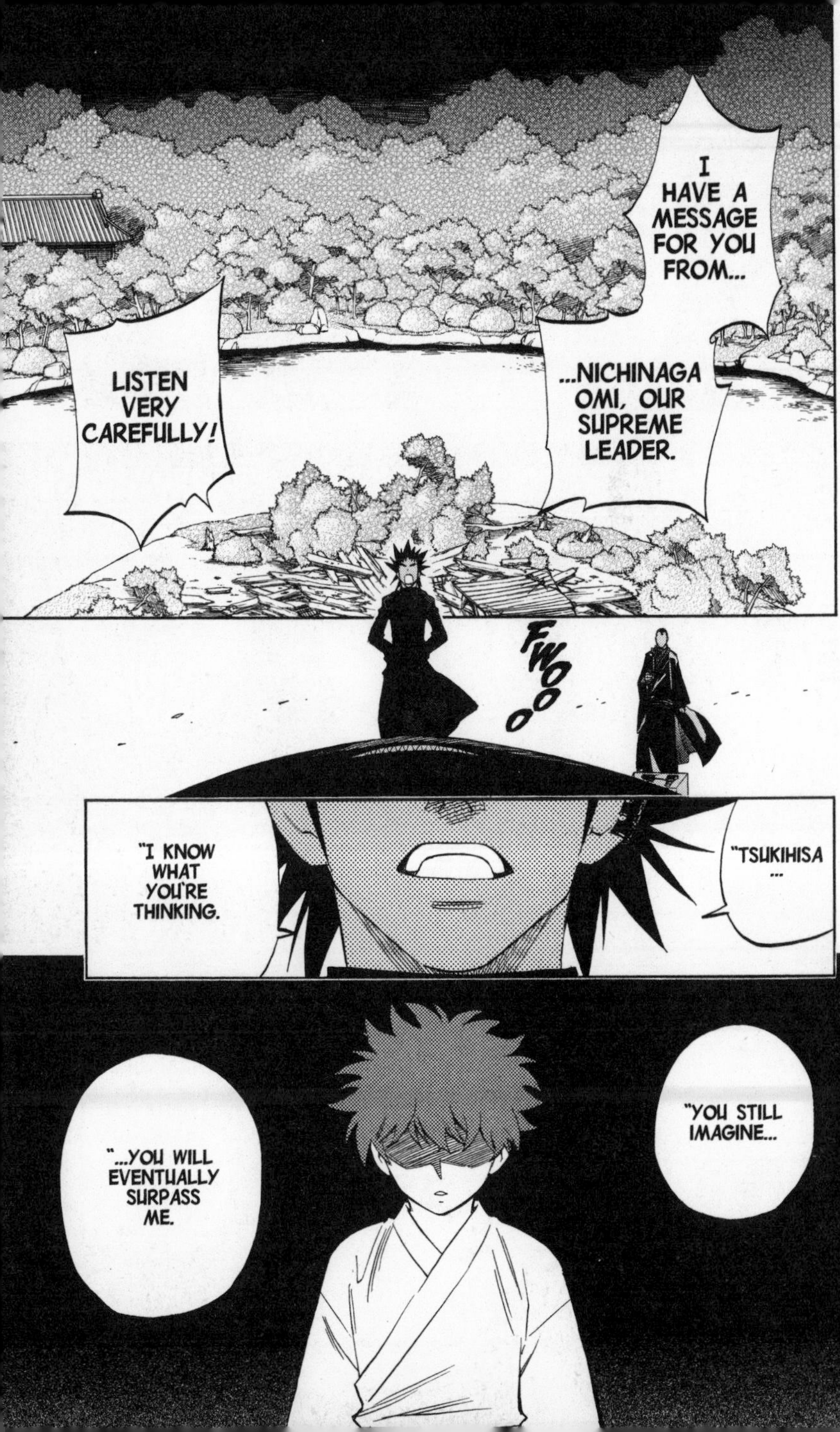
I HAVE A MESSAGE FOR YOU FROM...
...NICHINAGA OMI, OUR SUPREME LEADER.
LISTEN VERY CAREFULLY!
FWOOO
"TSUKIHISA...
"I KNOW WHAT YOU'RE THINKING.
"YOU STILL IMAGINE...
"...YOU WILL EVENTUALLY SURPASS ME.

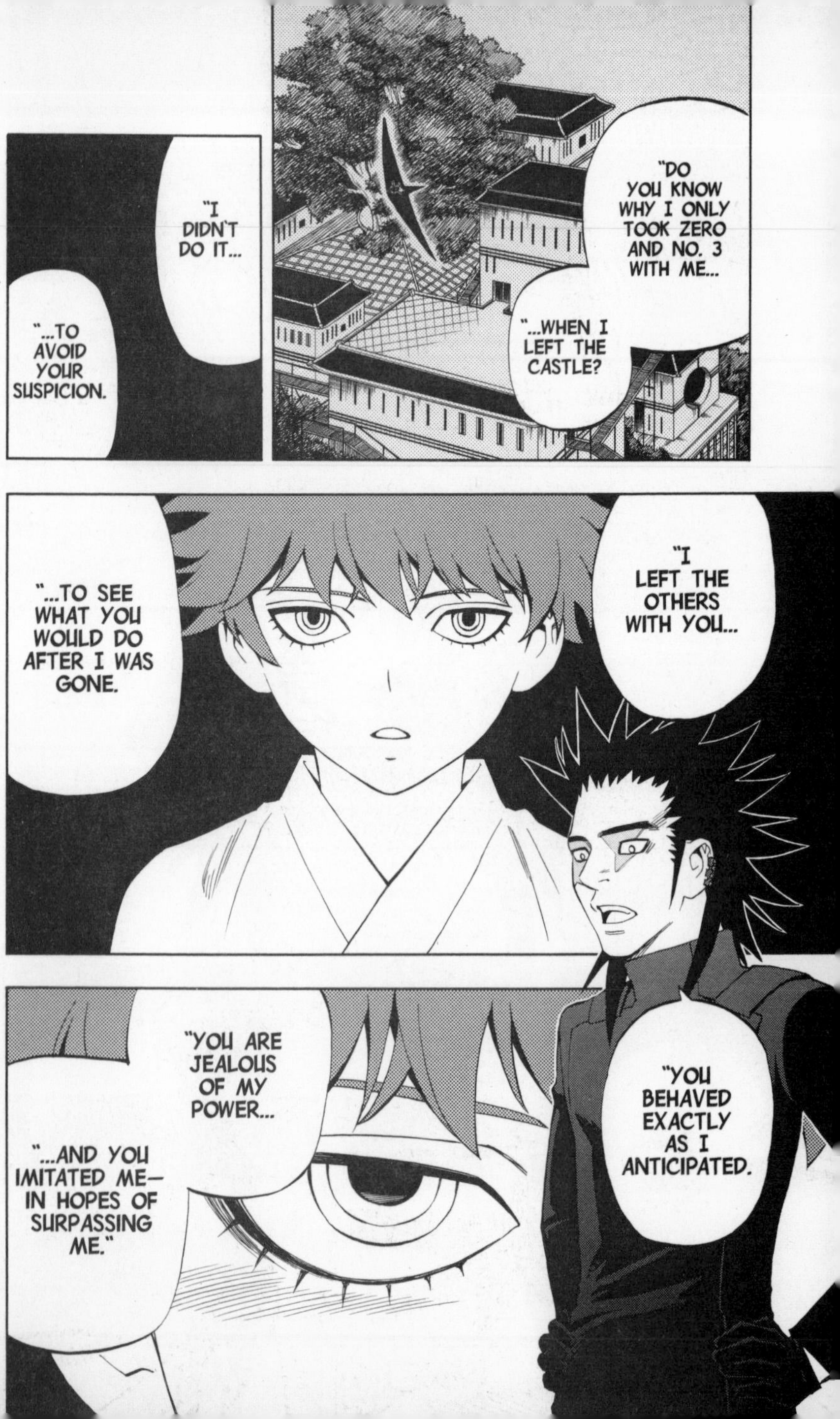
"DO YOU KNOW WHY I ONLY TOOK ZERO AND NO. 3 WITH ME...
"...WHEN I LEFT THE CASTLE?
"I DIDN'T DO IT...
"...TO AVOID YOUR SUSPICION.
"I LEFT THE OTHERS WITH YOU...
"...TO SEE WHAT YOU WOULD DO AFTER I WAS GONE.
"YOU BEHAVED EXACTLY AS I ANTICIPATED.
"YOU ARE JEALOUS OF MY POWER...
"...AND YOU IMITATED ME— IN HOPES OF SURPASSING ME."

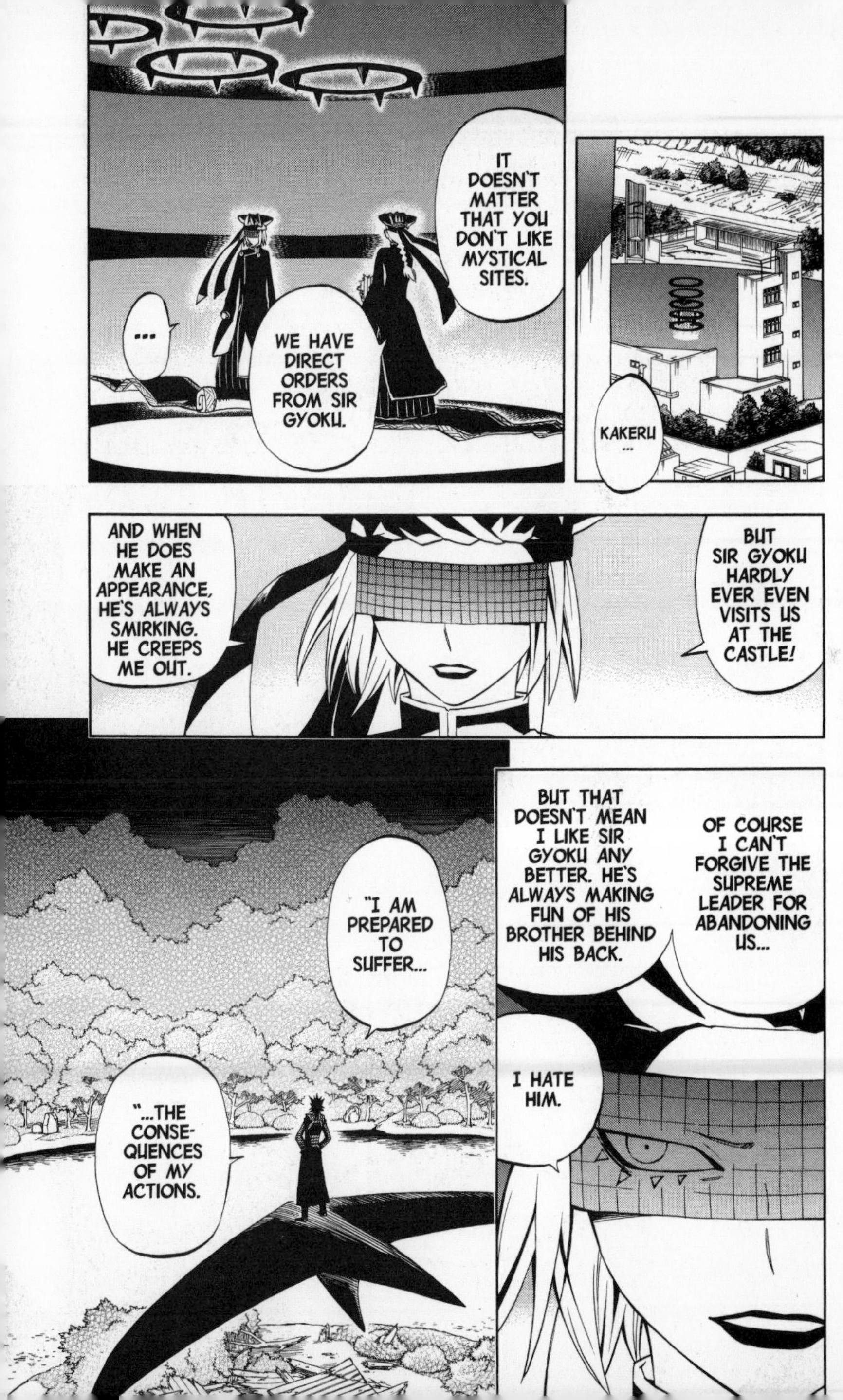
KAKERU ...
IT DOESN'T MATTER THAT YOU DON'T LIKE MYSTICAL SITES.
WE HAVE DIRECT ORDERS FROM SIR GYOKU.
...
BUT SIR GYOKU HARDLY EVER EVEN VISITS US AT THE CASTLE!
AND WHEN HE DOES MAKE AN APPEARANCE, HE'S ALWAYS SMIRKING. HE CREEPS ME OUT.
OF COURSE I CAN'T FORGIVE THE SUPREME LEADER FOR ABANDONING US...
BUT THAT DOESN'T MEAN I LIKE SIR GYOKU ANY BETTER. HE'S ALWAYS MAKING FUN OF HIS BROTHER BEHIND HIS BACK.
I HATE HIM.
"I AM PREPARED TO SUFFER...
"...THE CONSE-QUENCES OF MY ACTIONS.

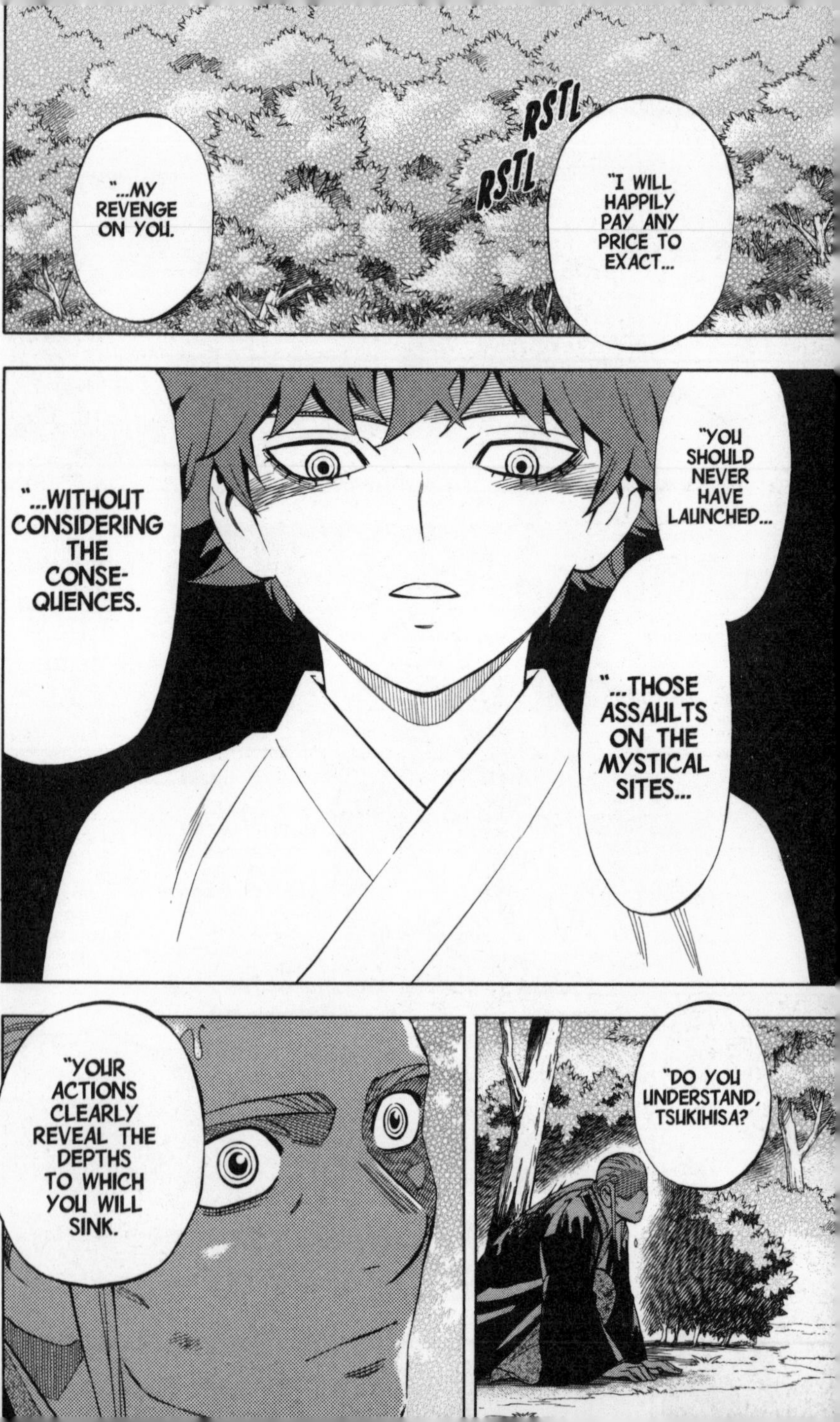
"I WILL HAPPILY PAY ANY PRICE TO EXACT...
RSTL
RSTL
"...MY REVENGE ON YOU.
"YOU SHOULD NEVER HAVE LAUNCHED...
"...THOSE ASSAULTS ON THE MYSTICAL SITES...
"...WITHOUT CONSIDERING THE CONSE-QUENCES.
"DO YOU UNDERSTAND, TSUKIHISA?
"YOUR ACTIONS CLEARLY REVEAL THE DEPTHS TO WHICH YOU WILL SINK.

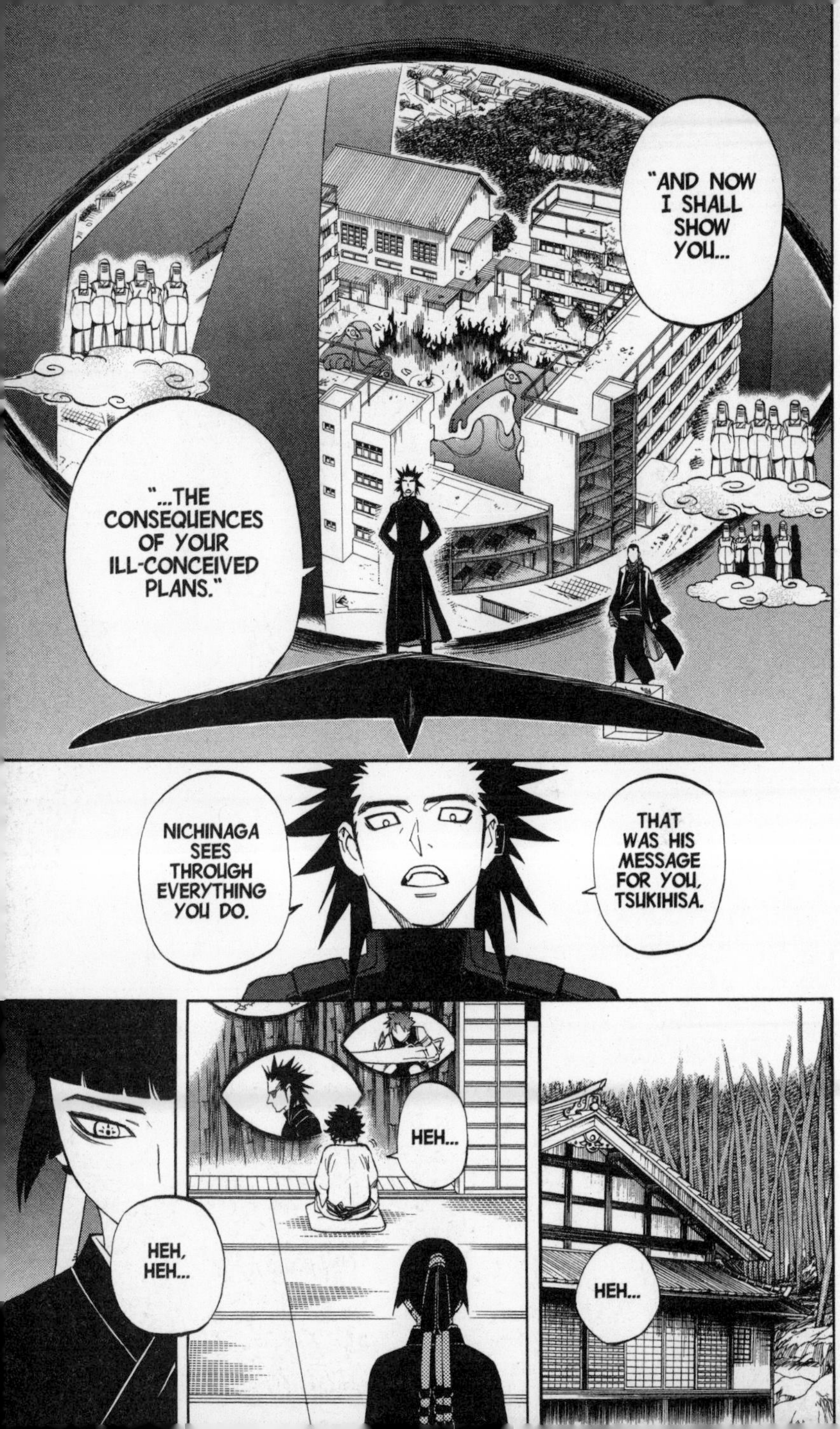
"AND NOW I SHALL SHOW YOU...
"...THE CONSEQUENCES OF YOUR ILL-CONCEIVED PLANS."
THAT WAS HIS MESSAGE FOR YOU, TSUKIHISA.
NICHINAGA SEES THROUGH EVERYTHING YOU DO.
HEH...
HEH...
HEH, HEH...

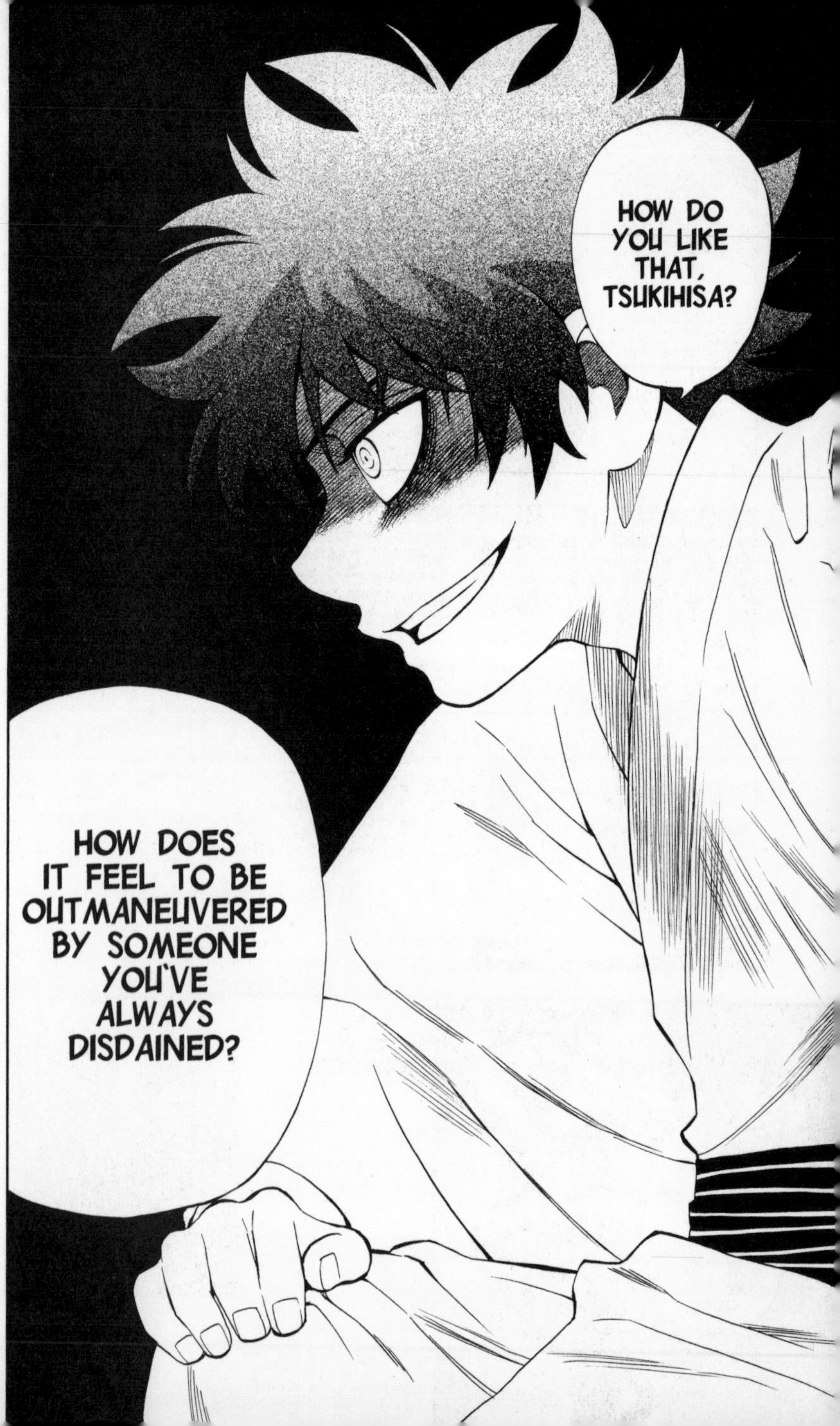
HOW DO YOU LIKE THAT, TSUKIHISA?
HOW DOES IT FEEL TO BE OUTMANEUVERED BY SOMEONE YOU'VE ALWAYS DISDAINED?

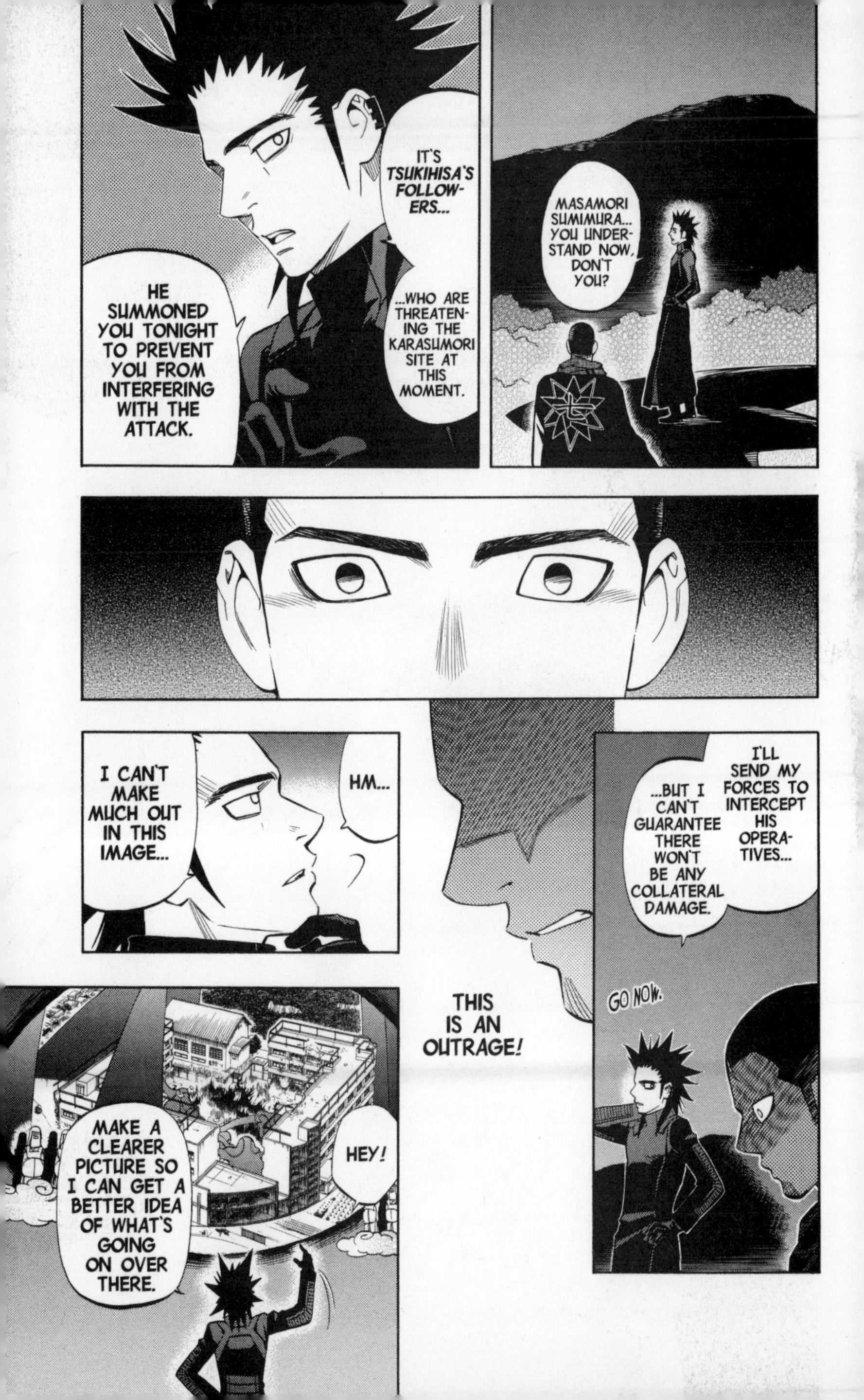
MASAMORI SUMIMURA... YOU UNDERSTAND NOW, DON'T YOU?
IT'S TSUKIHISA'S FOLLOWERS...
...WHO ARE THREATENING THE KARASUMORI SITE AT THIS MOMENT.
HE SUMMONED YOU TONIGHT TO PREVENT YOU FROM INTERFERING WITH THE ATTACK.
I'LL SEND MY FORCES TO INTERCEPT HIS OPERATIVES...
...BUT I CAN'T GUARANTEE THERE WON'T BE ANY COLLATERAL DAMAGE.
GO NOW.
THIS IS AN OUTRAGE!
HM...
I CAN'T MAKE MUCH OUT IN THIS IMAGE...
HEY!
MAKE A CLEARER PICTURE SO I CAN GET A BETTER IDEA OF WHAT'S GOING ON OVER THERE.

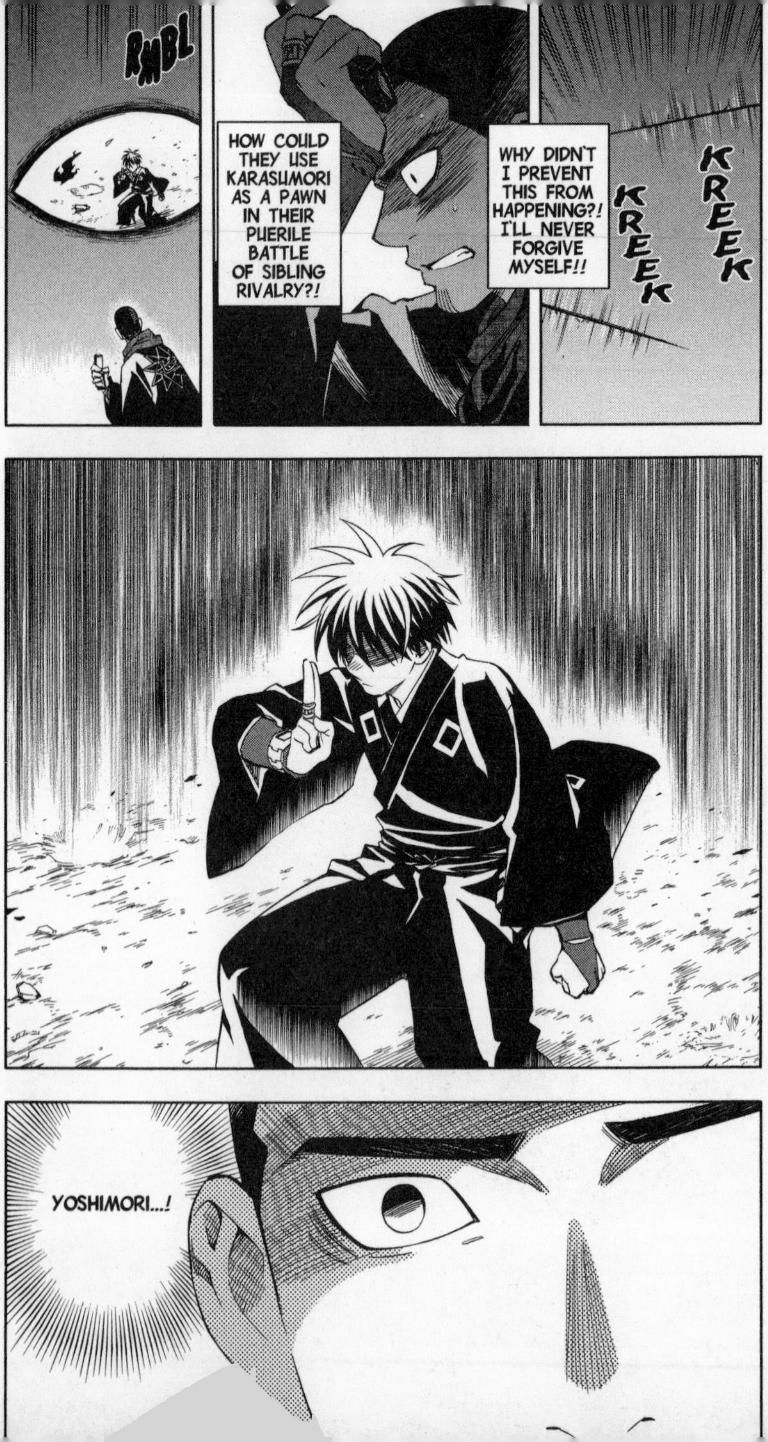
KREEK KREEK
WHY DIDN'T I PREVENT THIS FROM HAPPENING?! I'LL NEVER FORGIVE MYSELF!!
HOW COULD THEY USE KARASUMORI AS A PAWN IN THEIR PUERILE BATTLE OF SIBLING RIVALRY?!
RMBL
YOSHIMORI...!

I'LL EAT THE REST TOMORROW.

I DIVIDE MY ICE CREAM IN TWO...
→

SUPER

MESSAGE FROM YELLOW TANABE

As a shonen manga creator, I have tried to retain a childlike sense of wonder. However, I've noticed that my childhood love of sweets and snacks is fading. Well, I still like them, but I simply can't eat as much. Will I eventually start saying I like fish more than meat too?

KEKKAISHI

VOLUME 27

SHONEN SUNDAY EDITION

STORY AND ART BY YELLOW TANABE

© 2004 Yellow TANABE/Shogakukan
All rights reserved.
Original Japanese edition "KEKKAISHI" published by SHOGAKUKAN Inc.

Translation/Yuko Sawada
Touch-up Art & Lettering/Stephen Dutro
Cover Design & Graphic Layout/Julie Behn, Ronnie Casson
Editor/Annette Roman

Printed in the U.S.A.

Published by VIZ Media, LLC
P.O. Box 77010
San Francisco, CA 94107

10 9 8 7 6 5 4 3 2 1
First printing, August 2011

PARENTAL ADVISORY
KEKKAISHI is rated T for Teen
and is recommended for ages
13 and up. It contains fantasy
violence.
ratings.viz.com

www.viz.com

WWW.SHONENSUNDAY.COM

NO. 2

NO. 1

Half Human, Half Demon— ALL ACTION!

elive the feudal fairy tale with the
ew **VIZBIG Editions** featuring:

Three volumes in one
for $17.99 US / $24.00 CAN
Larger trim size with premium paper
Now unflipped! Pages read
Right-to-Left as the creator intended

**Change Your
Perspective—Get BIG**

大 **VIZBIG** EDITION

InuYasha

Story and Art by Rumiko Takahashi

ISBN-13: 978-1-4215-3280-6

On sale at
store.viz.com
**Also available at your local
bookstore and comic store**

www.viz.com

MANGA STARTS ON SUNDAY
SHONENSUNDAY.COM

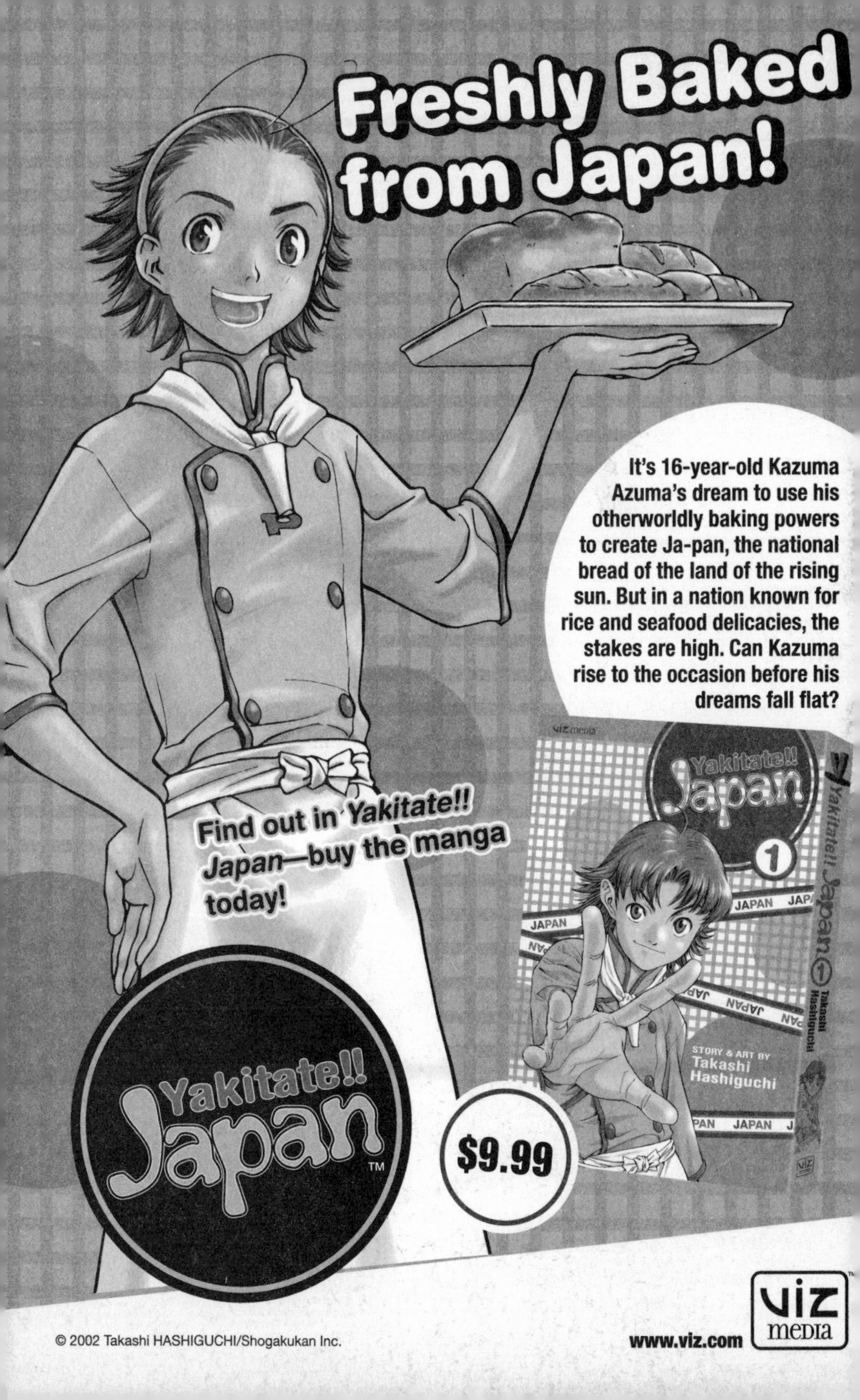
Freshly Baked from Japan!
It's 16-year-old Kazuma Azuma's dream to use his otherworldly baking powers to create Ja-pan, the national bread of the land of the rising sun. But in a nation known for rice and seafood delicacies, the stakes are high. Can Kazuma rise to the occasion before his dreams fall flat?
Find out in Yakitate!! Japan—buy the manga today!
Yakitate!! Japan 1
STORY & ART BY Takashi Hashiguchi
Yakitate!! Japan™
$9.99
© 2002 Takashi HASHIGUCHI/Shogakukan Inc.
www.viz.com
viz media

At Your Indentured Service

Hayate's parents are bad with money, so they sell his organs to pay their debts. Hayate doesn't like this plan, so he comes up with a new one—kidnap and ransom a girl from a wealthy family. Solid plan… so how did he end up as her butler?

Find out in *Hayate the Combat Butler*—
buy the manga at store.viz.com!

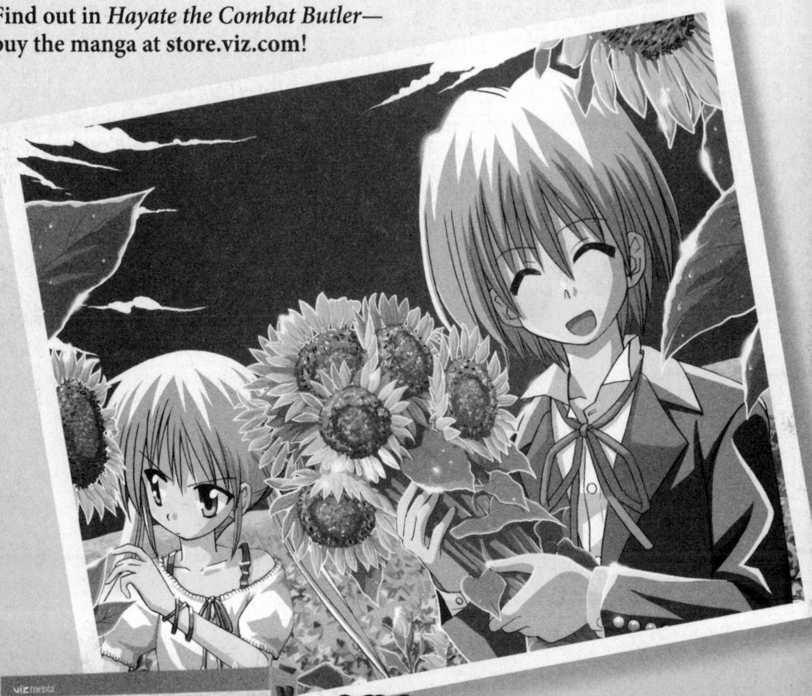

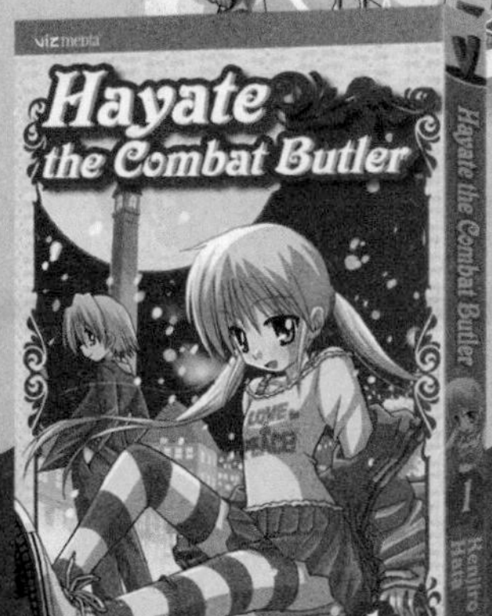
viz media
Hayate the Combat Butler
Hayate the Combat Butler
1
Kenjiro Hata
1
Kenjiro Hata

Hayate the Combat Butler™

viz media

www.viz.com
store.viz.com